# Women of Valor

# Women of Valor

*Orthodox Jewish Troll Fighters, Crime Writers, and Rock Stars in Contemporary Literature and Culture*

KAREN E. H. SKINAZI

RUTGERS UNIVERSITY PRESS
NEW BRUNSWICK, CAMDEN, AND NEWARK,
NEW JERSEY, AND LONDON

Library of Congress Cataloging-in-Publication Data

Names: Skinazi, Karen E., 1974– author.
Title: Women of valor : Orthodox Jewish troll fighters, crime writers, and rock stars in contemporary literature and culture / by Karen E.H. Skinazi.
Description: New Brunswick : Rutgers University Press, 2018. | Includes bibliographical references and index.
Identifiers: LCCN 2017056006 | ISBN 9780813596020 (cloth : alk. paper) | ISBN 9780813596013 (pbk. : alk. paper)
Subjects: LCSH: Jewish women—Religious life. | Jewish women in popular culture. | Orthodox Judaism. | Popular culture—Religious aspects—Judaism.
Classification: LCC BM729.W6 S58 2018 | DDC 296.8/32082—dc23
LC record available at https://lccn.loc.gov/2017056006

A British Cataloging-in-Publication record for this book is available from the British Library.

∞ The paper used in this publication meets the requirements of the American National Standard for Information Sciences—Permanence of Paper for Printed Library Materials, ANSI Z39.48-1992.

www.rutgersuniversitypress.org

Manufactured in the United States of America

Two unknown women and my grandmother
(far right), Poland, 1939

*In memory of my grandmother, Miriam Bajtelman Leszner Shuman
(19?–2004), z"l, who survived the Holocaust, in which she lost her parents,
sisters, brothers, nieces, nephew, cousins, friends, and neighbors; who spent
four years in a displaced persons camp when no country would give her
refuge; who was eventually transplanted to a new world, where nothing
was quite like it had been; who watched the father of her young daughter die a slow, painful death (the first of two times she was widowed);
who raised my mother on her own, working in and out of the house and
struggling to make ends meet; and who taught me strength, courage, and
the importance of* Yiddishkeit. *It is because of her I believe that the* eshes
chayil *is not only a* "woman of valor" *but also a* "warrior woman."

# Contents

# An Unorthodox Guide
# to Orthodox Judaism

*Phoebe described herself as Orthodox—to Chloe's ears, an unfortunate term—but there seemed to be a rather large range of value-systems lumped under the rubric of that one word. No wonder that "the Jerusalem of New Jersey," as small as it was, had five different Orthodox synagogues.*

—Rebecca Goldstein, *Mazel*

Two Jews, three opinions? Fourteen million Jews . . . many versions of Judaism. This book engages the ideas by and about Orthodox Jews, but it is important to point out that there are many divisions *within* Orthodox Judaism, which is itself usually distinguished from Conservative, Reform, and Reconstructionist Judaism (some might add "Conservadox" in there as well) or Liberal/Progressive and Masorti Judaism. Judaism is dynamic and evolving, as are all the denominations.

A number of these divisions will be discussed throughout the book, but I attempt here to provide a rough schematic for the reader, recognizing that this guide is unorthodox and will irritate as much as it will explain ("I am nothing like him!" the doctor, his small *kippah* carefully positioned to cover his bald spot, will proclaim as the yeshiva *bocher*, whose sable *shtreimel* is trapped like a fierce animal under a big plastic bag, makes his way past. "Does it make sense to call us both *Chasidische balabustas*?" the snooded mother of fifteen in her thick-seamed high-denier stockings might ask of the glamorous performer, who wears a high-lighted human-hair wig, balances on Jimmy Choo heels, and sings and dances for adoring crowds). And yet, here it is:

---

*Haredi*: literally, Haredi means "one who trembles" (i.e., before God). It is usually translated into English as "ultra-Orthodox" (though this is a term that is not embraced by the community) and is colloquially referenced by the black hats that the men in many of the Haredi communities wear. *Haredi* is a term that can be used to cover the following:

1. The *Yeshivish* sect, which is also known as (1) *Litvish/Litvaks*, as the culture is descended from Lithuania; (2) *Agudah* Jews, as Agudath Israel is the political and social movement associated with them; or (3) *Misnagdim*, as they are opponents of the Hasidim. Sometimes *Haredi* refers only to this group, in which case you might see *Haredim* and *Hasidim* as separate entities. This group is considered more intellectual than Hasidim and is called the "brain" of Orthodoxy.
2. The *Sephardi Haredim, who* are descended from Spain and North Africa and are primarily located in Israel.
3. The Hasidim, known as the "heart" of Orthodoxy. *Hasidism* is a term covering the followers of the Ba'al Shem Tov, an eighteenth-century mystical rabbi. The Hasidim are not a singular community. There have been dynastic wars, and Chabad-Lubavitch and Breslovers are exceptional for being welcoming to the secular world and, in the minds of many Hasidim, too liberal. The Satmars, on the other end of the spectrum, are thought to be "very Hasidic" or stringent (Fader 179). The Hasidic dynasties are multiple and multiplying, though there are also Hasidim unaffiliated with any particular court. In addition to Chabad, Breslov, and Satmar, the larger Hasidic dynasties are Bobov, Belz, Ger, Vishnitz, and Skver; there are also a number of smaller ones. In her study of the everyday lives of Hasidic women, Ayala Fader notes that "court distinctions are often important in marriage, school considerations, or distinctions in ritual practice" but that "these distinctions are rarely noted in everyday interactions in school, the streets, or at home by women" (21).

Between Haredi and Modern Orthodox Judaism is not a great chasm in the earth. They exist on a continuum, and a number of the cultural productions discussed in these pages feature not only mixed communities but also families composed of different sects and individuals who move between and among them. In Israel, the *Hardal* straddles the Haredi (*Har*) and Religious Zionist (*Dati Leumi*) communities, the latter being on the more liberal end of the spectrum (comparable to, if distinct from, North American Modern Orthodoxy).

---

*Modern Orthodoxy*: loosely defined with the phrase *Torah u'madah*—a combination of Torah and secular knowledge (or in the *Bnei Akiva* flavor, *Torah va'avodah*, "Torah and work"). This also includes many different beliefs and modes of practice. When I was growing up, I shunned my father's cramped, pungent-smelling man-cave *Mizrachi* synagogue and *davened* instead in the beautiful new Modern Orthodox synagogue dubbed "The Bayit." I sat in the balcony among giggly female friends from my Orthodox day school and mingled with the male members only during the kiddush. This was a Modern Orthodox institution in what I imagined was its most natural form: boys in knit *kippahs* (usually crocheted by girls who liked them), girls in knee-length skirts (sometimes *slightly* above the knee), women in once-a-week hats, food traditional Jewish and uninspired, Zionism unquestioned, and few if any challenges to religious dogma, as was clear by the (obviously male) rabbi's speeches (which, I admit, were assiduously avoided). The members were not undiverse, but most were in the usual upper-middle-class Jewish professions, and the variety of practice on a day-to-day level was idiosyncratic but within a range: for example, all "kept kosher," but this meant a number of things. Some members only ate in kosher restaurants, some went to nonkosher restaurants but ate only cold vegetarian food, some were fine with fish, and some kept strictly kosher kitchens at home but filled their plates with jumbo shrimp on Vegas junkets. Maybe this vision is nostalgic, but I think it will resonate with many still today.

Within Modern Orthodoxy is Open Orthodoxy, which is more egalitarian and inclusive, particularly in terms of women's religious participation, education, and leadership. I discovered it attending *Rosh Chodesh* services, led by women, at *Yedidyah* in Jerusalem in the mid-1990s. This is a movement known for the monumental figure of Blu Greenberg, such organizations as the Jewish Orthodox Feminist Alliance (JOFA) and Women of the Wall, and partnership minyanim. In the twenty-first century, Orthodoxy ordained its first *maharat*, or female clergy member, though it remains unusual within Orthodoxy to accept, never mind employ, women as clergy. (In February 2017, the Orthodox Union [OU], the overarching organization for Modern Orthodox synagogues in North America, explicitly barred women from serving as clergy, though it was not a decision that was accepted by all. "The OU should stick to tuna fish,'" declared the rabbi of Ohev Sholom, the National Synagogue in Washington, DC, which employs Maharat Ruth Balinsky Friedman [quoted in Nathan-Kazis, "Exclusive"].) It seems to me that this development and its backlash act as a testament to one of the many ways that women are at the heart of the Orthodox culture wars, defining boundaries and creating change within Orthodox movements. Most Orthodox women do not seek to become clergy members, to be sure; as will become clear on the pages of this book, though, women of various sects of Orthodoxy can be imagined and can imagine themselves as having many different opportunities for empowerment within their Orthodox communities that practice gender segregation for religious (among other) rituals.

There are other ways of marking the divisions in or gradations of Orthodoxy, and my method is by no means definitive. In *Sliding to the Right*, Samuel Heilman casts Modern Orthodox on the left against Haredi on the right. In *Strictly Kosher Reading*, Yoel Finkelman puts Orthodoxy in three camps: Hasidic to the far right,

Haredi as centric, and Modern Orthodox to the left. In *Becoming Frum*, Sarah Bunin Benor reads Orthodoxy on a continuum of Modern Orthodox through Hasidic and non-Hasidic "Black Hat" Judaism (as Benor remarks, though in common use, the term *Black Hat* "symbolically excludes women," which is one of the key reasons I eschew it), all of which she sees as complicated by *ba'alei teshuva*, those who were not born but became Orthodox (Benor 9). Categorization can have a very practical use, as on the matchmaking website frumster.com, which divided its members into Modern Orthodox Liberal, Modern Orthodox *Machmir* (strict), *Yeshivish* Modern, and *Yeshivish* Black Hat (my brother-in-law and his wife met on the site, for the record—so it did something right!). There is a good logic to many maps of the Orthodox world and also (and always) a degree of idiosyncrasy.

To conclude this unorthodox guide, I will note that in many instances, be they in news stories, novels, films, or in the names of schools and synagogues and other Jewish organizations, *Orthodox* appears as an umbrella term, a catchall word that seems to mean both too much and too little. Take this headline from 2017: "Smurfette Is Removed from Posters for the New Smurf Movie in Israeli City to Avoid Upsetting Orthodox Jews," cried the sensationalist *Daily Mail* (Al-Othman). The conservative *Jewish Chronicle* covered the situation similarly, stating, "In Bnei Brak, a predominantly-Orthodox suburb of Tel Aviv, a special version of the poster is on display" (Moran). As this language shows, there is no doubt that *Orthodox* is a problematic term; after all, I can hardly imagine a single member of "The Bayit," an Orthodox shul, objecting to Smurfette's three-apple-high blue image on a billboard. But it is also a productive term. There are as many similarities as differences among and across Orthodox communities; the general adherence to halacha, or Jewish law, binds the diverse members. We can take smaller and smaller slices of Judaism and put each under a microscope, or we can take a look at the breadth of possibilities within a culturally defined and commonly understood denomination. For this study, I've chosen the latter.

# A Woman of Valor

A woman of valor, who can find? Far beyond pearls is her value. Her husband's heart trusts in her and he shall lack no fortune.

She repays his good, but never his harm, all the days of her life. She seeks out wool and linen, and her hands work willingly.

She is like a merchant's ships; from afar she brings her sustenance. She rises while it is still nighttime, and gives food to her household and a ration to her maids.

She considers a field and buys it; from the fruit of her handiwork she plants a vineyard. She girds her loins with might and strengthens her arms.

She senses that her enterprise is good, so her lamp is not extinguished at night. She puts her hand to the distaff, and her palms support the spindle.

She spreads out her palm to the poor and extends her hands to the destitute. She fears not snow for her household, for her entire household is clothed with scarlet wool.

Bedspreads she makes herself; linen and purple wool are her clothing. Well-known at the gates is her husband as he sits with the elders of the land.

Garments she makes and sells, and she delivers a belt to the peddler. Strength and splendor are her clothing, and smilingly she awaits her last day.

She opens her mouth with Wisdom, and the teaching of kindness is on her tongue. She anticipates the needs of her household, and the bread of idleness, she does not eat.

Her children rise and celebrate her; and her husband, he praises her: "Many daughters have attained valor, but you have surpassed them all."

False is grace, and vain is beauty; a G-d-fearing woman, she should be praised.

Give her the fruit of her hands, and she will be praised at the gates by her very own deeds.

—Proverbs 31:10–31

# Women of Valor

Figure I.1. *Hereville: How Mirka Got Her Sword* (2010) by Barry Deutsch. Permission to reproduce by Barry Deutsch.

# Introduction

## SHE PUTS HER HAND TO THE DISTAFF

### I. The Contemporary Orthodox Heroine (Troll Fighter, Dragon Slayer, Time Traveler . . . with Knitting Needles)

In 2010, Mirka appeared. Hair braided, sleeves and hemline of her dress long, Mirka hovered over a giant ball of yarn, one arm reaching into the inky, starry sky, the other clutching a sword the length of her torso. Her head was thrown back, and she was smiling. Barry Deutsch's graphic novel carrying this front-cover image is called *Hereville: How Mirka Got Her Sword*, but the tagline running across the top of that dark sky, suspended over Mirka's head as she hovers over the yarn, is even more intriguing: "Yet Another Troll-Fighting 11-Year-Old Orthodox Jewish Girl" (see figure I.1).

The fact is—and Deutsch knows it, and we all know it—Mirka is probably the first troll-fighting eleven-year-old Orthodox Jewish girl. She is certainly the first to grace the cover and insides of a graphic novel, anyway! Eleven-year-old Orthodox Jewish girls, like thirty-year-old Orthodox Jewish women, have set images in modern societies. They are modest; they are meek; they are unquestioning. They don't fight trolls.

But Deutsch offers a different vision of Orthodox womanhood. Mirka is studying under the tutelage of her stepmother, Fruma, the only powerful adult in the series who is not a witch. That she is a representational Orthodox Jewish woman is suggested by her name; Fruma is the feminine of *frum*, which is Yiddish for "religiously observant." Fruma is efficient, intelligent, and the novel's source of love and comfort. She is always pictured competently running the household. When she speaks, she is imparting her wisdom, and she shows endless patience for her difficult stepdaughter. She is, in short, the embodiment of the *eshes chayil*—the "woman of valor."

The woman of valor is held up as the ideal woman in a hymn of the same name, which comes from Proverbs 31, verses 10 through 31. This biblical passage is today and has been for the last four centuries sung to the woman (or women) of the house in Jewish households around the world on Friday nights. The "Woman of Valor" is an acrostic poem, as each line starts with a letter of the Hebrew alphabet from *aleph* (the first letter) through *taf* (the last). It is, in part, a metaphorical poem, as we can understand the "woman" to also be the Sabbath, which is often personified as a queen. Or it could be the Torah. Or Wisdom. The passage is thought to be a mother's advice to her son (possibly King Lemuel) or her daughter, or it could be a eulogy (Abraham after Sarah's death). And it is read as a set of instructions as well as praise. The list of attributes the poem offers is long and detailed: a woman of valor is skilled at commerce as well as domestic arts, is intelligent as well as kind, and cares for her community as well as her family. There is nothing mentioned about troll-fighting specifically, but she is described as so thoroughly capable as to make the possibility imaginable.[1]

Yet what is most interesting about the woman of valor is the way she has been taken up in recent years—not only by Deutsch (a secular man) but also, and more fundamentally, by Jewish women writers and filmmakers—to invest strength and authority in the figure of the Orthodox woman, to reveal her true voice and agency.

The use of this trope to signify women's power is noteworthy because it runs directly counter to the bulwark of fictional and media depictions of Orthodox Jewish women—or, in fact, of women of any religious community rooted in traditional (typically patriarchal) mores. When we think, in the twenty-first century, of religious Jewish women, we still expect them to look a lot like the women featured in the literature that chronicled the history of Eastern European Jewish migration to America. Perhaps we might imagine them as we do Gitl, the dowdy first wife of Yekl, the eponymous hero of Abraham Cahan's classic novella. Poor Gitl appeared in 1896 with her "uncouth and un-American appearance . . . slovenly dressed in a brown jacket and skirt of grotesque cut . . . her hair concealed under a voluminous wig" (Cahan 34). Happily, Gitl rids herself of that voluminous symbol of Orthodoxy that defines and dogs her throughout the tale. Why would she want a wig that "made her seem stouter and shorter" and "also added at least five years to her looks"? After all, "In New York . . . none but an elderly matron may wear a wig without being the occasional target for snowballs or stones," according to Cahan's narrative (34). Other stories of the era similarly tell of women and girls getting rid of their hair coverings and frumpy old-world clothes. Young Shena Pessah, in Anzia Yezierska's 1920 short story "Wings," can't wait to trade her "old women's shawls" for "American dress-up," again suggesting that religious attire ages and unsexes a woman (Yezierska 20). And Genya, David's mother in Henry Roth's modernist novel *Call It Sleep* (1934), knows to transform herself even before setting foot on mainland America: "Her clothes were American—a black skirt, a white shirt-waist and a black jacket. Obviously her husband had either taken the precaution of sending them to her while she was still in Europe or had brought them with him to Ellis Island where she had slipped them on before she left" (H. Roth 10).

The unlucky ones, however, were those who didn't follow in Gitl and Shena Pessah and Genya's footsteps and instead became relics of an unwanted past and an abandoned Old World. Beginning in the 1980s, a proliferation of Gitls, condemned to their headscarves and modest dress were returning to haunt the pages of Jewish fiction. In *Lovingkindness*, Anne Roiphe's brilliant 1987 novel that critically tests the very Enlightenment ideals it espouses, a secular, feminist American mother resents her daughter's freedom to choose Orthodoxy, which the mother sees as freedom's opposite. The mother fears her daughter will "turn into one of those pious women in long dress with high neck and long sleeves, with a scarf tied over her hair, eyes demurely downcast, in sensible shoes with laces and thick stockings" (20). The downcast eyes are as much a part of the daughter's modest ensemble as her stockings. To her mother, both are signs of meekness and foolish anachronization. For this mother, practicing Orthodoxy means "sliding down the historical ladder," a process that she sees her daughter as complicit in (Roiphe 18). To an Israeli journalist covering a story about a descendent of a famous Hasidic rabbi, in the first scene of Naomi Ragen's 1989 novel *Jephte's Daughter*, Orthodox women are categorized as "dull, pale creatures, covered up from head to toe winter and summer, zealously successful in ridding themselves of any taint of womanly allure or feminine promise" (1). In Tova Reich's 1988 satirical novel *Master of the Return*, we get the story from an "insider"—but it is little different. Bruriah, an Orthodox woman, says, "To the outsider, it looks like we're downtrodden and oppressed, like we're low, lower than low. We eat the leftovers. We're barred from the study halls. We're regarded as inferior and unclean." To this, she adds, "That's how it looks from the outside.... But we know the truth, don't we?" (156–157). Nora Rubel, in *Doubting the Devout*, a study of "The Ultra-Orthodox in the Jewish Imagination," correctly surmises, "Reich's tone and the broader context of the novel suggest that Bruriah and her cohort are victims of false consciousness" (71). In other words, paired with Roiphe and Ragen's narrativized outsider perspective, Reich's telling from the inside, as it were, is a confirmation of every suspicion the secular reader harbors of Orthodox women: that they are backward, oppressed, overcovered, powerless, and dourly unattractive, to boot.

These end-of-the-twentieth-century stories suggest a failure of the secularization that was written as the natural and inevitable future for Cahan's characters a hundred years earlier. They tell of a damning failure, a pitiable failure—but a failure nonetheless. In fact, there has been a growing recognition in the twenty-first century of the failure of total secularization to take root, even as (or perhaps because) we have events like France banning the burka and feminists proclaiming that monotheism is a problem. In 1999, the *New York Times* foreign affairs correspondent Thomas Friedman published *The Lexus and the Olive Tree*, arguing that both secular and religious worldviews are still dominant worldwide. A

photograph Friedman includes in his book illustrates their potential synchronic-
ity: it portrays a Hasidic man holding his cellular phone up to the Western Wall
in Jerusalem so that his relative in France can say a prayer there. Here, the prayer
we consider ancient and the technology we consider modern come together as
one united expression of contemporary existence, religious and secular.

In the post–9/11 era, there has been increased interest in religion's role in the
lands of the Lexuses. American intellectual historian Wilfred M. McClay writes,
"The secular worldview, whose triumph once seemed so inevitable, now seems
stalled, and even to be losing ground, or being superseded" (127). And in a 2005
article in the *Chronicle of Higher Education*, Stanley Fish wrote of the growing significance of religion in all aspects of American life, including academia. "When
Jacques Derrida died," he recalls, "I was called by a reporter who wanted know
what would succeed high theory and the triumvirate of race, gender, and class as
the center of intellectual energy in the academy. I answered like a shot: religion"
(Fish). "For much of the twentieth century," write Ari Joskowicz and Ethan B. Katz
in their 2015 study of Jewish (post)secularism, "most secular and religious thinkers believed that they were living in an age of steady secularization. . . . Today, the
secular is no longer considered the norm" (1).

It seems strange, then, that with the new century, which is arguably *ambivalent* about secularism, we would hold on to the same old or old-world images of
Orthodox Jewish women in the pages of our fiction and on the screens of our
cinemas.[2] In some ways, though, this is what we do. If anything, Orthodox Jewish
women are all the more pitied for being clustered with images of other women
of oppressive religious communities in the twenty-first century. On the first page
of Eve Harris's 2013 novel, *The Marrying of Chani Kaufman*, we find a terrified
young bride and her mother, a woman who is like Gitl: she "sagged under the
weight of her mousy wig . . . an old woman at forty-five" (1). But the young bride
is no safer for her youth. The front cover of the novel bears a picture of a bride in
a veil so opaque as to render her faceless. Like Muslim women, who inspired the
sympathy of Western readers with their devastating autoethnographies (sometimes cowritten with the helping hands of white Western women) preceding and
during the incursions into Iraq and Afghanistan, this bride begs readers to unveil
her and liberate her from her (visibly rendered) oppression.

Throughout Harris's book, the Orthodox neighborhood of Golders Green
is contrasted with colorful, secular London by being painted in shades of gray,
a near-cinematic anachronization of the Orthodox community. This narrative choice recalls *Yekl*—or rather, its transformation to the big screen as *Hester
Street*, a 1975 film that transports viewers to New York at the turn of the twentieth
century through its black-and-white rendering of its old-world immigrants who
speak Yiddish and Yiddish-inflected English.[3] The women of *The Marrying of
Chani Kaufman* wear "the compulsory long skirt with a white high-necked shirt
underneath a plain navy blazer. The colours were purposely dull" (E. Harris 3).

The Orthodox women of Brooklyn in Julia Dahl's 2014 novel, *Invisible City*, fare little better: "The women look simultaneously sexless and fecund in aggressively flat shoes, thick flesh-colored stockings, and shapeless clothing" (13). The front cover of Dahl's novel bears an image that casts a spotlight on the nonreligious heroine, selectively colorized in a picture that has been desaturated of all other color. Turned (or turning) partially toward the viewer's gaze, she appears lit up with peach skin, chestnut hair, and a bright-red blouse, a dynamic image of a woman amid grayscale, static, faceless men in black hats and women in wigs. The visual images metonymically suggest the lifestyles that readers fear the flat-shoed women have, shut up in a dreary, antimodern, antifeminist Old World that somehow eludes, even as it is located within, the New World.

The picture in nonfiction is often no less monochromatic. *Unchosen*, Hella Winston's 2005 sociological study of the "hidden lives of Hasidic rebels," offers a scholarly examination of Hasidic life in America, but it has a sensationalist edge, another promise of "unveiling." Given access to a group of insiders of the "extremely insular Satmar Hasidic sect," Winston describes the women she interviews as "all dressed modestly, in long skirts, thick stockings, high-necked sweaters, and monochromatic cloth turbans that expose no hair" before she launches into the secrets they keep beneath their austere turbans (vii). Stephanie Wellen Levine's 2003 *Mystics, Mavericks, and Merrymakers*, a book about the author's year in Crown Heights, New York (home to a large Lubavitcher Hasidic community), stands as a rare counternarrative, even as Levine repeatedly tells readers that she, along with everyone she knew, thought the possibility that Hasidic girls and women "could be anything other than the Platonic essence of feminine subjugation seemed as unlikely as a suckling pig on a Shabbos [Sabbath] table" (13).[4] A 2017 London *Times* article defines Haredi women by their reproductive roles almost exclusively: "Once married, girls will stop their education and start fulfilling the biblical commandment to be fruitful and multiply" (Pogrund).

To most writers and readers, along with bewildered neighbors, the wigs and turbans, drab clothes, and thick stockings classify these women as *unable* to be part of London and New York and the twenty-first century. They are alien to the contemporary world, inhabitants of "hermetically sealed" societies or *paradoxical* "21st-century shtetl[s]" (Pogrund).[5] In popular and academic discourse, the Orthodox neighborhoods are regarded as *allochronic* or *anachronistic space*. I borrow these terms from anthropologist Johannes Fabian and postcolonial literary critic Anne McClintock, who write about the ways the anthropologist and colonizers, respectively, imagine their subjects as existing not only in a different space but also in a different time. And it is this distortion of time—these Daliesque renderings of these individuals' contemporary existence—that denies them their modernity and thus, to a degree, their humanity. Even David Hollinger, whose *Postethnic America* (1995) offers an important theory of diversity in America beyond multiculturalism's "ethnoracial pentagon," opens his book with the same logical fallacy, telling a story about seeing men in black hats and coats and thinking they were Pennsylvania Dutch, only to have his fiancée correct him: "No, those are Hasidic Jews. My *roots*, not yours" (ix, emphasis mine). On the one hand, Hollinger uses this anecdote to illustrate the diversity of Americans who affiliate in a variety of ways (as Hasidim, Amish, or "regular" people like his fiancée and him); on the other, by calling these contemporaries his and his fiancée's "roots," he creates a temporal boundary between these "others" and himself.

This desire to see in religious Jews a form of ancestry, I should add, is particularly pervasive in secular Jewish writing. In *Holy Days: The World of a Hasidic Family* (1985), Lis Harris, a secular Jew, says that she was motivated to write about a Lubavitch family and community because of a sense that "the Hasidim represented some *antique* version of myself" (11, emphasis mine). In *Mitzvah Girls*, a 2009 ethnography of Hasidic women and girls in Brooklyn, Fader is explicit about the complicated role the ethnographer has when she is from the same stock, so to speak, as her subject: "I . . . confess to harboring romantic notions about shared history and identity. I knew I would not share a common faith with Hasidic women, but my great-grandparents had been Orthodox and came from the same parts of Eastern Europe that many Hasidic Jews do" (17). Fader, ultimately, however, provides a clear-eyed reading of the women and girls and comes to see them as bridging the divides between modernity and tradition and between secularism and religion (33). Fader is perhaps not as dazzled as Levine by her Hasidic subjects, but neither does she imagine them as doomed to the oubliettes of history. Rather, she sees Hasidic girls and women as envisioning and constructing an "alternate religious modernity" (1).[6]

It is an odd fact that people look upon their neighbors and cousins (and even themselves)—people who are driving cars or riding subways, speaking into or tapping away on their iPhones, pulling from their wallets pound notes bearing the image of a living queen or coins issued in the current century, and intervening in local and federal politics—and relegate them to another time. Even the modesty rules that made Smurfette's image on a billboard unacceptable, which appear as laws of the past, are *modern innovations*, what sociologist Samuel Heilman has called Orthodox Jewry's "sliding to the right" (Tova Mirvis offers another image in *The Ladies Auxiliary*: "The whole Orthodox world had taken a giant step to the right, and like partners in a dance, we had followed" [Mirvis 137]). Contemporary orthodoxies are forms of modernity, whether or not they are desirable ones. This truth is often hard to ascertain in media depictions of Orthodox Judaism, particularly stringent Orthodox Judaism, though. And as a result of this confusion, dangerous practices are tolerated (in the spirit of honoring tradition) when they should be halted, even as distinct (but not necessarily better or worse) practices are condemned and obstructed with little benefit to anyone.

To illustrate this point, we can compare two examples out of Quebec in recent history. In the first, Lev Tahor, a Hasidic group based in Sainte-Agathe-des-Monts that is often referred to as the Jewish Taliban, was allowed to engage in behaviors that were sadistic to women and children while the media portrayed them as merely following a traditional lifestyle. "Girls and women walk amid the partly unpaved roads and modest homes in flowing black robes, with head scarves tied tightly under their necks and capes covering long dresses" reads a description of the group by Canadian newspaper the *Globe and Mail*, linking this image of the *frumka*-covered women and girls to the goal of maintaining "strict religious observance in an 'old-fashioned' way of life" (Peritz and Martin). Yet Lev Tahor was founded in the 1980s. It "fashions" itself on the newly spawned ideas of its recently deceased extremist leader, Rabbi Shlomo Helbrans, not recognized "old" ways or traditions, and many other Orthodox Jewish groups, even strict ones, are at pains to distance themselves from a group they see as abusive, cultish, and a distortion of Judaism.[7] Food restrictions are so severe that most of the Lev Tahor community is malnourished. Girls of fourteen and fifteen years old, like those in Fundamentalist Mormon communities, are forcibly married off to men twenty or more years their senior (Fisher, "Heart" 49).

Alternatively, from 1997 through 2013, the Côte-des-Neiges sports center in Montreal ran weekly gender-segregated swimming lessons for the benefit of Muslim and Orthodox Jewish women. For one hour of each week, these women were able to learn a skill, which they could not do under other circumstances because they did not want to be immodestly dressed in front of the general public. (In fact, there are many women who are not comfortable in bathing suits and do not care to be ogled by strange men while so scantily clad, and thus the safe space provided for the Muslim and Orthodox women had far-reaching benefits.) The *one hour* took away far less time from public swimming hours than children's swimming lessons and had clear benefits and beneficiaries. Yet in 2013, *one* person complained about this practice, and the complainant garnered the support of the Council on the Status of Women, the Quebec Secular Movement, and subsequently, Bernard Drainville, the provincial minister for democratic institutions, who fought to end the sessions at the sports center ("Côte-des-Neiges").[8]

To coexist in a genuinely multicultural society, it is crucial to distinguish between oppression and choice. It is also important to recognize the difference between tradition and innovation. Innovations can be red flags, signaling trends that threaten the rights of individuals—often, specifically, those of women. In 2015, Belz Hasidic rabbis in London's Stamford Hill stated that women could no longer drive because they were defying "the *traditional* rules of modesty" (Gani and Elgot). Justice prevailed: this led Britain's education secretary to declare that the edict was "completely unacceptable in modern Britain." However, the *Guardian* failed to note the irony produced by the man it interviewed, who said, "My mother drives, my mother-in-law drives" but his wife did not because "*this is our tradition*" (Gani and Elgot, emphasis mine). When innovations like these are rendered as traditions, they are justified within the sects as age-old and unchangeable. And for mainstream, secular readers, Orthodox women's modest dress and behavior, seen to be dictated by these long-standing, immutable "traditions" of the religion, render the whole practice of Orthodoxy outdated and oppressive and thus "completely unacceptable." That Orthodox communities construct their own modernities is hard to see. But they are indeed modernities, ones that embrace ideals distinct from those of mainstream culture and have, in fact, arisen in direct opposition to mainstream culture. "Haredization" is, in large part, a response to liberalization.

Playing on this popular representation of Orthodoxy as (always) anachronistic, the pages of Deutsch's graphic novel appear, at first, to be torn from the past. *Hereville* is depicted in sepia tones, like an album full of old pictures we might find in our grandparents' attic. In this sense, it seems not unlike the narrative grayness of *Chani Kaufman*, sending us into a static past. Furthermore, Mirka's hometown—with its rolling hills, densely planted trees, cavorting animals, and gothic buildings (not a car in sight), inhabited only by a witch and a troll and religious Jews in seemingly timeless dress—appears as a cross between a fairy-tale village and a prewar Polish shtetl. It might strike readers as an "anachronistic pleasure" (to quote a journalist's description of modern-day Satmar Williamsburg; Feuer L13). Yet it would be unfair to suggest that the limited palette and old-world imagery of Deutsch's graphic novel confine the characters to a spatio-temporal plane beyond the everyday world of the twenty-first century—except inasmuch as it *is* a fantastical, artistic novel beyond the everyday world of the twenty-first century. The sepia illustrations cannot really be mistaken for those of the old country, not with the rough-drawn cartoon features (a line and a dot for an eye, a triangle for a mouth) and onomatopoeic words flashing across the panel, Batman-style ("KRAK!"; see figure I.2). If *Hereville* has a generic predecessor, it is Shaun Tan's beautiful black-and-white 2006 graphic novel, *The Arrival*, an everyimmigrant's story of landing on foreign shores, which reproduces and artfully revises many tropes of early twentieth-century immigrant fiction. Like Tan's, Deutsch's book is a postmodern delight, and part of its charm is its ability to invert the "traditional"—to make the old new and the weak strong.

This inversion is certainly what is at stake in Mirka's domestic skills. On the first page of the book, readers see Mirka trying to justify her poor knitting skills to Fruma, who stands over her, counseling her. "Mirka," says Fruma, "you've dropped a stitch." "*Hashem* preordains *everything*, right?" retorts Mirka, referring to God's will. "So He must have *willed* me to drop that stitch." The inset text of a narrator reads, "Fruma's unreasonable *insistence* on teaching Mirka 'womanly arts,' like knitting, was hard . . . to live with" (Deutsch 1). Readers are encouraged to feel oppressed, along with Mirka, by her apprenticeship to this womanhood (a womanhood that's explicitly Jewish: along with ironing, cleaning, and knitting, Fruma models baking challah, the egg bread served with Friday night dinner, and teaching the children Torah). Fruma's smart rejoinder to

Figure I.2. Excerpt from *Hereville: How Mirka Got Her Sword* (2010, 9) by Barry Deutsch. Permission to reproduce by Barry Deutsch.

Mirka's justification—"Have you considered that Hashem *wants* us to have the *free will* to drop stitches?"—quickly sets Fruma's character as nobody's fool, but still, like Mirka, readers must wonder: How could such duties lead to an interesting and important life? What leaders, warriors, or people of power and influence are rehearsing "knit one, purl two" as they prepare for political summits, great battles, and board meetings?

Women of valor, it seems. Fruma's skill at knitting might allow her to clothe her household in scarlet wool, but it also gives her a warrior's strength. *Chayil* is from the same root as *chayal*, the word used in modern-day Hebrew for a soldier, and though almost always translated as the "woman of valor" or the "virtuous woman," *eshes chayil*'s best translation might be the title of Maxine Hong Kingston's much-loved memoir, *The Woman Warrior*. At the climax of *Hereville: How Mirka Got Her Sword*, the witch (or *machashaifeh*, as she is called) tells Mirka, "Whatever you need to know to beat this troll, you can learn from your stepmother" (75). Fruma's lessons are not in vain. When Mirka comes upon the troll in the forest, he says, "We will fight the noble way. With THESE!" and he holds up to her a pair of knitting needles, challenging her to a knit-off (121). The knitter of the better sweater would be the grand winner of the troll's sword (we are assured of Mirka's victory, of course, because the book's tagline and front cover promise it). Is it possible that the traditional instruments of female domesticity are also those of revolution? Could the very symbols of what Mirka (and readers) see as her—and by extension, Orthodox Jewish women's—oppression also become her means of liberation?

Mirka takes up the challenge and wins the sword. The book, however, does not end with Prada purchasing Mirka's magnificent wool creation to display in its flagship store in Soho while the troll is forced to work a rural Walmart's Christmas rush. Deutsch is hesitant to conclude *Hereville: How Mirka Got Her Sword* by reinforcing the idea that an Orthodox Jewish woman (or girl) can only find power in her clothes-making skills. And maybe it is true that knitting needles alone will never fully unravel the web of oppressive patriarchy. In a gentle narrative twist, Mirka attempts to knit a masterpiece, but the resulting sweater is a mess; ultimately, she wins with her wits.

If this ending does not satisfy all—and if the "womanly art" of knitting does not make good on the power that it has potentially been endowed with—it is perhaps because we imagine knitting and the like to be the whole of "womanly arts," or the whole of the role of women in Orthodoxy. We might assume then that Deutsch can only support this prescribed role to a limit before his (modern, secular) feminist impulse for revision inspires him to change the story, to free Mirka from the shackles of her religiously dictated duties.[9] But in fact, the strength of this ending is its *combination* of the heroine's domestic know-how with her intellectual ability. Furthermore, a glance at the hymn "Woman of Valor" (or "Woman Warrior") should remind us that Deutsch is hardly unique here by creating this combination. It is a message that we see again and again in the works of Jewish women writers and filmmakers: women can buy fields, plant vineyards, go to battle, *and* support the distaff. Domestic work is not, and has never been, the whole of the ideal woman in Judaism, Orthodox or otherwise. The woman of valor is multitalented.

## II. The Return of Religion

Why are we witnessing a profusion of Gitls in the pages of contemporary Jewish fiction? These Gitls appear as flat representations in a colorless world, but they can also be found at the helms of fictional businesses or fighting fictional crime: there are Gitls everywhere. McClay sees in the post–9/11 era "the perceived failure of secularist modernism, specifically its inability to provide an adequate framework for the great mass of Americans to lead meaningful, morally coherent lives" (127–128). This sentiment is evident in the increased engagement in religious Judaism as well as its popular and critical examination. Indeed, as novels, films, television shows, magazines, radio programs, and blogs are produced by and about Orthodoxy; as mainstream readers and viewers are consuming these cultural works; and as literary and cultural critics examine them, it is hard not to see this subgenre of Jewish literature and culture emerging as a significant manifestation of a kind of postsecularist engagement.[10] Thinking back to Hollinger's error, we might note the similarity of Orthodox Jews with the Amish, who are also a source of cultural fascination (and alienation and anachronization). According to the PBS series *American Experience: The Amish*, the community of about 250,000 people receives nearly twenty million curious tourists per year. Wondering about these visitors, an Amish individual interviewed for the show asks, "Are they yearning for something? Are they seekers?" We could ask the same of the viewers and readers (and some writers) of this contemporary Jewish genre.[11]

Orthodoxy, of course, has always played a significant role in Judaism. Yet Jewish literary history has long cast Orthodoxy as the site of rejection (if often laced with longing and nostalgia)—whether in the figure of a father-by-blood or a brother-by-association. At the turn of the twentieth century, narratives about Orthodoxy primarily highlighted children's abandonment of their fathers' dogmas. Israel Zangwill's London in his *Children of the Ghetto* can barely speak the language of their devout father, and the heroine of the novel, explicitly called an "allegory of Judaism," staggers and falls down when she is leaving the synagogue on the Day of Atonement (491). In New York, on Hester Street, the heroine of Anzia Yezierska's *Bread Givers* spurns her rabbi father and his old-world ways to the extent that she wishes the endless choices that defined America meant that "children could also pick out their fathers" (76).[12] Although there was a resurgence of Orthodox practice in the post-Holocaust era[13] in America after the influx of refugees and survivors from Europe, this was precisely the era of

the "universal" Jewish figure in literature. Perversely, the reinvigoration of Orthodoxy spurred a simultaneous reinvigoration of Orthodoxy as a site of rejection
in mainstream circles and literary representation—this time, a lateral rejection
(of one's "brother"). In 1959, Philip Roth took a brilliant dig at this fear in his
short story, "Eli, the Fanatic," wherein the Jews of Woodenton, New Jersey, are in
a new and thus tenuous position as American insiders. "It is only since the war
that Jews have been able to buy property here, and for Jews and Gentiles to live
beside each other in amity," explains Eli. "For this adjustment to be made, both
Jews and Gentiles alike have had to give up some of their more extreme practices in order not to threaten or offend each other," he adds (Roth 262, emphasis
mine). As such, the Jews regard a Hasidic newcomer as a threat to all they have
achieved—even as he is a symbol of all they have lost.[14]

Toward the end of the twentieth century, representations of Orthodoxy
became more varied than ever before. If fanatical societies that oppress their
women remains the dominant image, it is not the only one. Cynthia Ozick's
*Bloodshed*, which followed almost twenty years after "Eli, the Fanatic," tells a
story similar to Roth's: the story of the confrontation between the secular, Americanized Jew and his foreign, Hasidic cousin. But by the mid-1970s, Ozick was
able to offer us a story not of Woodenton, a typical American suburb "long . . .
the home of well-to-do Protestants," but of, more significantly, an upstate New
York Hasidic enclave in the image of New Square (Roth 262).[15] It is America made
over in the image of Orthodoxy, prefiguring the settings of Naomi Ragen, Faye
Kellerman, and Allegra Goodman's 1990s New York novels that immerse us in an
Orthodox Jewish American universe.[16]

Ozick's story is prescient in another key way: though told from the perspective of the "rational" secular character who comes to visit and pity his female
cousin (who had once planned to become the first female Jewish president of the
United States and is now a *mere mother*), our sympathies are with the Hasidim,
who are kinder, more insightful, and more honest. "Give the mother of four sons
a little credit too, it's not only college girls who build the world," the cousin's husband says "in a voice so fair-minded and humorous and obtuse that Bleilip"—
the secular figure determined to see the Hasidim as humorless misogynistic
zealots—"wanted to knock him down" (Ozick, *Bloodshed* 59). The Hasidim of
the story see what the secular man cannot—how comprehensive and yet how
limited the lens is through which Bleilip regards the "primitives," the "town of
dead men," who are not primitive or dead at all but thriving among their newly
built homes and modern appliances (Ozick, *Bloodshed* 58, 60). Here, the Hasidic
man recognizes and knows that he must resist seeing himself as he is seen; after
all, he is cast like Aimé Césaire's Caliban who, unlike Shakespeare's Caliban, can
tell Prospero, "You have lied so much to me / (lied about the world, lied about
me) / that you have ended by imposing on me / an image of myself" (Césaire 9).

In addition to Orthodoxy being a site of rejection, it can be a site of acceptance, aspiration, embrace, and investigation. This is apparent not only in Roth and Ozick's stories but also in the most sustained early engagement with Orthodoxy's potential: Chaim Potok's 1967 novel *The Chosen*, which was published between the two. This constellation of texts heralded a body of literature, which has taken a number of names: "liturgical" or moving "Toward Yavneh," in Ozick's words; an "Act II" as critic Ruth Wisse called it; or the "new wave" of Jewish writing, according to Thane Rosenbaum.[17] Admittedly, Potok's novel initially appears to be less nuanced than Roth's story. Like his turn-of-the-twentieth-century immigrant predecessors, Potok tells a story of a strict rabbi father, an oppressive religion, and the happy ending of Americanization by way of shaving *peyos* (earlocks) and getting a college education. But this is too simple a reading of *The Chosen*. After all, the foil to Hasidic Danny, Reuven Malter—in almost every way the typical American boy—is *also* Orthodox. We almost forget this detail when we watch the 1981 film version, in which the music and cinematography dramatically distinguish old-world Danny and the black-and-white-clad Hasidim from new-world American Reuven and his friends, who are decked out in baseball caps and other Americana. What Potok skillfully does—and this is a formula later repeated by writers like Ragen and Mirvis—is *normalize* Modern Orthodoxy through its contrast with ultra-Orthodoxy. The novel also drove Orthodoxy into the popular imagination.[18]

As Wisse pointed out in 1976, Ozick had "an almost complete lack of supportive evidence" when she famously "foretold the emergence of a new kind of literature" in her 1970 talk "America: Toward Yavneh" (Wisse, "Act II" 41). Yet Ozick's now oft-invoked image of the shofar, the ram's horn blown on the Jewish New Year, as the symbol of new Jewish writing appears nothing short of prophetic.[19] The body of turn-of-the-twenty-first-century Jewish writing discussed on the pages of this book constitutes that very "liturgical literature" that "has the configuration of the ram's horn: you give your strength to the inch-hole and the splendor spreads wide" (Ozick, "Yavneh" 280).[20] Allegra Goodman's *Kaaterskill Falls* (1998), for example, provides us with the full depth of humanity in the context of an Orthodox Jewish community that lives in New York's Washington Heights but does not even notice the Cloisters, so "absorbed in their own religion" as they are (4).

Of course, not every aspect of Ozick's prophecy—complicated, idealistic, demanding—has come to fruition in every example of the genre. Ozick imagined a literature that "will not be didactic or prescriptive; on the contrary, it will be Aggadic, utterly freed to invention, discourse, parable, experiment, enlightenment, profundity, humanity" (Ozick, "Yavneh" 280). Perhaps it is unreasonable (or simply too ironic) to ask a body of literature to speak to all these prescriptions. In any case, much of it is, in fact, didactic; not all of it is profound. Goodman's novel probably comes closest to Ozick's vision. Still, the engagement with the liturgical and the unabashedly Jewish, covenantal, ritualistic concerns—the Orthodox ethos Ozick imagined—is prevalent in contemporary Jewish literature. It is perhaps not as completely "free" as Ozick desired, but authors are "freer," closer in sentiment to Wisse's claim in 1976 that Jewish writers "no longer [have] to defend themselves from real or imagined charges of parochialism" and are thus "freer to explore the 'tribal' and particularistic aspects of Judaism . . . in its workable myths" (Wisse, "Act II" 41).[21]

Creating, in essence, a new genre, the writers were indeed "freed to invention": we see this in the diversity not only of forms of Orthodoxy but also of genres and modes of storytelling. The stories cannot be confined within American borders either, though most of the literary critics who examine them use this nationalistic lens. The fictions cross national borders and knit together different communities as they also distinguish one group from another. In 1978 and 1988, Tova Reich wrote Orthodox-themed satires—about American Orthodoxy in *Mara*, featuring a heroine with the same name, and Israeli hippy-cultist *ba'alei teshuva* (returnees to the faith) in *Master of the Return*, respectively.[22] In 1981, Canadian writer Nessa Rapoport published *Preparing for Sabbath*, which told the story of a Jewish girl named Judith from Toronto seeking love and spiritual fulfillment through Orthodoxy in Massachusetts, New York, and Israel. Well-known writers Chaim Potok and Philip Roth also returned to explorations of Orthodoxy during this time in new ways. Almost twenty years after publishing *The Chosen*, his best-selling book about Orthodox men and boys, Potok thought to write a book with a female protagonist; *Davita's Harp* (1985) delves into the *female* experience of and response to an Orthodox lifestyle. And in 1986, Philip Roth wrote *The Counterlife*, a book that takes readers on a spiritual and geographical journey, investigating Jewish life in suburban New Jersey, London's West End, a village in Gloucestershire, and a settlement in the West Bank. The same year, an American dentist named Faye Kellerman published the first book of her Decker/Lazarus crime novels, which feature Orthodox Misnagid Rina Lazarus at the helm of a mikvah (ritual bath), bringing together genre fiction and a primer on Orthodoxy. In 1987, Roiphe extended the ideas of Ozick's *Bloodshed* with *Lovingkindness*, which told the story of an American mother's horrified reaction to her daughter's choice to "return" to Orthodoxy and the homeland. In 1989, Ragen came out with *Jephte's Daughter*, the first book of her Haredi romance/thriller trilogy, a saga of a Hasidic woman sacrificed by her father to extremism of the faith—a tale that leads us from poolside California through Jerusalem and London.

By the end of the 1980s, it was obvious to literary critics like Thomas Friedmann (to be distinguished from the journalist Friedman) that "a growing number of contemporary novelists [were] concern[ing] themselves with issues that [were] thought to only trouble the Orthodox" (78). Reminding us of Ozick's prophecy, Friedmann writes, "The era of the covenantal Jewish novel, as Cynthia Ozick had predicted, is back" (73). A year later, scholar Alan Berger, building on Wisse's "Act II" of the 1970s, claimed "the decade of the eighties, for its part, constitutes nothing less than a third act" (221). In fact, he observed in a survey of Jewish studies, "Orthodoxy seems . . . once again to be a driving force in Jewish American literature" (223). Sylvia Barack Fishman also cites Ozick, writing in her 1991 account of American Jewish fiction from 1960 to 1990, "The new genre of American Jewish fiction has been unabashedly religious in its sensibility." It is, she writes using Ozick's words, "liturgical in nature" and "centrally Jewish in its concerns" (Fishman, "American Jewish" 35). Importantly, this genre offered a more interesting view (or views) of Orthodoxy. Indeed, as Fishman writes, "a bewildering array of diverse Orthodox societies and characters [are] . . . markedly different from American Jewish literature of the past, where Orthodox characters tended to be cranky old men or force-feeding characters and aunts" (39). And there was one more element that was clear, even in the early stages of this subgenre of Jewish literature: women dominated it.

### III. Women and the Literature of Orthodoxy

The body of liturgical Jewish writing emerging at the end of the twentieth century had a distinctly feminine cast. It was, of course, a time when women were realizing that they could tell their own stories—stories of women who were not merely the appendices, accoutrements, or accomplices of men. It was a time when women began to look for their own role models, their foremothers. In 1977, Elaine Showalter published her groundbreaking study *A Literature of Their Own: British Women Novelists from Brontë to Lessing*, proclaiming a tradition of women writers. This was closely followed by Sandra Gilbert and Susan Gubar's *The Madwoman in the Attic: The Woman Writer and the Nineteenth-Century Literary Imagination* (1979) and the launching of a new field of feminist literary studies. Jewish women's writing also resurfaced to challenge and revise dominant literary and cultural histories: In 1969, Elizabeth Gertrude Stern's *I Am a Woman—and a Jew* (1926), the autobiography of "Leah Morton," was recovered and reissued. Stern writes of leaving her family's Hasidic traditions and marrying a non-Jew, thinking the marriage would make her not Jewish as well ("How mistaken I had been" [Morton 2]).[23] In 1975, Alice Kessler-Harris republished Anzia Yezierska's *Bread Givers* (1925). "'There wasn't anybody who didn't know Anzia Yezierska,' commented a woman recently of the 1920s. Today, there is hardly anyone who does," wrote Kessler-Harris in the introduction to the new edition. The work of recovery continues into the twenty-first century. Lori Harrison-Kahan, for example, has been recovering a pantheon of forgotten early twentieth-century Western American Jewish women writers. Among these women, prolific, sassy, and at times profound suffragist Miriam Michelson has been a source of discursive delight for Harrison-Kahan and me in our ongoing collaborative research.[24]

It would surely be unsurprising to discover that Jewish women have always had their own traditions, experiences, and practices—and their own stories. It is telling that many of the sites of resistance to the rejection of Orthodoxy in the early twentieth century appear in the stories of women: in Cahan's *Yekl*, Gitl loses her wig but keeps a hat and her Jewish name (despite Yekl/Jake's attempt to make her a "Gertie") and is set to marry a religious scholar after the divorce from her off-the-*derech* (off the path of Orthodoxy) husband. Mary Antin tells, in her memoir *The Promised Land* (1912), of her father forcing her mother to abandon her *sheitel* (Jewish marital wig) and the rest of her "mantle of orthodox observance," suggesting Antin's mother's resistance to relinquishing her religious practice (247). Chaim Grade describes his mother's continued observance in his memoir, *Der Mames Shabasim* (*My Mother's Sabbath Days* [1955]). "Old Gran'ma Lowenthal," the "gentle, timid, sweet, little old-fashioned Jewish mother," is the only conspicuously Jewish character in Michelson's 1905 novel *A Yellow Journalist* (157). She is a sympathetic and generous foil to her "daughter-in-law of another religion, another caste, an 'outlandish woman' lightly contemptuous of the man who was sacrosanct in that clean, simple temple—his mother's heart" (159). Old Gran'ma Lowenthal prays over the body of a dying man, invoking the *selichot*—the penitential prayers—of the Ten Days of Repentance and Yom Kippur, the Day of Atonement: "'O Eternal, our God,' she prayed passionately, bending over him, 'pardon all our sins and forgive all our iniquities and grant us remission for all our transgressions'" (167)—or, as it is better known among Jews, "*Selach lanu . . . mechal lanu . . . kaper lanu . . .*"

In *Strands of the Cable: The Place of the Past in Jewish American Women's Writing* (named after a line in Mary Antin's introduction to *The Promised Land*: "We are the strands of the cable that binds the Old World to the New"), Ellen Serlen Uffen argues that women's place in Jewish American literary history has been underrecognized. "Their view of reality adds to that of the men," she writes. "The world, as discovered through women's eyes, is not the world men see" (2). The problems of that underrecognition include an obscuring of women's religious practices. Uffen notes that women in literature struggle with questions of identity: "How does one live, they all wonder in various ways, as a Jewish woman in secular America?" She adds in parentheses,

> Women, who were not formally schooled in religion beyond a familiarity with a few basic prayers, ironically, were not so quick as men to abandon religious practice. Religion was a definitive link with the Old World, identified by the women with home and family and not, as it was by their husbands, with poverty and oppression and lack of freedom. If the Shabbos candles continued to be lighted in the crowded tenement apartments of New York or Boston, then, it was the women who made sure to do it, although few of them could read the prayers that all of them recited from memory. (3–4)

Although Uffen's work is not specifically or only about Orthodoxy in women's literature, she captures the ways in which Orthodoxy is wedded to and embedded in female characters of women writers over the course of the twentieth century. There is no question that many women writers rejected Orthodoxy, like their male counterparts—Antin rejects it, along with her father—but still, we are left with the sense that Orthodoxy lingered in specifically feminized ways. Yet never has that link between female experience and Orthodoxy been as explicit as it is in contemporary Jewish literature.

In the last few decades, scholars have been actively engaged in studying the literature of Orthodoxy, reading it, as Sara Horowitz does in a 2006 article, as a "crucial shift from considering Jewishness as a North American ethnicity or subculture to thinking about Judaism as a religion" (236). Similarly, in his 2007 book, *American Talmud*, Ezra Cappell asserts that what unites early twenty-first-century Jewish American literature is "an abiding interest in representing Judaism and its traditions" (175). He further notes that the recent representations of Orthodoxy in this literature have been both prominent and controversial—and like Horowitz, he takes this controversy to be a sign that Jewish American literature is in the throes of a revolution. "Although the discussion on Orthodox representation has only just begun," writes Cappell, "one idea seems underscored by this literary debate concerning Orthodox representation: [Irving] Howe's conception that 'American Jewish fiction has probably moved past its high point' could not be more wrong" (176).

Many scholars choose the nexus of women and Orthodoxy as their primary focus of study—and with good reason. Berger calls the "role of gender in Jewish practice" a central concern (A. Berger 222). Fishman adds, "Feminist exploration is one of the most significant new generic movements" (Fishman, "American Jewish" 46). Alyse Roller devotes her 1999 study, *The Literary Imagination of Ultra-Orthodox Jewish Women*, to the self-help books, anthologies, personal narratives, Holocaust testimonials, and incipient fiction that Orthodox women began writing for each other in the late twentieth century. Judith Lewin argues in a 2008 article that the "salient feature of . . . [new Jewish] writing [is] the return of contemporary Jewish women to a religious practice, to a Jewish sense of self and community, and to a Jewish spirituality and family" (2). Barbara Landress's 2012 monograph, *All Her Glory Within*, explores the conflicts between feminism and Orthodoxy in Jewish women's fiction, arguing that these literary texts "support the historian Menahem Friedman's thesis that women are the agents of change in Orthodox society and more generally in Jewish culture" (172). In the 2016 *Edinburgh Companion to Modern Jewish Fiction*, Rachel S. Harris calls the "fourth generation" of Jewish American women writers "the medium in which the tension between the longing for and the rejection of a traditional and religiously observant world is addressed" (77). And in the same volume, we see that the link between women and Orthodoxy is not confined to and should be studied outside of American literature. Phyllis Lassner argues that British Jewish women's literature has remained on the margins of both the multicultural study of women writers and British Jewish Studies, even though "their plots contrast men's and women's struggles with acculturation to British social culture [and] women's relation to Jewish religious observance" (Lassner 199).[25]

## IV. Ask Her

Interviewed about *The Marrying of Chani Kaufman*, which was long-listed for the Man Booker prize, Eve Harris admitted to being both beguiled and repelled by Haredi life (Kean). Certainly, many Jewish writers have used Orthodox Jewish women in their fiction to express and negotiate their anxieties about their otherness, as Rubel's *Doubting the Devout* demonstrates. And others have engaged it in ways that suggest condemnation, romanticization, nostalgia, and kinship. It is a chance to flirt with the concept of postsecularism. Some of these writers are "seekers." But surely writing about Orthodox Jewish women is a project also open to Orthodox Jewish women. Can the Orthodox woman, to channel Gayatri Spivak's famous question, speak? Is it possible to attend not only to the voices of secular Jewish and non-Jewish writers imagining Orthodox women but also to the voices of the Orthodox women imagining secular Jews, and non-Jews, along with themselves? Can we see how Orthodox women imagine and negotiate their experiences and relationships and the roles and images projected on them? Or are Orthodox women too confined and defined—too policed by their communities—to tell their own stories?

There is reason to think they are. Although we must be wary of the sensationalism of news accounts about "non-Western" (anachronistic, primitive, backward) communities, the sheer number of accounts of women's subjugation under Orthodoxy, which began escalating in the twenty-first century, forces us to take seriously the rising fundamentalism in these communities. In New York, it was discovered—and widely reported—that on the B110 in Brooklyn, Orthodox women were being sent to the back of the bus, which called to mind for many Americans an era of racial segregation. The laws of the land were disregarded in favor of those supposedly decreed by God: "If God makes a rule," a Hasidic man told a woman who asked why she had to move from the front of the bus, "you don't ask 'Why make the rule?'" (Chavkin, "Women Ride"). In a small town in Quebec, the Lev Tahor community's abuse of women and girls was exposed when the police raided the community (Mezzofiore). And in Beit Shemesh, Israel, a group of Haredi men attacked young Orthodox (non-Haredi) girls going to school for what they saw as their immodest dress. The men spat on the seven- and eight-year-old girls; threw food, feces, and bricks into their schoolyard; and called the girls and their caregivers harlots. Although there have been several examples of Israel's Haredi community leading the way in what

Elana Maryles Sztokman calls Orthodoxy's "war on women," this attack was the incident that garnered international attention.[26] Furthermore, the men inspired little sympathy with the justification of their behavior. As reported in the British newspaper the *Guardian*, "when community activist Rabbi Dov Lipman asked one protester why they were focusing on the way small girls dress, he was told 'even an eight-year-old draws my eyes'" (Sherwood). After the story was aired on television, the BBC reported that the broadcast covering it "inflamed secular opinion" ("Beit Shemesh").

At stake in all these incidents is an obsession with women's roles and bodies, as evident in the literature Orthodox rabbis were producing. In 2012, an influential Israeli Religious Zionist leader, Rabbi Zvi Tau, published a pamphlet called "Who Created Me as He Willed," telling women, in the words of the English-language headline of the left-leaning Israeli newspaper *Haaretz*, that "A Woman's Place Is in the Home." Tau writes, "Home is the natural habitat for women to express their special tendency . . . not the domain of social activity. At home, without the bustle . . . is where a woman can fully live her life." Tau also clearly states that women should be consigned to their biological reproductive role. Motherhood is a woman's "natural vocation, and God created within her the necessary talents and an inner orientation for these issues." Any alternative "will harm the quality of life of the nation and society, since the true female character will not be realized and will be missed by the world. Society and the nation should rather be built on perfecting the special attributes imprinted in women" (Levinson).

Following news of Tau's pamphlet, in December 2012, I learned that Rabbi Shlomo Aviner, another leader of the Religious Zionist movement, had issued a strict set of modesty decrees in "Be'ahava U'be'emuna (With Love and Faith)," his synagogue leaflet. Aviner's leaflet was essentially an update on *Modesty: An Adornment for Life*, or what's called *The Tznius Bible* (*tznius* being Yiddish for "modest")—a 1998 book by Rabbi Pesach Falk, complete with pictures of faceless or feature-vague women in an extreme version of TLC's *What Not to Wear*. This near-exhaustive book tries to account for all possible immodesties in dress. For example, Falk warned against the wearing of white undergarments, which could immodestly appear through outer clothing and which Falk recommended dying with a tea bag. He also discouraged the carrying of a heavy shoulder bag, which could pull on a garment and reveal flesh. And what if the woman were to lose weight? Had she checked that her old clothing still fit as snugly around the neck as it once did to maintain its kashruth—its kosher status?

Apparently, however, Falk's compendium was not thorough enough. Although Aviner begins with complimentary language about how "wonderful and pleasant" women's modesty is, "how much nobility and honor, purity and holiness is there," the media picked up on the misogynistic undertones of his communiqué (Aviner). In addition to a list of problematic fabrics (jersey, Lycra, tricot) that could be tight and/or revealing, Ynet news reported Aviner's very specific account of expectations for female clothing and hair, which girls ought to be educated on by the age of three:

> The rabbi rules that a skirt must be "10 centimeters (4 inches) longer than the body dimensions in the widest place, and 50 centimeters (20 inches) in the knee area." Another method [of measurement] is "to examine the skirt's width by lifting your leg onto an ordinary chair." According to the rabbi, the body must be fully covered by the garment . . . "the neck must be covered: A. On the sides till the place the body curves. B. in the back till the first vertebra. C. In the front till the bones. The upper button must be fastened of course, a high neck is even better." The arms, according to the rabbi, must be covered "till under elbow in any case." Sleeves with wide edges must be avoided "as the arm is revealed when the hand is lifted or any other movements are made." (Nahshoni)

The article goes on to reveal Rabbi Aviner's forbidden colors (red, nude, orange, yellow, green, gold, silver, or anything shiny), the required length of a skirt, the required thickness of stockings, the kinds of fasteners that are acceptable (buttons are generally not), the appropriate style of shoes, and the rabbi's favored hair coverings and hairdos for women and girls ("For single women . . . a braid is the best option"; Nahshoni). Few elements of female appearance escaped Aviner's notice.

News of this nature has spurred some awareness about how Orthodox womanhood was being controlled, and not only in Israel: journalists in New York reported that modesty patrols were being put on duty to check women's clothing, and in London, street signs were calling for a segregation of the sexes.[27] As with the response of the British education secretary to Belz Hasidic women being banned from driving, the response to these actions was simply that they were, in the modern world, "completely unacceptable."

But what is lost in the mainstream media representation is this: *Orthodox girls and women were (and are) not all sitting silently in their dun-colored, floor-length, appropriately fastened clothing at the back of the bus or locked in their homes, despairing their helpless fate.* Many enjoy very satisfying lives. Levine argues that Lubavitch girls are, in fact, a *beacon* for mainstream girls, who often suffer from low self-esteem in a culture that valorizes unrealistic beauty and inspires competition for men's affection. Hasidic girls, who lead lives removed from consumerism (to a degree) and sexual excess and are segregated from their male counterparts, according to Levine, have an "exquisitely refined sense of their feelings and thoughts," "are open about their insights," and "handle intense conflict with poise, grit, self-understanding, and courage" (211). Additionally, Fader, writing of Hasidic women, even of the very stringent courts, avers that despite being "forbidden to participate in many forms of . . . leisure activities such as going to the movies, watching television, reading certain books . . . they are neither isolated nor oppressed in their lives" (Fader 25).

Moreover, to some of the rabbinical decrees, there was and is a clear backlash. This is beautifully depicted in the 2016 Israeli film *The Women's Balcony*, written by Shlomit Nehama. In the film, the women's balcony of a synagogue collapses. The old, revered rabbi and rebbetzin of the synagogue take ill, and a handsome, charismatic, single rabbi (played by Avraham Aviv Alush, who resembles a young Omar Sharif) tries to persuade a happy and pious congregation to adopt a series of practices that severely compromise the women's lives. Rabbi David offers compelling rhetoric for his decrees. He argues, for example, that men need to study Torah and women do not because women are always already holy. He says that women should cover up in a fashion similar to the Torah to protect their holiness. He excludes women from the synagogue not because they can have no place there but because, he explains, construction of their space cannot be prioritized over the cost of a scribe for a new Torah. He rules out the courtship of a male congregant with a young woman who is a serious student and poor housekeeper. In response to their new headscarves, placelessness in the synagogue, and declared unsuitability, the women bond together, raise money, stage protests, and convince their husbands that this rabbi is leading them astray. By the end of the film, the women have triumphed. The new rabbi is removed, and the old one—whose devoted murmurings to his wife are essentially the only words he mutters throughout the film—is returned to his rightful place, as are the female congregants to the synagogue and the young woman to her suitor (the film, in the classic tradition of comedies, ends in a wedding).

This film is not mere fantasy. Real women are responding similarly. Batsheva Neuer, for example, who self-identifies as a member of the Religious Zionist community, showed her defiance to Rav Aviner's decrees when she wrote a *Jerusalem Post* op-ed titled "Will the Real Religious Zionist Leaders Please Stand Up?":

> As a (modest) woman who has always identified with this sector, Aviner's ostracizing clothing regulations are enough to render his understanding of the religious Zionist cultural climate obsolete. His words are also enough to dissuade young, religious Zionist women from attempting to take their engagement in Judaism seriously. How can we really relate to a leader who hypersexualizes women, objectifying them as mere inducements to sin?
>
> I couldn't help but feel violated as I read through the regulations—Aviner, a talmid chacham (wise student) who spends his day immersed in Torah learning, seems more aware of the inches of a woman's body than most girls I know.
>
> Does a man publicly highlighting every nook and cranny of women's physiques reflect the so-called "modesty" that we are aspiring to? Is this what God had in mind when He declared: "Let your Camp be holy"?
>
> When asked why his wife did not cover her hair, Rabbi Joseph Soloveitchik, the great halachic and philosophical authority of the last generation, reportedly responded: "ask her." When will religious Zionist rabbis like Aviner follow

suit and maintain a more "ask her" policy toward women's behavior and dress? (Neuer)

Citing this story from the great halachic authority from the last generation is a way of reminding us that contemporary rabbinical decrees reflect the "Haredization" or hyperbolization of Judaism, the sliding to the right of Orthodoxy. It is also Neuer's way of rejecting contemporary characterizations of Orthodoxy without rejecting Orthodox Judaism. And there are other kinds of responses to contemporary Orthodox Judaism and to contemporary Orthodox Judaism's position within a "modern" world—a world framed in terms seemingly antithetical to Orthodoxy's. We might find that these responses favor egalitarianism, individualism, science, and reason; there are many possibilities. But to know how the Orthodox woman responds to the worlds around her, Jewish and secular, and negotiates both her constraints and the images projected on her, we must, to echo Rabbi Soloveitchik and Batsheva Neuer, "ask her."

## V. Calling on the "Woman of Valor"

"The authors who focus on Jewish spirituality often seem to share a symbolic language, a loosely connected system of themes and metaphors," writes Fishman, adding that "the fact that such a kinship exists is significant and notable, because it indicates the richness of this most intensive incarnation of contemporary particularistic American Jewish fiction" ("American Jewish" 48). When we "ask her," we get, as we should expect, many answers. We cannot reduce the voices of Jewish women to a single voice, just as we cannot reduce Orthodox women to the images imposed on them by their communities or the secular world.[28] But there is a trope that has emerged in these voices, and that is the invocation of the "woman of valor" from Proverbs 31, long a staple in Jewish religious and cultural life. The woman of valor functions as a symbolic figure in contemporary Jewish women's fiction to present and represent (and problematize) the ideals of Orthodox Jewish womanhood.

Over the course of this book, I will discuss the novels, stories, memoirs, films, blogs, television shows, radio programs, cover art, magazines, and music that offer new ways of envisioning the woman of valor. To limit this project to high literature would be to miss the rich variation in the articulation of this trope, the multiple forms it takes, and the contexts in which it emerges. That this project is a transnational one is crucial too: as national borders rarely fully separate Orthodox communities, they also fail to fully separate Orthodox literary and cultural productions. American Jewish fiction leads the way, but it also shares the path.

In this emergent body of liturgical literature, the woman of valor is the Jewish model that writers and thinkers rely on when constructing their pictures of Orthodox girls and women who might devote themselves to the rituals of

Judaism, solve mysteries, lead communities, run businesses, and play music for women to "rock out" and enjoy themselves. Or in biblical parlance, these women of valor are G-d-fearing women who can find. They are women who open their mouths with wisdom and sense that their enterprises are good. They will be praised at the gates by their very own deeds.

As we will see, the woman of valor is not a universally accepted image of agency. A number of writers and filmmakers critique the model as antifeminist and unrealistic. Scholars and activists frequently see in this model the Orthodox woman's consignment to the domestic sphere. "The household management skills of the hardworking wife are the subject of much praise in Prov. 31:10–31. As always in male-centered scripture, the positive and negative roles of women are viewed primarily from the perspective of what they provide for the men involved," writes Carole R. Fontaine in the *Women's Bible Commentary* (154). Other feminist exegeses highlight the patriarchal nature of the praise, arguing that the woman of valor is "auxiliary" (Carmody 73), a "slave-woman" (qtd. in Fox 93), and complicitous in her own enslavement. In 1972, a group of women calling themselves *Ezrat Nashim* challenged the Conservative movement with a manifesto, "Jewish Women Call for a Change." They wrote, "It is not enough to say that Judaism views women as separate but equal, not enough to point to Judaism's past superiority over other cultures in its treatment of women. We've had enough of apologetics: enough of Bruria, Dvorah, and Esther; enough of *eshet hayil*" (Bloomberg 116). One of these women, Paula Hyman, went on to write the landmark text *Jewish Women: New Perspectives* (1976), in which she declares, "While men are allowed to define themselves through a wide spectrum of activity in the world, women are defined in sociobiological terms as wife and mother and relegated almost exclusively to the home and family life" (106). Even in the twenty-first century, we see the same arguments arise. Yael Israel-Cohen notes in her 2012 book, *Between Feminism and Orthodox Judaism*, that although Orthodox women receive weekly praise for their duties in the song "Eshes Chayil," their duties are (only) domestic, and "the fact that women are given praise for their duties does not change their status in the literature from being limited and inferior" (18).

In many ways, then, the interpretation of the *eshes chayil* is at the heart of these debates about the Orthodox woman. The lines of debate do not necessarily run along authors' religious affiliations, contrary to Wendy Shalit's well-known *New York Times* rant against writers who depict Orthodoxy but are not themselves practicing.[29] For example, Ragen, who identifies as Orthodox, offers sharp critiques of women's roles under Orthodoxy in her "Haredi trilogy." We can more easily see her alignment with "off-the-*derech*" writers like Deborah Feldman, whose 2012 memoir of Satmar Hasidic life, *Unorthodox*, was a bestseller. Conversely, Allegra Goodman has moved between Conservative Judaism and a liberal Orthodoxy (the vision of her "Kirshner" Jews stemmed from visits to her mother's familial home in upstate New York, where she witnessed a tight-knit Orthodox Jewish community), and she writes one of the most sympathetic and nuanced depictions of the strictly Orthodox woman in *Kaaterskill Falls* (1998). More importantly, the debates are not only intertextual but also intratextual, deeply embedded in individual works by and about Orthodox women.

To analyze these debates, I will begin by examining the "hottest new trend" in New York publishing, as declared by *Tablet Magazine*: the memoirs and novels that chronicle women's experiences under (the oppressive conditions of) Orthodoxy and, typically, their departures from their communities. In the 1980s, Ragen set the stage with her first novel, *Jephte's Daughter*, which the *New York Times* dubbed a "Jewish Gothic." In the twenty-first century, we see her legacy in the proliferation of "off-the-*derech*" writing, which I discuss in the first chapter, "A G-d-Fearing Woman, She Should Be Praised." Many memoirs emerged, in concordance with the era, as blogs, enabling authors to have direct contact and dynamic interaction with their readership; some blogs were later transformed into print editions. Though men joined this fray—chiefly Shalom Auslander and Shulem Deen—the field has been dominated by women: Deborah Feldman, Frieda Vizel, Leah Vincent, Reva Mann, Leah Lax, and Chaya Deitsch. Alongside these memoirs sits the complementary fiction by "off-the-*derech*" writers such as Judy Brown, Anouk Markovits, and Naomi Alderman. Crucially, unlike Ragen's "Jewish Gothic," this new body of writing offers a more nuanced picture of the faith than has been assumed by Shalit and other critics.

Read as authenticating documents supporting a secular thesis, these narratives, which express deep dissatisfaction with the roles of women in Orthodoxy, often ironically reclaim the tenets of Orthodoxy for women. With sensationalist paratextual features, they appear in line with the "veiled bestsellers" of Muslim women in a post–9/11 era, stories that scholars have shown to be packaged for and misread by a Western, mainstream, feminist audience that prizes its ability to liberate the oppressed. Yet the stories demonstrate an ability to liberate from within. And it is as much Orthodox Judaism as the women themselves requiring liberation. Repeatedly comparing the religion to its practice, the authors and artists of these works insist that it is the current articulation and not the fundamental beliefs of Orthodoxy oppressing women. By way of example, I turn to the 2010 semibiographical novel *Hush* by Judy Brown (writing as "Eishes Chayil"). A novel that recounts the story of a young Orthodox girl who is sexually abused and commits suicide, *Hush* demonstrates how Orthodox communities can silence individuals who speak out about their deep-seated problems and thus fail to alleviate them. When the heroine of the novel speaks out against the atrocities she has witnessed, she is criticized. But the heroine is vindicated in the end by the novel and by her husband, who reminds her what a woman of valor really is. Writers like Brown employ the model of the woman of valor to expose the suppressed problems of Orthodox communities, engaging in dialogue about them and seeking remedies.

Also spawned in the R(e)agen era—a time of Cold War fears, peak U.S. crime rates, and rediscovered religious influence—was another kind of "Jewish Gothic": Faye Kellerman's Decker/Lazarus series, which I investigate in the second chapter, "A Woman of Valor Who Can Find." Here, the "Jewish" absorbs and diffuses rather than fuels the "gothic," rendering it harmless in the face of the more powerful forces of good and God. Kellerman has taken this series from the 1980s through the present day (*Walking Shadows*, published in 2018, is the twenty-fifth book in the series). The longitudinal nature of the series has allowed readers to track the heroine, Rina Lazarus, from her early twenties to her middle age, learning, stage by stage, about the whole life of a "woman of valor." She is not always perfect (she makes a few errors in judgment) and not always as chaste as some might imagine a woman of valor to be, but when the rabbinical sage of the series, old-world Holocaust survivor Rabbi Schulman, takes the hero aside and explicitly says of Rina, "She's an *eishes chayil*," the reader already knows (Kellerman, *Sacred* 206). She's beautiful, she's industrious, she's mostly modest, she cooks and bakes and teaches and cares for her children, and she is ever the dutiful wife. Shamelessly didactic, Kellerman only allows resistance to this image in order to contain it. Cindy, Rina's stepdaughter, hears the "Woman of Valor" and believes "the gist of it centered around a woman slaving away without complaint to support her husband and family" (Kellerman, *Street Dreams* 113). But Cindy's role is to reflect the skeptical reader. Kellerman has Cindy soon come around, and she, like her father, begins to embrace the religious dimension of her Judaism, becoming, like Rina, something of a woman of valor herself.

Although Kellerman deftly transports readers through the vagaries of Rina's life (as Rina's children grow up and leave for college, Kellerman offers her ways of expressing her role that are not bound to motherhood), there is something unrealized in Kellerman's depiction of the woman of valor crime-fiction heroine. Perhaps that is why Rochelle Krich invented Molly Blume, a heroine who follows in Rina's footsteps but is more nuanced, more sensitive to competing notions of truth, and less idealized—a twenty-first-century woman of valor who combines mystery-solving with the lighting of *Shabbos* candles while also questioning everything about her role along the way. This character is educational as well: the friction between Molly's "modern" American life and "traditional" religious ideals are not easily resolved, and it is a friction that Krich forces readers to wade in. Of course, with violence and sex (though Molly Blume, despite favoring cleavage and short skirts, is chaster than Rina), neither Kellerman nor Krich's series is appropriate for the strictly Orthodox reader. But Rebecca Lyon, sheltered from violence and too young for sex or romance, is perfect. In Rebecca, heroine of the Ezra Melamed/Jewish Regency Mystery Series, readers find another literary descendent of crime fiction's queen woman of valor Rina Lazarus. Young Rebecca is the creation of Haredi writer Libi Astaire, who crafts each mystery book as a history lesson about the lives of Orthodox Jews in early nineteenth-century London. There, no life is more interesting (or less visible in fiction and history) than that of a smart, plucky, inquisitive, and pious woman-of-valor-in-training.

If mystery novels can act as primers of Orthodoxy, "mom-to-mom" stories can also instruct—and in so doing, forge bonds between warring communities. In the third chapter, "She Opens Her Mouth with Wisdom," I look at the inspirational work of Malka Zipora, the pseudonym of a Hasidic writer, who was born in Israel to Hungarian parents, moved to New York, and ultimately settled on the north side of the border in Montreal. There, she discovered a sharp clash between the large Hasidic communities and the policy of laïcité, or French secularism, which—unlike the American model of separation of church and state that includes "free exercise" of religion—denies religious practices, particularly those thought to interfere with gender egalitarianism. In her short story collection, Lekhaim!: Chroniques de la vie hassidique à Montréal (later published in English as Rather Laugh than Cry [2007]), Zipora situates us in this context. Yet her book is not overtly political or reactionary. Instead, it plays the role of a cultural bridge, universalizing the experiences of Hasidim, particularly the mothers of the households, and telling their tales in a manner that relates to secular francophone readers.

Remarkably, publication of this book seems to have set off a chain of events in which Hasidic women have taken prominence in mediating the culture wars of Quebec: in 2008, a young Hasidic woman hosted a public wedding in Sainte-Agathe-des-Monts, a frequent site of anti-Semitism, inviting the entire town and the press in order to render visible and familiar Jewish customs and rituals. In 2013, Mindy Pollak, a Hasidic woman of the Vishnitz community ran for and was elected to public office in Montreal, a significant first and a direct response to the Quebecois fears that Hasidic men were oppressing their women. In 2014, a filmmaker aired his documentary Shekinah, about the "intimate life of Hasidic women," using Chanie Carlebach, a formidable rebbetzin, the founder and director of an international women's seminary, and a mother of twelve, to showcase the strength and drive of Hasidic women. Quebec's growing interest in the Hasidic woman almost took a walk down the red carpet: in September 2015, Canada chose Félix et Meira, Maxime Giroux's film about a married Hasidic woman who falls in love with a Quebecois man, for its foreign-language submission to the Oscars (see figure I.3).

Still, the terrain tread by the heroines of "off-the-derech" memoirs and fiction, by crime-solving educators, and by Hasidic moms who extend their ideas of kiruv (outreach) beyond their fellow Jews is all, in some ways, unsurprising: it centers on community, a traditionally feminine sphere. In chapter 4, "She Senses That Her Enterprise Is Good," however, I interrogate the economic role of the Orthodox woman. This role is hotly contested, an apparent oxymoron. Whether it is

Figure I.3. Scene from the film *Félix et Meira* (2014). Produced by Metafilms. Photo by Julie Landreville.

National Security Agency chief risk officer Anne Neuberger in the United States, or the women's editor for *The Telegraph* Emma Barnett in Britain, Orthodox Jewish women in high-profile positions are repeatedly asked to account for the perceived incompatibility of their professional and religious lives. Suggesting that this seeming incommensurability stems from Victorian-era Christian models of womanhood, not traditional Jewish ones, this chapter revisits the entrepreneurial aspects of the woman of valor, focusing on Allegra Goodman's critically acclaimed novel, *Kaaterskill Falls* (1998).

Goodman's novel is a clear intervention in American Jewish literary history; for the first time, we read the story of a dedicated wife, a mother of five, and a wig-wearing observant Jew—who is also an ambitious businesswoman. Like her predecessors, Goodman presents selective verses of the hymn "Woman of Valor," here focusing on the economic elements of the role. Readers join the members of an Orthodox family around the table as they laud Elizabeth, the wife and mother of the house, for her ability to financially support them: "*Ashes chayil miyimtza? V'rachok mipnimi michrah*'" (Goodman, *Kaaterskill* 157). This first line is translated, along with the subsequent one: "She seeks wool and flax, and works with eager hands" (158). The key to reconciliation between the Old World and the New, Orthodoxy and feminism, and community and capitalism in the book, the *eshes chayil* is here deployed precisely to exalt the Orthodox woman's *non*domestic duties. Elizabeth's husband asks, "Is it really such a question whether a woman can start a business?" He concludes, "This is the work of the virtuous wife, the '*Ashes Chayil*' in the ancient song" (Goodman 158–159). Through Elizabeth, her fictional businesswoman, and Isaac, her supportive husband, Goodman opens a window on a potentially feminist Orthodox Judaism where women *are* valued, in the words of Rebecca Goldstein's doubtful protagonist of *The Mind-Body Problem*, "for bringing home the kosher beef fry."

The recognition of the importance of Orthodox women's paid work is a common theme in films by Orthodox women—but unfortunately (or not), men never see these films. In the final chapter of the book, "She Will Be Praised at the Gates by Her Very Own Deeds," I investigate the idea of the Orthodox artist and the exclusive entertainment that Orthodox women generate and consume, films foremost among them. As we see, there is a creative tension that ensues in the nexus of Orthodox women's artistic yearnings and a culture of gender segregation. This tension gives rise to a feminocentric cultural canon: films, stories, magazines (online and print), and music by and for women only. Although presumably constructed entirely apart from mainstream culture, these works often adopt and adapt popular genres and cultural productions for female Haredi audiences. In these works, then, we might find a little orphan Annie who is a refugee from pogroms or Mary Poppins quoting Torah, direct from Stamford Hill. Here I extend the work of Yoel Finkelman, who argues that Haredim have a vested interest in creating kosher entertainment to prevent community members from being lured by the outside world.

These women-only spaces are discursive as well as literal, and this chapter provides close readings of the films of Tobi Einhorn and Robin Garbose, who screen their all-female-performance productions for women-only audiences and restrict their release on DVD. We see a focus on contemporary issues for Orthodox women: women needing to work while also being charged with caring for their households, women coping with being unwed or childless in a community with cultural imperatives to marry and procreate, and women being sent to the back of the bus to avoid contact with male passengers. The films are used to work through fears and anxieties and offer support for viewers.

The chapter concludes with a discussion of the history, music, and reception of the all-girl alt-rock indie Hasidic band, Bulletproof Stockings, and its derivative, PERL (the latter featured on the front cover of this book, illustrated by the Orthodox Jewish woman artist, Elke Reva Sudin). As in the secular world, Orthodox women's stories, in novels and on screen, fashion, develop, and sustain a community. It is a community that is primarily virtual: between the making and viewing of a film or the writing and reading of a book lies a temporal and spatial gap. This gap is embodied on the screen on which the film is projected and the paper on which the words are printed. Performances by bands like Bulletproof Stockings offer examples of Orthodox women's cultural productions that audiences encounter in a direct and unmediated fashion. Moving beyond the "imagined community" of the literary and film industries, Bulletproof Stockings—bold, inspiring, engaged with women who are observant Jews (engaged with women of all kinds, in fact)—produced a radical vision of what Orthodox Jewish women can do. I argue that their concerts provided a revision of the Chabad-Lubavitch *farbrengen*, a traditional spiritual gathering of single-sex participants who come together, most famously at "770," Chabad's headquarters, to sing and dance and drink and celebrate. At the twenty-first-century concerts of Bulletproof Stockings, located at such legendary Manhattan venues as Arlene's Grocery or Webster Hall, these participants (Jewish and non-Jewish) coming for Hasidic-inspired music were all women. And through these Hasidic rockers, they united to form a modern, spiritually empowered sisterhood.

Throughout the works examined in *Women of Valor* is the desire to educate readers, viewers, and listeners; to revise misconceptions; and to explore the possibilities of the "woman of valor." We also find a great deal of ambivalence. For example, Deutsch's taglines indicate a number of positionings of the Orthodox girl. His second *Hereville* graphic novel, *How Mirka Met a Meteorite* (2012), bears a tagline that, unlike the first, makes his heroine an *exceptional* rather than *typical* specimen of her culture: "Boldly Going Where No 11-Year-Old Orthodox Jewish Girl Has Gone Before." His third tagline, for *How Mirka Caught a Fish* (2015), returns to the representational while also reinstating this portrayal within her more expected sphere as caregiver: "Yet Another 11-Year-Old Time-Traveling Orthodox Jewish Babysitter." But it is precisely in this ambivalence that we can see the richness of the woman of valor. Just as the *eshes chayil* in the song can be a woman of the home and a woman of a trade, so too can a modern Orthodox woman, even if the two lifestyles don't and can't always act in harmony. Today's narratives by and about Orthodox women are an engaging, at times provocative, counterargument to the mainstream media's picture of the Gitl of the twenty-first century. They are in constant battle with that picture, often manage to reinforce it, and have not emerged as the dominant image—or images.

Still, the literature is here. And it is growing. So let us soar with Mirka above the ball of yarn in the sky and see how we can unravel its many and varied tales.

# CHAPTER 1

# A G-d-Fearing Woman, She Should Be Praised

### EXPOSURE, DIALOGUE, AND REMEDY IN "OFF-THE-*DERECH*" NARRATIVES

### I. INTRODUCTION: STILL JEWISH

*IN MY DREAM . . . I was in a car with Larry David, driving through Brooklyn. As we entered an Orthodox Jewish neighborhood, Larry said, "Oy gevalt! It's Passover!" and piously bowed his head. "Larry," I said, surprised, "I didn't know you cared about this stuff." And in my dream Larry David replied, with great solemnity: "I don't believe in God, but I do believe in Jews."*
—James Parker, "The Joy of Vex," *The Atlantic*, July/August 2011

*I've come to a conclusion. I can't be an Orthodox Jew. I don't have it in me and I never did. But I can't not be one, either.*
—Ronit Krushka in Naomi Alderman's *Disobedience* (2006)

What does it mean to reject the Jewish God or religious practice but not a commitment to Jews and Jewishness? Why is it that not only the avowedly "cultural" Jews like Larry David but also those raised in the "religious" world of Judaism insist on some kind of essence of Jewry that begs distinction from dogma?[1] After all, James Parker's imagined Larry David is suggestive of a far greater phenomenon, which can be seen in the proliferation of narratives by men and women who have left Orthodox communities and describe a religion rendered archaic, stifling, and alienating but also, oddly, unabandoned. The women, in particular, tell stories of oppression, abuse, and silencing. Living in an Orthodox community, they have suffered under the weight of their wigs and their wombs. They have watched the suffering of others. And because they have left this harrowing environment, we might expect a wholesale denunciation of it. Yet they fail to reject Judaism and its laws or figuratively walk away from their communities even when they have literally, suggesting that these stories have a different purpose.[2]

"Off-the-*derech*" (off the path of Orthodoxy) narratives, like much of religious literature (whose antithesis we might imagine them to be), are indeed purposeful—didactic, instructive, and exegetical. The books flaunt images of naked women on their covers, promise sex and drugs, and are marketed as sensationalist tell-all exposés akin to Muslim "veiled bestsellers" and other ex-religious (misery) memoirs. They are sold as authenticating tales for the polemics of New Atheism and incite the feminist calls to arms and demands for liberation. But if the purpose of these narratives is liberation, it is not only (or even primarily) liberation of the individual women but also, more crucially, liberation of Orthodox Judaism itself. Rather than resigning themselves to condemning Orthodox Judaism as an instrument of women's oppression, the authors reconceive it as a space of female empowerment and activism. They recall to readers that the *eshes chayil*—the "woman of valor," whose praises are weekly sung to Orthodox Jewish women—is not held down by the interpretative foot of contemporary Orthodoxy, and neither does she need to be elevated by the saving hand of secularism; she is, fundamentally, in her own right, a woman with agency.

In this chapter, I will explore women's contributions to "off-the-*derech*" narratives, a remarkably large new subgenre of Jewish literature. A product of modernity, the narratives have their roots, as often as not, in the internet, which, by virtue of its accessibility (and anonymity), has eroded the boundary between "insular" Orthodox communities and the "Outside World."[3] These contemporary contexts structure the ways that readers understand the narratives and also shape them. The interactions between writers and readers form modern nonrabbinic *responsa*. This is significant because, at the heart of "off-the-*derech*" narratives, both the naming of the problems of contemporary Orthodoxy and a shared discussion of them can be found. As these writers demonstrate, the two steps of exposure and dialogue are necessary before there can be a movement toward remedying the ills of contemporary Orthodoxy and a reimagining of the promise of Jewishness that lies behind its modern manifestation.

---

In 2007, when Shalom Auslander published *The Foreskin's Lament*, he inaugurated what would become the "off-the-*derech*" memoir genre with his story of abandoning Orthodoxy, told as a searing, uproarious denunciation of God and Judaism. Nothing is too sacred for Auslander; God swears like a sailor, and biblical heroes are the stuff of slapstick.[4] We find, in his retelling of the Torah, a "man named Job who was sad and asked,—Why?, so God came down to the Earth, grabbed Job by the collar, and howled,—Who the fuck do you think you are?" There is also "a man named Moses who escaped from Egypt, and who roamed through the desert for forty years in search of a Promised Land, and whom God killed just before he reached it—face-plant on the one-yard line—because Moses had sinned, once, forty years earlier. His crime? Hitting a rock" (Auslander 2–3). To say the book is irreverent is an understatement: the young Shalom Auslander, like the young Alexander Portnoy, guiltily masturbates across the page (minus the raw liver). He creates an invisibility cloak of religious garb and compulsively shoplifts random items, from chewing gum to radios ("On my head, the biggest yarmulke I could find, pinned prominently to the front of my head. My white *tzitzis* dangled conspicuously from the sides of my pants. . . . Wearing a skull-cap made me vanish" [157–158]). He smokes weed, defies his family's Ortho-dox strictures by riding in a car on Shabbat (the Jewish Sabbath), and feasts on unkosher food (132). Although none of his crimes are heinous under American law, Auslander represents them as the gravest of sins in Judaism (describing the Shabbat car ride, for example, as "finishing what Hitler started" and offering up his wasted sperm to the reader as serial genocides according to halacha—Jewish law [132]).

For all that Auslander's story is one of a boy and later a man who is deter-mined to unbind himself from the covenant with God (to which the novel's title alludes) that Judaism professes, Auslander's story is *not* the story of an atheist, though it is true that his anecdotes at times resonate with James Parker's dream. Here, for example, he tells a story that would suggest his own allegiance with atheism:

> I learned that in the late 1980s, when Soviet Jews began immigrating in large numbers to Israel, an Israeli newspaper reported that the first thing tens of thousands of them did, young and old alike, was to have a circumcision, lining up all over the Promised Land in assembly-line fashion to undergo the proce-dure as soon as possible.
>
> —Do you believe in God? the reporter asked an older man who was await-ing his turn.
>
> —No, he replied,—I am an atheist.
>
> —Then why have a circumcision? he asked.
>
> The man, fighting back his tears, answered proudly.—Because without a circumcision, he said,—it is impossible to be a Jew! (147)

This snippet of history that Auslander shares has in common with his own path the almost compulsive need to maintain a sense of Jewishness. While no good expla-nation is offered for this need, it is one that arises again and again in twenty-first-century Jewish literature. In *Disobedience*, Naomi Alderman's "off-the-*derech*" character, Ronit, compares her Jewishness to her lesbianism—both invisible, both immutable. "You don't choose it. . . . If you are, you are," she declares. "There's nothing you can do to change it" (255–256). The whole of Auslander's memoir, like his fiction, reveals that for Auslander, there is nothing he can do to change it either; it is impossible to *not* be a Jew.

In his telling of his life and his path "off the *derech*," Auslander laments his *inability* to *dis*believe: "I had spent twelve years trying to eke out some space for myself, trying to build a family where I was loved for who I was, and not hated for what I wasn't, and I had just begun to succeed, a success that led to joy, a joy that led to a baby, and a baby that now threatened to bring that family crashing right back into my life. And with me, always, like venereal disease, the Lord" (200). Not your typical rabbi's testament of faith, perhaps, but Auslander's is oddly unwavering. It leads him back *on* the *derech* when he is off, even if he cannot ultimately remain in the Orthodox fold. When he falls "off the *derech*" again, separating him from his family and all the trappings of an Orthodox lifestyle, he confesses, "I believe in God. It's been a real problem for me" (307). What this story is about, then, is not loss of faith in God or in Jewishness; it is about a need to rethink what (inextricable) Jewishness can do and what Judaism is. Unfortunately, Auslander never lets us know how he has redefined Judaism.

For most readers, though, this book likely offers something other than a redefinition of Judaism; it offers a peek into the lives of people who are both visible and unknowable. To New Yorkers in particular, Orthodox Jews are fascinating. Around the time of publication, more than a million and a half Jews were believed to be living in New York City (almost two million including the surrounding areas), and according to a 2012 study, 60 percent of Jewish children in New York were being raised Orthodox (Nathan-Kazis, "Changing Face"). At the same time, Orthodox Jews were depicted in the press and popular culture as both anachronistic (outside of time) and anatopistic (outside of space: *in*, but not *of*, New York). A 2009 *New York Times* article on Williamsburg serves as a perfect example. Titled "A Piece of Brooklyn Perhaps Lost to Time," the article features this local-yet-foreign space where one can delight in the "anachronistic pleasure" of "knifegrinders on the street" and "bearded men in 19th-century frock coats."[5] A kind of wonderland, then, and it's only a subway ride away! "Be forewarned," though, the author cautions: "some of the residents do not take kindly to intrusion and may greet strangers with a brusque look" (Feuer LI3). And yet here, thanks to Auslander, an invitation for intrusion! And no forewarning needed. After all, the reader can intrude on an Orthodox Jewish community from the comfort of his or her home and openly express all the skepticism and derision he or she feels. In fact, there is an invitation for this too. On the back cover, Auslander's *A Foreskin's Lament* is labeled a book about the "isolated religious nutjobs on the fringe of American society."

Ironically, while American audiences were apt to see Orthodox Jewish communities as "isolated" and "on the fringe of American society" (setting aside the "nutjobs" comment for the moment), the easy movements between Orthodox Monsey and the "American" Palisades Mall in Rockland County, between

yarmulke and baseball cap, suggest a distinct *lack* of isolation. The incorpora-
tion of Americana in Auslander's daily life (e.g., sports games on the radio)
further supports the permeability of borders. This integration can be found in
most "off-the-*derech*" memoirs to greater and lesser degrees. Chaya Deitsch, a
Lubavitcher, talks about watching cartoons and reading Maud Hart Lovelace's
Betsy-Tacy stories as a child, for instance. In narratives of "stricter" Hasidic sects
(Shulem Deen of Skverers, Deborah Feldman of Satmars), Americana appears
more stealthily (a television hidden in a cabinet, a VCR rented for a day, books
quietly borrowed not from the local library but rather from the one on the other
side of town).

Sometimes, as in Deitsch's story, this outer world helps makes sense of the
inner one: Deitsch compares the different perspectives she and her family members hold to those in *Rashomon*, a film she watches with her mother. Further
complicating the inside/outside divide, Feldman reads *The Chosen*, Potok's classic tale of a friendship between a Hasidic and a Modern Orthodox boy, and *The
Romance Reader* (1995), Pearl Abraham's bildungsroman of a Satmar girl who
struggles with her family's lifestyle. Through these novels, Feldman sees how
Hasidim appear to "real" Americans when they discover the strange groups for
the first time (the cover of Abraham's book promises readers that *The Romance
Reader* "lifts the veil from a sealed-off world"). Deen, like Feldman, takes in *The
Chosen*, although in this case it is the film version, which mainstream Americans
apparently embraced (according to the *New York Times*) as an "introduction to
the isolated world of the Hasidim" (there's that word *isolated* again—about a
film that begins with an all-American baseball game; Maslin).

Sometimes cultural artifacts are modified to fit the Orthodox ones: to "kosher
up" the children's classic song, "On Top of Spaghetti," Deitsch's mother sings a
dairy-free version (the original mixes milk and meat, which is taboo under the
laws of kashruth).[6] And sometimes, they remain intact, pieces of "real" America
that exist as just that. Along with *The Chosen*, Deen watches *Ferris Bueller's Day
Off*, *Beethoven*, and *Under Siege*, about which he writes, "I had yet to learn the
term 'escapist entertainment,' but never before had I felt so transported from
reality" (Deen 171). Of course, if Steven Segal antics, Navy SEALs, submarines,
sixteen-inch guns, and Tomahawk missiles are not part of his everyday "isolated"
Hasidic "reality," it is hard to say in whose reality they are the norm.

But also, Auslander suggests to readers, the "fringe" group of Monsey, New
York, is little different from peer communities in Jerusalem, where he goes to
live, and North London, from which his wife hails. In other words, if his New
York community is made up of "isolated religious nutjobs" *separated from* its
American neighbors in certain (penetrable) ways, it is also *connected to* communities of "isolated religious nutjobs" worldwide. Auslander establishes the existence of this global Orthodox Jewish network for readers not by taking us from
the United States to the United Kingdom (as Leah Vincent and Chaya Deitsch

do when they tell of going from New York/New Haven to girls' seminaries in Manchester/Gateshead, respectively, in their memoirs) but rather through his caricatured conversations with his family. "Is she Jewish?" asks his mother when he tells her of meeting his wife-to-be. He confirms that she is. "Jewish from London?" Explains Auslander, "Jews in Monsey have a hard time imagining there are Jews anywhere else in the world, and if there are—if—they are certainly less devout. My mother phoned a rabbi in Monsey, who phoned a rabbi in Manhattan, who phoned a rabbi in central London, who phoned a rabbi in North Finchley." Auslander's mother is satisfied with the report she receives: "I hear she comes from a good family" (250). The minimal degrees of separation—here, we see enacted a game of "Jewish Geography, The Orthodox Edition"—illustrate the ties to and trust in the extranational communities of like-minded "isolated nutjobs" on the fringes of a number of societies.

The connection to London's "isolated nutjobs" that Auslander illuminates is all the more relevant when we consider that the publication of this American memoir coincided with the publication of the first British ex-Orthodox memoir, suggesting the advent of the genre occurred across these linked communities. But there *is* a national context as well. When Reva Mann published *The Rabbi's Daughter* in 2007, she did so on the tail-end of a British sensation: Alderman's *Disobedience*, which was a work of fiction that made its debut in households across Britain on BBC's *Woman's Hour* and was reviewed by the *Times Literary Supplement*, *The Guardian*, *The Telegraph*, *The Times*, and *The Observer*. *Disobedience* went on to win the Orange Award for New Writers, the Sunday Times Young Writer of the Year Award, and a Waterstones Writer for the Future Award (in the United States, Alderman was also shortlisted for the National Jewish Book Award for Fiction and the Sami Rohr Prize). Alderman's story is about a rabbi's daughter from Hendon in North London, who falls in love with another woman of the community and who, after many years in New York, returns to face the community and her former lover.

Perhaps this is why Mann's tale—also the tale of a rabbi's daughter—had such a strong impact. Mann is both the daughter of a rabbi (Rabbi Maurice Unterman of London's Marble Arch Synagogue)[7] and the granddaughter of Rabbi Isser Yehuda Unterman, chief Ashkenazi rabbi of the State of Israel. If Alderman's story of a rebellious daughter of an eminent rabbi was "only" fiction, Mann's held the allure of the "real." Although the book lacks the careful plotting of Alderman's tale and its grand revelation at the end, in some ways, it replicates Alderman's bifurcated structure that gives readers insights into the lives of two women—a believer and a nonbeliever, an adherent and one who left the fold. The narrative voices are both sympathetic and cutting; only in Mann's story, the lives and voices belong to one woman.

According to her memoir, Mann was raised in an Orthodox household, but her initial rebellion against her father's Judaism was actually a return to her grandfather's stricter Orthodoxy. Her story reads like Ann Roiphe's *Lovingkind-ness* or Philip Roth's *The Counterlife*; it is the tale of a liberally educated individual who reaches out for the confining comfort of traditions conceived as belonging to the past. Like the daughter in *Lovingkindness*, she moves to a women's yeshiva in Jerusalem (another international, intracommunal leap) and is matched with a *ba'al teshuva*, a fellow "Master of Return." She is married and raises three children in an "ultra-Orthodox" home before deciding to leave her husband and the atten-dant lifestyle. Thus marks another rebellion against men's rules and desires in the story—and the reader is swept into the world of a writer who learns to bring *her* rules and *her* desires to the fore.

In many ways, these twin originators of the genre, Auslander's *The Foreskin's Lament* and Mann's *The Rabbi's Daughter*, are a study of contrasts. Where Aus-lander is funny, Mann is sensual; where he is flippant, she is earnest; where he is damning, she is forgiving. Moreover, where Auslander offers as perhaps his greatest transgression in the post-Orthodox world his attendance at a baseball game on Shabbat, Mann takes us on a journey of drugs, lesbianism, hepatitis, philandering, and random, very explicit sex. In the era of reality television and horror-infused memoirs such as James Frey's (less-than-"real") *A Million Little Pieces* (2003), Mann tops the charts in sensationalist appeal. Despite those serial genocides Auslander commits with his sperm, *The Foreskin's Lament*, compared to *The Rabbi's Daughter*, seems a little tame.

For Mann, though, the elements of sensuality and sensationalism are not arbitrary; rather, they are crucially tied to her spiritual journey. Perhaps one could make the same argument about Auslander; the need to read masturba-tion through the lens of the Holocaust, after all, might not be entirely glib for a people consumed by guilt and haunted by a brutal collective memory. American short story author and essayist Norma Rosen (of an earlier generation than Aus-lander but equally distanced from the Holocaust by blood and geography) explains, "For a mind engraved with the Holocaust, gas is always *that* gas. Shower means their shower. Ovens are those ovens" (47). In British novelist Howard Jacobson's *Kalooki Nights* (2006), a character similarly declares, "You don't say 'gassed' to Jews if you can help it . . . gassed, camp, extermination, concentration, experi-ment, march, train, rally, German. Words made unholy just as ground is made unholy" (49). And yet Auslander takes this gesture, already satirical in Jacobson, and drives it into the realm of the absurd. Mann's sexual escapades, in contrast, are less a manifestation of an embedded Jewish (or Holocaust) consciousness than an active engagement with, and even embodiment of, Jewish rite and ritual.

Take, for example, Mann's description of her encounter with a near stranger: "Sam takes my hand and pulls it down to feel him hard. I undo his belt and open his fly, then feel for him through the slit in his Y-fronts and cup his balls in the palm of my hand. He is big. God loves me, I think, as I feel him swelling even more. He has not forsaken me after all" (Mann 262). For all that this passage has the elements of soft pornography, God is forced into the story at a moment where we might least expect religious zeal. And while it is easy to read this "God loves me" flippantly, ascribed as it is to the size of the stranger's penis, Mann makes it difficult to do so. She figures her relationship to God as both personal and structured, a response within a system. "He has not forsaken me after all," she writes, invoking the line from Tehillim (Psalms): "My god my god why hast thou forsaken me?"[8] Tehillim, like Mishlei (Proverbs), in which we find "Eshes Chayil," is part of Ketuvim, the third section of the Tanach (*Torah-Nevi'im-Ketuvim*), the collection of canonical Jewish texts. Tehillim is an integral part of daily and ritualistic Jewish life. There is a tradition to do a "psalm of the day," and Tehillim is read on one's wedding day, before a journey, and over a body continuously from death until burial. In Mann's portrayal of her husband, however, Tehillim becomes connected to neither solace nor inspiration—only the denial or delay of carnal pleasure. On their wedding night, Mann prepares for the marital consummation with perfume and candles yet finds herself "waiting and waiting" for Simcha; he is "standing in the corner of the living area reciting from the Book of Psalms, communing with his true love" (146). By invoking Tehillim again in her tryst with Sam, Mann reveals *her* communion with God (*also* her "true love")—not through the reading of a mere book filled with *questions* but through the reading of the swollen penis as the *answer*: "He has not forsaken me after all."

In *Standing Again at Sinai*, the first book of Jewish feminist theology, published in 1990, Judith Plaskow argued for the return of sexuality to the realm of the sacred. She wrote, "Feminist images name female sexuality as powerful and legitimate and name sexuality as part of the image of God" (201). And it is specifically in these bodily, carnal, seemingly gratuitous images that Mann's faith and commitment are repeatedly given voice, although Mann sometimes requires the reader's immersion in religious knowledge to recognize her claim. In a moment similar to the passage above, one that is, at first glance, a cheap justification of an extramarital affair, Mann—a married mother of three—describes her need to sleep with Joe, her handyman, as *"pikuach nefesh"* (231). Mann is a writer who appeals to a wide public, even (perhaps especially) one deeply unfamiliar with the territory she covers. She is a writer who is careful to translate both language and customs, even when such translations feel contrived. "I dedicate the day to study, trying to access the *neshama yetera*, the extra soul promised on the Sabbath," she explains at one point, offering clarity. "Are you going to introduce me only to someone from a secular background who has become religious—a *ba'al tshuva?*" she claims to ask the matchmaker at another point, although this wording as direct quotation seems highly unlikely (45, 62). A matchmaker would know what a *ba'al teshuva* is, as she would know the acronym FFB, which Mann also defines (this time explicitly for the reader) immediately following its use:

"*frum* (religious) from birth" (62).⁹ So where is her definition of "*pikuach nefesh*," a term unfamiliar not only to non-Jewish readers but to the vast majority of Jewish readers as well?

Building on the DuBoisian idea of a "double consciousness," James Weldon Johnson wrote a century ago of a "double audience," an idea literary critic Werner Sollors extends to ethnic writers at large: "Ethnic writers in general confront an actual or imagined double audience, composed of 'insiders' and of readers, listeners, or spectators who are not part of the writer's ethnic group" (249). Although Mann gestures toward explanation by saying, "I decide that my grandfather would decree that having my vitality squelched and my femininity repressed for years has put me in emotional danger," Mann refrains from telling outsiders explicitly that *pikuach nefesh* is the Jewish principle declaring that the preservation of a life overrides almost any other religious considerations. This choice is significant because on a surface level, the justification for the affair could be one that a reader of any background could imagine as her own: if my femininity were squelched in my marriage, I too might turn to another man. Better still, a reader could say, If I were a woman living under the tenets of *repressive, patriarchal Orthodox Judaism*, no doubt my femininity would be squelched in my marriage, and I *surely* would turn to another man. This version of the memoir, as a tale of imprisonment and liberation, is exactly the version that mainstream readers are likely to desire. Yet to the insider, at least, Mann is not condemning Orthodoxy; by employing this fundamental Jewish principle to validate her sexual relationship, she is instead reclaiming it.

This reclamation is, in part, a refutation of the current practice of Orthodoxy, which Mann experienced as negating female sexuality, leaving her "waiting and waiting." The refutation, however, is a gentle one, whispered, it seems, by the deemed *apikores*, who stands at the gates of the synagogue, knowing her words might not reach the faithful congregants as they stream out after services. Still, *The Rabbi's Daughter* is culturally significant, as it stakes the claims that *true* Orthodox Judaism ought to be as much a part of the body as the soul, and as much a woman's as a man's. It is interesting to note that for women, whose religious expectations are bound to their biological identities (women are exempt from many commandments, such as daily praying, because of their commitments to childbearing/rearing), Orthodox Judaism, even in its reenvisioned form, remains embodied.¹⁰

And so Mann creates a paradigm for the "off-the-*derech*" narrative. Her graphic depictions of sexuality, writ as necessary, serve to illuminate the repressive sexual nature of contemporary (ultra-)Orthodox Judaism. Her code-switching suggests an engagement with different readerships, an attempt to put her ideas into conversation with both the pious and the scandal-seeking. Furthermore, her ultimate take on women's Judaism is grounded in reimagining the oppressive as liberating, the ill as remedy.

But still, it is easy to read this book as mere sensationalist antireligious propaganda, a modern-day *Maria Monk*.[11] Whispers are not always heard at the entrance to the synagogue or above the shouts and hollers at a rock concert, which is what the field of memoirs has become.

## II. AMONG THE MEMOIRS

In 2014, *Tablet Magazine* declared "Ex-Frum Memoirs" to be "New York Publishing's Hottest New Trend." Soon after, the *Jewish Daily Forward* followed with, "Ex-Hasidic Writers Go Off the Path and Onto the Page," a long article on these memoirs. Though primarily made up of memoirs, the genre, by my reckoning, includes fictional and semifictional accounts of departures (physical, ideological) from Orthodox communities. In the wake of Alderman, Auslander, and Mann's books, Judy Brown (as Eishes Chayil), a Ger Hasid, published *Hush* (2010), a semifictional novel of sexual abuse and suicide in her community (the departure here is ideological; the narrator refuses to share her community's herd mentality). Deborah Feldman soon after came out with *Unorthodox* (2012), a memoir of walking away from a repressed life in the Satmar community, after years of writing a popular blog. The same year, another ex-Satmar writer, Anouk Markovits, published her novel, *I Am Forbidden*, imagining the fates of two women of the community: one who stays and experiences great hardship and one who leaves and is free. Frieda Vizel, an ex-Satmar blogger like Feldman, depicted her exodus from Satmar life visually in *Oy Vey Cartoons* (2012–2014).[12] Leah Vincent ensured that readers recognized it was not only Hasidic Jews who suffered in her memoir of life among the Yeshivish and the subsequent challenges of freedom in *Cut Me Loose: Sin and Salvation after My Ultra-Orthodox Girlhood* (2014). Shulem Deen chronicled breaking with the Skverer Hasidim in Brooklyn and New Square in his heartfelt memoir, *All Who Go Do Not Return* (2015), after years of blogging on Unpious.com. Leah Lax described both entering and exiting Lubavitch Hasidism in *Uncovered* (2015), a book touted as the "first ex-Chasidic gay memoir" (Dreyfus). Then Chaya Deitsch offered a positive spin in her memoir of leaving Lubavitch Hasidism, *Here and There* (2015), which exalted her continued relations with her family. Readers of the genre are, as I write, anticipating the memoir of Abby Stein, a (female) transgender Columbia student who was formerly a (male) Satmar rabbi. Already, Stein has many fans of her blog—where she writes about, among other things, her childhood, her transition, and the journey "off the *derech*" of her cousin, actor Luzer Twersky (who specializes in Hasidic/ex-Hasidic roles, playing the Hasidic husband in *Félix et Meira*, Paris in *Romeo and Juliet in Yiddish*, Mendel in *Transparent*, himself in the documentary *One of Us*, and Baruch in the *High Maintenance* episode called "Derech").

By the time Deitsch published her narrative, some readers were beginning to find the genre repetitive. Writes a critic in the *New York Times*: "I am still not entirely sure how to feel about this phenomenon. Some publishers are clearly exploiting our prurience, slapping one sensationalist subtitle after another onto these books, as if a great feast of anthro-porn awaits (See: 'Unorthodox: The Scandalous Rejection of My Hasidic Roots' published in 2012, and 'Cut Me Loose: Sin and Salvation After My Ultra-Orthodox Girlhood,' published in 2014.) . . . The emotional arc of these stories is almost always the same: The narrator starts out in a cloistered world of stringent laws and customs, suffers a crisis of faith and eventually summons the courage to break away" (Senior). The criticism here is astute, the term *anthro-porn* brilliant. And the reviewer does admit that "unless their audience's sole objective is titillation or condescension, readers can learn lots about a subculture they once knew little about." But she also wants less *sameness*: "There are now enough of these reminiscences sloshing around the market that any new addition must explain its presence in some way" (Senior). And I can't blame her.

So what caused the proliferation of these narratives that were and are "almost always the same"? One answer is timing. In 2001, Leigh Gilmore described memoir as "*the* genre in the skittish period around the millennium," an idea Julie Rak extended in her 2013 study, *Boom! Manufacturing Memoir for the Popular Market*. Rak argues that since the 1990s, "the success of memoirs by previously unknown writers [as opposed to celebrity memoirists] is a major reason why memoir is one of the most highly visible and popular non-fiction genres today." She examines the public's fascination with and deep *investment* in these life narratives (such as, famously, James Frey's; 9). Of the variety of memoirs, "misery lit" topped the list. In 2007, the BBC reported that "the bestseller lists are full of memoirs about miserable childhoods and anguished families" and that the popular British bookstore, Waterstones, had an entire shelf devoted to "Painful Lives" (O'Neill).

Furthermore, there was another "boom" happening at the time: the boom of the antireligious tract. If the twenty-first century was beginning to hint at the rise of "postsecularism," not everyone was having it. Antireligious sentiment—or "New Atheism"—was developing as its equal and opposite force. In *Between Naturalism and Religion* (2005) and again in "Notes on Post-Secular Society" (2008), Jürgen Habermas writes of seeing the resurgence of "orthodox . . . groups within the established religious organizations or churches . . . on the advance everywhere," remarking that liberal rule of law and multicultural societies were particularly and necessarily open to change by this resurgence (18). Yet according to Habermas, the secularists continued to imagine a foreseeable end to religion despite evidence to the contrary, and "laïcistic" intellectuals, unrealistically, wanted all matters of religion to be safely tucked into the private sphere. The New Atheists proved unsatisfied with either of these light-touch options: they wanted Reason, without God, *now*. When Auslander and Mann emerged with their stories, they did so amid a series of polemical texts blasting religion: *The*

*End of Faith* (2004) and *Letter to a Christian Nation* (2006) by neuroscientist Sam Harris; *The God Delusion* (2006) by eminent British evolutionary biologist Richard Dawkins; *Breaking the Spell: Religion as a Natural Phenomenon* (2006) by philosopher and cognitive scientist Daniel Dennett; and *God Is Not Great* (2007) by the famous, controversial Anglo-American journalist Christopher Hitchens. Shortly thereafter, HBO political talk show host Bill Maher came out with *Religulous* (2008), which turned out to be the biggest documentary of the year and almost as irreverent as director Larry Charles's earlier mockumentary *Borat* (2006).[13]

A mug full of misery memoir, then, mixed with a dash of religious oppression, could not, at that moment, have offered a more perfect brew. In fact, Auslander and Mann were not unique in their recipe: from the early twenty-first century on, everyday people (mostly women) who had left religious communities were daily airing the proverbial dirty laundry of their former faiths and loyal adherents. Published to critical acclaim, for example, was *Persepolis*, Marjane Satrapi's successful graphic novel about leaving Iran, originally appearing in four parts in French over the years 2000 to 2003. It is a book that is nuanced in its examination of life under Islam, or, metaphorically, "under the veil." Gillian Whitlock observes that the shift from (fundamentalist) East and (liberal, secular) West lacks the dramatic contrast readers expect (192). How different are the veiled women of austere Iran from the veiled women of an austere convent in Austria? Still, as Rak points out, the publication of the English-language editions of the book fit nicely into the genre of women's liberation narratives. It appeared first, excerpted, in *Ms. Magazine*, the liberal feminist magazine founded by Gloria Steinem and other second-wave feminists. Furthermore, though Whitlock remarks on the failure of contrast between East and West, Rak argues that English readers would not know of this failure at the conclusion of the first book:

> *Persepolis 1* and *2* were published together as *Persepolis: The Story of a Child-hood*. This is an important detail, because the change of title means that readers of the 2003 English-language version of *Persepolis* were not made aware that the book was part of a longer series. English-speaking readers would not know, and did not seem to know at the time because reviewers did not remark on it, that Satrapi's story did not in fact end with Marji escaping Iran and traveling to Europe. Instead it was possible for readers of *Persepolis* to imagine Europe, and western cultures, as part of the "happy ending" for Satrapi as she leaves her war-torn, intolerant, fundamentalist country of origin. (Rak 165–166)

*Persepolis*, then, functioned to tell the story America and other Western countries already wanted to believe: there was no greater misery than oppressive (patriarchal, misogynistic) religion and no greater memoir than a religious one.

But it was not only tales of the far-flung religious communities that Western readers were consuming. Foreign (mostly Muslim) women's liberation autoethnographies were interspersed with American (defamiliarized) ones. In 2005, Martha Becks published a memoir of her American life—in a homegrown American religion. In *Leaving the Saints: How I Lost Mormons and Found My Faith* (2005), Becks recounts, among other sins of the Church of Latter Day Saints, the sexual abuse she suffered at the hands of her father, a prominent member of the community. This memoir provided a nice bit of insider ethnography, authenticating, in essence, Jon Krakauer's 2003 investigative book *Under the Banner of Heaven*, which led to an uproar in the LDS community. Mike Otterson, managing director of public affairs for the LDS Church, regarded Krakauer's book as a sign of the war between the religious and the secular ("His basic thesis appears to be that people who are religious are irrational, and that irrational people do strange things") and an exaggeration of every stereotype available for a "full-frontal assault on the veracity of the modern Church." Otterson angrily declared, "Krakauer . . . puts himself in the same camp as those who believe every German is a Nazi, every Japanese a fanatic, and every Arab a terrorist," promising readers that Krakauer's was hardly an account to be believed—or even read ("Church Response"). But then came a book by Becks, a tell-all by one who *was* to be believed; after all, the life she describes is the life she lived.

After Becks's very American memoir, in 2007, Somali-Dutch activist Ayaan Hirsi Ali's *Infidel* (2006) was released in English, and readers learned about barbaric practices such as female genital mutilation performed in the name of Islam. People regarded this memoir too as an authentic and authenticating document, recognizing Hirsi Ali's name as linked to that of Theo van Gogh, whose murder in the Netherlands for his work (with Hirsi Ali) on *Submission*, the 2004 short film criticizing women's treatment in Islam, triggered an anti-Muslim outcry and a demand for restrictions on Muslim immigration. Hitchens, still on his *God Is Not Great* high, praised the book in the *Sunday Times*, and then wrote the foreword for the 2008 paperback edition of *Infidel*.

And back in America again, readers were riveted by local American communities of terror. In *Escape* (2007), Carolyn Jessop, a former member of the Fundamentalist Church of Jesus Christ of Latter Day Saints, told of being forced, at the age of eighteen, into a marriage with a man thirty-two years her elder. Jessop's husband already had three wives and more than thirty children and, within months of his marriage to Jessop, would gain two more wives. Jessop suffered through a series of dangerous and ultimately life-threatening pregnancies before escaping her community.[14] A couple of years after *Escape* appeared, Jayanti Tamm published *Cartwheels in a Sari* (2009), describing the life of her family and community in a Queens-based cult with a caste system and seemingly arbitrary prohibitions (Mormons, it turned out, were not the only oppressive American-born religious group). This was followed by the memoir *Why I Left the Amish* (2011), in which Saloma Miller Furlong, who was featured on PBS's *American Experience: The Amish*, revealed the darker side of her family and community that was not appropriate for public television, sharing stories of physical and sexual abuse and male domination.[15]

Ex-Orthodox Jewish writers, like their ex-religious, non-Jewish peers, had and have a good deal of ground to cover to fill in curious outsiders on the secrets of their little worlds. Answering her own question of why there are so many ex-Orthodox Jewish memoirs, Senior tells of a conversation with Deitsch, who explained, "'It was a lapsed Bobover who told me that other Hasidim barely consider Lubavitchers Hasidic.'" Senior concludes, "And therein lies the case for Ms. Deitsch's book. Despite their core similarities, no two memoirs in this unlikely category are alike." She develops this point further: "Outsiders may look at Hasidim and see an undifferentiated blur of men and women armored in stern attire, but Satmars are not Skverers, who are not Breslovers, who are not Lubavitchers" (Senior). This is true, but it perhaps belies the bigger issue at stake in the collective Orthodox identity, which is estrangement from mainstream society. Yes, Lubavitch Hasidim interact with secular and non-Jewish communities, whereas Satmars are far less to likely to, but both still practice their rituals with a degree of privacy and segregation that the general public finds alienating—and discomfiting.

People are curious. Take, for instance, the opening gambit of Oprah Winfrey's February 2012 episode of *Oprah's Next Chapter*, called, dramatically, "America's Hidden Culture." It began with Oprah conspiratorially telling viewers, "This past Sunday, I spoke about sexuality and modesty in front of a group of ultra-Orthodox rabbis." Over the course of the episode, Oprah speaks not only to rabbis but also to Orthodox Jewish women. She knocks on their doors, sits in their living rooms, and asks nosey questions about their personal lives. (It was as though, for those of who grew up wondering if our frumpy, bewigged, Orthodox teachers "do it through a hole in the sheet," the juvenile whispers in the back of the lunchroom suddenly had a place on the global stage.) A similar scenario was reproduced in 2017, with Britain's Kate Humble interviewing Haredi women for her (even more dramatically named) show, *Extreme Wives*. In the age of reality TV, everyone wants to know what's going on with everyone—in their lives, in their homes, and in their beds.

In other words, we want to get under Orthodox women's wigs—or as they call them, their *sheitels*. Those *sheitels*—or turbans, or kerchiefs, or *shpitzels*—simultaneously conceal and reveal, telling us, in essence, everything we *don't* know. They comprise the visible marker of Orthodox women's difference.

### III. The Sheitel

*"Here everything is so different."*
  *She colored deeply.*
  *"They don't wear wigs here," he ventured to add.*
  *"What then?" she asked, perplexedly.*
  *"You will see. It is quite another world."*

—Abraham Cahan, *Yekl* (1896)

Like the veil, the *sheitel* of an Orthodox Jewish woman is interpreted as a symbol of her oppression, a reading that much of Jewish literature underscores. As *Yekl*'s Gitl cannot be Americanized and liberated until she sheds that "voluminous" sign of Orthodoxy in Abraham Cahan's 1896 ghetto tale, so too do all other such religiously clad female figures modestly creep past the yellowed pages of Jewish fiction of the twentieth century that follow, failing, it would seem, to gain subjectivity while under the weight of their wigs. Readers encounter this idea in Reich's *Master of the Return*: "They used to call her Ivriya the Beauty, and some of the old charm still hovers over her face. All vanity. When she would race, her rich hair blended into the chestnut mane of her favorite stallion." This female religious character is imagined riding against the wind, her beauty drawn as much from her freedom as her features. But without pity, the male narrator continues, "Now [her rich hair] is losing its thickness and shine. What does it matter? She obeys me and conceals every strand under a kerchief, even in bed." The subjugation of this woman is endless: day and night. The commands of the patriarchal husband are absolute. And lest they be insufficient, the commands of the patriarchal God loom above those of the man: "I remind her of the righteous married woman who, despite her exemplary charity and virtue, once inadvertently allowed a single hair to show, and though at her death she was admitted to the Garden of Eden, she was condemned to be stuck to the door for eternity by that rebellious strand of hair" (18–19). This cautionary tale has a familiar flavor for students of Jewish lore: another classic story tells of the Jewish woman who, about to be tied to a horse and dragged through the streets until death by Cossacks, sticks pins through her skirt into the flesh of her legs to protect her modesty.[16] "Vain is beauty; a G-d-fearing woman, she should be praised," we hear in the description of the woman of valor in Proverbs 31. Indeed, these pitiful women of valor—man-fearing, God-fearing, and with only enough agency to perpetuate their own oppression—tell a story that no modern, egalitarian reader could bear.

Scanning the fiction, it would seem that Orthodoxy does even more than oppress women; it erases them, as Haredi newspapers do their faces in photographs.[17] Orthodox women as dynamic characters are near absent in the canon of twentieth-century Jewish fiction. In part, this is because Orthodoxy itself fades

from the literary landscape. By midcentury, we could only catch a rare glim-
mer of it, as in the black-hatted male representations of old-world Orthodox
Judaism in the 1959 stories of (Canadian) Mordecai Richler and (American)
Philip Roth.[18] Their treatments of these figures are not identical: Roth's "Eli, the
Fanatic" brings the past close to home through a figure who turns out to be the
cultural doppelgänger, the other possible version, of the whitewashed American Jew. Richler's *The Apprenticeship of Duddy Kravitz*, on the other hand, distances his secular, striving Canadian from the black-hatter; ancient, irrelevant,
the Orthodox Jew is the immigrant grandfather in the background of Duddy
Kravitz's modern Canada, attempting to inspire his grandson, only to see his
old-world values transformed into new-world corruption and greed. Roth and
Richler's stories converge, however, on the monolithic maleness of the symbolic
figure of Orthodoxy.

This gendering of Orthodoxy is echoed in the British text *Rodinsky's Room*
(1999), Rachel Lichtenstein's search for "the *frummer* in the attic," a ghostly figure of a black-hatted Jewish man who disappeared from his London East End
flat in the 1960s and becomes, in the 1990s, representative of a lost, forgotten, or
imagined Jewish past (3). Rodinsky haunts the assimilated, half-Jewish ("wrong"
half) Lichtenstein, materializing as an apparition marked by his piety and his
otherworldliness. These traits are bound up in one image: "He looked ancient,
his skin was so pale and transparent it gave off a bluish hue, and hanging majes-
tically underneath his nose was a long trailing white beard. His coat and large
black hat were tattered and worn but unmistakably the costume of a Hasidic Jew"
(49). His paleness speaks both to the classic trope of the weak and wan yeshiva
*bocher*, the emasculated Jewish man who is cloistered in the study halls, and to
his ethereality.[19] He is outside of place and time, wearing what now appears the
"costume" of a foreign or ancient tribe. The "trailing" of his beard suggests his
distance from the here and now, much as Richler's "trailing grandfather with
his beard and black hat" is juxtaposed with contemporary Jews ("the short husbands with their outrageously patterned sports shirts arm in arm with purring
wives too obviously full for slacks, the bawling kids with triple-decker ice cream
cones, and the squealing teen-agers"; Richler 75).

Perhaps the lack of Orthodox women as either symbols or characters, however,
is most acute in Potok's novel, *The Chosen*, where the lives of men and boys, both
Modern Orthodox and Hasidic, are explored in depth and detail. Here, women are
almost entirely invisible but for those who appear as covered wombs: we see them
in "long-sleeved dresses, with kerchiefs covering their heads, many with infants in
their arms, others heavily pregnant" (119). That is all for Potok; even these women's
children come only in the male variety (because they are "all," we read, "with their
fringes and earlocks"; 119).[20]

A rare exception is Leonard Michaels's 1969 short story, "Murderers." Here, we
discover that the wig, like the veil, can work as a different kind of instrument of

patriarchal power.[21] That which desexualizes (remember how Gitl's wig "made her seem stouter and shorter than she would have appeared without it . . . [and] added at least five years to her looks"?) also sexualizes—always keeping the wearer subject to interpretation by the male gaze. The wig on Michaels's rabbi's wife is an alluring, changing beacon to the boys who look upon it. And yet, the woman herself is no more and no less than her wig. Examining the rabbi's wife, Michaels's boy narrator says, "Today she was a blonde. . . . She had ten wigs, ten colors, fifty styles. She looked different, the same, and very good. A human theme in which nothing begat anything and was gorgeous. To me she was the world's lesson. Aryan yellow slipped through pins about her ears. An olive complexion mediated yellow hair and Arabic black eyes. Could one care what she really looked like? What was really?" (97).

If the Orthodox woman herself is not portrayed as a dynamic individual, her wig certainly has more play. The rabbi's wife's wig exoticizes, eroticizes, and turns her into a creature of the Occident and the Orient, the domestic and the foreign. It defines her. Yet the definition is anything but clear. "A human theme," says the narrator, "the world's lesson." What is learned in that lesson? Though she is fornicating as the boys surreptitiously watch her through the window and looks "very good" (dowdy Gitl's literary obverse), the rabbi's wife is in fact Gitl's twin: she too lacks individuality, a chance for development, and any potential heroism. "Could one care what she really looked like?" is perhaps a greater cruelty from the perspective of a teenage boy than "Could one care what she really is like?" and encompasses the latter as well.

When Orthodox women are finally granted a voice at the century's end, the kerchiefed or bewigged women despair their lot. "That awful wig!" cries Batsheva Ha-Levi, the heroine of *Jephte's Daughter*, who is trapped in an abusive marriage to a Hasidic zealot. "She took it off and flung it to the floor" (141). The wigs don't symbolize lost traditions. There is none of the nostalgia that we find in Cahan's David Levinsky, a rich, successful, secular business owner, whose story closes with him bemoaning the fact that he lost his way by abandoning Orthodoxy. Women are pictured resenting their roles, which often take the form of their metonymic head coverings. "I don't even want to wear a wig. I think if all women refused to shave and cover their heads, the rabbis would have to rethink the laws, change them," reports Rachel, the heroine of *The Romance Reader*. "But I don't know anyone who agrees with me," she concludes (Abraham 219). It would seem, in fact, that almost *all* the fictional Orthodox heroines of the twentieth century *do* agree. In Jewish literature, the wig is anachronistic, oppressive, dehumanizing, and unfeminist. Ironically, *sheitels* need, at times, to be metaphorically wrenched from Orthodox women's heads. Gitl, for example, resists the removal of her *sheitel* throughout *Yekl* and only agrees to it once it is replaced by a hat (a hair covering that can signify Americanness and comply with Jewish modesty simultaneously).

But this resistance to uncovering is seen, at best, as a sign of false conscious-ness, as is the choice to don a head covering in the first place. The latter can be observed in Roiphe's *Lovingkindness*, when the mother worries about her daughter, Andrea (now Sarai), who has chosen Orthodoxy: "Will they cut off her hair and *hide her* under a wig?" (87, emphasis mine).

The fiction suggests it's ideal, as in *Call It Sleep*'s Genya, to dispose of such apparel before landing on American shores. Even in late twentieth-century retell-ings of the early part of the century, the impossibility of the wig's retention seems certain. "When my grandmother came to this country," Ruthie says in "Hair," Myra Goldberg's 1993 short story, "she got married, you know, over there, and all her beautiful hair got cut off, which is what those Jews in Europe did." "But secretly," Ruthie confides, "she knew she was coming here, so she grew it a little under the wig. And when she saw that Statue of Liberty, she took off her wig with her children beside her and threw it into the harbor" (170). This anecdote pro-vides a perfect complement to Dara Horn's story of male liberation in her novel *In the Image* (2002): "They were throwing their tefillin overboard," the story recounts about those early immigrants, "because tefillin were something for the Old World, and here in the New World they didn't need them anymore" (50). In his analysis of the feminocentric canon of short Jewish fiction, David Brauner notes the way that Goldberg's Ruthie "distances herself from the traditions of orthodox Judaism" by implying "that the cutting of the hair of married women is a benighted practice carried out only by 'those Jews' 'over there.'" Brauner reads the grandmother's discarding of the wig as symbolizing "the sense of freedom instilled in her by her first sight of the new world" as well as "the journey of a whole generation of Jewish immigrants to America at the end of the nineteenth and start of the twentieth centuries, from the religious tradition. . . . of the old world to the assimilation demanded . . . by the new" (110). To be at the end of the twentieth century, then, and still donning that archaic headwear, still hiding her (necessarily beautiful) hair, still hid[ing] *her* (to echo Roiphe)—How could it happen? Why would Batsheva or Rachel or Sarai want it to?

These twentieth-century fictional accounts, which situate the wig in the foreground, set the stage for readers' recognition and understanding of female Orthodoxy. The wig had a totalizing effect. Whether it desexualized or sexu-alized, whether it was desired (wrongly) or despaired, it was oppressive and obscuring—a denial of personhood.

But the twenty-first century offers a more nuanced version of the wig. Nathan Englander takes it up in his acclaimed short story collection, *For the Relief of Unbearable Urges* (2000), in a story called "The Wig," the title of which immedi-ately suggests the garment's prominence. Ruchama the wigmaker, mother of six, is presented as a woman fulfilling her Jewish roles as mother and breadwinner and helping the women of the community fulfill theirs: "They circle the globe

to see Ruchama" for their wigs (87). Here, Englander begins to imagine the ways
that head coverings might also liberate. Even as symbols of modesty, they can be
a path to freedom, individuality, independence—if always a constrained freedom, a tempered individuality, and a limited independence. Significantly, this
is not a story of embracing the tenets of Orthodoxy. It is not because Ruchama
fosters her customers' modesty or deepens their connection to their religious
practice through their head coverings that the women come to her but "because
they are trapped in their modesty and want to feel even as illusion, the simple
pleasure of wind in their hair" (87). As in Reich's novel, the conceit of freedom
appears as wind through the hair, though here the possibility exists even if the
hair is synthetic or has been tonsured in a Hindu ritual in India.

For Englander, ultimately, what the wig offers is not enough. Rather, the investment in its meaning suggests a failure to invest in real, activist modes of empowerment. Ruchama, like her customers, seeks a form of escape in a wig. She is a
mundane version of the typical Orthodox heroine of the "Jewish Gothic" genre—
not locked up and forced into marriage with a brute but merely unhappy, frustrated with having to tend to her husband and children, and lured by the secular
woman who comes to her shop in smart slacks and a "confidence [that] can get
anything done in this world" (Englander 89). To achieve her desire of "freedom in
a wig," Ruchama becomes obsessed with the perfect mass of human hair and must
destroy everything in her path to get it. She deprives the man whose hair she takes
of his "defining" characteristic (the wig is thus "defining" before it even evolves
into its wig-like state). She is so absorbed in the details of the wig that she cannot
perform work functions. She spends such a large amount of money on the hair
that she fails to pay her bills. And finally, she sacrifices her reputation and potentially her marriage by claiming she is philandering rather than admit she is simply
wig-making. "The Wig" is thus not a success story for Orthodox women; on the
contrary, it's a kind of cautionary tale. And yet, it's a game changer.

In fact, in revisiting "that awful wig!" in the twenty-first century, Ragen, the
original "Jewish Gothic" writer, presents a narrative, and a heroine, quite different from those in *Jephte's Daughter* (1989), *Sotah* (1992), and *The Sacrifice of
Tamar* (1994). In *The Saturday Wife* (2007), Ragen's eponymous heroine (not,
this time, a victim but very much the villain) tells readers about the gamut of
head coverings, which she uses to distinguish among the good, the bad, and
the ugly. Around her, Delilah (her name gives away both her villainy and her
link to hair affairs) sees rebbetzins as "overweight Jewesses in bad wigs wearing dowdy calf-length skirts and long-sleeved polyester blouses" (18). She also
observes the alternative, the "younger married women" who wore wigs that
"were long and smooth and sexy, in daring shades of blond and red, bouncing
around their shoulders as they walked or danced" (49). Perhaps these two versions of women and their wigs speak to the two poles of Orthodox womanhood

in twentieth-century fiction: Cahan's and Michaels's. But Ragen, even in her glib figuring of (Delilah's glib readings of) the wig, soon reveals that there is more to these head coverings than Delilah's superficial accounting initially suggests.

On her first Saturday as the rabbi's wife, Delilah "agonize[s]" over what to wear on her head at synagogue. I quote at length here to suggest the significance of the head coverings not only for the character but also for the reader, who is, perforce, drawn into the many personalities and histories the head coverings take on:

> Should she wear a wig, the only one she owned, a long, blond number purchased for exactly such an occasion, or a stylish hat in which most of her own hair would show? Or should she wear one of those horrid hair snoods so popular in Boro Park among the women who took the Woman of Valor song literally (*Charm is a lie, and beauty is worthless; a God-fearing woman brings praise upon her self*). She had one in her closet, purchased to wear to the ritual baths if she wanted to shampoo her hair before she got there, saving time. It was black with little silver sparkles, hugging her head like those towel turbans in the shampoo ads, making her look like an Italian film star in the forties. The wig, on the other hand, made her look like Farah Fawcett when she was plastered on the bedroom walls and lockers of every horny teenage boy in America. She finally chose the hat, which, though it showed most of her long hair, still looked the most respectable, with its cool white straw, band of apricot silk, and large apricot bow. (Ragen, *Saturday* 63–64)

The detailed options of women's head coverings suggest an uncritical modernization of Michaels's story of forty years earlier, but the perspective in Ragen's book urges us to resist this interpretation. In Michaels's story, we see the rabbi's wife through the eyes of voyeurs—horny teenage boys who would plaster Farah Fawcett posters on their bedroom walls and lockers. There, we are positioned as the "murderers," as the rabbi accuses the boys when he discovers their "ocular perversion," giving the story its name (98, 96).[22] In Ragen's novel, *we are* the rabbi's wife, *our* eyes roving over the possibilities of invented selves. The wearer can be sexy, repellent, an actress in shampoo ads, a 1940s Italian film star, a 1970s American TV star, or respectable. Who should she be? Who can *I* be? In the most generous reading of Ragen, we might say that her shifting object into subject allows the head covering to be full of potential, a transformative object, its ritualistic power—if perhaps light-years removed from its original religious context—bestowing agency on the wearer.

IV. Veiled Bestsellers and Their Sister *Sheitel* Tales

*You've never seen anything like* Persepolis—*Marjane Satrapi may have given us*
*a new genre.*
                                          —Gloria Steinem, back cover of Marjane Satrapi's
                                                    *Persepolis: The Story of a Childhood* (2003)

*A story that millions can recognize, told with spirit, courage, and honesty.*
                                          —Gloria Steinem, front cover of Leah Lax's *Uncovered* (2015)

The wig, as it appears in Englander and Ragen's twenty-first-century stories, is a
far cry from the wig in Cahan's nineteenth-century tale of (necessary, enforced)
progress and Americanization. It is no longer merely a synecdoche for the
Orthodox woman—downtrodden, old-world, enslaved to modesty. Its meaning
is slippery and ambivalent. And here too, we find a nice analogy with the Muslim woman's veil, long a metaphor for her imprisonment. I return to *Persepolis*,
where the veil represents the religious fundamentalism of Iran after the Islamic
Revolution but also exists as a thing unto itself: a versatile swathe of fabric. Reading the scene where the veil is first introduced, Whitlock notes it is done so "with
high drama" as well as "irony" (189): "Satire prevails as we see the playground
scene of schoolchildren using the newly acquired veils as toys: to skip and to
play hide and seek and to put the veil into a different frame: it is after all a piece
of cloth and its fetishization by adults can seem strange" (190). If the wig is not
similarly turned into a mop-head or animal tail for a child's costume in fiction
or memoirs, it certainly loses some of its serious edge (and why not?) when it can
turn the wearer into a '70s television star.

But the "fetishization" of religious covering is pervasive in mainstream culture, and as a result, there is a need to make veiling, in "modern, liberal" countries,
impossible. In 2009, French president Nicolas Sarkozy declared, "The problem of
the burka is not a religious problem, it's a problem of liberty and women's dignity. It's not a religious symbol, but a sign of subservience and debasement. I want
to say solemnly, the burka is not welcome in France" (Crisafis). A year later, the
French Senate voted almost unanimously to ban the burka. Canada nearly followed suit on the same logic. There, the Conservative government banned face
veils during oath-taking ceremonies, such as citizenship ceremonies, marking
the veil as "unCanadian" and "unlawful" and the wearing of it "rooted in a culture
that is anti-women" (Chase). When the bill was struck down, Prime Minister Stephen Harper reintroduced the "niqab issue" as part of his 2015 reelection platform.

If veiling is "anti-women," *unveiling* is rendered a feminist act. Yet writers
like Englander, Ragen, and Satrapi make us rethink this logic. And perhaps their
nuanced approaches exist beyond the realm of literature. Perhaps this mode of

thinking explains Stephen Harper's 2015 election loss to Liberal leader Justin Trudeau—who responded to the niqab debacle by saying it was "unworthy of someone who is prime minister for all Canadians" and then, upon being elected, quickly won over feminists across the globe in a social media frenzy with his "Because It's 2015" explanation of the (radical) new gender parity he established in the cabinet (Bryden). Apparently, accommodating multiculturalism *and* feminism is possible.

Still, it is not only on the right but also on the left that there is a struggle to marry these ideologies, which became evident across the border where another (some might say far more significant) election was in the works soon after the Canadian one. In his pursuit of religious debunking, Bill Maher brought Steinem, icon of second-wave feminism, onto his show in February 2016. This was a key moment in American politics: Hillary Clinton was discovering a formidable foe in Bernie Sanders, her opponent for the Democratic presidential candidacy. Maher recalled to Steinem "one of Hillary Clinton's greatest moments as First Lady," which was when Clinton declared, "Women's rights are human rights." Turning Steinem's attention to women in Muslim countries, Maher asked, "Is feminism something that goes beyond our borders?" "Yes, absolutely," responded Steinem. "It is totally beyond borders. *All* monotheism is a problem." Here, Maher and Steinem put a new spin on Clinton's attempt to universalize both the experiences and the need for rights of women in different (and distinct) communities. The human rights violations that prompted Clinton to make her pronouncement occurred in China, a country that has nothing to do with monotheism. Revisited in Steinem's rhetoric, however, the call for women's rights cemented Maher and Steinem's anti-Muslim and, more broadly, atheistic agendas, insisting on the divorced aims of feminism and religion.

But perhaps here is where the left goes so far around it meets the right. And perhaps, in their treatment of Islam as a problem, Maher and Steinem did less to bolster Clinton's campaign than Trump's. After all, if Harper's use of the niqab in the 2015 Canadian election had strong racist undertones, Islamophobia in the 2016 Trump campaign was explicit—and pernicious. As a presidential nominee, Trump proposed a "complete and total shutdown of Muslims entering the United States," called for increased surveillance on mosques, and cited a dubious story of a U.S. general who shot Muslims with bullets dipped in pigs' blood as a way of illustrating his point that "we better start getting tough" (Johnson; Johnson and DelReal). Similarly, in anticipation of the 2017 French presidential election, right-wing populist Front National candidate Marine LePen decried "Islamist globalization" as an ideology that "wants to bring France to its knees" (McAuley). Banning the burka was only the first battle cry, it would seem, in France's move toward a war with Muslims.

In the United States too, there has been an unveiling of Muslim women. Although not enshrined in law, unveiling has become part of the cultural imagination. Muslim women's memoirs, in particular, promise first-person, authentic, metaphorical unveilings; they are texts that function not only to educate but also, fundamentally, like Trump's apocrypha, to warmonger. Tellingly, the proliferation of these narratives coincided with the American invasions of Afghanistan (2001) and Iraq (2003). Whitlock argues, "There can be no mistake: these autoethnographies are deployed as propaganda to represent and justify a military intervention in the name of (among other things) the liberation of women oppressed by Islamic fundamentalism" ("Burqa" 56). The texts "pull Western readers into this dark and confined space of the *burqa*, to share this discipline of views vicariously at least," and non-Muslim readers feel they are given access to the women's feelings, experiences, and beliefs. This is a (metaphorical) lifting of the veil: "The veil or the *hijab* (of which the *burqa* is an extreme form) is an icon that covers this life writing at every turn, a trope which shapes its metaphorical repertoire and which it in turn embraces—sometimes unexpectedly" (Whitlock, "Skin" 55). With access, readers can sympathize, and then they can help—through war.

"George W. Bush," wrote Shulem Deen in 2003 in his first blog post to garner a substantial readership, "should've sent troops to New York's Hasidic neighborhoods. If Americans were so insistent on spreading freedom, there were places closer to home that needed it. Before we went off to bring democracy to Afghans and Iraqis, maybe Williamsburg and New Square could be liberated first" (206). There is little to suggest that the negative spotlight on the Orthodox Jewish community has a direct relationship to the War on Terror, except as a ripple effect, in that "all monotheism is a problem." Some scholars, like David Hirsh, argue that anti-Jewish sentiment at large was turbocharged during this period by a combination of related factors (collapse of the peace process in Middle East, growth of anti-imperialist rhetoric, declaration of Zionism as a form of racism at the UN conference in Durban). It appears to be of greater significance, however, that despite tensions between Muslim and Jewish communities, certain practices and attitudes in both, especially in regard to women, became increasingly suspect at this time (sometimes with very good reason).[23] Deen's criticism of the community he left is clearly underpinned by what he saw on the news with regard to the invasion of Muslim countries. There was a growing intolerance for "extremism," whatever its source.

The Muslim and Jewish memoirs, which appeared to chronicle "extreme" practices in closed-off communities, thus came to inhabit a shared discursive space. Note the way Steinem equally praises Satrapi's memoir of leaving Iran and Lax's of leaving Jewish Orthodoxy. Lax's personal note to Steinem in the acknowledgments that follow her memoir furthers the interface of Muslim and Orthodox Jewish women's experiences Steinem has helped engender: "Special thanks to . . . kind Gloria Steinem, who, on long walks at Hedgebrook, made me aware of the era I missed while *under the veil*" (Lax, emphasis mine). Of course, neither Steinem nor Lax was entirely original here. Recall the blurb promising the originality of *The Romance Reader*: it "lifts the veil from a sealed-off world."

Yet as scholars like Whitlock contend, the "veil" and its removal form a knotty metaphor in the narratives, and the "access" is fraught. Whitlock asks how feminists in the West can "understand the veil, catch its meanings, and use it to fabricate more subtle and perceptive cross-cultural communication? No one can read the veil from a neutral, disinterested space (Young 80), so how then can we read the stories of these women who speak through the *burqa?*" (Whitlock, "Skin" 55–56). Similarly, Judith Butler questions the narrative read into unveiling by telling a story in *Precarious Life* of visiting a political theorist who displayed pictures of Afghan girls whose burkas had been removed on his refrigerator door. They were tacked "right next to some apparently valuable supermarket coupons," she adds snarkily, "as a sign of the success of democracy" (141). Despite Muslim women arguing for the burka's significance in "belonging-ness to a community and religion, a family, an extended history of kin relations, an exercise of modesty and pride, a protection against shame," Butler writes, "According to the triumphalist photos that dominated the front page of the *New York Times*, these young women bared their faces as an act of liberation, an act of gratitude to the U.S. military, and an expression of a pleasure that had become suddenly and ecstatically permissible. The American viewer was ready, as it were, to see the face, and it was to the camera, and for the camera, after all, that the face was finally bared, where it became, in a flash, a symbol of successfully exported American cultural progress" (140). The gap between the women and their representation (or consumption) looms large. But the American reading of this imagery is culturally and emotionally satisfying, and it is aided by the language of the texts, particularly the titles of the autoethnographies of these Muslim women: Cheryl Benard's book is called *Veiled Courage*, Harriet Logan's is *Unveiled*, and Batya Swift Yasgur's is *Behind the Burqa*.[24]

In titles that showcase Western feminism's demands for, and celebrations of, women's liberation, the prefix reigns supreme. Turning back to the body of Jewish writing, we can see that, reviewing Alderman's *Disobedience*, Alan Cooper separates prefix *dis* (or *diss*) from noun *obedience* to read the title in terms of its claim to not only shed but also actively spurn the obedience of Orthodoxy (Cooper). Titles that echo *Unveiled* use the prefix *un* to mark the before and after, the entrapment and liberation, beginning with Hella Winston's 2005 *Unchosen*, an antecedent to the memoirs, which dwells on the stories of Hasidic rebels. This *un* is echoed in Feldman's 2012 memoir, *Unorthodox*; Lynn Davidman's 2014 collection of memoir-stories, *Becoming Un-Orthodox* (she doubles up on her prefix work with the subtitle, *Stories of Ex-Hasidic Jews*); and Lax's 2015 memoir, *Uncovered*, an almost perfect mirroring of *Unveiled*.[25]

If the prefix is not enough to position the texts as stories of a break or breaking out, many of the titles and subtitles set an internal boundary, which, once traversed, cannot be reversed (the ex-Orthodox Jewish memoirist's version of Thomas Wolfe's *You Can't Go Home*). "Go" is forever separated from "Return" in Deen's title, *All Who Go Do Not Return* (a man's narrative, but one of liberation nonetheless).[26] "Left" sits in contradistinction to "Came" in Lax's subtitle, "How I Left Hasidic Life and Finally Came Home." "After" marks an impermeable temporal border in Vincent's subtitle, "Sin and Salvation after My Ultra-Orthodox Girlhood," and the *joining* conjunction "and" acts, as well, to *disjoin* in Deitsch's title, *Here and There.*

But the ultimate paratextual signifier for the memoirs' triumph of liberation is the cover art. Cover art for memoirs carries special significance. Memoir covers often present images that deliberately blur the lines between writer and subject. See, for example, Caitlin Moran's sassy 2011 memoir, *How To Be a Woman*, which offers a close-up picture of the bold (white, British, feminist, familiar) writer/subject, whose shades-of-gray hair, sweater, and skin complement the background and lettering, leaving her blue-green eyes center-stage, wide, and defiant to pierce the icy patina of the book cover and the soul of every reader (or bookstore browser) to come along (see figure 1.1). There are no secrets here. No enforced modesty. No coy hesitation to tell all. *Come on in, reader, pour yourself a stiff drink, and let's talk vaginas.* In contrast, the Muslim liberation memoir presents the veil/burka/hijab as a curtain between reader and writer, enticing you to open the cover to make your way toward knowing the writer. This is a story that will be hard to read; this is a person who will at first seem unfamiliar; this is not a chat but a rollercoaster of emotions. *Keep your box of tissues handy. This is the book that will open your heart and your mind.* Ironically, of course, the way readers approach the text is often not *open* at all; what they read generally confirms what they already believe.

Whitlock imagines or infers the Western reader's reaction to the jacket art of Muslim women's life stories when she begins her 2005 *Biography* article, "The Skin of the *Burqa*," by asking, "What does one do but recoil at the sight of the *burqa* on the cover of Latifa's life narrative *My Forbidden Face?*" (54). It is a question she returns to, in less outraged manner, in *Soft Weapons*: "How can we read the image of the burka on the cover of *My Forbidden Face?*" (45; see figure 1.2). Latifa's book, graced with the image of "the totally effaced woman in the burka on the purple cover," is one of a number of "veiled bestsellers" that Whitlock reads (or recoils from), locating it among its peers: Jean Sasson's *Mayada: Daughter of Iraq* ("the more erotic sexualized gaze over the chador on the glossy back cover") and Azar Nafisi's *Reading Lolita in Tehran: A Memoir in Books* ("the dark monotone of the young veiled women in chador on the sepia cover"; 45). Despite the "different modalities of life narrative . . . : the autoethnography by Latifa, the veiled bestseller by Sasson, and the academic memoir by Nafisi," together they form an "exotic display . . . of Muslim life narrative," she argues (Whitlock, *Weapons* 47). These life narratives are carefully produced

Figure 1.1. Caitlin Moran for the cover of *How to Be a Woman* (2011). Photo by Chris Floyd. Permission to reproduce by photographer.

and marketed to interpellate the reader "as a liberal Western consumer who desires to liberate and recognize [the women] by lifting the burka and bringing [them] alongside us, barefaced in the West" (47).

An investigation of ex-Orthodox memoir book jackets suggests a degree of variety beyond the ubiquitous veil of Muslim women's life narratives, but the significant difference is perhaps less the variety than the message to readers. In

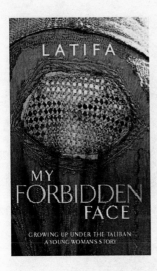

Figure 1.2. Cover of Latifa's *My Forbidden Face* (2001). Permission from Frederick Courtright, Hachette Book Group.

the Orthodox narrative, the change has begun or, more often than not, been completed. The hero or heroine is visibly en route to "liberation" if he or she hasn't already been "liberated" or, as the title of Lax's book makes clear, "uncovered" (Logan's book, in contrast, might be called *Unveiled*, but the female face on the book's cover is anything but. Like the figure on Latifa's book cover, the face is completely obscured by a burka, eyes peering through a heavy mesh mask). Although we might want to read Muslim and Jewish covers as similarly marking the transitions from benighted to enlightened, the Muslim narratives demand we focus on the before; the Orthodox Jewish narratives highlight the after.

Some versions of this visual narrative are rendered as a chronology—not, say, from 2008 to 2015 but rather from time immemorial to the modern era. In these versions, we are presented with images that resonate with the *New York Times*' "lost to time" sentiment. Though once "lost to time," these narratives promise that the writers, freed from the anachronization of their religious upbringing, are now found (an ironic inversion of the logic of the Christian hymn "Amazing Grace," in which the singer is "lost" because of faithlessness and "found" through his spiritual conversion). The cover art on Deen's book, for example, is almost abstract and certainly lacks a sense of time or place: a monolithic turquoise background is bisected with white lines that appear to be trees in a forest but on close inspection are the fringes of a tallis (a Jewish prayer shawl). In a movement toward the horizon on the top right-hand corner of the cover, a Hasidic cutout figure, devoid of detail, walks away. *Go, little man! Flee from the abstract to the concrete, the mythical to the scientific, the past of* there *to the present of* here (see figure 1.3).

Along these same lines but bringing us all the way to the present is Deitsch's book, actually called *Here and There* (see figure 1.4). This book heavy-handedly presents two pictures, one for each of the title's demonstrative pronouns, banded

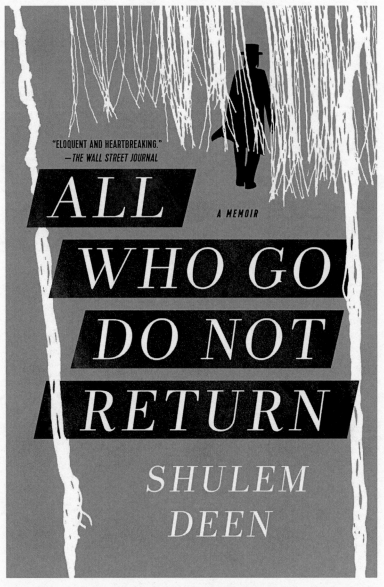

Figure 1.3. Cover of Shulem Deen's *All Who Go Do Not Return* (2015). Cover design by Kimberly Glyder. Permission to reproduce by Kimberly Glyder.

CHAYA DEITSCH

# HERE

# AND

# THERE

LEAVING HASIDISM, KEEPING MY FAMILY

Figure 1.4. Cover of Chaya Deitsch's *Here and There* (2015). Jacket reproduced courtesy of Schocken Books.

across the cover. Deitsch's Hasidic "there," like Deen's, is abstract, unreal(istic), and dream-like. It is a painting ("The Proposal" by Chabad artist Hendel Lieberman [1900–1976]), romantic blues and taupes faded. The figures are slightly crude, decentered, in ancient dress, and their eyes are turned from ours. "Here," in contrast, is a photograph (the medium itself announcing its modernity), the author at its exact midpoint with her hair short (again, signaling modernity) and her smile wide as she faces the camera straight on. If Deen, as a cutout Hasid, was once "lost to time" and is now on his way home to modern civilization, viewers can rest assured that Deitsch, as a glossy photograph, has already made it.

Perhaps figuratively closer to the veil fronting Muslim narratives is the hair that appears on "off-the-*derech*" dust jackets. The long, loose hair acts as a proclamation of freedom (see figure 1.5). Ivriya from Reich's *Master of the Return* is back on her horse, her hair streaming in the wind, rich again like the chestnut mane of her favorite stallion. The word *roots* in *The Scandalous Rejection of My Hasidic Roots*, the subtitle of Feldman's 2012 book, *Unorthodox*, is a pun, referencing both Feldman's (liberation from) family/community and her (covering of her) hair. Viewers instantly recognize this, as the book's front cover image shows Feldman's newly uncovered hair adamantly free, flying up behind her unnaturally, as though blown by an offstage fan (think Marilyn Monroe's iconic subway scene but with locks of brown hair instead of a fabulous white dress). Blue Rider Press apparently inherited Feldman's invisible fan for her subsequent book, *Exodus* (2013), as the image is remarkably similar.

Feldman's hair affairs help form the "display" of Jewish life narratives. Along with the book covers on Lax, Mann, and Vincent's memoirs, the story they tell is one erotic in nature. And yet they differ from the Orientalist covers of Muslim narratives like Jean Sasson's *Mayada*, where readers encounter a woman with a "sexualized gaze over the chador" (Whitlock, "Burqa" 45). In the images on the Jewish books, there *is* no gaze: turned away from the reader, the women on the covers neither offer nor are subject to a gaze of any kind. Furthermore, the chadors here—the *sheitels*, kerchiefs, and turbans—are long gone. This is but one reason that the women on these cover images seem less exotic. We can also hardly fail to miss the fact that Muslim veiled bestseller covers appear elaborate to the point of ostentatious. The lids on the women are too heavily kohled, the lashes too thickly mascaraed, the eyebrows too boldly painted on, the irises too blue or too amber. The women in the pictures wear rhinestones, glitter, and chadors made of filigreed gold and pearls.

In contrast, we might almost call the erotic covers of the Jewish narratives modest, despite the fact that they exhibit naked, or mostly naked, women's bodies. Take *Uncovered* (see figure 1.5): though the author's picture reveals an older woman with short white hair and a genial smile, perhaps in her late fifties, the front cover of the book presents a different image. Here we find a naked young woman, whose (uncovered) hair flows down her back. We cannot see the woman's

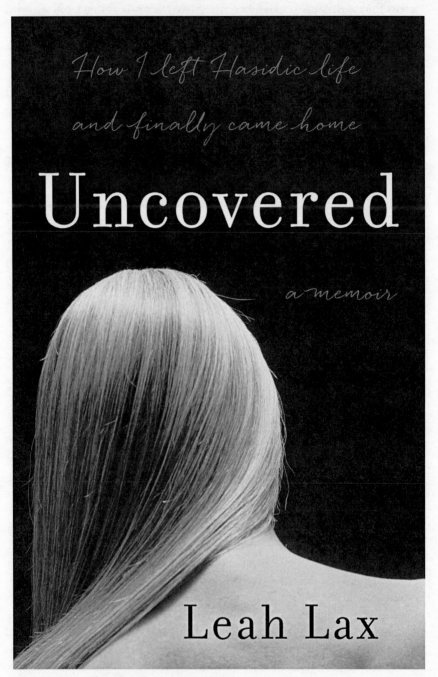

How I left Hasidic life
and finally came home

# Uncovered

a memoir

Leah Lax

Figure 1.5. Cover of Leah Lax's *Uncovered* (2015). Permission to reproduce by author.

face, but we see that her skin is flawless, unmarked by age. The hair, in contrast, is a soft gray, easily mistaken as flaxen. It is significant that it is *not* flaxen. The hair is intended to be a jarring juxtaposition to the youthful body, the overall image working to suggest a coming-of-age story that has been long delayed. In full adulthood, the woman is at last awakening to herself and to her sexuality. "If I hadn't been a lesbian," Lax told me, "I could have stayed in that world. But once I knew, I couldn't stay. I had to start over" (personal communication). In this visualization of her late-stage rebirth, the figure of the memoirist is naked as both an unadorned babe in arms and a wholly realized sexual woman. And with her back turned to the viewer, she is at once enticing and modest ("Look but don't look").

Similarly, each of the two front covers of Mann's *The Rabbi's Daughter* features an unembellished nude—again shyly, it seems, with her back to the viewer. In the first version, the woman's hair is pulled into a loose bun, and the bare skin of her back dominates the bottom half of the cover. The top half, like Deen's, is a background made of a tallis; the foregrounded title and author are inscribed on it. In the second version, the background looks like paper, crumpled and then flattened, promising access to not only "a memoir" (which is written across the background) but also the process of the memoir itself: the act of memorializing, the moments of memorialization. As in Lax's cover image, the woman faces away from the camera, her long, straight hair gracefully draped on one side, exposing the flesh of her neck and back, the length of her spine, her sharp shoulder blades. Her lowered, averted face might indicate shame or humility—or a refusal to be subject to a viewer's gaze. Here, the tallis does not appear behind the title as background art but rather as the thing that clothes the woman, albeit tenuously. This is perhaps the most sexually charged part of the image: the precariousness of the covering.

The picture on the hardback edition of Vincent's *Cut Me Loose* features a woman—or rather, a *piece* of woman, a woman *cut* (see figure 1.6). We view only her lower half (and even this part of her is turned away from us). Running our eyes down the picture, we see the bottom of her skirt, which modestly hits below the knees, followed by the backs of her calves in brutally ripped stockings, and then the feet; one heel is nestled into the other. This cover suggests duality: as the length of the skirt and the stockings (the ladders seeming to appear on the backs of the legs only) indicate, she might still appear the "good" religious girl when seen from the front, even as we are privy to the "bad" girl side that she hides. (The image calls to mind the tagline from a 1980s B-film called *Angel*: "High School Honor Student by Day. Hollywood Hooker by Night.") Alternatively, this is a picture of transition: if the skirt harks of the religious life, the stockings, dominating the foreground, tear into that image, and we look to the feet about to take flight. She is in the act of liberation; she is cutting loose (a pun; Vincent is a cutter).

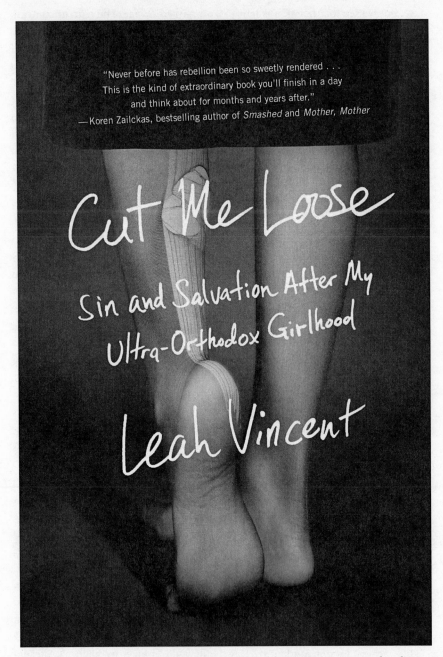

Figure 1.6. Cover of Leah Vincent's *Cut Me Loose* (2014). Permission to reproduce by Random House.

On the cover of the paperback edition, however, Vincent's transition appears complete, the woman in the image already liberated. Although the woman in this picture is positioned toward the camera, she is no Caitlin Moran. This figure is almost faceless, her head turned to the side, the picture cropped along the border of her lower lip, leaving us with a woman's naked form from chin to waist. The shift from back to front is not, of course, insignificant: though the woman's face, marker of her individuality, is absent, the presence of her neck, collarbones, chest, and décolletage—signs of femininity—are in full view. The breasts, in particular, draw the eye as the cover, like Mann's, gestures to its own writerliness, with its title's cursive letters scrawled across the woman's chest. "Leah" and "Vincent" each curve along the upper arc of a breast. Suggestive without being graphic, the skin is concealed below the inscribed décolletage. And what is it that lends the cover its modesty? As in Mann's picture, the "veil" that separates the viewer from the woman's breasts and abdomen is none other than a clutched tallis.

Why the tallis? Significantly, the tallis is not, like the chador, a religious female garment, and cannot be mistaken as a symbol of the "before." On the contrary, the prevailing Orthodox custom is that women are forbidden from wearing tallises, on the basis that they are explicitly men's garments. The Chabad.org website informs us that a "woman who fulfills this mitzvah, which she is not obligated in doing and is not performed by the vast majority of her gender, draws undue attention to her excessive piety in an inappropriately ostentatious manner" ("Is It Appropriate"). Although both chador and tallis are clothing that indicate piety, the tallis worn by a woman acts as a *subversion* of that piety. If this is an image of the "after," it is an "after" that complicates the expectation of a clear chronology, a departure and an arrival, a linear movement from religious imprisonment to secular freedom.[27]

Like the erotic image of the woman in the chador, the image of a nude woman standing under the fringes of a tallis, or the image of a demure midi paired with ripped stockings, might appear to be a marketing ploy, mixing sex appeal and sensationalist transgression. We miss the point, however, if we think sex and sin are all these books have to offer. Instead, we might recognize these covers as alluding to their texts' missions: to keep, embed, and contextualize Judaism. Cloaking naked female bodies can be both carnal and modest, and the subverted tallises on these books' covers demand attention be paid to the reinvented and reinvested Judaism the books denote. Bodies wrapped in tallises, flesh marked with women's names, hair that has been reclaimed from exaggerated decrees on modesty show embodied, feminized Judaism. These covers might be trafficking in salaciousness, but it is not wholly gratuitous salaciousness; the texts, to return to Mann's "*pikuach nefesh*," her Jewish saving of herself through unsanctioned sex, are about liberating Judaism as much as liberating the Jewish woman's body.

## V. Still the *Eshes Chayil*

*It is a grave sin for a man to spill seed, one punishable by death according to
our rabbis. But women face similar restrictions. Birth control obstructs sperm
and prevents new souls from being born. A wife who takes it is a dangerous
sinner, a damaged vessel. Such a Jew does not have a place in paradise. . . . I became a person the day I stopped being a vessel. It is difficult to describe the sense
of wonder, the freedom of stepping out of survival mode and into motherhood.
I learned the joy of children because I could finally be a mother, because I could
devote my energy to the three children I had, not to the ones I still needed. And
for first time, I began to feel complete.*
—Judy Brown (Eishes Chayil), "Cracks in a Holy Vessel," *Forward*, March 11, 2013

In response to Judy Brown's public reclamation of her body in the *Forward*, a
woman named Rachel Freier responded online with a counterargument, telling Brown and fellow *Forward* readers that "A Mother Is Who I Am." She said
there was nothing holier than motherhood; she maintained a law practice without compromising her dedication to Haredi Judaism or her role as a "*yidishe
momme*." Brown in turn fired off "I'm a Mother, Not a Baby Machine," accusing
Freier of shutting up not only her but also all the other women in the neighborhood in a similar state of agony. What did this public debate do for readers?
Did it, as one reader wrote, play up the image that "all Orthodox Jews are living
in cages, barred from ever leaving the boundaries of their communities because
they can't read the exit signs due to their lack of secular education" (C. Feldman)? What do online debates and blogs and stories emerging on the internet
and in memoirs from the deep, dark recesses of Orthodox communities tell their
readers? Do these writings feed readers the sensationalism they crave?[28] Or do
the writers—think of the nude and seminude women on the front covers and the
promise of "good stuff" in the subtitles, like Vincent's *Sin and Salvation after My
Ultra-Orthodox Girlhood* and Mann's even better *A True Story of Sex, Drugs and
Orthodoxy* (Oh my!)—redirect that craving? And if so, to what?

Ragen, who I like to think of as the stepmother of the contemporary genre
of "off-the-*derech*" narratives, knew long ago that sex, scandal, and shock tac-
tics were crucial selling features of stories about religious Jewish communities.
When she published *Jephte's Daughter* (1989), the *New York Times* dubbed it a
"Jewish Gothic." Here, Batsheva Ha-Levi, who could have been a character on
the prime-time soap opera *Dynasty*, which was in its last season when the book
was published, is a beautiful young woman (raven-black hair tumbling down to
her waist, pale-blue eyes that "people stared at and often got lost in," firm breasts,
slim thighs, the whole bit) residing, like the Carringtons, in a California mansion
and the heir to a dynasty—only in her case, it's a Hasidic one (Ragen, *Jephte's
Daughter* 36). Over hundreds of pages, from sun-kissed California to Jerusalem's

cloistered *Mea She'arim* to the art scene of London, we follow Beautiful Batsheva's journey into selfhood. The novel is a bildungsroman and a *Künstlerroman* and a soap-operatic romance. The book was a trendsetter that led to such popular Hollywood films as *A Stranger among Us* (1992) and *A Price above Rubies* (1998), as well as the Israeli film *Kadosh* (1999)—all featuring hot-and-bothered Hasidim, sinister schemes, and victimized women.[29]

Ragen, however, appears to have seen her role not as a sensationalizer of the community but rather as an activist, and responses from readers helped encourage her belief. Looking back on the publication of *Jephte's Daughter*, Ragen writes in the foreword to the 2001 edition, "*Jephte's Daughter* was my first published novel. I wrote it in a rush over a year's time, little realizing in the innocence and passion of bringing to life the tragedy of a local ultra-Orthodox girl, what a storm of controversy would greet it's [*sic*] birth." She explains further that the "rich inner life of ultra-Orthodox women—a subject hardly touched in American Jewish literature of the time" as well as "domestic abuse in Chassidic circles" were felt by many to be "an unwelcome intrusion into that very private community" (ix). Ragen argues that this "intrusion" is precisely the domain of literature: "Literature is the way mankind speaks to each other and to itself" (ix).[30]

More than her initial action, it was the *reaction* (to which she in turn reacted again) that inspired her to produce *Sotah* (1992), the story of a Haredi woman wrongly accused of adultery, and *The Sacrifice of Tamar* (1994), the story of a Haredi woman who keeps her rape a secret for fear of being cast out of her community. And it is perhaps with thanks to Ragen that other people began producing serious investigations into the problems of Orthodox communities at the turn of the twenty-first century. In 2001, for example, Sandi Simcha DuBowski produced a documentary about homosexuality in the Haredi community, *Trembling Before G-d* (a play on the literal translation of the term *Haredi*). I remember seeing it at the Film Forum in New York City, sitting a row behind an unshowered Ethan Hawke (remember that, Leila?), thinking it was brilliant and so important but also not likely to be interesting to the general public. I was wrong. *Trembling Before G-d* broke opening-day box office records, received ten award nominations, and won seven, including Best Documentary awards at the 2001 Chicago and Berlin film festivals (Hernandez and Brooks). In 2005, with less fanfare but an audience that far exceeded the typical academic readership of a PhD dissertation-turned-book, Hella Winston's *Unchosen*, investigating Hasidic rebels, appeared. If the ex-Orthodox writers themselves were slower to add to the volume of works exposing and examining problems of Orthodoxy, they still joined. And in so doing, they offered voices that were treated as those of authority and authenticity—voices to incite action.

Long before the memoirs and semiautobiographical fiction of ex-Orthodox writers appeared in the twenty-first century, Ragen foregrounded three important aspects of literature about Orthodox Jewish communities: exposure, conversation, and a movement toward remedy. These elements appear time and again in "off-the-*derech*" narratives. Just as the narratives require that we recognize that the writers are still (inextricably, undeniably, incomprehensibly) Jewish, so too do we find that these Jewish writers are still dedicated to the betterment of their (former) communities. They are still taking on the role of *neshot chayil*, "women of valor," still "spread[ing] out [their] palm[s] to the poor," still "extend[ing their] hands to the destitute." Leaving does not mean abandoning; it means taking a step back, taking on a new perspective (think of Deitsch and her mother watching *Rashomon*), and taking to task problems not acknowledged from within.

––––––––––

If we conjure the making of a memoir, we imagine it in the loneliest and most singular of terms. In fact, one need not look too deeply into the etymology of the word to recognize that *mémoire* is French for "memory." We are reading a person's memory, something that can only come from that person and would not be the same told by another. It is uniquely individual and private. But Rak argues for a different way of understanding memoir: "Memoir," she writes, "is a way of thinking and perhaps even of being *public*, as it remains a way to construct, package, and market identity so that others will want to buy it. . . . Memoir is about . . . how private individuals communicate within, against, and to a public" (7, emphasis mine). This idea of the public memoir is heightened in an era when anyone can publish a memoir—a musing, a memory—for free online, named or anonymously, and others can respond, refute, or offer memories of their own that change the meaning of the original. Ex-Orthodox narratives, memoirs and fiction alike, engage the responses of both current community members and the general public.

Much of this interaction happens via the internet. Not all ex-Orthodox memoirs and narrative writers got their starts on the internet, but it is interesting to consider that many did: Shalom Auslander, Deborah Feldman, Shulem Deen, Frieda Vizel, and Leah Vincent, among others. Though this authorial origin is not unusual in the twenty-first century, it holds a special significance for writers for whom foraying into the "outside world" is fraught and unusual. The stories often echo, eerily, ones we find in slave narratives as the enslaved tell of budding literacy as the path to liberation. Similarly, digital literacy becomes the way out for these writers. Deen offers the most detailed narrative of his experiences, beginning by recounting ordering a computer as a teaching aid and discovering in the box "a 3.5-inch floppy disk with a label: *America Online. 30-Day Free Trial*" (127). Soon he gets mail—"Look at this! . . . I'm having a conversation!"—and his journey down the virtual rabbit hole begins: "All of a sudden, I was connected to millions with whom I could interact, and soon I discovered a world of people entirely different from anyone I knew" (127–128).

This community-building aspect of Deen's engagement with the internet becomes the key one. Although being online offers him other significant pieces of information that change his life (like the existence of birth control), it is the people who respond to his digital persona who allow him to make the leap into the unknown and to take control of his destiny:

> The Internet provided a small remedy, a therapeutic outlet through which to express what felt like an unending inner battle over how to negotiate my circumstances. Interacting with others online helped to solidify my identity as a heretic. . . . It wasn't long before I discovered my own fellow travelers. We found one another, scattered across various discussion groups, and proceeded to create our own: "Hasidic and Enlightened," "Frum Skeptics." . . . All of us were hiding in our homes and offices, seeking forbidden knowledge and forbidden connections. From around the world, Brooklyn to Tel Aviv, Montreal to Antwerp, from all sects and subgroups, we were able to say to one another: I, too, am asking forbidden questions. (200)

As in Auslander's book, readers are reminded that these are not truly isolated communities—only what connects them here is not a rabbi who knows a rabbi who knows a rabbi but a series of modems communicating through fiber-optic cables. Years after Deen's narrative, the internet—replete with hashtag reassurances like #itgetsbesser—continues to be the gateway to a new community for those who leave the path of Orthodoxy (although the nonprofit organization Footsteps, founded in 2003, which Deen and Vincent and others have been heavily involved in, has done tremendous work in person to provide support for leavers).[31]

At last, Deen comes to his writing. He starts a blog and begins to write about issues affecting him and his community. As noted, the post that attracted attention was a call for President Bush to bring liberation to the Hasidim of America. He discovers the lures of a (hungry) responsive readership. "Across the Internet, I found other bloggers who linked to me, excitedly, with a discovery they seemed to think astonishing: 'Look at this! A Hasid writing in secret about his insular world.' Apparently people wanted to read about my world," he realizes (206–207). Soon he begins writing in earnest and is profiled by the *Village Voice*, at which point he realizes that readers want more than stories of insular Hasidim: they want sensationalist stories.[32] Deen, however, situates himself as other writers who have left the community do. He comes to his work with a mission to find a "remedy" not only for himself but also for the people he left behind. In-members of Hasidic communities are not helped by sensationalism alone.

Moreover, sensationalist renderings of Orthodox communities can be dangerous for the in-members. Responding to Deen and others who promote or consume the rhetoric of the liberation narrative, Vizel illustrates this point in her blog, *Oy Vey Cartoons*. In Vizel's cartoon image, we see men in military uniform, armed with guns, in three rows of three and four, legs swinging wide. They march aggressively toward a Hasidic woman, their faces impassive. The Hasidic woman appears unimpressed by the testosterone collective approaching her. She stands in a line, pushing ahead of her a baby carriage; behind her, forming the frailest of human defense chains, two small children walk, hands linked. The children frown; the baby peers from the pram, startled. Rather than appearing in need of the soldiers' protection, she looks in need of protection *from* the soldiers. But the title indicates the general dismissal of the needs, desires, or beliefs of the Hasidic woman herself in the quest to free her from the shackles of her religious life. "Finally," reads the ironic title overhead, "they're coming to liberate the Chasidic woman" (see figure 1.7).

Although Vizel left the Satmar community herself, she has insisted on a measured approach to Orthodox communities in her work, repeatedly giving readers a sense of why not all Hasidic women are running for the metaphorical fire exits of Crown Heights and Williamsburg. "Hasidic women live in a radically different culture than the secular American culture, and their world is more complicated and nuanced than the mere sum of these rituals. Things that seem strange and unjust to outsiders are natural and non-issues to Satmar women," she explains (Vizel, "On Hasidic Women"). Furthermore, she writes, "They invest themselves in the home and find power and passion within the framework of their available religious outlets." Devaluing the potency of the liberation narrative in explicit language, Vizel says, "We can decry Satmar women's oppression and demand their liberation. But we'll be missing the point. Satmar women don't want to be saved." Still, Vizel sees her role as not only a cultural translator but also, significantly, an activist on behalf of the Orthodox community and its (not always or

# FINALLY.

## THEY'RE COMING TO LIBERATE THE CHASIDIC WOMAN

Figure 1.7. Cartoon panel from the blog post "On Hasidic Women" (2012) by Frieda Vizel. Permission to reproduce by the author.

only) benighted and oppressed women. Despite the difficulties in-members of Orthodox communities face in acknowledging their problems and out-members have in knowing about or properly understanding them, Vizel insists that "problems exist in the community that need to be addressed. Increasing awareness and resources for Hasidic victims of domestic violence . . . are some of the ways we can have a conversation about the problems in the Hasidic community without narrowly judging a people from the prism of our own culture" (Vizel, "On Hasidic Women"). Her work offers exposure, engages in conversation, and calls for remedy: Vizel might not be a practicing Satmar, but she maintains her role as an *eshes chayil*, here clearly meaning a woman committed to bettering her community.[33]

## VI. *HUSH* BY EISHES CHAYIL

*Her husband, he praises her: "Many daughters have attained valor, but you have surpassed them all."*

—Proverbs 31:29

In 2010, Judy Brown published the semiautobiographical novel *Hush* under the pseudonym Eishes Chayil. For the remainder of this chapter, I use this novel as a case study to show how a woman who left her Orthodox community can continue to work toward its betterment and still play the role of the *eshes chayil*. Only here, the woman of valor has an enlarged perspective and an ability to interact with people not only within but also well beyond the insular community in which she was raised. This is significant because *Hush* is a novel that, like *Jephte's Daughter*, breaks fresh ground: it tells the story of sexual abuse and suicide in a Hasidic community. It describes the cries of the abused Hasidic girl as desperately silent: "She did not cry out loud. Her mouth opened and closed and opened and closed as if it did not dare make a sound, and I heard the long, silent screams of agony again and again" (Brown, *Hush* 127). This silence of the girl is echoed by that of the community that fails to tell, or act on, the girl's suffering and death.

The issue of sexual abuse among Orthodox Jews is one where there has been scant awareness due to the insularity of the Orthodox communities and the efforts made to "hush" victims and witnesses. In the novel, a woman, whose son was molested by a rabbi who taught him, spoke to the principal of the school, the teachers, and the police, but "even the police told her that they couldn't help her. They said gathering evidence of molestation in the Orthodox community was impossible and that she would lose the case" (Brown, *Hush* 198). In her January 2017 regional Limmud talk, Yehudis Fekete echoed this fictional episode with her real account of being sexually abused by a Haredi teacher in Manchester and her challenges in bringing the man, Todros Grynhaus, to justice. Fekete told of Grynhaus's wife walking in and finding Grynhaus abusing her—a fifteen-year-old girl who was boarding at his house, under his protection—and how the wife called a leading rabbi in America, whose solution was to remove Fekete from the Grynhaus home. When Fekete attempted to contact the rabbi's wife, she was of no help. "My husband will decide what my husband will decide," she reportedly said. Fekete spoke to a rabbi in Israel as well, but he deferred to the American rabbi. From the rabbinical authority, the only injunction to eventually come forth was on the Grynhaus daughters: to not leave their bedrooms without their dressing gowns. Fekete took her evidence to the *Beit Din*, the Jewish court. But they did not help her. Her evidence disappeared. She knocked on doors. She warned people. Years passed. "Nobody wanted to know," she said. Only when another survivor of Grynhaus's abuse went forward to the police did Fekete dare do the same. And even then, Fekete realized that it was not enough. The support of the community was too strong—logistical, financial—and Grynhaus was given someone else's passport, which he used to flee to Israel. Although Grynhaus was eventually brought back to England, found guilty on all counts, and sentenced to thirteen years in jail, the story Fekete told—of deceit, collusion, the silencing of victims, and the enabling of abuse—was not a happy one. "It takes a village to raise a child," said Fekete. "And it takes a village to abuse one." She added, "It took one man to hurt me and many more to look away, helping him to hurt me."

In a rare instance of publicity, in 1984, four Italian American Catholic boys accused Ger Hasidic psychologist Avrohom Mondrowitz of molestation and sodomy.[34] Only after Mondrowitz fled to Israel (escaping justice) did his *Jewish* victims come forward—and in such large numbers that the leaders of Agudath Israel issued a statement condemning Mondrowitz: "Great Rabbis and Roshei Yeshivah have heard first-hand testimony from his victims, and were horrified to hear of these terrible crimes which cause one's hair to stand on end. Anyone who helps or defends him will be liable for his actions, and will be considered responsible and as an accomplice to his crimes. And for this the punishment is severe" (Orbach).

In the Haredi community, sexual abuse takes on a strong element of shame—for the abused as much, if not more so, than the abuser. And there is nowhere for a victim (doubly victimized) to run: the "connectedness" of the Haredi community expounded by Auslander and Deen means nowhere is safe. In a 2014 *New Yorker* investigation of sexual abuse and the subsequent casting out of Haredi victims following the conviction of Nechemya Weberman ("the Devil of Williamsburg," who was sentenced to 103 years in prison for sexual abuse), we read that one Satmar victim "never contemplated moving, because all the major Hasidic communities—in upstate New York, Jerusalem, London, Montreal, and Antwerp—were connected, and he assumed that everyone already knew his story" (R. Aviv).

Much of the discourse surrounding abuse in Haredi communities is speculative, but even speculation has caught the attention of the secular world—unfortunately, because the topic traffics in sensationalism. It has also led to tangible results. Robert Kolker, a contributing editor of *New York Magazine*, brought an abuser to justice (and was nominated for a National Magazine Award) on the basis of his 2006 article, "On the Rabbi's Knee." Writing about the case of an alleged abuser, Kolker says, "What is perhaps most troubling about [the] case is the idea that Kolko, if culpable, *could just be* the tip of the iceberg" (emphasis mine). He then goes on to claim that "rabbi-on-child molestation is a widespread problem in the ultra-Orthodox Jewish community, and one that has long been covered up." What he does not do is provide evidence, numbers, statistics—because, as he admits, he cannot. This problem came up again at the 2015 U.K. Limmud Conference when Manny Waks, a survivor and leading Australian campaigner against child sex abuse, pointed out, "There is zero research in the community."

Yet each of these pieces—the Agudath Israel's statement, Kolker's article, Fekete's talk, Waks's testimony, and more recently the Netflix documentary *One of Us*—contribute to the knowledge and understanding of the problem. *Hush* is also important because it dramatizes an issue that has been silenced—in part because it can't be proven to have statistical significance—even as it persists.

*Hush* is told in the voice of young Gittel, the friend of the abused and deceased girl, Devory. Through Gittel's eyes, we see how the values of the community, particularly that of modesty for its female members, enable the silence. Comparing an insufficiently modest woman to her mother, as well as a "great *Eishes Chayil*," Gittel explains,

> [Tovah's] mother covered her hair at home with a snood, leaving one whole inch of her hair showing in the front. My mother, who tucked every last strand of hair into her turban when she took off her wig, strongly disapproved of such behavior. She said that a true married Jewish woman does not show as much as one piece of hair, and that in the Talmud it said Kimchas—a great *Eishes Chayil*, a Woman of Valor—mothered seven sons who all grew up to be high holy priests because even within the four walls of her home they never saw her hair. Now that was modesty. (Brown, *Hush* 13)

This rhetoric is, by now, familiar: we read it in relation to Reich's Ivriya and again in Feldman's *Unorthodox*. Yet if this version of the woman of valor—a woman who protects her children from seeing her hair—is passed down to Gittel through her mother and other members of the community, it is not the one she ultimately believes in. This version teaches a woman that modesty means hiding, effacing, and silencing herself and that a man's attention is her fault alone. And aren't there more important things to protect children from?

The authorial "Eishes Chayil" is far less concerned with an inch of hair or an uncovered thigh than justice or remedy. The true woman of valor, she asserts, is the one who pushes forward with her mission even when it means potentially alienating her husband, despite the importance of *shalom bayis*, the Jewish concept of peace in the home. In *Hush*, Gittel grows up, repressing the memory of Devory, as the community at large does. But once married and pregnant (her proper place in her community secured), she becomes driven to expose Devory's abuse by her brother. As a result, she estranges her family, particularly her husband, Yankel, who fails to understand both the nature of the crime (the word *rape* is unfamiliar to him, suggesting the vast ignorance of the community) and her need to expose it.

In the end, readers are brought back to the true meaning of the woman of valor. Gittel's "husband's heart trusts in her" (as per Proverbs 31), which acts as the ultimate vindication for her behavior. Although this need for male absolution might seem problematic for a mainstream egalitarian readership, it serves as an effective tool for a Hasidic readership accustomed to women looking to husbands and rabbis for support and permission. Yankel's willingness to see his wife's righteousness despite the community's *unwillingness* is made evident when he wraps his arms around her before Devory's recovered gravestone. "Why are you holding me outside, where people can see?" Gittel asks him, bewildered at her husband's flouting of Hasidic custom (326). "Because you are in pain," he answers, and the two cry together. At this point in the novel, we see a "happily ever after" foretold—as much as there can be in a novel about molestation. Gittel writes a letter to the newspaper and, more significantly, persuades the editor to publish it. In the letter, she reveals Devory's secret and apologizes not only for her own complicity in Devory's abuse and death but also for that of the whole community. "You didn't have to die," she writes. "But for our ignorance, for our deliberate blindness, for our unforgivable stupidity, you did. I hope this letter will stop others from sharing your fate" (335). Although not all the responses to her letter are favorable, Yankel supports his wife adamantly. Surie, Gittel's sister, tells her, "That is not the way an *Eishes Chayil* acts. A Woman of Valor does things quietly—at least anonymously. And how *dare* you talk about the *rabbonim* like that? How will your children ever get married? And don't even try to go near my children with that garbage mouth of yours" (336). But Yankel (a pious Jew, a good husband, a *man*) declares, "*You* [Gittel] are the *Eishes Chayil*. . . . *You* are the real one. You are the only one protecting the children, and that is what a real mother does" (336). The meaning of the *eshes chayil* is at last defined.

Brown's choice of pseudonym, of course, mimics the label given to her character (with the added value of modest anonymity that Surie calls for). In fact, the two are closely linked in other ways: just as Gittel writes about sexual abuse and spurs a readership into conversation and debate ("the letters came by the tens, then by the hundreds"), so does Brown (336). On the website Jewishmom.com, however, one response—from a woman who referred to herself only as "A Lubavitcher"—accused the author of airing the community's dirty laundry "for the sake of sensationalism": "Although the insights about child abuse (how the victim felt, how her best friend felt, how the molester acted) might be valuable, and it is certainly wrong to protect molesters and silence witnesses in order to protect some idyllic reputation, it is too miserable to see in print that someone obviously on the inside, someone who clearly knows better, has decided to badmouth our entire society, our way of life and the Torah itself for the sake of sensationalism" ("A Lubavitcher's Response"). "A Lubavitcher" is also offended by the author's choice of pseudonym ("a strange compliment to pay herself"). Yet it is clear that, like the in-text fictional letter, the real-life artifact *Hush* is doing crucial work in its exposure of abuse. And not all Orthodox respondents agreed with "A Lubavitcher." In *Jewish Magazine: The Magazine of the Orthodox Union*, Rabbi Tzvi Hersh Weinreb, the emeritus executive vice president of the Orthodox Union, writes that although the book "has been described by some as a sensationalist exposé"—a point he does not wholly refute—he believes in the importance of the exposure and the courage of the author, whom he commends for her choice of pseudonym. "If this book provokes awareness of these phenomena and results in constructive efforts to ameliorate them, the author will have achieved her goals," he concludes.

Brown is the daughter of a prominent woman in the Haredi world, Ruthie Lichtenstein, the editor in chief of the Brooklyn-based ultra-Orthodox daily newspaper *Hamodia: The Daily Newspaper of Torah Jewry* as well as the weekly women's magazine *Binah*. Brown may have chosen to omit her real name as the author from a sense of modesty. It is also likely, however, that she felt the need to protect her family and community, as the book was loosely based on her experience witnessing a friend being molested. But after a rare instance of the media reporting on an internal community crime—an eight-year-old Hasidic boy called Leiby Kletzky was abducted and murdered by an Orthodox Jew in New York in 2011—Brown decided to declare her real name in a *Huffington Post* article as a way of adding to the "unhushing" she saw occurring as a result of the widespread publicity.

As Judy Brown, the writer has continued in her *role* if not the *name* of "Eishes Chayil," the woman who is dedicated to the betterment of her metaphorical family. She has proceeded to "unhush" herself about challenges in her community and her experiences in articles and responses in such fora as *The Forward*'s sisterhood blog, the *Huffington Post*, and Jezebel, and she has written a memoir titled *This Is Not a Love Story* (2015), focusing on her brother's autism (another community shame).

From *Disobedience*, *The Foreskin's Lament*, and *The Rabbi's Daughter* to the proliferation of memoirs in the second decade of the twenty-first century, the "off-the-*derech*" narrative has become a popular genre. But it is more than that. It provides an opportunity for writers to present issues confronting Orthodox communities, such as repressed sexuality for women, which leads them to be unable to commune with God, or distorted sexuality, which leaves them unable to commune with anyone. And presenting these issues is not necessarily done for the purpose of profit. It is done to lead to dialogue and, ultimately, a remedy.

The authors write from the position of "after." They have, as their book cover images so often suggest, been "unveiled." And remedy is challenging when writers, like Brown, are known to be "off the *derech*"; they are regarded by those who have remained "on the path" with suspicion. Still, the need to expose, discuss, and fix the problems of Orthodox communities comes up in "off-the-*derech*" narratives again and again. Despite (or through) their often-salacious titles and covers, the authors engage seriously with Orthodoxy and its challenges. They are not, on the whole, standing outside the cave of Orthodoxy, beckoning their former fellow prisoners to come into the sunlight and leave the shadows behind. They are not openly condemning monotheism alongside Gloria Steinem either—even if they share her feminist stance. They are, instead, encouraging Orthodox women to discover the agency in their own positions and within their communities and to act as true *neshot chayil*, women of valor—not concerned with a rogue hair but rather with a lost child, an abused wife, a suffering soul.

———

In the following chapter, I will cover the ways that women from *within* Orthodox communities also represent women of valor as concerned with lost children, abused wives, and suffering souls—and, perhaps, rogue hairs. These are not characters of books considered serious or literary. They are the creatures of a kind of genre fiction that is serial, formulaic, and distinctly lowbrow. Still, these characters—and the books at large—have more to offer than we might assume. There is a lot to learn from crime fiction . . . so long as readers don't mind stumbling over a corpse or two along the way.

# CHAPTER 2

# A Woman of Valor Who Can Find

## CRIME FICTION AS PRIMERS OF ORTHODOXY

### I. Introduction

*The world of ultra-Orthodox women can seem to be a mysterious one.*
—Ira Spitzer for Jewish News One (JN1) in New York City, covering
Feredrica Valabrega's photography exhibit "Bat Melech," July 20, 2013

*It's a good story. A sheltered, beautiful young woman falls in love with a hand-
some drug addict who kills her because her Orthodox Jewish parents forbid her
to see him. . . . It's not exactly the truth, but it's a good story. Maybe they'll write
a book, or make a television movie. Is that what you want . . . ?*
—Rochelle Krich, *Grave Endings* (2004)

"A woman of valor, who can find?" begins the hymn "Eshes Chayil." Is she "shrouded
in mystery and forbidden," like all Orthodox Jewish women, as many writers suggest (see Beaudoin, back cover)? Or is she easily found—that is, by murderers
and rapists and thieves? Is the unknown Orthodox "woman of mystery," in other
words, the ideal woman to feature in mainstream mystery novels? It would seem
the answer is yes. In her 2010 study, *Doubting the Devout*, religious studies scholar
Nora Rubel argues that a dominant narrative of Haredi culture is the "new Jewish
gothic," a genre of antireligious novels that has its roots in the English anti-Catholic
Gothic literature of the eighteenth century, which originated with Gregory Lewis's
*The Monk*. "Mirroring cultural stereotypes and indicative of an increasing hostility
toward the haredim from the Jewish American mainstream," Rubel writes, "these
characters permeate Jewish literature, film, and even popular television dramas.
These gothic-style captivity narratives [Ragen's, filmmaker Boaz Yakin's] featur[e]
haredi men as villains and haredi women as victims in mysteries, romances, and
crime dramas" (Rubel 81). As a departure from the texts that Rubel studies, the
perpetrators in some twenty-first-century novels are *not* Haredi men but rather
women, complicating the flat image of patriarchy inherent in earlier narratives.

Furthermore, we might note that gay Haredi men can apparently occupy similar roles to Haredi women. Take, for example, the dead, gay, "off-the-*derech*," would-be messiah junkie figure at the heart of Michael Chabon's strange but fascinating mystery novel, *The Yiddish Policemen's Union* (2007).

Still, twenty-first-century versions of these Haredi-women-as-victims mystery tales abound. *The Big Nap* (2002), the first of Ayelet Waldman's "mommy-track mysteries" (from which Chabon, her husband, borrowed and repurposed the fictional "Verbover" Hasidim for his *Yiddish Policemen*) has Hasidic babysitter Fraydle coming to work for secular, sharp, Harvard-educated, intermarried, former public defender Juliet Applebaum ("You'll help out a nice Jewish neighbor lady and maybe you'll show her how to light the *Shabbos* candles while you're at it," Fraydle's aunt tells her; Waldman 15). Fraydle, who is a victim of Haredi culture from the start ("Eighteen years old and already being forced into marriage and a life like her mother's—baby after baby with menopause as the only end to it") soon becomes a victim of violent crime, her dead body discovered in a freezer serving as a catalyst for Juliet's reengagement with her career (21). Similarly, in Julia Dahl's *Invisible City* (2014), a secular Jewish (raised-as-Christian) reporter stumbles on the scoop of a lifetime when she starts to investigate the mystery of a dead Hasidic woman found at the bottom of a quarry in a community that turns out to have surprising ties to her own past.

Interestingly, Orthodox Jewish women writers also seem to consider the Orthodox Jewish woman to be the ideal woman to feature in mystery novels—but with a difference. In the crime fiction of Orthodox Jewish women, she does more than play the victim and contribute to the cultural logic that deems Orthodox Judaism a mysterious and therefore potentially dangerous practice. In other words, she is not only the answer to the question "A woman of valor, who can find?" The Orthodox woman character of this fiction is not waiting to be found. She is a woman who takes charge: of souls, of sins, of crimes, of her life, and of her image. And thus she is also the *statement*: She is a woman of valor who "can find."

Faye Kellerman's Decker/Lazarus series—starring detective Peter Decker and his wife, Rina Lazarus—began in 1986 with *The Ritual Bath* and is still going strong more than thirty years and twenty books later. Yet the series is hardly unique now. Some of Kellerman's literary descendants, like Rochelle Krich, have extended the roles of their Orthodox female characters from wives or helpers into the primary role of detective novels: the detectives. Looking at writers such as Krich, a Modern Orthodox German-born American woman, and Libi Astaire, an American Haredi woman living in Israel who writes Jewish historical mysteries situated in England, we might say Kellerman birthed a genre of Orthodox women's mystery fiction—transnational, narrative-driven fiction that puts Orthodox women characters at the heart of the seemingly least *tznius* (modest) kind of story.[1] The women of these novels, whether they are detectives, aides, or narrators of the tales, occasionally play the victims as well. But for the most part, these are the empowered women of the stories. For a woman's agency to appear in these tales, readers don't require the intervention of a Harvard-educated secular lawyer or the Melanie Griffith-style caricatured shiksa-detective featured in *A Stranger among Us*. The authors instead use the Orthodox women's intelligence, their positions in their communities, their commitment to the home, and their faithfulness to the Torah to revise the popular image of Orthodox women as victims and make these women into lay rebbes. These are rebbes of a living and livable creed who teach—through examples from their own mundane lives that often include cooking, childcare, community work, and internal struggles with their beliefs—what Judaism is all about. And significantly, these imagined creatures anticipated the real women advisers on Jewish law who have come into being in the twenty-first century: *yoetzot*.[2]

A *yoetzet halacha* is a woman of advanced Torah scholarship. Her primary job is to teach and provide counseling and support for women with questions about Jewish law as it pertains to women (in particular, marriage, sexuality, and women's health). This focus on teaching Jewish law with an emphasis on women is the theme that runs through the work of Kellerman and her descendants, often pushing the mysteries of the mystery novels from the fore. Judaism, particularly women's Judaism, is almost a character itself in the books. Other characters love it, hate it, and struggle with it, but they cannot forget it, ignore it, or fail to learn something from it. Readers too cannot fail to learn from it: what Jewish law asks its people to do, how they do what they do, why they do what they do. At their cores, these conventional mystery novels found on the shelves of supermarkets and airplane terminals are primers of Orthodoxy.

## II. The Highbrow Aims of Lowbrow Genre Fiction

*Since any reader of detective fiction knows that the smallest detail can serve as a clue and is therefore willing to pay close attention to every aspect of the world evoked, ethnic mysteries can fulfill the function of anthropological handbooks and provide their readers with exciting introductions to unknown cultures. Because these narratives, due to their generic conventions, do not purport to inform but simply to entertain and because their readers receive incidental cultural information along with thrilling action and often almost without recognizing it, the inadvertent learning effect can be, and frequently is, all the greater.*

—Peter Freese, *The Ethnic Detective* (1992)

*"Detective, you said your wife told you to stop the guy whom you didn't know at all. . . . In other words, you blindly listened to your wife."*

*"She knows the nuances of . . . the religion. . . . I didn't listen to her because she was my wife. I listened to her as one listens to an expert witness."*

—Faye Kellerman, *Sanctuary* (1994)

Kellerman's books can be said to fit into a subgenre of fiction called religious detective fiction, in the tradition of G. K. Chesterton, whose Father Brown stories ran from 1910 to 1936. A Catholic priest, Chesterton's Father Brown turns to his faith to help him solve crimes.[3] He is often thought to be the obverse of Sherlock Holmes: intuitive rather than deductive, spiritual rather than scientific. In a review of a contemporary BBC series of Chesterton's stories, *The Guardian* called Brown's "most conspicuous feature . . . his inconspicuousness" and remarked that "neither film nor TV is a medium built for the celebration of humility" (Newton). Of course, this is also true of detective novels, which generally celebrate a strong, smart hero. What Kellerman seems to have learned from Chesterton is not only how to use the stories and morals of religion to solve mysteries but how to do so with modesty and humility. Peter is the brawn and a brain. Yet Rina's gentle Jewish insights—often quiet asides over dinner, a mention of this or that passage from the Torah or Jewish history—help Peter solve his crimes. In *The Burnt House*, for example, a mysterious body is found in the ashes of a burned apartment house. Peter complains that no clues can be found, but Rina tells him of *habayit hasaruf* (the Burnt House), an archaeological discovery in Jerusalem that, despite its charred state, reveals much about the culture of the era in which it was built and the Roman war (in 70 CE) that destroyed it. Peter then goes back to the apartment house, digs in the ashes, and finds a ring that helps him identify the body and solve the crime.

Kellerman's books also fit into the larger scheme of American ethnic detective fiction, which often has the dual objective of solving crimes and teaching about a nonmainstream ethnic or racial group. This category is exemplified by fiction by writers like Chester Himes, with his brilliant comedy-caper series about black Harlem police detectives Grave Digger Jones and Coffin Ed Johnson; Walter Mosley, who is known for his character Easy Rawlins, a black private detective in Los Angeles[4]; Tony Hillerman, a white writer famous for his Navajo Tribal Police mysteries; and the writer most often considered Kellerman's direct predecessor, Harry Kemelman, whose Rabbi Small is an armchair detective and a voice of Judaism.

Kemelman's series ran from 1964 to 1996. Here, we do not have a lay rebbe but rather an ordained rabbi solving mysteries. In each of Kemelman's novels, readers are served up a teaspoon of Judaism with their cup of crime. William David Spencer, a theologian, calls *Friday the Rabbi Slept Late* "a potent defense of American Judaism" (35). This defense was outward-facing: Peter Freese argues that it was Kemelman's "ecumenical message of religious tolerance and peaceful coexistence between diverse ethnic and religious groups which appealed to his wide non-Jewish audience" (97). Similarly, Wendy Zierler writes that Kemelman's novels "serve the function of cultural mediation" for gentile readers ("A Dignitary" 263–264).

To distinguish the objectives of Kemelman, who began writing his series more than twenty years before Kellerman, we need to consider how Judaism was represented in the American arena at each moment. In the pre–Six Day War era, it would be hard to imagine a Jewish figure like Decker: big, tough, and religious (in fact, outside of Haredi men's action films, the "religious" element makes him an unusual figure even today). On the contrary, as critics have argued, Rabbi Small "is a popular cultural example of [Daniel] Boyarin's feminized Jewish male" (L. Roth, *Inspecting* 19).[5] Furthermore, the American Judaism that was defended in Jewish American literature in 1964 was the very American Judaism that—like the protagonist in "Eli, the Fanatic"—often made itself recognizable and acceptable to America by attacking the otherness of itself that it saw in Orthodoxy.[6] After all, even though Rabbi Small makes it his ambition to convince the women of his congregation to keep kosher (though they are serving shrimp cocktail at their luncheons) and revere scholars over athletes, it is obvious that the congregation is composed of *assimilated Jews*. And though Small fights to make them more religiously observant, the very fact of their assimilation makes them familiar figures to the common reader. Here, we find no woman insisting on tucking each last strand of hair under her kerchief or tam, no detailed description of the rites of *niddah* or what it is to be *shomer nagiyah*, no mystery solved because the suspect was wearing a *shtreimel* on a weekday. Small's voice teaches, but it is presented as something of a lone voice crying in the wilderness, with his Jewish congregation playing the part of wilderness.

Kellerman, in recounting her evolution as an author, writes that Kemelman's books failed to inspire her: "The books were informative, but they were also as much about temple politics as they were about murder. The series was far from the crime novels that I had found so compelling" (Kellerman, "Peter Decker and Rina Lazarus" 181). It is hard to imagine that a crime series that dispenses Jewish lore had no impact on Kellerman's oeuvre, but it is clear that the Judaism Kemelman presents and what Kellerman offers readers are vastly different from one another. Rina is not just a moral voice or a hopeless reminder of traditions lost; rather, she represents a distinct, unassimilated form of Judaism—from her covered hair to her refusal to shake hands with men—and she represents this form in a similarly distinct, separate, and unfamiliar community in which she is participating. That Rina is *participating* and not merely instructing is crucial to understanding Kellerman's project. Rina is a voice of Judaism, but she is not a *lone* voice; rather, she is part of a larger body that *davens* and eats kosher and works together to paint the synagogue when it is vandalized. By writing Rina into the enclosed space of the yeshiva and later the open space of an Orthodox synagogue-centered community, Kellerman offers the individual representation of unassimilated Jewishness and simultaneously reclaims what Kemelman despairs as lost: the modern, living, practicing *community*.

Diana Ben-Merre has a different reading, seeing Kemelman's as the markedly Jewish series and Kellerman's as offering the universal feeling of redemption that comes from (any) religion. For instance, Ben-Merre reads the story of Peter's evolution from secular non-Jew to Orthodox Jew as an "existential" quest, not a story of Jewish engagement. At the outset of the series, readers encounter what is obviously a taboo relationship between Rina and Peter; at this stage, Rina is an Orthodox Jew, and Peter is Baptist. But Kellerman does a Big Reveal near the end of *The Ritual Bath*: just as Henry Fielding's famous foundling, Tom Jones, can marry his wealthy neighbor because he turns out to be the nephew of the wealthy squire who (*by chance!*) raised him, so too does the big, fair-skinned, ginger-haired Peter Decker turn out to be Jewish by birth, adopted and raised by Baptists.[7] Ben-Merre sees Decker, who reclaims his Jewish birthright, as a modern-day Daniel Deronda.[8] After recounting the plot of George Eliot's philosemitic novel—Deronda, a gentleman with an unknown heritage, grows up Christian only to discover his Jewish roots—Ben-Merre notes that the "Daniel Deronda principle is particularly useful because Decker's desire to return to his origins becomes more than a strategy to deflect criticism—it becomes a way of making his quest to understand his religious origins *less a special Jewish quest than an existential one*" (Ben-Merre 62, emphasis mine).

Thus whereas Ben-Merre sees Kemelman "insisting on the differences between Jews and others," she argues that "Kellerman is interested in suggesting that the differences between Jews and others are *illusory*" (62, emphasis mine). Ben-Merre takes as her example the title of the second novel of Kellerman's series, *Sacred and Profane*. The "profane" refers to the ethic of violence and cruelty of pornographers, which is so far removed from the values of the "truly enclosed" yeshiva that the yeshiva's values, in turn, "seem private and irrelevant," according to Ben-Merre. Therefore, she claims that it is not the yeshiva of Judaism that is the "sacred" of the novel but rather "the very possibility of religious belief." Even when the novel wraps up with prayer, Ben-Merre chooses to read the prayer as suggesting the generic peace that ends the chaotic detective novel: "The feelings evoked by the passage are universal" (63).

Ben-Merre's reading of Kellerman's texts is compelling, but ultimately the idea that Kellerman's Jews can be any Americans, that the *davening* can be any prayers, does not ring true. For one, the yeshiva is not, of course, "truly enclosed." The crime is not being investigated apart from Decker's engagement with the yeshiva world but *because* he is taking two yeshiva *bochers* (Rina's sons) out camping in the woods.[9] Likewise, when Peter goes to say his "evening prayers," we are told the specifics of his physical engagement with the prayer, marking the prayer as not universal but rather patently Jewish: he turns to face "east" (as Diaspora Jews do to direct themselves toward Jerusalem) and "took out his siddur [Jewish prayer book]" to say them (Kellerman, *Sacred* 311). It is a small gesture but a deliberate one.

More significantly, in the larger context of the series, the claim of universalization falls flat. To be universal, a religious belief or ritual must be translatable if not instantly recognizable. But many of Kellerman's almost obsessively detailed accounts of rituals are neither. In *The Ritual Bath*, the first of the series, for example, we learn all about the mikvah—how an Orthodox woman goes to the ritual bath to be completely immersed each month when she completes her period of *niddah*, the time of the month she is menstruating and for seven days afterward. We learn about the role of the mikvah lady, how she inspects the women who come to the mikvah and guards the place. And in case we have still not learned enough about this rite of *taharat ha'mishpacha* (family purity) in *The Ritual Bath*, we get an extension to our lesson in *Serpent's Tooth*, when Rina explains to a board of police officers how often and when and why she and her husband have sexual intercourse.[10] First, we cover what has become for the Kellerman reader common ground. (The need for repetition is there: *The Ritual Bath* was, after all, published eleven years earlier and is nine books back in the series—and also, there is no need to read the series in order. Despite the ongoing drama of the series, each book can be approached as the first.) Rina says,

> We're Orthodox Jews. . . . The religion prohibits sexual encounters during a certain period of every month—during the woman's menses and for seven days afterward. Then she undergoes ritualistic purification by bathing in prescribed waters. When she is done, she is permitted to resume relations with her [husband]. . . . Generally, it works out to two weeks of abstinence followed by two weeks of sexual activity. (Kellerman, *Serpent's Tooth* 229)

Then we get our new piece of information, not available in *The Ritual Bath* or the books that follow. "In our specific case, it's a little shorter—more like twelve days off and eighteen days on," Rina explains, leaving the reason for variation a cause of "medical factors" (229). The police might not know that Rina has had a hysterectomy, but the avid Kellerman reader does. Is the reader curious whether a woman needs to visit the mikvah once she has undergone a hysterectomy? She need be curious no longer. After an evasive response to the police officer, Rina confides to her husband, "For a moment, I considered telling him about my hysterectomy," to which her husband roars, "Don't you dare! None of the bastard's business!" And it is not. But it is *ours*, and Rina says to her husband, for our elucidation, "Besides, then I'd have to explain why I got a period at all. And how a period is defined by Jewish law. In reality, I didn't think the sergeant was up to grasping the intricacies of remnant endometrial tissue sloughing from a subcervical hysterectomy" (234). Good thing *we* were up to it!

Despite distinguishing between Kemelman's and Kellerman's presentations of Judaism, Ben-Merre concludes that the demystification of the Jewish character through universalization is an important feature the two oeuvres share. She sees this demystification as helping create "an environment in which black-bearded Jews—or any Jews—no longer are viewed in the context of traditional stereotypes. Once Jews are seen as subjects rather than objects, they no longer appear inordinately materialistic or overly clever. . . . The contributions of these writers of the Jewish-American mystery novel have helped make the Jewish American experience universal and therefore comprehensible" (66). It seems here that Ben-Merre's universalist reading of Kellerman's "black-bearded Jews" is meant to be affirmative, a constructive revision of a long-standing negative image of Jewry in American literature. Curiously, however, Ben-Merre questions the value she has posited, essentially asking, as it is often phrased in popular Jewish culture, "Yes, but is it good for the Jews?"

Ben-Merre is unsure. She writes, "Ambiguities remain. Rabbi Small's clean-shaven suburban style and his close friendship with Hugh Lanigan may be reassuring for the wrong reasons. Kellerman's black-bearded Jews, whose religious concerns are universal, may offer similar reassurances. Both suggest that to be acceptable, the outsider has to be recast in terms that the dominant culture can understand and accept" (66). I want to reassure Ben-Merre and others who worry that Kellerman has stripped her Orthodox characters of their distinct religious observance and belief. Despite or perhaps because of (the safety of) her incredible popularity, Kellerman is defiantly *not* universal, and even when she brings into her fiction communities that seem *like* Orthodox Judaism—at least to the outside, secular world—she attempts to destroy any sense of resemblance the communities might share (as in *Jupiter's Bones*, the story of a corrupt and dangerous cult, à la Jonestown).

Thus although Kemelman might seem the obvious comparison to Kellerman, being a Jew writing Jewish detective fiction, Tony Hillerman's motives seem to mirror Kellerman's more closely. His novels, featuring two Navajo policemen, teach readers (who are tremendous in number) about the customs and values of the tribe. On his death in 2008, the *New York Times* described Hillerman's near-universal acceptance: "In the world of mystery fiction, Mr. Hillerman was a rare figure: a best-selling author who was adored by fans, admired by fellow authors and respected by critics. Though the themes of his books were not overtly political, he wrote with an avowed purpose: to instill in his readers a respect for Native American culture" (Stasio B17). Reading the general description of his work, one can easily substitute Kellerman's name for Hillerman's: "His stories, while steeped in contemporary crime, often describe people struggling to maintain ancient traditions in the modern world. The books are instructive about ancient tribal beliefs and customs, from purification to incest taboos" (Stasio B17). Hillerman's reason for such instruction is quoted: "It's always troubled me that the American people are so ignorant of these rich Indian cultures" (qtd. in Stasio B17). He then goes on to talk about the continued relevance of "ancient Indian ways" in the modern world.

That Hillerman writes from outside of the culture and Kellerman writes from within makes little difference. In fact, through her use of Peter as Rina's student (later Peter's daughter Cindy takes on this role, and later still, it's Peter and Rina's foster son, Gabe), we often feel that we are getting a similar external position. Writes Freese in *The Ethnic Detective*, "Hillerman's mysteries . . . make their readers realize, not through theoretical reflection but through exciting stories, that one needs openness, tolerance, and empathy in order to overcome one's culturally transmitted ethnocentrism" (8). Freese goes on to argue that the formulaic nature of mystery novels, when paired with what he refers to as a "foreign-language text" (but seems to be, more accurately, a foreign-culture text), creates "vehicles of first-hand information about ethnic interaction in the 'multicultural' society of the United States" because of the audience's strong desire to *know* "whodunit" (9). As I will demonstrate, the same applies to the Decker/Lazarus series.

### III. The Decker/Lazarus Series

*To make the murder mystery genre my own, I needed to give my book a voice. I needed a narration that told the reader that this was a different kind of suspense novel from a new author named Faye Kellerman. I felt that I could put my imprimatur on my story only if I wrote from a point of expertise, i.e., if I wrote what I knew. . . . I considered the fact that I was female. That was more relevant than you might think, because in the early '80s, women PIs were coming into their own. I thought about writing from the perspective of a woman PI—I certainly admired Sue Grafton and Sara Paretsky—but I had been married for a very long time. As a wife and mother, I didn't see myself as chasing down bad guys and wielding a gun, so the idea of writing a character like that really didn't strike a chord. . . . [Also] I was a Jew. My Judaism has always been important to me, and I have always loved the rites and traditions of my religion. . . . Judaism was such an integral part of my being that I had no real sense of self without it. . . . As I thought about my Judaism and how much it had made me who I was . . . [and if] I wanted to write about what I knew, it was a good start for my books to have Jewish content, and what better way than to have my protagonist be an Orthodox Jewish woman? . . . Since I enjoyed reading novels that took me into other worlds, I figured that there had to be readers out there who would enjoy learning about religious Jews.*
—Faye Kellerman, "Peter Decker and Rina Lazarus" (2009)

Kellerman's Decker/Lazarus novels are booming bestsellers. According to Kellerman's website, twenty million copies of the novels are in print. The books fit squarely into the genre of popular detective fiction: they are formulaic, serial, conservative, and mass market, and their hypermasculine crime-solving hero and plethora of female victims seem to reinforce the male hegemony.[11]

As popular rather than literary fiction, Kellerman's series has not been subject to a great deal of literary criticism.[12] But of note is the engagement with her texts by Ellen Serlen Uffen, who championed women's "lowbrow" writing, publishing an article in defense of the study of genre fiction in 1978 (years before Janice Radway wrote her landmark *Reading the Romance*, the reader-response theory that elevated romances to the stuff of academe). Uffen treated Kellerman's series as an important contribution to Jewish writing.[13] In her reading of the series, Uffen demonstrates the ways that the form of the mystery novel and the form of Orthodoxy mirror each other—suggesting that Kellerman's choice of genre for the dissemination of information about Orthodoxy is ideal. Using religious language to frame the detective novel as a novel of *order*—the novel establishes a contract with the reader, has its good guys and its bad, follows conventions "religiously," and inspires the hope (in the happy ending) that "we, too, will be saved"—Uffen argues that "the detective novel . . . despite some appearances to the contrary, is the most orthodox literary form" (195, 196). Because of this formal rigidity, Uffen contends, the reader can have faith that regardless of the drama at hand, order will necessarily be restored by the book's author "both to the social world and to the individual soul" (196). Uffen writes that Kellerman "takes the orthodoxy of the detective form more than usually to heart and makes it one with the stories," as it is not only the "literary order" that needs restoring but also "the world and soul of Detective Sergeant Peter Decker of the Los Angeles Police Department . . . which need to be saved, to be retrieved from chaos and restored to order" (196). And what will save him is Orthodox Judaism—via Rina.

Although Uffen, writing in 1992, was examining the series in its early stages—only four books had been published at that point—her commentary remains remarkably accurate. Considering the path that Kellerman has taken since 1992, as well as the changing climate in which she has been writing, I want to extend Uffen's argument by demonstrating how significant Kellerman's didactic novels have been in revising Orthodox Judaism's popular image.

In Kellerman's novels, a reader is immersed in Judaism through the titles (many are biblical), the crimes to be solved, and the ongoing subplot of Jewish instruction that is transmitted from maven (Rina) to novice (Peter). The ongoing subplot, in fact, is the key feature that sets the series apart from the rest of the mystery subgenre of detective fiction featuring a police officer that the Decker/Lazarus series otherwise occupies. To integrate the unusual subplot into the series, Kellerman relies on another convention of genre fiction: romance.[14] Kellerman distinguishes her hero, Detective (later Lieutenant) Peter Decker, from literary tradition by adding his pursuit of a woman, Rina Lazarus, to his pursuit of violent criminals. He must solve his cases by overcoming a series of obstacles, reflecting the difficulties of his personal life too. And by pursuing Rina, he is pursuing a "return"—a return to Orthodox Judaism, the course of which readers follow all the way from his complete ignorance of the inhabitants of the first novel's "Jewtown," as he calls it, to a complete immersion in the life (Kellerman, *Bath* 10).

From the outset, the roles of the heroes in this genre fiction challenge convention. Certainly, it appears to have the conventional male hero: Peter Decker is the insightful, loveable detective who solves the crimes and appears as the prime hero of Kellerman's early Decker/Lazarus series. He is the one who (with his sidekick, Marge, and several other marginal cops) can get inside the mind of the bad guy, can stake him out, and can capture him. But the female heroine hardly seems heroic. Rina is not a detective but a helpmeet, the one who bakes the challah and the knishes, soothes Peter's body and ego, the traditional wife waiting for her hardworking man to return at the end of the day. If Peter is characterized by his intelligence and his toughness, Rina is primarily characterized by her beauty—and to drive this point home, Kellerman has Peter carry a picture of Rina in his wallet to shut up anyone who dares question his loyalty to his wife. Her beauty is *that* compelling.[15]

Yet despite Peter's seemingly unquestioned superiority, his de facto position as the detective hero of the series, the books begin with Rina—a heroine, Kellerman suggests, of another kind. As Laurence Roth sagely observes, her last name, Lazarus, "signifies the contemporary perception that Jewish tradition is being resurrected and embodied by American Jewish women" ("Unraveling" 187).[16] She is guardian of a yeshiva's mikvah, which the first novel of the series tells us is a "mainstay of Jewish life—as much a part of Orthodoxy as dietary laws, circumcision, or the Sabbath," although it is likely to be less known to readers than the other mainstays cited (211). Rina is thus presented to us as a maintainer and defender of the community's rituals. At the opening of this first book, Rina is at the mikvah, attending to an older woman and learning how make her famous potato kugel after teaching the Jewish laws of purity to a younger woman, a seventeen-year-old bride. Her role in the community, therefore, if not the genre, is rendered visible: student, teacher, and an integral part of the yeshiva's community, despite the fact that a yeshiva is traditionally a man's world—the place where a man studies among other men.

In this novel and the ones to follow, Rina, then, even more than Rav Schulman, the yeshiva's official spiritual leader (a classic old, bearded, old-world rabbi), is established as the mouth of Orthodoxy as well as its heart. Roth writes, "Despite the fact that Decker is the detective and solves all the crimes in Kellerman's stories, Rina Lazarus is the spiritual hero of the series—and thus its real hero—because it is she who saves Decker from biological merger by explaining and adamantly defending the mystifying fences that Orthodox Judaism erects around Jewish women and between Jews and gentiles" (187). This role becomes central to a mystery series that also reads as a primer for Orthodox Judaism. Yet being the mouth and heart of Orthodoxy gives Rina a murkily defined place in the mystery novel genre itself—a genre with a clearly defined set of conventions. In fact, an early practitioner and critic of detective fiction, S. S. Dine, published a famous set of conventions in 1928 called "Twenty Rules for Writing Detective Stories," most of which are broken by Kellerman. Of particular note is rule number sixteen, which declares that there should be no "side-issues" or "preoccupations." Dine writes, "A detective novel should contain no long descriptive passages, no literary dallying with side-issues, no subtly worked-out character analyses, no 'atmospheric' preoccupations. Such matters have no vital place in a record of crime and deduction. They hold up the action and introduce issues irrelevant to the main purpose, which is to state a problem, analyze it, and bring it to a successful conclusion" (Dine). Orthodoxy in the novels is not only a "side-issue" but also, often, a "front" issue.

Whereas Peter conforms to his generic role by being both a stereotypical (coffee-guzzling, donut-eating) and all-too-smart cop who can put together the pieces of each puzzle (because in the genre, unlike in life, the puzzle pieces *always* fit together), Rina seems to play to a number of generic roles. Were she merely a recurring character rather than a main one, we could say she occupies different generic roles at different points in the series: traditional love interest, Watson, victim. None of these terms stick, however, even when she seems to conform to them. To wit:

1. Traditional love interest: Rina is easily characterized as the detective's young, dramatically beautiful love interest (Dine, for the record, pronounced, "There must be no love interest. The business in hand is to bring a criminal to the bar of justice, not to bring a lovelorn couple to the hymeneal altar," but this rule has been very widely ignored since his declaration). Sometimes this is her main role. Even more on point to the genre, she is called a *femme fatale*, a term Peter uses even after he marries her (Kellerman, *Serpent's Tooth* 158). Kellerman tells us, "He would have done anything to *get* her. Anything at all. And had another man entered the picture, he would have done anything to *keep* her. Lie, cheat, steal . . . Maybe even murder" (158). But Rina is no Brigid O'Shaughnessy. What Peter actually has to do in order to get and keep Rina is become and stay religious . . . which hardly sounds like the motives of a femme fatale.[17] It also seems as though "traditional object of romance" is a flimsy title for a female character who is not abandoned by the author when conquered by the male hero. Even Dorothy L. Sayers has willful, feminist Harriet Vane, a reader's delight in several of the Lord Peter Wimsey detective stories (1923–1942), only reappear in one novel after Lord Peter wins her over; arguably, Lord Peter's marrying of Harriet Vane (in *Busman's Honeymoon* [1937]) took the life out of the series (making her fatal in another way).

In contrast, Rina is more a stereotype of a Jewish wife than femme fatale, for, despite her ravishing beauty, she has an exaggerated attention to the kitchen and mothers Peter's colleagues as well as her children. It is key to note that all of Rina's traditional womanly characteristics are complicated by her chosen relationship to her Jewishness, whether it is the way her beauty is revealed (and covered—with a hair covering and modest clothing) or the fraught issue of maternal obligation in an Orthodox lifestyle.

2. Watson: Not infrequently, Rina's role is to assist in solving the crime—the steadying and sober Watson to the manic Sherlock Holmes. There are moments when Rina is less spiritual guide and more detective, and her role and Peter's blur. In the fourth novel, *Day of Atonement*, for example, Rina joins Peter to canvass the Hasidic residents of Crown Heights, using her facility with Yiddish and insider knowledge to gain access to the yeshiva *bochers*, who might offer a clue as to the whereabouts of a missing Haredi child of Boro Park. Later in the novel, she saves Peter's life by, significantly, pulling off the kerchief that modestly and conveniently covers her hair and using it as a tourniquet on Peter's shot arm (*Atonement* 428–429). She again uses her knowledge—of Hebrew and Israel—in *Sanctuary*, the seventh book, helping Peter solve a crime centered in the Tel Aviv diamond bursa. Her deep familiarity with the history of the Holocaust comes into play in *The Forgotten*, which deals with a hate crime by a neo-Nazi group. She has useful information about Russian art in *Murder 101* due to the Chabad lawsuit against Moscow (where forty thousand works of the Schneerson collection are being held).[18] But unlike Peter's daughter, Cindy, who evolves into a cop like her dad over the first ten books, Rina chooses to be a detective as a hobby only; her talent never parlays into paid employment.

3. Victim: If the "death of beautiful woman," as Poe contended more than 150 years ago, "is unquestionably the most poetical topic in the world," ravishingly beautiful Rina makes for a great victim—though, of course, she cannot actually be a dead one (163). This is her starting role: though she is not the one raped at the mikvah in the first novel, she is the intended target, an almost victim. And there are other moments when she is an intended target. Whenever she interferes in Peter's work or leaves the safety of his shadow, readers must worry for her. But Rina's almost-victimhood remains essentially that throughout the series: *almost*. Unlike Ayelet Waldman's beautiful Hasidic babysitter in *The Big Nap* and the unhappy Hasidic mom in Julia Dahl's *Invisible City*, Rina is never found lifeless, stuffed in a freezer or at the bottom of a quarry. And though she does suffer at the hands of criminal men, she is never raped, robbed, or murdered—making her a pretty poor victim of crime fiction.

The last of these three roles that Rina occupies (poorly) allows Kellerman to respond to the characterization of Orthodox women in popular culture as well as to Poe's beautiful dead woman and the legacy of female victims in the mystery genre.

## IV. Not a Victim

*Cleaning was a way of not only negating what had taken place, but of doing something.* Action *as opposed to sitting around and being victimized.*
—Faye Kellerman, *The Forgotten* (2001)

Meet Rochelle Krich's Molly Blume: ever conscious of the length of her skirt, skeptical about the covering of her hair after marriage, worried about what it means to be the "rabbi's wife." She is always considering options and making choices about her religious observance (when she's not researching a crime or under attack from a criminal). Molly is, like her author, a writer of crime stories. She is also an amateur sleuth. In each of Krich's novels, where the police fail, Molly succeeds. Molly appears to be the ultimate *anti*victim—and not only because *she* (and not her man) is the one who successfully solves crimes (while leading a halachic life) in her eponymous series.

But Kellerman too is conscious of making Rina a creature of choice. Introducing Rina to her readers in the first Decker/Lazarus novel, Kellerman not only indicates the Orthodoxy of Rina and her community but also immediately clarifies for her readers that Rina's religious lifestyle is one that she chooses for herself. Rina's story is distinguished from the stories of women who feel victimized by the Orthodox life—the stories that make for the sensationalist marketing of "off-the-*derech*" memoirs and popular films, as discussed in the first chapter. Kellerman specifies that Rina makes this choice with the recognition that it is outside the comfort zone of her modern family (and by extension, Kellerman's readership): "Of all the religious obligations that Rina had decided to take on, the covering of her hair was the one that displeased her mother the most" (*Ritual Bath* 2). She also sets Rina against the grain by having Rina recognize the incongruity of the values of Orthodoxy and mainstream American life but still prefer to see the good in the former, even if others do not. At the outset of *The Ritual Bath*, the age of the bride Rina is helping is conspicuously mentioned, for example, and Rina muses, "Rivki was barely seventeen with little knowledge of the world around her. Sheltered and exquisitely shy, she'd gotten engaged to Baruch after three dates" (1). "But" we are told—and this "but" allows us the perspective less common to readers—"Rina thought it was a good match" (1). The narrative follows the various reasons this is true, teaching us far more about Rina and her faith in the Orthodoxy's values than about the bride and prospective groom, who never resurface in the novel.

If Rina is not victimized by being born into an oppressive community, she is also not victimized in the classic ways that crime fiction victimizes women. As noted, in this first novel, Rina is pursued by a madman, and in many ways, we might believe we are reading the typical New Jewish Gothic Haredi-woman-as-victim plot. But though the man is intent on raping her, he fails. In another novel, in which a number of people have been kidnapped or killed by a carjacker, Rina finds herself pushed against her car, with a gun in her back, but she acts quickly and saves herself; the perpetrator is killed. Repeatedly, Kellerman diverges from the stock plot—from a strategic point of view, the Decker/Lazarus series requires both Decker and Lazarus: Kellerman needs her heroine to survive.

Still, Kellerman risks echoing and even magnifying the image of oppressed Orthodox womanhood through Rina's various compromised positions. As Kellerman works so hard to present the Orthodox woman's role as powerful, it seems against her best interest to put Rina in these scenarios. Unsurprisingly, we find that the victimization of the Orthodox heroine is masterfully contained and refocused in the novels. It is not that Rina is *not* victimized. In the end, it is that Rina is not victimized by her Orthodox lifestyle or (people's) crimes against women. She is a victim of life's crimes: she is widowed at a young age after caring for her husband through a painful illness, she falls in love with a man she cannot marry (he's a priest), and she has a complicated birth leading to a hysterectomy at thirty, despite her desire for many children. None of these tragedies are part of the genre; they are simply part of women's lives.

Furthermore, Rina is repeatedly able to defy her victimhood or almost-victimhood—without, as Rubel observes of the victim-heroines of "the new Jewish gothic," ultimately "finding safety and fulfillment outside of the haredi community" (83). If Kellerman's Haredi communities seem to be the walled off, isolated spaces that call to mind the Gothic era's Italian caves and Spanish monasteries where monks and priests commit rape and murder without being observed, they do not bear out this image. Ben-Merre, in fact, sees the focus on crime in the "enclosed orthodox Jewish community that is organized around a yeshivah" to be a measurement of "how un-self-conscious the Jewish mystery has become" (62–63). She also suggests that Kellerman's yeshiva is the obverse of the hell typically found in "Jewish gothic" fiction when she refers to the yeshiva as an "Edenic community [made up of] a society of black-bearded Jews" (62). Admittedly, this description strikes me as odd; after all, readers encounter the yeshiva through the story of a rape (and also, it's hard to imagine that all the men have black beards with nary a *gingy* in the crowd). Nonetheless, it is significant that Rina does not flee the yeshiva because she is pursued by a rapist; she chooses to leave only *after* the rapist is caught by the police, suggesting that rather than fleeing an unsafe space, she is leaving a space imperfectly suited to her. Similarly, she leaves the Borough Park community where her brother-in-law is harassing her in the third book, though again, her departure occurs only *after* he is caught by the police in a massage-parlor raid, suggesting the cause for departure is not fear. More importantly, her choices to leave these specific Orthodox communities never indicate her departure from Orthodoxy itself.

Krich brings the subversion of the Orthodox woman-as-victim to the fore in *Grave Endings*, the third novel in her Molly Blume series. In the first two books of the series, the victims are not Orthodox women, allowing us to see Orthodox womanhood only through the guise of Molly, a strong, determined, intelligent woman who solves the crimes of Los Angeles despite personal risk (and who, at the same time, is revealed as feminine, romantic, and falling in love with her handsome beau—a Modern Orthodox rabbi, no less). By the third novel, however, Krich asks us to examine the literary and cultural history of Orthodox women as victims by giving us the backstory that has been obliquely circulating in the shadows of the first two novels: the murder of Molly's best friend, a fellow Orthodox Jewish girl. The crime at first appears to be a salacious one, the kind readers "want": "a sheltered, beautiful young woman falls in love with a handsome drug addict who kills her because her Orthodox Jewish parents forbid her to see him" (Krich, *Endings* 216). It's a "good story," the father of the murdered girl admits. It has the elements of a gothic novel: the mysterious setting of a foreign, religious community; oppressive parents; a young, beautiful heroine; star-crossed love; and murder. The Romeo-and-Juliet-style love between an Orthodox Jewish girl (or married woman) and a non-Jewish man has particular resonance. In Quebec, where the friction between Hasidim and non-Jews is ongoing (see chapter 3), Myriam Beaudoin uses the theme in a subplot of her novel *Hadassa* (2007), and Maxime Giroux brings it center stage for his film *Félix et Meira* (2014). But as the father points out, and as we come to see by the end of Krich's book, "it's not exactly the truth" (216).

## V. Feminism and the Orthodox Jewish Woman's Detective Novel

[Peter:] "The law is so archaic as well as sexist. It's unfair enough to raise even your underdeveloped feminist hackles."

[Rina:] "Peter, where is it written that you can't be traditional and a feminist at the same time? One doesn't preclude the other."

—Kellerman, *Sanctuary* (1994)

[Cindy (Peter's daughter):] "I don't think Gloria Steinem would approve of your methods."

[Rina:] "Oh, forget about Gloria Steinem! She never nursed a husband through cancer, only to watch him die! She never labored in childbirth. She was never a widow with two small children. She's never been married to a police lieutenant. She's never had a hysterectomy at thirty. And she's *not* an Orthodox Jew. So she has no concept of *shalom bais*—peace in the house. Which, in my humble opinion, is to her detriment!"

—Kellerman, *Serpent's Tooth* (1997)

Rina: housewife, mom, and husband's helper. Perfectly clever, but willing to let the big man take on the big action. She is no V. I. Warshawski or even Nancy Drew. Most scholarship on feminist detective fiction elides Kellerman's work altogether.[19] But is Rina a character that affords a marriage between Orthodox Judaism and feminism, or is she, as Laurence Roth argues, a "missed opportunity"? Roth writes that because of Rina's evident strength, "it is all the more disconcerting that Rina spends the majority of her stage time . . . cooking, crying, tending to her children and teaching Judaism to Decker" ("Unraveling" 198). Roth recognizes both Rina's iron core, one Kellerman demonstrates time and again, and her importance to the series, but he argues that she is too often offstage. She has power and resilience, yet she is too often in fear or tears. While she offers us the sense that women's Judaism can empower, it is only used to empower men. "Kellerman," he writes, "is not interested in Rina's overturning middle-class American Jewish gender divisions or reclaiming the mystical power of Jewish female spirituality in a way that truly transforms her character" (202). Roth here suggests that the only way Judaism can be feminist is if it "overturn[s] . . . gender divisions." But this understanding, I argue, fails to see what's actually at stake in Kellerman's Decker/Lazarus series: Kellerman is emphatic about *using*, not *overturning*, gender divisions to create a clear role for women in Orthodox Judaism, which is too often seen in terms of men's agency.

Roth's reading of Rina—"cooking, crying, tending to her children and teaching Judaism to Decker"—is not inaccurate so much as selective. She *does* cook, cry, tend to her children, and teach Judaism to her husband and a number of other characters who appear in the series, but she also runs the mikvah, is employed as a schoolteacher, does the yeshiva's bookkeeping, and is the unofficial caretaker at her synagogue (Kellerman, *The Forgotten* 1). If Roth sees Rina's highlighted feminine behaviors as an indication of Kellerman's construction of Rina as "a standard bearer of middle-class 'norms,'" I see them as a resistance to a masculine portrayal of heroism (198). Rina might not solve a lot of the series' crimes (though when she does offer suggestions, Peter is always wise to listen to them), but she takes charge in ways that speak to readers' daily lives. Just as her "victimhood" is of life's crimes, her responses are ones we can imagine. Rarely do we see her on a stakeout, rarely are bullets whizzing past her head, and she never seems to stumble upon rotting corpses like her husband (at least not until the twenty-fourth book!). But her synagogue is vandalized in a hate crime we can all imagine (particularly in the Brexit/Trump era), and she takes on her victimhood and the victimhood of the community targeted with resolve, scrubbing the swastikas from the synagogue's walls. Yes, she is taking on traditional women's work. But to what end? We learn, "Cleaning was a way of not only negating what had taken place, but of doing something. *Action* as opposed to sitting around and being victimized" (Kellerman, *Forgotten* 54).

It is *through* this picture of traditional Jewish womanhood—not against it—that Kellerman makes Rina, in Roth's own words, "the real hero" of the series ("Unraveling" 187). In fact, just as Peter has to be schooled on Judaism throughout the series (thus offering a forum of education for the reader), he also has to be schooled on feminism, particularly in terms of respecting women and the work they do. In *Sanctuary*, Rina tells him that "it's not feminists who look askance at us stay-at-home moms. It's everyone else. Especially the *men*" (Kellerman, *Sanctuary* 308). She then provides a detailed list of the things a stay-at-home mother does.

Kellerman and her literary descendants can be located among women mystery writers engaged in revising the images of women-as-victims in the genre at large by using "an established popular formula in order to investigate not just a particular crime but the more general offenses in which the patriarchal power structure of contemporary society itself is potentially incriminated," as Priscilla L. Walton and Manina Jones argue in *Detective Agency: Women Rewriting the Hard-Boiled Tradition* (4). Yet their feminist agenda is not always obvious to a reader. Citing a review of *Prayers for the Dead* in which a *Los Angeles Times* critic refers to Rina's explanation of *shalom bais*, Roth is struck by the fact that Rina's explanation, quoted by the critic, comes as Rina is wiping a dish clean: "Wiping the dish, Rina thought about the Jewish concept of shalom bais, the keeping of marital peace" (qtd. in Kaufman 8). To Roth, this is Kellerman's fundamental problem: she has Rina doing traditional women's work while her husband is investigating a murder. Roth takes this critic's remark as a clear indication that Kellerman's readers are equally uninvested in overturning gender roles or having gender roles overturned for them. But to be fair, Kellerman also offers an almost identical description of Peter, who, after cooking veal chops and preparing a salad for his family, "wiped the last dish, his face a study in concentration. He was thinking about the case" (*Forgotten* 183). For Kellerman, for men and women, cooking and cleaning are not merely traditional women's work, they are the work of *everyone*, the work of *every day*, and using them as quiet moments of contemplation seem like a great lesson for any reader. (I, for one, am happy to take the lesson to heart!)

A similar criticism comes from Roth in terms of Rina as a mikvah lady—a woman who helps other women in the community prepare themselves and go through the ritual of immersing themselves in the spiritual bath. While Roth is correct to point out that Rina's explanation singles out women's obligation and "avoids mentioning when and how men make use of the mikvah," it is not as though the two (women's use and men's) are equitable. If women are obligated to attend the mikvah based on their menstrual cycle (thus, typically every month), men might choose to immerse themselves at various times: following ejaculation, before holidays (most commonly Yom Kippur) or one's wedding, or in anticipation of the Shabbat—but these visits to the mikvah are a custom, not an obligation.[20] Apart from the looseness of men's custom (few men, even Hasidic men, hold themselves to the standard of going to the mikvah after each ejaculation), the men's mikvah would typically be a separate entity, and Rina would have nothing to do with it and perhaps even little knowledge of it. But more significantly, Kellerman is constructing a woman's role that is hers alone, an important role, and one that allows her to help other women in a women-only space. Is this characterization really unfeminist?

I would contend that it is not so much that Kellerman "misses the opportunity" as Roth misses Kellerman's point: Kellerman's primary goal is to teach readers about Orthodoxy (the *Los Angeles Times* reviewer declares she learned more about Judaism reading *Prayers for the Dead* than in twelve years of Sunday school!) and about the feminism that is built into it. If it is "disconcerting" to Roth that Rina spends her time engaging in activities relegated to the traditional feminine sphere, it is likely because he does not accept Kellerman's elevation of these activities to be on par with Peter's work. Kellerman imbues these activities with strength and dignity, with a significance that overshadows Peter's ability to solve unfathomable crimes (198). Roth recognizes Kellerman's motives—hence calling Rina "the real hero" of the series—but he cannot reconcile the image of a powerful hero with the image of a wiper of dishes and baker of excellent salsa chicken (recipe provided in the back of *False Prophet* by author).[21]

If Kellerman is overturning anything, it is the *perception* of gender roles. Rina does all the things traditionally allotted to women in Anglo-American culture, but this is the wrong category in which to locate her. Instead, we need to view Rina through the lens of the woman of valor, who runs her household and is an active participant in commerce and community:

- *She rises while it is still nighttime, and gives food to her household.* Her lieutenant-husband holds terrible hours. ✔
- *She considers a field and buys it; from the fruit of her handiwork she plants a vineyard.* It's an English garden, actually, and it's so impressive, it's photographed and featured in magazines. ✔
- *She senses that her enterprise is good, so her lamp is not extinguished at night.* Her enterprise is her knowledge, and she is peddling it at school by day and home by night. ✔
- *She spreads out her palm to the poor and extends her hands to the destitute.* It's not incidental that her last name is Lazarus, as in Emma Lazarus, who wrote the iconic verses on the Statue of Liberty. ✔

- *She opens her mouth with Wisdom, and the teaching of kindness is on her tongue.* She is a *bit* of a know-it-all sometimes, but mostly she's sweet as sugar! ✔

The problem of the model of the woman of valor is that the feminine characteristics are regarded as antifeminist characteristics, and Roth, certainly, will not be the only one to read them this way. The evocation of Steinem in *Serpent's Tooth* demonstrates Kellerman's recognition of this reading. In turn, Kellerman attempts to provide a model of feminism based in Jewish tradition.

As always, Peter plays the role of student for Kellerman's lessons. In *Sacred and Profane*, Rina is presented to us as an *eshes chayil* through Peter's free indirect discourse. Peter thinks, "She never ceased to surprise him—so utterly feminine yet so competent. He saw firsthand how she handled crises, and her strength and willpower were scary. Maybe it was the religion; the women in the Bible were not known for their passivity—Judith lopping off the head of Holofernes, Yael driving a tent peg through Sisera's temples" (Kellerman, *Sacred* 112–113). Here, we see Rina placed in a long history of strong Jewish women, of *neshot chayil*. Yet we might note that the very ambivalence that Peter has toward Orthodox women is one that we might expect a reader to hold. For Peter, as for critics, "feminine" and "competent" run counter to each other (Peter's partner, Marge Dunn, is described over and over as wearing cheap, ill-fitting clothes, having mousy brown hair, and of needing to go to the gym—all of which seems to reinforce Peter's idea that she makes an excellent partner). The language "feminine *yet* competent" suggests an oxymoron. But the "yet" is Peter's "yet"—not Kellerman's. Kellerman is insistent that the "yet" is illusory.

Distinguishing Rina from other women in the series (like Marge), Kellerman is clearly at pains to make Rina dramatically feminine. Rina's femininity is elaborated on in each book, making us see it as a key feature of the character. And at no point does Kellerman trade in femininity for competence, or suggest that it ought to be downplayed for a feminist cast to her novels. Still, femininity serves an interesting role beyond "Hollywoodizing" the Haredi housewife. Kellerman repeatedly highlights Rina's beauty and constructs her devotion and willingness to do things for her husband as so dogged as to seem subservient; Rina is all long, swinging, sexy hair and *let me pack a lunch for you, honey*. But again, I would stress that these characteristics do not come to us straight from the bodice-ripper menu or from Stepford, Connecticut. Rina's hair is her best feature, but it is also the feature that marks her religiously. Crucially, we only see it if she is alone or alone with her husband. If in each and every book a crime is committed, a main character is faced with a life-threatening danger, an innocent person seems guilty, and the mystery is solved, in each and every book, we read about Rina's hair coverings. And as for her busyness in the kitchen, which we might take as Rina playing the traditional Western woman's role there (minus the barefoot and pregnant bit, ironically in a book about an Orthodox woman), we come to see that her packed lunches and cookies dropped off at the department are the manner in which Rina is controlling the food consumption of her new beau/husband, aligning it with her belief in keeping kosher—or rather, allowing Kellerman to teach us, through Rina's cooking and controlling, about keeping kosher. (Along with solving a mystery and mentioning head coverings, generally every book discusses what foods can be eaten, what foods can be eaten *outside the house*, where we can find kosher restaurants in Los Angeles, why Orthodox Jews have to use a hot water urn for tea instead of a kettle on Shabbat, and how long they have to wait between meat and dairy.)

Ultimately, this femininity, this *qualified* femininity or *religious* femininity, goes hand in hand with Rina's power and independence, because the model of the *eshes chayil* suggests no contradiction there and Kellerman refuses to admit any. Almost victimized in the first book, Rina chooses, initially, not the shelter of a husband—in fact, she holds off for several books before agreeing to marry the Rambowitz-figure who desires her—but a system of self-defense. Peter, whose vision of femininity excludes gun-handling, tries to dissuade her from the purchase and use of such a "manly" weapon. Even when she already has the gun in hand, he tries to control its office: he proposes to clean the gun and break it in for her. But Rina responds with a "teach a woman to fish" suggestion, saying, "I've got a better idea. Why don't you offer to show *me* how to clean, oil, and break in the gun?" (Kellerman, *Sacred* 78). Readers later learn that Rina, who once lived in Israel, was hardly ignorant of weaponry when she bought her gun.

Peter remains the readers' companion in (lessening) ignorance and (healthy) skepticism through much of the series, even as he learns about Judaism and begins to sing the hymn "Eshes Chayil" every Friday night as religious Jews do, coming to recognize his Orthodox wife's competence and agency. Peter, like many readers, cannot fully shake the image of Orthodox women as passive possessions of their men. He tells Rina, "I think some of the [Jewish] laws are nonsense." He elaborates on his point in their conversation, referring to her marriage to her first husband:

[RINA:] "Such as?"
[PETER:] "The separation of the sexes. Women are considered chattels—"
[RINA:] "That's not true."
[PETER:] "Honey, your *ketubah* is nothing more than a sales receipt. Your husband bought you." (Kellerman, *Sacred* 227)

This is not an uncommon reading of Orthodox marriage, and here, we might find that Peter is offending Rina but perhaps not our own sensibilities.

There is a shift in our attachment to Peter, though, when his skepticism becomes oppressive. In terms of believing in the theoretical idea of the husband buying the wife in Orthodoxy, we can sympathize with Peter. After he marries

Rina, though, *Peter* is the husband who has bought his wife, and he actually says to her, "You're my *wife!* According to Jewish law, I *bought* you" (Kellerman, *Atonement* 196). This declaration, in the switch from third person to first, from theoretical to practical, changes the texture of the claim. Suddenly it is not Orthodox marriage laws that are at fault for oppressing a wife but Peter, who is being misogynistic. It is not the practice but the practitioner who is the problem, and Peter, being a novice, is relying not on Jewish learning and law but his own misperceptions of Orthodoxy. And so we move away from Peter. We never see Rina as chattel. And *we* immediately side with her here. In fact, as Peter is not the narratorial voice of the books (though we often read the stories through his lens), we get to hear Rina's thoughts on Peter's attitude and share in her reactions. "So condescending," she thinks in this conversation (Kellerman, *Atonement* 197). And again later, "he could be very parental. Lecturing her all the time" (392). The same kind of exchange appears in *Murder 101* when Peter complains about having to "babysit" Rina, and she returns, "I'm an excellent shot. And FYI, I don't need your babysitting" (294). Peter has many redeeming qualities, but his thoughts often indicate the need to control his woman, as in *Milk and Honey*: "He couldn't control his own woman; how could he presume to control felons?" and later "How could she have been so stupid as to disobey him? Disobey him. As if she were a child. Sometimes it felt that way" (216, 276). When he takes his impulse too far but tries to blame it on the Orthodox system rather than recognizing the flaw in himself, we cannot help but bristle and, in so doing, realize that perhaps Orthodoxy itself is not the underlying problem. "*She* was fine, but *Peter* was having a hard time adjusting to her independence," we read, following Rina's thoughts (*Atonement* 392). It is not that the Orthodox woman lacks independence; it is that we are primed to read her that way, as Peter does.

Kellerman's feminist agenda in creating an "empowered female subject . . . not just [as] a formal but . . . also political gesture" is complicated by and hinges on her commitment to Orthodox Judaism (Walton and Jones 4). Laurence Roth is hardly the first feminist critic of Orthodox Judaism's treatment of women; he comes from a long line—an entire branch of criticism, in fact. And it is this criticism that animates what Rubel calls the "new Jewish gothic." *Kal vachomer*, as the Talmudist (and Talmudist detective) would say, suggesting an a fortiori logic, Orthodox women mystery writers have an even bigger job than other women mystery writers in revising their versions of the disempowered female subject. The widespread image of the oppressed and silenced Orthodox woman, who is taught that "women have no real place in a conversation," as Feldman writes in *Unorthodox*, is replaced in the novels of Kellerman and her literary descendants by the woman who speaks, who does, who teaches—even as she wipes a dish (200). Rather than presenting Orthodox women cloaked in mystery, the writers of *these* novels are using the mystery genre to demystify and empower Orthodox women as they live—*not*, for the most part, as they would live were they super-sleuths packing heat.

And to return to the *Los Angeles Times* critic who learned more from Keller-man's novels than twelve years of Sunday school, among the gender-traditional yet gender-empowering offerings made by the women of these novels, education is first and foremost. Roth writes that "Kellerman's audience . . . is not about to embark on a wholesale transformation of their lifestyle" (L. Roth, "Unraveling" 207). But they might, I would suggest, embark on a wholesale transformation of their knowledge and understanding of Orthodox women—and Judaism at large. The writers of Orthodox women's mysteries use their fiction to teach, making their heroines able to save not only the bodies of would-be victims but also the souls of their companions *and readers*. Although Kellerman's novels are as familiar to mystery readers as those of Sue Grafton, Janet Evanovich, or Patricia Cornwell, they must be distinguished by their overpowering need to teach the lessons of Orthodox Judaism, which supersedes even the need to solve the crimes of their novels.

## VI. Primers of Orthodoxy

*Orthodox Judaism was a religion of routine, and at the dinner table, the first order of business was always welcoming the metaphorical Sabbath Bride in a song called "Shalom Aleichem." This ode was followed by a tribute to the real woman of the house—a poem from Proverbs called "Eshet Chayil," or "Woman of Valor." I've read the English a couple of times, and the gist of it centered around a woman slaving away without complaint to support her husband and family, words that seemed quaint and a bit shallow in the postmodern feminist world. . . .*

*My father sang, of course. But this time, the Loo was joined by my stepbrothers, who were fluent with the Hebrew text and sang with grace and meaning, their voices ringing clear as they smiled at Rina. But it was Koby who gave me pause, his voice deep and crystal, singing along note perfect with my stepbrothers in crisp, beautiful Hebrew. Here was a black man from Africa sitting with my white family from Los Angeles, people he had known for less than two hours, and he was more integrated than I was. It brought it all home that a traditional Sabbath cut across cultural lines. When the chorus came and the men broke into spontaneous harmony, an involuntary lump formed in my throat.*

—Faye Kellerman, *Street Dreams* (2003)

Like her father, Cindy is moved, over the course of Kellerman's series, to come to view Orthodoxy as a desirable and deeply satisfying lifestyle. Even the "quaint" elements of its representations and expectations of women come to be valued. Rina, of course, is her primary teacher. Rina is everyone's teacher; in several books, Kellerman has Rina employed for pay as a teacher, and in those she is not, Rina is always and ever *our* teacher. And like any good primary school teacher, Rina teaches the "who," "what," "where," "how," and "why" of Orthodoxy, explaining the beliefs and rituals. We might think of her as a teacher in an American classroom, sharing with students the history of the immigrants who had come on the Mayflower and the Arbella, the doctrine of the Calvinist Church in New England, the problems of the term *Puritan*, the conflicts with Anne Hutchison and the Antinomians, the great figures of John Cotton and Richard Mather, and the belief that they must act like a light of the world. And how much more would the students believe their lessons were their teacher John Winthrop himself? In similar fashion, Rina instructs in Orthodoxy and lives it; and readers can imagine her as an authentic embodiment of Orthodoxy—specifically, women's Orthodoxy.

There are moments when the teaching is explicit. "Time for the Mideast geography lesson!" we read in *Sanctuary* (Kellerman 297). This novel is full of (awkwardly) explicit lessons in Hebrew, geography, and, of course, the Jewish people of Israel. The journey is an attempt to authenticate Judaism, making readers see that Judaism comes from something concrete and real, thus justifying the faith that Rina spends so much of the series professing.[22] And as always, Rina knows best: she has lived in Israel before and knows the country well. Although Rina's lessons about "black hats" are old hat by now, they are in a new context—not the yeshiva of Los Angeles or the enclaves of New York. Here, the people are a part of their landscape in a new way. She tells Peter and readers, for example, that it would make sense for a religious Jewish person to seek sanctuary in Israel because of all the "black areas." She then has to explicate for her American husband/reader, who decodes the word *black* in terms of skin: "A semantic misinterpretation. Not black as in Afro-American, black as in *black hat*—the ultrareligious area. The Black Hatters—the *Charedim*—must make up at least a third of Jerusalem—Sanhedria. The Ramot. Har Nof. Sha'arey Chesid" (Kellerman, *Sanctuary* 155).

Yet in Israel, Rina does not only offer lessons about the "Black Hatters." Through Peter, we see the "slums" of Tel Aviv and wealthier Ramat Aviv and the Diamond Bursa, and with him, we repeatedly misread people and situations ("You're just thinking like an American," Rina tells him/us, and "I'm learning," Peter says and we think; Kellerman, *Sanctuary* 242, 244). Rina shows us the country directly as well, and we gaze through her romantic vision of the land. In Jerusalem, we see the mix of people: Haredi Jews, modern Israelis, Arabs in kafias, Coptic priests, and nuns. We pass pushcarts, malls, and the *Knesset*. The last of these comes with a bit of commentary: "The seat of Israeli government, the Knesset was architecturally modeled after the Acropolis, the ancient seat of Greek government. Why Jews would deliberately copy Greek architecture was beyond Rina's comprehension. For the past eighteen hundred years, the religion had assiduously celebrated Channukah—a festival commemorating the Jewish overthrow of enforced Hellenic rule" (269). It is not the last piece of commentary Kellerman offers. As she takes Rina through Hebron, a city in the West Bank, she tells us about the history and makes a pointed political statement through her idealized heroine: "Though Rina knew that Hebron was still a *Jewish Holy City*, would always be a *Jewish Holy City*, it was time to be realistic. Hebron was no longer *Jewish*" (272).

If *Sanctuary* is a forum for education about Israel, *The Forgotten* is one for the Holocaust. The inciting incident of this book is a hate crime committed to Rina's synagogue; the walls are covered in swastikas, the floor is littered with pictures from concentration camps, and everything of value has been stolen. To understand the crime, readers must understand its source, and Rina (yet again) has insider knowledge: she is the daughter of Holocaust survivors.[23] In this novel, Kellerman has Rina make good on her name "Lazarus," allowing her to "raise the dead" (201). Rina talks about her family's experience in the Holocaust, and we are introduced to a survivor of Treblinka. (As there were very few survivors of Treblinka, which was strictly a death camp, this choice shows that Kellerman is determined to give a fictional voice to a historical lacuna.) The central question of the book asks, Who are the "forgotten" people of the Holocaust? *The Forgotten* gives readers a taste of what happens when history is not passed down from generation to generation, which is precisely what the rituals and teachings of Orthodoxy seek to avoid. ("They'll never be forgotten," Rina tells a Holocaust survivor who laments the nameless bodies piled on each other in the death camp. "Jewish law won't allow it" [318].) The teenager who vandalizes Rina's synagogue does so because he is trying to make meaning of his identity after coming across pictures of concentration camp prisoners in his grandfather's belongings. He also discovered that the dates he had been told for his grandfather's arrival in America (pre-Holocaust) did not match those on the grandfather's papers (post-Holocaust). The boy does not know his family's real history. He assumes that his grandfather, who told his family he was Jewish, must have really been a Nazi. Thanks to Rina's sleuthing, readers learn that the grandfather was neither Nazi nor Jew; he was a young Polish boy during the war, one who risked his life to photograph the prisoners and to feed them. The nameless victims documented by the fictional character (undocumented, unphotographed in history) may be one group of "the forgotten," but another is made up of the unknown, unsung heroes.

Whereas Israel and the Holocaust are both familiar to most American readers, particularly as touchstones of Judaism, Ethiopian Jewry (Beta Israel) is much less so. Little has been written on the history of Ethiopian Jews outside of Israel. There are virtually no novels or films that tell the story of the Amharic-speaking black Jewish community that lived in villages in Ethiopia for centuries before being brought to Israel, almost in its entirety, over the last forty years. Koby, Peter's son-in-law, gives readers the chance to learn about Ethiopian Jewish culture and history and to recognize Judaism as a multiracial and multicultural religion. We learn about Koby's food, his history before and in Israel, and his customs, which differ from Ashkenazi customs. We also learn about his encounters with racism. (Importantly, while Peter, the Jew-in-training, has reservations about Koby's color, Rina has none. To her, a coreligionist, particularly a practicing one, is always and immediately a part of her in-group. This is lovely but not a particularly realistic reflection of the experiences of Jews of color.) In other novels, we are introduced to a Persian Jewish community and to Columbian Jews.

So in the end, we are treated to one of the least monolithic depictions of Jews imaginable. Each group is divided and subdivided. In *Sanctuary*, when Rina's childhood friend Honey, a member of a strict Hasidic sect, gives her a call, we are taught about the subdivisions, which often occur as a result of Haredization. Honey, we learn, is using a payphone because her rebbe has outlawed home phones. Rina is surprised by this prohibition, which seems outside of the usual restrictions. "Rina," we are told, "knew lots of religious people who didn't own television sets or go to the movies. She knew plenty of Orthodox adults who shied away from popular fiction and magazines like *Time* and *Newsweek*. The stories were too lurid. The pictures were prurient" (Kellerman, *Sanctuary* 10). However, the phone seemed unusual to her. Honey says, "I know it sounds like every year some group is trying to *outfrum* the other. That another group goes to more and more extremes to shut out the outside world. But the Rebbe's not trying to do that" (11). At this point, Kellerman has Rina wonder, "*Which* Rebbe?" (11). This thought process is significant because, rather having Rina appear ignorant (although it is nice for a reader to think even briefly that all-knowing Rina might share some of her ignorance), Kellerman makes it clear that Rina's question comes from a place of *superior* knowledge about the Hasidim: "Most people thought the Chasidim were one cohesive group. In fact, there were many Chasidic sects, each one interpreting the philosophy of the *Ba'al Shem Tov* a little differently" (11).[24]

With each Orthodox community she visits with her readers, Kellerman revises the image of the insular enclave as anachronistic space. When Rina still resides in the yeshiva, it is a popular opinion among the police that the Orthodox Jews are living vestiges of the past. The Foothill cops of which Peter is a member "were . . . baffled by the enclave, imagining it a slice of old Eastern Europe that had been frozen in a time warp," we read in *Sacred and Profane*. Kellerman corrects them and us: "Actually, the yeshiva embodied aspects of both past and present" (Kellerman, *Sacred* 14). Similarly, the unnamed upstate New York village (presumably based on New Square or Kiryas Joel) where Rina's friend Honey lives makes Peter scoff and ask, "What's wrong with living in a city or at least a *town*? Since when is upstate New York sixteenth-century Poland?"[25] Although Rina replies, "It's a psychological thing, Peter. Blocking out the outside world. Less distraction. Easier to learn Torah," we learn this is not strictly true (13). Contemporary America and the world are not blocked out; instead, their value has been transformed by the villagers. The buses that run from the village to New York City, where the men are employed in the workaday world, have been "altered": they have "tables and benches for learning, and a bookcase full of *sepharim* [holy books]. . . . A *bais midrash* [house of learning] on wheels." Almost as an aside, when we read about the men's buses, outfitted for their Hasidic lifestyles, we are also told, "The women have their own bus, too, but we don't use it very often. Everything we need is in the village" (75). This physical segregation is not highlighted or lingered on. A separate space for women in and of itself, Kellerman suggests, is not the great problem of women in Orthodox Judaism. Rather, this is an instance in which we need to worry about the separate *laws* for men and women. Specifically, we should be concerned about the problem of the *get*, the Jewish divorce. In Judaism, only a man can grant one.

*Sanctuary*'s main mystery has little to do with Honey, and though Honey's story provides a forum for a number of issues in Orthodoxy (the divisions among sects, the growing Haredization Honey denies), it significantly opens a window on this key problem of practicing Jewish women: namely, the plight of the *agunah*. The *agunah*, the anchored woman, is a woman who is considered in a state of limbo; she is separated from her husband physically but not legally, and she cannot remarry. He might be missing or presumed dead, but if he is not verified as dead, she is chained to him as a serf to an absent landlord. If the man is present but simply refuses to grant a divorce when she requests one, the same applies: the woman remains married to the man. In other words, according to this Jewish law, a woman has *no agency*. She is entirely disempowered, and she is often victimized; a man whose wife desires a *get* can demand money, custody of children, or anything else he wants in exchange for the piece of paper that grants her freedom.[26]

In many ways, Kellerman's book, published in 1994, is prescient, anticipating awareness of the plight of the *agunah*. At the time, perhaps the only organization helping *agunot* was Agunah International Inc., cofounded by activists Rivka Haut and Susan Aranoff—and it was run out of Haut's living room. Formed in 2002, the Organization for the Resolution of Agunot (ORA) was one of the first major organizations to offer advocacy, support, education, and resolution (ORA has resolved almost three hundred *agunah* cases as of 2018). Around the same time, people began participating in International Agunah Day on *Ta'anit Esther* (the Fast of Esther). JOFA—the Jewish Orthodox Feminist Alliance—made the *agunah* one of its prime causes, hosting conferences, publishing the *Guide to Jewish Divorce and the Beit Din System* (2005), and offering links on its webpage with instructions for advocacy and resources for *agunot*. The film *Women Unchained* (2011) propelled public awareness, and the mainstream media began to cover the saga of the *agunah* as well. The story of Gital Dodelson was featured in the *New York Post* in November 2013 (Lewak), followed by NPR's *This American Life* episode "Sun-Rise, Sun-Get" in January 2014. The *New York Times* entered the fray with a powerful front-page human interest story in March 2014 about a man who remarried despite refusing his first wife, Lonna Kin, a divorce (Medina A1). Other headlines have appeared in the time since, sometimes trafficking in blatant sensationalism (the British *Daily Mail*'s June 2014 article about a Brooklyn *agunah* named Rivky Stein was titled, "'Raped, Tormented and Locked in a Room to Starve with Her Two Babies': The Shocking Claims of a Young Jewish Mother Who Found the Courage to Flee Her Husband but Is Still 'Chained' Because He Refuses to Grant Religious Divorce"). Finally, the situation of *agunot* was termed a "crisis" by Orthodoxy, leading, in June 2014, to the creation of an international *Beit Din*—religious court—to hear divorce suits.

Traditionally, the plight of the *agunah* has been dealt with in a deeply problematic manner, one that comes to light in Kellerman's 1994 book. Modern Orthodoxy has approached the problem through (non-Jewish) legal circuits; many rabbis require that grooms sign a prenuptial agreement promising to pay a woman a certain amount of money, indexed to inflation, for each day that she demands a *get* and he refuses to give one. This document can be enforced as a binding arbitration agreement in the state courts. Haredi Orthodoxy, however, has dealt with the matter differently: through public shaming and, if necessary, violence.[27] In October 2013, the *New York Times* reported on a scandal long known to those within these communities with the headline, "U.S. Accuses 2 Rabbis of Kidnapping Husbands for a Fee" (Goldstein and Schwirtz A18). According to the article, an FBI sting operation uncovered the "kidnap team" led by Rabbi Mendel Epstein: "For hefty fees, he orchestrated the kidnapping and torture of reluctant husbands, charging their wives as much as $10,000 for a rabbinical decree permitting violence and $50,000 to hire others to carry out the deed" (Goldstein and Schwirtz A18). (It is noteworthy that this article was published a month before the one on Dodelson; the media seems to have become interested in *agunot*'s situations only after it uncovered the potential consequences to their husbands.)

*Sanctuary* provides a nuanced discussion of the Jewish laws pertaining to marriage and divorce as well as the consequences. Though Rina is always quick to defend traditional Judaism, even she recognizes, through her conversations with her husband (who has not spent years immersed in the Torah way of thinking), that there are serious problems with the methods currently used in the Haredi world. She initially wants to argue that beating a husband who refuses to give a *get* is reasonable—that even *killing* him can be acceptable ("the ultimate liberation of his *yaitzer harah*," or evil side, she calls it; 309). She accuses her husband of "judging by American jurisprudence standards" (311). But Rina is *also* a product of America, and she too comes to judge by the same standards: "Peter was right. It was still murder" (318). So though it seems that Rina almost always defends Jewish law when it conflicts with American culture or law, Kellerman is more invested in establishing Rina as a reasonable authority than a fanatic. This is important: as our teacher, we need to believe her and believe *in* her as a righteous and reasonable person.

After all, she is instructing us on questions like, What is Orthodoxy? What is *women's* Orthodoxy? What does it involve? We are told the rules pertaining to eating rituals and relations between the genders and rituals for the dead. We are instructed on the things the Orthodox woman does (go to the mikvah) and might not do (see movies) and what she can but does not have to do (go to synagogue on Friday nights). She sometimes goes to *shul*—but only sometimes. She does not sit with her husband because men and women sit separately. She benches *gomel* for her endangered husband in almost every book, and Kellerman explains each time that it is a prayer of thanks for surviving a dire situation.

However, the Orthodox woman is defined by not just her rituals but also her maternal expectations, and the deep and sustained focus on (in)fertility in the series suggests that the author cannot help but think of these expectations. In fact, *in*fertility, more than fertility, is a driving force in Kellerman's books. Hence Rina does not spend the pages of the series in an endless state of pregnancy and childbirth. Already a mother to two boys, Rina gives birth once over the course of the series and never again. After delivering this child (her third, and the first girl, allowing her to fulfill the mitzvah of "be fruitful and multiply," which is defined by the *Shulchan Aruch*, the standard Jewish legal code, as bearing one boy and one girl), she is rendered infertile (*Shulchan Aruch*, Even HaEzer 1:5).

Rina's infertility hits her very hard, and Kellerman lingers on Rina's disappointment. The first two chapters of *Grievous Sin*, in fact, are given over entirely to Rina's delivery and the complications that arise from it, making this book glaringly different from the rest, which, per the genre, always begin with a crime. The title also comes from Rina's experience. But even when Kellerman's narratives are not focused on Rina's disappointment with her limits of fertility, the topic resurfaces (and not only in *Grievous Sin*, whose crime revolves around a woman who aborted one baby and stole another). *Milk and Honey*'s mystery is solved when Peter realizes that it has to do with the lengths to which the murdered mother, who struggled with fertility, had gone to conceive her child. (Rina helps him with the case by sharing a biblical analogy: "Look how long it took Rachel to have a baby." Peter displays the results of his learning when Kellerman writes that he "was well aware that she was referring to the biblical matriarch" [310].) Two brothers in *False Prophet*, both suspects, are obstetricians; one specializes in abortions and the other in infertility. In *Sanctuary*, Rina visits Rachel's Tomb (which also plays a significant role in the third book of Krich's Molly Blume series), a place in Bethlehem traditionally visited by infertile women coming to ask God for children as the matriarch Rachel once did.

But crucially, fertility is not only a woman's domain. Men's testicles are missing, inactive, surprisingly active, or replaced in her series, such that men too are brought into a problem so often defined as a women's issue, particularly in Orthodox Judaism. (The failure to properly include Orthodox men in testing and responding to infertility is also central to Anouk Markovits's novel *I Am Forbidden*.)[28] In *Justice*, men's infertility rears its head with a young mobster who was abused as a boy and lost a testicle; his belief in his infertility leads to his abandonment of his son, who becomes Peter and Rina's foster son, a new character for the series and student of Rina's Jewish teachings. In *Prayers for the Dead*, men's infertility arises again, and we learn that after long years of infertility treatments, one of the suspects has been given a testicle by his twin brother (also a suspect) to enable procreation with his wife. Although the brothers are religious Christians, not Jews, their reason for the unusual surgery (rather than a far less complicated sperm donation) comes out of the biblical prohibition against "spilling seed," allowing us to see how it might be a consideration for observant Jews as well.

Kellerman's ability to provide alternatives for problems of infertility is not limited to the wonders of modern science. The key option she provides comes through Rina's example of taking in those who need her. In *Hangman*, it's a waif, Gabe Whitman; in *Murder 101*, it is a debilitated young police officer. When Gabe, son of Peter's nemesis, is dropped at their door, Rina does not hesitate to invite him into their home and their lives, though Peter points out that they are finally done with parenting—his daughter Cindy is married and a police officer, Rina's son Sammy is married and in medical school, Rina's son Jacob is in university, and their shared daughter Hannah is about to leave for seminary in Israel. Why begin anew? Why take on a child not their own?

Rina's answer comes by way of a story about a childhood acquaintance her own parents once took in—a girl with whom she was barely friends but had met in an art class and brought home one day after the girl was orphaned. "She lived with us for a year," Rina explains. "Then she went back east for two years. Then she came back and lived with my parents for another six months after I got married. . . . And my parents did it because they're wonderful people and probably, being Holocaust survivors, knew what it was like to be lost" (Kellerman, *Hangman* 113). Parenting, we see, does not begin and end with childbirth. And families can be composed of many additions and renovations, like an old house continually being refitted for modernity. As Hannah explains to Gabe, who is like a sad pup, following Rina around and regularly asking her to adopt him, the Lazarus-Decker household has room for everyone (Kellerman, *Games* 363). It consists of a daughter from the current marriage, a daughter from the dad's first marriage plus her husband (an Ethiopian by way of Israel), two sons from the mom's first marriage (adopted by the dad), a dad who was adopted from deeply religious Jewish parents by deeply religious Baptist parents, and a lot of other uncles, aunts, ex-aunts, grandparents, and ghosts that make up what Hannah calls the "pathology" of their family (Kellerman, *Hangman* 117). Gabe does not get adopted (he's too old when he comes along), but Rina takes good care of him: "Rina had a way of making him feel calm but not smothered. . . . She let him make his own choices, but if he had questions, she'd offer advice. She also had a great sense of humor. She was kind of like your favorite teacher" (291). In fact, Rina teaches so much about Judaism, her specialty, that soon Gabe adds to the mix not only by living with the family but by beginning his conversion to Judaism. And in the future, his choice of mates seems likely to be Yasmine, so a Persian Jew might add another hue to the spectrum of the family.

Interlaced through all these questions of who and what and where and how is, of course, the why. Why do we need Orthodoxy? Roth writes, "The crime Decker investigates in each mystery is really a pretext for Kellerman to appropriate pop culture's capitalist critique of America and transform it into a moral critique of secular American society. By doing so she exposes its vapidity as well as the real crime that Rina the spiritual hero prevents in this series—biological merger with such a society and the loss of a distinctive identity that provides a moral compass with which to plot one's path through life" (204). There is a problem with this reading, however. The religious or spiritual societies seem as damned as the nonspiritual. For example, the New Age gurus in *False Prophet*, the Christian fundamentalists in *Prayers for the Dead*, and the cult members in *Jupiter's Bones* are all spiritually involved, and yet they defraud, kidnap, and murder. Even Rina's Haredi brother-in-law is morally corrupt. Kellerman is critiquing not only secular culture but all cultures and behaviors that fail to live up to the ideals of Orthodox Jewish dogma (as she defines them). Orthodox Judaism is the beacon unto other nations—but only in its purest, best form, which, for Kellerman, is a feminized form. It is Rina's version—the version of the *eshes chayil*.

## VII. KELLERMAN'S LITERARY DESCENDANTS

*Call me crazy but I don't see an Orthodox Jewish woman who bakes chocolate chip cookies and makes sandwiches as a gritty crime fighter.*

—Faye Kellerman, *Murder 101* (2014)

At the outset of Rochelle Krich's novel *Blues in the Night*, we are given a note on pronunciations of Yiddish words—as if to suggest that to understand this book, we first need to know our Yiddish (the second book in the series does the same and also ends with a glossary of Hebrew and Yiddish terms, wrapping the whole book in Yiddish translations).[29] From there, we dive into the exciting career of Molly Blume, beginning with the details of the novel's whodunit she is to solve: "An unidentified woman in her mid- to late-twenties, wearing a nightgown, was the victim of a hit-and-run accident that left her unconscious and seriously injured. There were no witnesses" (Krich, *Blues* 1). Before we can start to sort out this mystery—who is the woman? Why was she in the street in her nightgown? Who ran her over?—the narrative is interrupted. Molly, trying to write her "true crime" column about the case, gets a panicked call from her mother. Yet her mom's fear is not that Molly will get embroiled in the unidentified woman's affair and be imperiled herself (she will) but rather that Molly will miss a potential *bashert*, or destiny (in love).

"Edie let us have a five-minute break from class," begins her mom's call (no "Hi, how are you?"). We are told that her mom is at the weekly Israeli dance lessons Molly's sister, Edie, teaches. Her mom continues, "She wants to set you up with someone. He's very special. Brilliant, funny, sensitive, handsome." Before Molly replies, she shares a Jewish joke with us:

> One of Bubbie G's favorite jokes is about a *shadchan* (matchmaker) who raves to a young man's parents about a girl who has everything: beauty, intelligence, a sterling character, wealth.
>
> What *doesn't* she have? ask the skeptical parents. A long pause before the *shadchan* replies: Teeth.
>
> It's even better in Yiddish. (Krich, *Blues* 4–5)

The introduction to Krich's series, then, outlines what much of our reading experience will be like: We will solve a terrifying and mysterious crime. We will learn about modern Jewish culture (like Israeli dancing). We will meet Orthodox women who work in a variety of fields (in addition to Molly, the true crime writer, and her sister, the Israeli dance instructor, Molly has two other sisters and a sister-in-law—a lawyer, a student, and a nutritionist, respectively). We will experience the intensity of the close-knit Jewish family (the sister who teaches the mom; the mom who seems overbearing, per Jewish mother stereotypes; the Jewish grandmother, called Bubbie G., whose influence looms large). We will be subject to Jewish jokes and will pick up a few Yiddish words. And we will be reminded of the expectations of the Jewish Orthodox woman, even as she is also acting as our brave detective—marriage and children.

Could Kellerman have imagined such a heroine?

*Murder 101*, Kellerman's twenty-second Peter Decker and Rina Lazarus thriller, stands out in Kellerman's oeuvre for resembling a Dan Brown novel—it is packed with famous stolen works of art, a Harvard symbologist, and big government cover-ups. But it also stands out because Kellerman is less coy in this novel about revealing who is behind the curtain. It is not surprising to find Rina acting as an unpaid detective (she does much of the thinking that solves the case) or even as a negotiator, demanding the Russian government's return of the Schneerson art to Chabad, because she is still saying, "I'm fine in the background" and working "with a soft voice and a smile" (Kellerman, *Murder* 436, 439). No one else in this book—not Peter; his old colleague, Scott, whom he has pulled out of retirement; or his new partner, Tyler, who seems more interested in screenwriting than acting as a police officer—plays as powerful and important a role as Rina does. What changes, however, is Kellerman's explicit recognition of her choice to keep Rina in the mystery genre's backseat (even if she is the driver of the series in all other ways).

After twenty-eight years of writing about Rina and Peter's lives, Kellerman has semiretired her characters, if not herself. Peter is no longer a lieutenant but an everyman police officer in a small town that sees little crime. Rina is teaching students at the university and hosting Shabbat dinners for them, no longer raising children or running a synagogue. Perhaps they will have more adventures, but they seem to be winding down. In *Murder 101*, with the inclusion of a young screenplay-writing character, Kellerman almost seems ready to pass the baton. (It is perhaps not coincidental that in 2006, her son Jesse, a Harvard graduate playwright like Tyler, wrote his first thriller novel.) She encourages the young fictional writer to do what she has not. "Maybe I should make my protagonist a woman," Tyler says after watching Rina in action. Peter seconds his idea, saying, "Model her after my wife." In 2014, when *Murder 101* was published, it was almost impossible *not* to imagine a woman at the forefront of bloody crime investigations (think AMC's *The Killing*; the Swedish/Danish show, *The Bridge*; BBC Two's *The Fall*).[30] Yet Kellerman knows there would still be resistance to one aspect of Rina's character. "Call me crazy," says Tyler, "but I don't see an Orthodox Jewish woman who bakes chocolate chip cookies and makes sandwiches as a gritty crime fighter." Rina, who is literally sitting in the backseat of the car, reminds the young man of her ability to drive. "Cookies notwithstanding," she tells him, "I've had as much input in this case today as you have, Tyler" (Kellerman, *Murder* 358).

For his failure to see the Orthodox, cookie-baking *eshes chayil* as a good and interesting fictional hero for crime fiction, Tyler blames the limits of his imagination. Perhaps he is not the only one to have such limits. But Kellerman insists that a leading lady of this nature is possible (if not certain). On the final pages of the book, Peter and Rina say good-bye to Tyler, who is leaving the force, and Rina again stands up for herself and the Orthodox woman and says, "About your screenplay, Tyler. . . . What about making the protagonist a woman?" Tyler is ambivalent, but he seems swayed: "It's a possibility. I do have some good role models for it." Then he backs down again. "I don't think I could write it as good as the real thing." Rina gives up. "So make it a man," she says (Kellerman, *Murder* 454–455).

Yet it seems that Kellerman was too hasty in suggesting the world is not ready for a cookie-baking Orthodox woman protagonist fighting crime. Since 2002, Krich has been offering readers just that in her "Molly Blume" series. Krich's books, like Kellerman's, are about educating readership about the roles and rules of Orthodoxy, particularly in terms of women. As we will see with Malka Zipora's stories in *Lekhaim!* (and Burshtein's *Fill the Void*), Krich imagines her fiction as opening a window onto the lives of Orthodox women. This is evident in *Dream House*, the second book of the series, when Krich describes the ankle-length sable and velour robes the women of the house wear for Shabbat dinner. Molly, who is both the protagonist and our first-person narrator, speaks directly to us when she says, "If you peek into Orthodox homes across the country, you'll probably find a number of women and girls similarly clothed" (Krich, *Dream* 53). Of course, we don't have to, because she has already told us what we would find. In other words, if we are already familiar with the ways that Orthodox women appear and behave in public, Krich takes the opportunity to instruct us on what they are like in private. In many ways, Krich's project is much like Kellerman's. But by creating an Orthodox crime-solving woman protagonist for her mysteries, Krich is burdened with acknowledging the ways that Molly's career and lifestyle relate to each other and even come into conflict with one another. And this she does, lending Molly an ambivalent attitude and a need to constantly negotiate the divergent and often contradictory spaces of her life.

After all, if Krich has Molly offering readers a peek into an Orthodox household, she also makes it clear that Molly's job allows Molly a peek into the non-Orthodox world, which would not, as Molly explains, otherwise be readily accessible to her: "The job is great. It's been a window onto the complex, layered identity of the city I love and from which Orthodox Judaism has insulated me most of my life. If you're Orthodox, you tend to live in close-knit communities that provide the necessities: Orthodox private schools; kosher markets, butchers, and bakeries; a ritual bath; synagogues within walking distance" (Krich, *Grave* 28). She goes on to say that most of her friends are friends from childhood and are also Orthodox, though she states, "I also enjoy the camaraderie with many of the detectives I've come to know, and I still feel a thrill of anticipation when I step into a police station" (Krich, *Grave* 28).

The exposure to the outside world affects Molly's relationship with her Orthodoxy, and in turn, her relationship with her man. "Okay if I wear pants?" she asks Zack during their courtship (Krich, *Dream* 66). The question is multivalent. Although the literal reference is to religious observance/appearance, Molly is also questioning her ability to metaphorically wear the pants in the romantic relationship and the novels.

The pants make clear that Krich's main character practices Orthodoxy differently than Kellerman's, though we see in Molly's family a diverse Orthodoxy that resembles Rina's family's. Molly's sister, Liora, for example, is more *frum* than Molly, which we know by her clothes ("ankle-length skirts and sweater sets"), her level of participation in choosing her spouse ("My family had already vetted his, and his family, ours, and both sets of parents had agreed to supplement the salary Liora would earn for those first years of marriage"), and her plan to support her "black-hatted young man" who "rock[s] on his heels," indicating that even as he comes to meet his potential wife, he is so spiritual that his mind is still deep in prayer or the intricacies of the Talmud (Krich, *Blues* 125, 124). Other members of the family are less *frum*. For example, *Dream House* begins on Halloween, the kind of holiday we might assume is entirely outside of Rina's sphere (certainly it would be at the yeshiva, but even beyond, non-Jewish holidays are given virtu-ally no mention in Kellerman's books). In Krich's hands, the non-Jewish holiday has a role to play, albeit a small one. "Even if Halloween hadn't fallen on Friday night," Krich explains via Molly, "Mindy [Molly's sister] and Norm wouldn't have taken their two girls trick-or-treating (despite its commercialization and allure, the holiday has its origins in religious ritual), though they always stock up on Hershey's Kisses and Reese's Pieces for the children who come to their door" (2–3). Judaism is more important than American holidays, but there is a recognition and an accommodation of the mainstream culture in which they find themselves.

Molly's relationship to men is dictated by her religious practice: its signifi-cance and its relative liberalism. If Rina Lazarus's name evokes spiritual rebirth and freedom, Molly Blume's name evokes a well-known figure from Irish literature; she is named, of course, after James Joyce's lusty Molly Bloom, the less-than-faithful wife of Leopold in the epic novel *Ulysses*. It is unsurprising that in Molly's first interaction with a man (a police officer of *Irish* descent), she is flirting: "We chitchatted for a minute, flirting comfortably the way we always do, both of us knowing that nothing would come of it for many reasons, includ-ing the fact that I'm Modern Orthodox Jewish and he's Irish Catholic" (Krich, *Blues* 10). Rina might bring the officer cookies, but she would never flirt with him (unless he's Peter, who might have looked Irish Catholic with his flaming red hair, but was secretly Jewish. Rina's soul must have recognized Peter's inner Jew for Kellerman's universe to stay standing). Still, Molly knows and we quickly learn that this is not a tale of going "off the *derech*." Molly pushes boundaries but never crosses them ("nothing would come of it"). A more realistic potential beau for Molly is Zack, a Modern Orthodox rabbi (and indeed he turns out to be "the one").

Yet Krich uses Zack's comparatively more religious status to reveal the degree of Molly's ambivalence toward elements of Orthodoxy. Zack wears a "black suede yarmulke much larger than the teeny colorful cotton ones a succession of girlfriends crocheted for him," suggesting that he has slid to the right, or become more observant over time (*Blues* 29). (The passage also indicates to us one way that young observant girls participate in a tradition of head covering before they are married and supposed to cover their own heads.)[31] Molly, on the other hand, pushes boundaries with clothes as she does with her interactions with men. For her date with Zack, Molly contemplates but then discards the "conservative navy suit" and instead chooses "a black Lycra skirt hemmed well above the knees and a short-sleeved, scoop-necked clinging white silk sweater that stopped just short of offering a peek at [her] Wonderbra-enhanced assets" (Krich, *Blues* 28). Show-ing knees, elbows, and collarbones and hinting at everything else, Molly makes it clear that she is not rigorous with the strictures of *tzniut*—modesty. In another scene, she's "tugging down [her] short black wool skirt, which had slid up during the ride and exposed an expanse of black-tights-covered thigh" (Krich, *Dream* 35). Yet as with her flirtation with the police officer, she is still within the range of acceptable dress for *Modern* Orthodoxy (note that she does stop short of offering a peek at her Wonderbra-enhanced assets and her thighs are clad in tights). And as her relationship progresses, she evaluates her choices: "Sleeves and skirts falling short of strict Orthodox rules, necklines a little too low. Nothing risqué, but not appropriate for a rabbi's girlfriend." She thinks about her sister's question, "Is a couple of inches such a big deal if you love someone?" She is also asked by Zack if her individuality is defined by her hemline (Krich, *Dream* 38, 68). The answers she gives are not immediate. Molly is a character who does not take the rules of Orthodoxy lightly, even if she follows most of them. Ultimately, as a married woman, she chooses to take on customs of modest dress, but only because her groom *doesn't* demand them: "I was doing this for Zack, who had asked but hadn't insisted that I cover my hair, and not wear pants in public, and lengthen my skirts and sleeves" (Krich, *Grave* 71). "It's your call," Zack tells Molly when she wavers about wearing a wig after marriage (she's already decided to keep her name for her career). "*Shalom bayit* is more important," he adds (Krich, *Grave* 97). We might recall the wise reply of the towering rabbinic figure of twentieth-century Orthodox Judaism, Rabbi Joseph Soloveitchik, when his students demanded to know why his wife didn't cover her hair. "Ask her," said the *Rav*.[32]

Krich also uses Molly's relationship with Zack to resist the fairy-tale structure that would seem to work perfectly for an Orthodox woman's narrative: the progression from sad singlehood to married-with-children bliss. When Molly and Zack, who meet at the start of the first novel, finally become engaged at the end of the second, the proposal is so offstage and unemphatic as to easily be missed. After Molly solves the book's crime (the issue of primary importance), she visits someone, and this is how we find out: "Last week I baked chocolate chip cookies"—of course she did, she's Rina's literary descendent—"and took them to Charlene's. We had tea in the living room, and she cooed over the princess-cut diamond engagement ring Zack gave me last Saturday night. It was the second night of Chanukah, and he'd put it in a large yellow plastic dreidel along with Godiva chocolates, so how could I say no?" (Krich, *Dream* 342). Even as her wedding date nears, Molly continues to prioritize her work life over her romantic/religious one (romantic and religious being deeply intertwined), interrupting a wig-fitting early for an important call and canceling a meeting with a *ketubah* (marriage agreement) calligrapher—twice—for an interview (Krich, *Grave* 74). But she *does* get there eventually. And as the series builds, slowly, to the marriage of Molly and Zack (which happens at the end of the third novel), readers have ample opportunity to learn about the many rituals that accompany a Jewish wedding (who pays for which parts of the wedding, how a *ketubah* is written, what happens at the *bedecken*, whether a *mechitzah* is appropriate for their level of observance, how long the bride and groom can't see each other before the wedding, why the mothers of the groom and bride break a plate after the ceremony, what prayers are said, etc.). *Mazel tov!* (But don't expect to soon see the "be fruitful and multiply" commandment in action—Molly will spend the fourth book giving us updates on her menstrual cycle, but the series ends without a pregnancy).

Despite Molly's ambivalence about her role as an Orthodox woman and her relatively liberal practice of Orthodoxy, Krich's books are far more "kosher" than Kellerman's. That is to say, if Kellerman's characters curse like sailors (or the scum-of-the-earth criminals that they are), it is notable that there is an utter lack of profanity in Krich's books. Similarly, if sex figures in Kellerman's novels, it is again notable for its complete absence in Krich's books. The courtship of Molly and Zack is sexually suggestive but ultimately painfully chaste. At the opening of the second book of the series, Molly is sleeping late the day after Halloween, the "result of another late-nighter with (Rabbi) Zack Abrams," she says, adding, "although you'd think by now my body would have adjusted to sleep deprivation" (Krich, *Dream* 2). But lest we think this is subtle, offstage sex, Krich reins in her readers' fantasies, not even allowing her lovers to close a door behind them. There *is* no offstage: "When the man who makes your heart race and various body parts tingle is a rabbi, and the way he looks at you says he feels the same way," Molly clarifies, "but the physical contact is verboten—well, unless you're into masochism, the privacy of an apartment is not a good idea" (Krich, *Dream* 20–21).

Even after they are engaged, Molly and Zack are *shomer nagiyah*—guarding against having any physical contact with each other because they are of the opposite sex. When Molly cries, Zack "blotted [her] eyes with a tissue, a gesture that, given the Orthodox rules, was as close to a caress as he could offer," Krich explains. As always, Molly shows both resistance and restraint: "I would have loved to lean against his shoulder, to take comfort in his arms. Solace, not sex. Sometimes the rules are hard to follow" (*Grave* 21).

With her Yeshivish character who rarely questions the strictures of Orthodoxy, Kellerman gives into the generic demands for sex (mystery novels, after all, can often be found beside Harlequin romances). Although it is already clear that Kellerman's stories are *not* strictly kosher—which is to say, novels a Haredi rabbi might endorse for their appropriateness and modesty—premarital sex between a rigorously Orthodox woman and a not-Jewish (or so we think at this point) beau comes as a surprise (or at least it did for me!). Kellerman justifies this sex in the novel: "Premarital sex isn't that big a deal in Judaism" (*Sacred* 268). Rina, who, as we might remember, works at a mikvah, which is used to preserve family purity laws built around distinguishing between times of physical intimacy and separation, tells Peter this before they hit the bedroom. Krich prefers to wait for the couple to stand under the chuppah before they do the deed (much as Stephenie

Meyer, the Mormon writer of the *Twilight* series, keeps the lust-driven teenage girl and sparkling vampire physically apart until they've said their "I dos").

But neither Kellerman nor Krich remotely approaches the chasteness, the "strictly kosher" form of writing—to reference the title of Yoel Finkelman's study of Haredi literature—as Libi Astaire, a Kansas-born, Israel-living writer of Regency-era, *Northanger Abbey*–inspired novels with cameos by Rabbi Nachman of Breslov (founder of the Hasidic Breslov movement). In a write-up of Haredi literature in *Tablet Magazine*, Astaire shared her rules for writing:

1. No murders or gratuitous violence.
2. No unredeemable characters.
3. No inappropriate language or sexual immorality. (Z. Berger)

Journalist Zackary Berger notes, "Of course, she doesn't write for the same audience that reads Laura Lippman or John Grisham. Astaire writes mysteries for Haredi women."

Astaire's Ezra Melamed series involves mysteries that take place in London's Jewish community. Most of the crimes are committed by non-Jews. If Jews commit crimes, they are either petty or done from ignorance, and Jews show great remorse when they do wrong, whereas non-Jews do not. The crimes are solved by a character called Ezra Melamed, a wealthy man and recent widow who spends the time he isn't solving mysteries playing chess with his business partner or frequenting a Jewish café, where we can learn about kosher food. Like Kellerman and Krich, Astaire uses her novels to educate readers about Jewish customs and beliefs. Though many of the rituals practiced by Astaire's characters are near identical to those practiced in the novels of Kellerman and Krich, the setting of the novels—1811 London—allows Astaire to teach us about Jewish history of the Regency era (her stories are set in London, but characters come along to teach us about Jews in Manchester and Alsace and Gottingen and Bohemia) as well. In fact, it is the sameness of these rituals—in a very different time and place—that enable readers to recognize the power of Jewish traditions, which are essentially consistent, as Astaire writes them, across time and space.

What makes Astaire's fiction interesting is that it features as its actual teacher a young, female narrator/transcriber of "not quite marriageable age"—which is quite convenient because, had she been younger, she would not have been able to write the tales, and had she been older, she (presumably) would have been consumed with issues of marriage and children. (Yet again, the writer of Orthodox women's mysteries shifts the focus away from a female Orthodox character's fertility.) The sleuth, as in Kellerman's books, is a man, but he is the "teacher's helper" (a rough translation of "Ezra Melamed"); Rebecca Lyon is our central consciousness and the instrumental character for solving the books' mysteries. Admittedly, Rebecca is often undermined by her naive determination to see the world through the lens of an Ann Radcliffe novel and by her family's refusal to take her seriously. However, Rebecca contributes much to the development of the stories and progression of the mysteries, and through her character, Astaire provides readers with a feminist Orthodox heroine.

"Ah, I know what you are thinking," our narrator challenges readers in *The Disappearing Dowry*. "She is a talebearer? I want nothing to do with a young lady like her!" (Astaire, *Dowry* 7). But Astaire justifies the unladylike behavior with a Jewish logic: "My tale . . . is a tale written in the tradition of our people: a family *megillah*," she says, referring to both the long scroll best known for the Jewish holiday of Purim and the colloquial Jewish term used to describe a protracted story (7). Rebecca, nonetheless, is careful, telling us in the first story that her tale has been written "with the permission and blessings of all concerned," as one would imagine a Haredi writer would receive from the rabbis of her community. At the start of the second novel, Rebecca voices the proud but humble pleasure of the author who has achieved success with her (rabbinically sanctioned) megillah. She says, "With what surprise, joy, and gratitude to the One Who bestows all good did I receive the news that the manuscript of *The Disappearing Dowry* [the shared title of Rebecca and Astaire's books] had been read by many members of London's Jewish community" (Astaire, *Ruby* 3).

Like Krich's Molly, Astaire's Rebecca fits imperfectly into the mold of the "woman of valor" (as Rebecca's mother is called) or even the "Daughter of Israel," as the younger generation of girls is called, due to her reading (of Radcliffe) and her sleuthing (borne out of her reading), which seem to cause conflict with the paradigm of Orthodox womanhood (9, 16). She is messy and disorganized. Like Mirka's, her stitches don't lie flat, and her dreams of aiding the poor are, as she describes it, "so grandiose that they could not be accomplished in their entirety," which meant that "she would lose heart and accomplish nothing at all" (Astaire, *Dowry* 17). Yet the work she does and the assistance she provides over the course of the novels are more important, ultimately, than flawless embroidery and more realistic than ending world poverty.

Although Astaire is not a household name like Kellerman, she offers something that Kellerman—and Krich—cannot: access to Haredi homes. A writer for *Mishpacha Magazine*, the website of the Breslov Hasidic community, and the website of Aish HaTorah (a major Jewish outreach organization), Astaire has the stamp of approval, the "permission and blessings" of the community of whom and for whom she writes, much like the women filmmakers I introduce in chapter 5. Thus Astaire is not only revising the image that mainstream America has of Orthodox women but also, significantly, revising the image and the paradigm that Orthodox women have of themselves.

---

The feat Kellerman and her descendants have accomplished is not to be easily dismissed. They have provided a wealth of information about Judaism through fast-paced mystery novels, a tool of mass culture, reaching millions of readers. Moreover, in the hands of Kellerman, Krich, and Astaire, women are not victims—not of Orthodox Judaism, certainly, and not (much) of crime. They are the heroines, whether they wear the detective badges or not. Finally, these writers have challenged the criticisms of second-wave feminism in relation to religious women. Yes, these women might bake and cover their hair. But these acts do not make them oppressed. And neither are the women limited to these acts, as the writers inform secular readers as well as Haredi ones.

Of course, writers can do more than inform. They can also reach out. We might not think that a writer like Astaire, who sent most of her stories to magazines for other Orthodox women, would be able to intervene in the fraught relations between Orthodox communities and hostile neighbors. But as the next chapter demonstrates, the writer Malka Zipora, who published most of her writing in the same magazines as Libi Astaire, did precisely that. And she is not the only Orthodox Jewish woman in Quebec to use her voice to build intercultural bridges.

CHAPTER 3

# She Opens Her Mouth with Wisdom

## THIS BRIDGE CALLED MY VOICE

### I. Introduction

*And do you, madame, do you know Israel? Madame, Madame, do you—do you speak Yiddish and know Shabbos? Madame! Do you know this? The real name is dreidel. It's for Chanukah. Do you celebrate Chanukah?*
—Myriam Beaudoin, *Hadassa* (2007, my translation)

*On November 3rd, 2013, thanks to you, I won my election, becoming the first Hasidic woman to ever hold political office. As borough councillor of the district of Claude-Ryan in Outremont, I promise to represent the interests of my citizens to the best of my ability. I will use this website to keep you posted on borough news, council meetings, local events, items of interest, and so on. Please don't hesitate to write me or leave a comment.*

*Join me as we build bridges, promote dialogue and understanding, and spread peace and harmony in the neighbourhood!*
—Mindy Pollak, http://www.mindypollak.ca/about

In places across North America and beyond, where there are insular Orthodox communities, there are frictions between those Orthodox communities and their neighbors. Some of these frictions seem to be the same the world over: There are bylaw battles over *eruvs* and over the erection and duration of sukkahs. There are disputes about educational provision. There are concerns about gender segregation in swimming pools and on city buses. There are also those frictions that are locally specific: nowhere else but Crown Heights has seen the likes of the riot that took place there after a Guyanese child was accidentally killed by an automobile in the Chabad rebbe's motorcade in 1991. And only in East Ramapo has there been a massive lawsuit because Orthodox Jews staged a takeover of the local

115

school board (in 2005) and then diverted funds to their parochial schools; the 2017 lawsuit accuses the board of degrading and disenfranchising black and Latino citizens. What village other than Kiryas Joel has received official permission of the U.S. Supreme Court to exclude female drivers from its school buses? Quebec's tensions, therefore, are both emblematic of the larger picture of Hasidic life in a secular society and also, as the only place in North America that threatened to ban religious symbols on public employees, unique (see figure 3.1). And one of

Figure 3.1. Poster for Quebec's "Charter of Values" (2013). Public domain.

the things that makes them unique is that they have led to the rise of the Hasidic woman's voice in dialogue with her neighbors in what has been called, time and again, an act of bridge building.

This act is not insignificant. If the Hasidic characters in francophone non-Jewish Quebecois writer Myriam Beaudoin's 2006 novel *Hadassa* are curious about what a non-Jewish person in Quebec does, thinks, and knows, the same sentiment could be said to exist tenfold in reverse, both within and outside of the book.[1] Beaudoin's French-language book purports to be about "un monde à part, enveloppé de mystère et d'interdits, mais séduisant et rassurant" (a world apart, shrouded in mystery and taboos, but seductive and reassuring). It was nominated in 2007 for the Prix des libraires du Québec and won, the same year, both the Prix littéraire des collégiens (awarded by a panel of college students throughout Quebec) and the Prix littéraire France-Québec. In 2011, another non-Jewish francophone writer in Quebec named Abla Farhoud also took on the subject of local Hasidim with her book titled *Le sourire de la petite juive* (The Smile of the Little Jewess). And in 2014, non-Jewish Quebecois filmmaker Maxime Giroux directed *Félix et Meira*, a film about a married Hasidic mother and a single Quebecois man, star-crossed lovers of Montreal's Mile End, which won "Best Canadian Film" at the 2014 Toronto International Film Festival and was submitted in 2015 to the Academy Awards as Canada's foreign-language contender. By virtue of their chosen subject, these books and film appear to follow in the success of the short story collection *Lekhaim!: Chroniques de la vie hassidique à Montréal* (later published in English as *Rather Laugh than Cry*), which was written by a Hasidic woman in Quebec in 2006. Yet in many ways, Beaudoin, Farhoud, and Giroux's tales more closely resemble the narratives of secular Jewish writers like Eve Harris and Julia Dahl that render Hasidic life exotic—and somewhat tragic. Beaudoin's story includes a romance between a gentile and a Hasidic woman, Farhoud's highlights the growing internal struggle of a Hasidic girl who feels confined by her religious identity, and Giroux mixes the two scandalizing ingredients to produce his stirring drama.

The author of *Lekhaim!*, on the other hand, writes her stories about and *within* the Hasidic community. The stories of the Hasidim she presents are the stuff of everyday, made interesting not through sensationalism but through humor and pathos. Despite the quotidian subject matter, the book was met with much success in francophone Quebec. "In the book *Lekhaim!* Malka Zipora portrays the ultra-Orthodox Hasidic Jewish community in Montreal and breaks down cultural barriers," exalted one French review (M. Singer, my translation). There is little doubt that the success of *Lekhaim!* stemmed, in part, from the audience's desire for an "authentic" Hasidic voice, particularly a woman's. A fear in secular Quebec, which was highlighted during the province's reasonable accommodation debates, was that women in minority groups such as the Hasidim were being oppressed and silenced. Through the book, francophone Quebecois could find a way to connect to the "bizarre" neighbors described in the media as "like 'bogeymen'" with a "mentality that's separate" (Côté A1; Heinrich, "Laurentian"). Indeed, the stories in *Lekhaim!* are relatable, as though to say, "You wonder who we are, and I will tell you. In many ways, we are like you. If we knew each other, we would probably get along."

The writer, whose real name is known to many residents in Outremont, the Montreal borough in which she resides, calls herself Malka Zipora for her book, though she refers to herself throughout, more significantly, only as "a Hasidic mom," making herself a representative of her community. In writing her stories for a general audience, Zipora "gingerly" draws "aside the shades to the window in [her] home" to provide "glimpses of many universal emotions and stories," which are essential to the Hasidic residents' communication and coexistence with their neighbors (Zipora 12). The language suggests hesitation and also a sense of modesty, more so than that of Krich, an author who brashly shares with us the brand of her characters' brassieres. Still, if Hasidic communities are known for their insularity and difference, Zipora is undermining both by drawing aside her metaphorical shades. But she is also doing something else surprising, which she does not name. She is giving voice to a group that has often been spoken for (in the media and literature, by non-Jewish Quebecois and secular Jews) but has rarely spoken: Hasidic women. This speaking is a speaking back, for when they are spoken for, Hasidic women are doubly rendered silent through the erasure of their own voices and the voices that represent them. The Hasidic heroine of Boaz Yakin's film *A Price above Rubies* is, in Rubel's words, "silenced and exiled" (93). Judy Brown called her book about the sexual molestation of a young Hasidic girl *Hush.* Deborah Feldman writes in her memoir of a common adage about women in her Hasidic community: "An empty vessel clangs the loudest" (21). This expression is understood to mean that the "louder the woman, the more likely she is to be spiritually bereft, like the empty bowl that vibrates with a resonant echo" (Feldman, *Unorthodox* 21).

The Talmudic prohibition against *kol isha* (literally "voice of a woman") comes from two sources: Berachos 24A and Kiddushin 70A, both of which describe a woman's voice as "nakedness" (*kol b'isha erva*) and argue that a woman's singing voice could sexually arouse men and distract them from their holy work or prayer. By describing Hasidic women as silenced—unable to speak aloud, tell their tales, define their own existence through their words—writers like Yakin, Brown, and Feldman suggest the idea that the prohibition against a woman's voice is extended, in the Hasidic communities, well beyond her singing voice. Yet Hasidic women in Quebec, as elsewhere, are taking charge of their own voices.[2] *Kol isha,* for Zipora, might mean a voice of peace diffusing a hostile encounter between communities. It might mean a political voice arguing for change. Or it might simply mean the voice of a "Hasidic mom," gently explaining the customs of the unknown neighbor and inspiring sympathy and camaraderie through a language that carefully wends its way between universalism and difference. Each voice, as it diffuses, argues, explains, or inspires, also narrates a self—woman—in her community.

## II. The Background: Out of Eden

Quebec has a Jewish problem. But it is not the problem of the 1930s and 1940s, when *Le Devoir*, the leading francophone newspaper, advocated a denial of civil rights for Jews; French Canadians supported Nazi ideology;[3] and Abbé Lionel Groulx, known as the "patron saint of independists," called for a boycott of all Jewish shops.[4] It's true that the Jews have long been called the "third solitude" in Quebec—a play on the title of Hugh MacLennan's 1945 classic Canadian novel *Two Solitudes*, the story of the divide between the English and French. And the Quebecois do have a rich anti-Semitic history, which was one of the central concerns of Montreal's most controversial native son, Mordecai Richler, in and beyond his 1992 book *Oh Canada! Oh Quebec!* (an outgrowth of his September 1991 *New Yorker* article and a book that was heavily condemned by the French press of Canada and even compared to *Mein Kampf*[5]). But as elsewhere, the majority of anti-Jewish policy and propaganda in Quebec mostly lies in the past. Admittedly, echoes of older anti-Semitism continued in the late twentieth and the twenty-first centuries, in such instances as when Parti Quebecois leader Jacques Parizeau blamed the failure of the 1995 referendum on Quebec's sovereignty on "money and the ethnics," a term read almost universally to mean Jews (as well as Greeks and Italians), and when a Jewish school was firebombed in 2004. For the most part, however, Jews and Jewish culture thrive in Quebec. Montreal is home to a large Jewish community; the hip magazine *Shtetl: Your Alternative Jewish Magazine*; the hipper webseries *Yidlife Crisis* (2014–); and the Segal Center for Performing Arts, which runs Yiddish theater. North of Montreal, the town of Kiryas Tosh is a self-sufficient community of Tosher Hasidim (not unlike Kiryas Joel or New Square in New York) with its own governing bylaws. The mountain town Sainte-Agathe-des-Monts hosts a major Yiddish/Jewish cultural program, KlezKanada, which draws participants from around the world and is the largest of its kind. Jews and Quebecois, it seems, have made a sometimes-uneasy peace. In fact, with the "brain drain" since the 1970s of anglophone Jews and the influx of francophone Jews from Morocco, Algeria, and Tunisia, Jews and Quebecois have found a common ground on the basis of language—the key instrument in the Quebecois cultural reformations. As a sign of recognition of this culturolinguistic connection, in 2013, Université de Montreal introduced a course titled "Culture et expérience juives au Québec," the first course about Jews in a francophone university in Quebec (Arnold, "New U of M Course").

And yet, Quebec has a Jewish problem, though today's Jewish problem is mostly specific to the Hasidic communities.[6] Populating Montreal's borough of Outremont, Boisbriand, and the idyllic mountain towns of the Laurentians, the Hasidim, living in the province since the aftermath of the Holocaust, have for the last quarter century found themselves at odds with the Quebecois communities they border. Tensions between the Hasidim and Quebecois have been palpable since "l'affaire Outremont" of 1988, when the Vishnitzer Hasidim petitioned the Quebec Superior Court to rezone an empty lot on a residential section of Saint-Viateur Street for the building of their new synagogue.[7] Their opponent was Gérard Pelletier, leader of Le Parti du Renouveau d'Outremont, who declared, "We do not want Outremont to become a Hasidic town" (Herman 155). The requests of the Vishnitzer Hasidim were denied, but the incident did not end there. It spurred French newspapers *Le Journal d'Outremont* and *La Presse* to publish anti-Hasidic sentiment, notably *La Presse*'s "Outremont se découvre un 'probleme juif'" (Outremont discovers a Jewish problem) that described Hasidim as "cette minorité bizarre" (this strange minority) in which the men were "'a couettes,' tout en noir comme des 'bonhommes sept heures,' ces femmes et ces enfants habiliés comme des oignons" (in "pigtails," all in black like "bogeymen," the women and children "dressed like onions"; Côté A1). "L'affaire Outremont" is much discussed in academic literature because it anticipated a generation of problems between Hasidim and their neighbors. In this first incident, we see a focus on disputed property, questions of accommodating difference, the language of exoticization and alienation, and the slippage between "Hasidim" and "Jews," issues that are all present in a number of later incidents, such as the 2011 hostilities over the Bobover synagogue's request to add a bathroom to their facility.

By the middle of the first decade of the twenty-first century, the conflicts between Hasidim and their neighbors in Quebec seemed near constant. In 2005, Val Morin, a town in the Laurentians north of Montreal, spent $100,000 in court against a Belz sect of Hasidic Jews that converted two residences into a religious school and a synagogue; the court ruled in favor of the municipality. In 2006, a number of Hasidim with summer homes in the area reported that in their absence, their homes had been raided and kitchen knives stabbed through their walls. In 2007, in Val Morin, returning Hasidic vacationers similarly found themselves without their air conditioners, bicycles, and scooters, and two months later, a series of suspicious fires were started in Hasidic homes in nearby Val David. Also that summer, a group of Hasidic Jews bought Miramont-sur-le-Lac, an estate in the town of Sainte Adolphe d'Howard; the resort had been listed for sale for two years before the Hasidim put in their $3.5 million offer, and no one else had shown interest. Yet when the Hasidim made their bid, the townspeople rallied against it.

The rhetoric of the media coverage, even in anglophone papers, is rarely favorable toward the Hasidim and their requests. In Montreal, in 2006, the Yetev Lev Satmar synagogue and school in the Mile End district asked the YMCA next door to put frosted glass on their windows so that their yeshiva pupils would not have a direct view of the women exercising in their gym clothes. The YMCA consulted with members and chose to comply, and the Hasidim paid for the renovation. Despite the easy resolution, there was a media outcry. Although one article noted that "only four people [have] . . . complained" in the nine months after the windows were replaced, the media coverage created precisely what it claimed the initial request did: a "tempest in a teapot" ("Faith, Fitness"). The flurry surrounding this incident is often cited as one of the reasons for the creation of a reasonable accommodation commission.

Furthermore, media coverage in Quebec (and beyond) often evokes the fear Richler's French-Canadian characters have in *The Apprenticeship of Duddy Kravitz* (1959): that Jews are going to invade the Edenic lands and destroy them.[8] An article on the purchase of Miramont-sur-le-Lac, which appeared in the *Winnipeg Free Press* and *Edmonton Journal*, begins, "St. Adolphe d'Howard is not accustomed to the spotlight. Under cover of Quebec's Laurentian hills and nestled among more than 80 lakes, the town 100 kilometers north of Montreal tends to be overshadowed by more popular areas nearby. Lately, they include the towns of Val David and Val Morin, which over the last few years have been making headlines for controversies surrounding Hasidic Jewish families who have summer homes there. Slowly but surely, the controversies have made their way over the green hills to small, sleepy St. Adolphe" (Blain, "Controversy"). The pastoral language of the article (the "green hills," the "sleepy" town) stands in juxtaposition to the words of the general manager of Miramont-sur-le-Lac, who predicts that the estate will now become "ghettoized" in the hands of the Hasidim (Hamilton).

In a similar vein, the *Montreal Gazette* reported that the Laurentians town of St. Jérôme had a "new thorn in their side: Jews. Ultra-orthodox Jews, more precisely—the Hasidim." A town meeting aired the following complaints about the "unreasonable" demands of the "ever-growing" number of Hasidic Jews:

> "The last shot they directed at us, was they set themselves up next to the baseball field and asked us to shut off the lights when they pray on Saturday evenings," reported one resident.
>
> "It's really a mentality that's separate," St. Hippolyte resident Lise Casavant said of the Hasidim, adding that immigrants should sign a new Quebec citizenship charter "or choose another province," a sentiment several other speakers also evoked. . . .
>
> And Lise Provencher, of St. Jérôme, said immigrants are "buying their way in" to Quebec and that Jews are the worst because they're "the most powerful. . . . It's always been said that the Jews are the trampoline of money in the world." After she spoke, the crowd applauded. (Heinrich, "Laurentian")

The comments move from a criticism of Hasidic isolation to a classic stereotype about Jewish money, an unfortunately unsurprising leap.[9] And even more problematically, the article reinforces the charges against the Hasidic community by concluding that "Hasidic Jews stand out by their separateness—even last night. There were none in the crowd to defend the community" (Heinrich, "Laurentian"). This apparent silence, read as a refusal to engage in the discussion, is one Zipora recognizes in her book of stories. "I was reminded that many of the misconceptions and misunderstandings about Hasidic life exist precisely because there has been very little explanation from the source," she writes (11–12). Yet the article's final statement, condemning the Hasidim to discrimination of their own making, blatantly neglects to note that the Hasidim typically do not reside in St. Jérôme after the summer and, based on the timing of the meeting (which fell two days after the holy day of Yom Kippur and a day and a half before Sukkoth), were likely consumed with holiday preparation, such as building their sukkahs.[10] Although Zipora makes the move to show that Hasidim can also be involved in neighborhood discussions, such discussions have and are too often arranged in a way that excludes the Hasidim. In yet another example, in June 2013, Quebec set its first fixed-date election, to take place in 2016—on Rosh Hashana.

Although not present to speak on behalf of their community during the town meeting, Hasidic women *did* speak up in response to the media depictions of Hasidic insularity and their property purchase when given a chance. One Hasidic woman, interviewed by sociologist William Shaffir, asked, "If Meharesh Yogi [a local yogi with a thriving studio in town] would have bought this place, what would anyone have said? They don't interact either, they're busy meditating. So who brought all this attention to the media?" (Shaffir 45). Why was this (logical) response not showcased in the media? Did the Hasidim really not care how they were being represented? Or were their responses being (yet again) silenced?

### III. Rather Engage than Isolate, Rather Speak than Be Silenced, Rather Act than Be Passive

*I originally wrote these stories for small magazines sold or distributed for my community. They covered issues that I discussed, laughed over or complained about with my friends as we sat on park benches nursing our babies, cleaning their faces of the sand they ate and threw at one another. In moments of inspiration, I would jot down my ideas on tissue boxes or make notes on junk mail while I stirred the soup.*

—Malka Zipora, *Lekhaim!* (2007)

*This book is in memory of my dear mother, who was my biggest motivator. She lived with incredible wisdom, creativity and purity of soul, dedicating her life*

*and energies to my father and to the children at the expense of denying herself*
*the things her heart may have liked to pursue. Through my book, I feel that in*
*some way I am fulfilling her aspirations and talent.*
—Malka Zipora, dedication to Lekhaim! (2007)

In *Lekhaim!*, Zipora shares intimate stories from her home—the carnivalesque nature of the "bedtime routine" with twelve children; the overwhelming expense of orthodontics, complicated by retainers that get tangled in *peyos*; and her desperate attempts to control a bad temper through emulations of rabbis of old. Zipora writes the book as a play on all the magazines, books, and blogs that address parenting issues, offering her own Hasidic-specific spin on them. She writes, in part, for her peers in Montreal, New York, and London—the other Hasidic women who also, daily, have twelve piles of homework to oversee, twelve lunches to pack, twelve burgeoning individuals to foster. And apart from their material similarities, these other women follow the same rules, religious and cultural, in Outremont, Crown Heights, and Stamford Hill. And one of these cultural (unwritten) rules is to observe *tznius* (modesty)—and not only in her attire. As we see from the opening lines of her book, it is crucial that Zipora foregrounds her commitment to motherhood, to activities like nursing and cooking, while leaving writing—her paid, creative work—on the "back burner" of her life. Her *tzniustic* attitude toward her writing is imperative: she tells readers, "I believe that the details surrounding the publication of the book, leading up to it, the characters involved in its conception and its publication were orchestrated by a Higher Hand. There were a series of events that *just so happened* to lead to a French publication of these stories" (9–10). She concludes that it was *bashert* (destiny) that landed her the publication of her book, and she "took it as a message that it was G-d's will that this book be published" (10). Her language echoes her religious commitment, of course, but also her unwillingness to assume credit for her work and therefore suggest she is an ambitious career woman or successful writer. She is, instead, a wife and mother who dabbles in writing while stirring the all-important soup. This is a language her Hasidic women readers understand and appreciate and would even perhaps recognize as a coded message. It is within the norms of Zipora's community for women to work outside the home (or in this case, for a venue outside the home), but dedication to the household is supposed to be given top priority.

Even as Zipora reaffirms the Hasidic woman's traditional primary obligation, she also shows Hasidim that they can do more, be more, and act more. A Hasidic woman does not have to act immodestly to fulfill her ambition; neither does she have to dedicate her life and energies to a husband and children "at the expense of denying herself the things her heart may have liked to pursue." In Zipora's book, every page attests to her role as a woman of valor in her home, but the publication of the book, and its dedication to a mother who did not see such endeavors as possible, attests to her role as a woman of valor in her community.

Yet Zipora is writing for more than Hasidic women across the globe; she is also writing for her non-Hasidic peers in Quebec. Her imagined local audience is not necessarily an unsympathetic francophone Quebecois audience, an audience that thinks the Hasidim of Quebec should "choose another province" or that "Jews are the trampoline of money in the world." But her audience is also not aware. Throughout the book, Zipora names, explains, and engages an unfamiliar reader. She intervenes in the conflict between Quebec's Hasidim and their neighbors—carefully, tactfully. She gives voice, through her writing, to women whose voices have not been heard—for the sake of her fellow Hasidic women, to show that their voices can be heard, and for the sake of non-Hasidic readers, to help them come to know her, even if only in some small way. By writing her stories, Zipora is ultimately redefining the Hasidic woman and her role in cultural relations.

"A truly Hassidic house is devoid of any external influences such as public media, whose entertainment prevails at the cost of values," writes Zipora (18). Nevertheless, in the twenty-first century, the internet has crept into many Hasidic households, and there are "kosher" novels and films. And then there are the ever-popular women's pan-Orthodox glossy magazines—primarily *Ami*, *Mishpacha*, and *Binah*. (From 2004 to 2013, there was also *Yaldah Magazine*, a *tznius* tween magazine started by a thirteen-year-old girl and run by an editorial board of twenty-odd international girls. The magazine focused on the age demographic of eight to fourteen years old; at its peak, its circulation was about three thousand!)[11] These are the kinds of magazines that Zipora mentions in her reference to her writerly past: "I originally wrote these stories for small magazines sold or distributed for my community" (9). The stories contained therein are rarely controversial. Instead, they are informative and entertaining and highly relevant to Haredi lifestyles. Zipora, for example, has an article in *Ami* about Hasidic life in Montreal that wouldn't have been out of place in an in-flight magazine, filled with details like the best kosher bakery and the option of $7 per day *frum* daycare. The stories and articles in these magazines follow strict, often unspoken, guidelines. As Montreal writer for *Mishpacha* and *Ami* Effy Fisher explained to me, a contributor to these magazines knows she is walking a fine line. Writing has to be interesting, but topics are limited. So is language. Authors can write about babies and motherhood (of course), but they can't use words like *abortion* or *embryo*. In one issue of the tween version of *Binah, called Binah Between—Binah* being the most liberal of the Orthodox women's magazines—a columnist uses the word *adapt* to discuss a South American plant. This term, suggestive of Darwin's *muktzeh* theory, became the cause for an angry letter to the editor (Daina 3). You can write about current events in the Haredi communities around the world (in fact, many of the readers get the majority of their news from these magazines), as Fisher explained, but most of the magazines avoid taking strong stances on divisive issues (Fisher, personal interview).[12]

The rules of these magazines are clear to the writers who contribute; they are often the same writers who, like Zipora, write children's stories and educational articles for forums with identical rules. Turning to a wider audience, however, is a challenge, one that emerging Orthodox filmmakers have learned in recent years: for example, Shuli Rand with *Ushpizin* (2006) and Burshtein with *Fill the Void* (2012) and *Through the Wall* (2016). Similar to Krich and Zipora, Burshtein imagined herself, with the production of *Fill the Void*, as "open[ing] a rare window into an insular world" (Miller). In an interview, Burshtein explained, "For me, [making the movie] was like opening a window . . . it's a window for you to look through. People will form their own opinions based on what they see. If I had tried to explain it, I think that window would have closed and it would have seemed like I was trying to make a documentary. When people are inside that world, living their lives, they're not explaining why they're doing this or that" (Miller). Despite the common use of the "window" metaphor, however, Zipora takes a different tact in her approach to showing non-Hasidic readers the lives of Hasidim. "If I wrote about visiting someone in the hospital on the Sabbath," she explains in the opening of *Lekhaim!*, "my Hassidic readers would know the unwritten part was that I had walked two miles to the hospital, climbed eight floors of stairs and walked two miles back, because on the Sabbath it is forbidden to use transportation or take an elevator" (11). This knowledge cannot be assumed when writing for a larger audience, and Zipora feels too much context is lost. So the tales become part fiction and part library reference book—and as a result, Zipora often seems didactic, not unlike Kellerman when she is instructing her readers on what *niddah* is and what it means for a woman posthysterectomy (not an area Zipora would touch!). But this instructive element is precisely how Zipora's small stories of a household take on their political significance. This is how they participate in an unspoken dialogue between disparate neighbors. After all, much of the friction between conflicting groups comes from unawareness: if the students in *Hadassa* cannot know whether or not their Christian teacher celebrates Hanukkah, Zipora's readers cannot be expected to be familiar with *negel vasser* or *kreplach*. So Zipora provides an index for her readers: an eight-page dictionary of Yiddish terms and their English translations that she gently titles, "A Little More Information."

While the index provides quick definitions for unfamiliar readers, Zipora's in-text translations might strike readers as odd. When she refers to the "Sabbath," the English term is followed by the parenthetical, italicized Yiddish: "(*Shabbos*)" (11). Rather than the Yiddish term followed by an English translation, in other words, one finds the reverse. *Destiny* is followed by "(*bashert*)," and the full expression "A person thinks, and G-d laughs" includes "(*a mentch tracht und der aibishter lacht*)" (11, 13). This continues apace. It is almost as though Zipora is translating for the outsider and then back again for the insider (i.e., *Dear fellow Hasid, what I'm trying to get across to our gentile friends is this concept we have, in case it wasn't clear*). Perhaps she is also suggesting that the meanings of expressions sometimes change along the way—which even an insider might forget. In any case, she does not limit herself to shifting between Yiddish and English but also throws in Hungarian, another old-world "how it was at home" language. "'That is how it was at home (*udj volt othon*),' she used to say," Zipora writes of her mother, giving us the translated English followed by Hungarian. She then follows the text with an interpretation of the meaning: "She meant that was how things should be" (16). Hasidic life comes to us aurally and polylingually; it is made up of different languages and customs that cannot be easily or directly translated. And awareness of Hasidic customs is not just for the foreigner. Zipora also aims to educate the Hasid about what is true and meaningful in *Hasidut*.

In teaching all her readers to be "fellow brothers and sisters," as she calls them, Zipora challenges the way that people in Quebec regard Hasidim as living anachronisms—great-grandfathers and foremothers (88). We see a legacy of this thinking in Quebecois culture. In 1954, non-Jewish Quebecois writer Yves Thériault wrote a novel called *Aaron*, in which the primary conflict is between Orthodoxy and modernity, made manifest in an old grandfather and his young grandson. More than thirty years later, non-Jewish writer, journalist, and filmmaker Jacques Godbout described Hasidim as earlier versions of himself and his fellow Quebecois: "We do not like to see the Hasidim proliferate because they remind us of who we were, our national decline, our rejection of the century, and that at that time of orthodoxy we had solidarity, concerned with our survival. The Hasidim want to be unique and distinct—us too" (180, my translation).

Of course, we see this anachronization by local secular Jews too. In 2005, for example, Montreal-born Dov Charney, CEO of American Apparel (who himself had been compared five years earlier by the *New Yorker*'s Malcolm Gladwell to the nineteenth-century *handschumachers*, the Eastern European immigrant Jewish glovemakers), created an advertisement featuring Hasidim (Gladwell 71). It consisted of a tableau of nine pictures of a Montreal Hasidic tailor depicted above the line, "There's nothing like the shmata business." The seemingly timeless image, paired with the Yiddish word for clothing, suggested that with American Apparel, Charney was upholding a long-standing Jewish tradition. Yet the Hasidic tailor was his contemporary, a twenty-first-century man engaging in a parallel business. Two years later, American Apparel returned to this theme, plastering the image of Woody Allen as he appears to his non-Jewish girlfriend's grandmother in the film *Annie Hall* on their billboards: in Hasidic garb. Unfortunately that didn't go so well for Charney: Allen sued him for unauthorized use of the image and won.[13]

By distinguishing between Hasidim living *in* history and living *through* history, Zipora's book forces readers to rethink their characterizations of Hasidim. Crucially, the characters are never, themselves, anachronisms. In her stories, the Hasidim speak on cell phones (in fact, phones loom large in the book, reminding us that communication and community share more than a common etymological ancestor). They visit physiotherapists. They use computers. There are two stories devoted to computer use, in fact, and they are followed by a chapter called "Women's Communication Network," suggesting an underlying relationship between yenta-ing and the internet. This modernity is not depicted as antithetical to the fundamental belief in passing down historical values to children and "sing[ing] the same songs their grandparents sang" (she adds, in a Whitmanian vein, "as they [the children] sing the story of Hanukkah, they sing of themselves and their parents and great grandparents from generations back"; 102). The twin desires—to be a part of their living world (involved in their community and their daily lives) and a part of history—appear thoroughly intertwined. Only through the lessons and rituals and traditions of history can they live in and interpret the modern world. Of course, it is also through the modern world that new lessons and rituals and traditions are invented (Haredization, we might recall, is a reaction to growing liberalism).

While this conceptual issue of image (of the Hasidim at large as well as the Hasidic woman in particular) is fundamental to Zipora's collection, she also confronts specific political conflicts head-on. One of these issues is that of the sukkah, the temporary structure that observant Jews construct and eat in during the fall holiday of Sukkoth to commemorate the "sojourn of the Jews in the desert while living under the protection of the clouds" (Zipora 152). In Outremont, sukkahs have been contentious since the turn of the twenty-first century. In Syndicat Northcrest v. Amselem, a condominium complex had them declared illegal in 1998 by the lower and superior courts of Quebec. The case went all the way to the Canadian Supreme Court before being overturned in 2004. Still, another law was passed in Outremont that a sukkah can only be up for two weeks (this law continues to be revisited nearly every year). In "Malice in Montreal," an article in *Ami*, readers can find a rich description of the scene:

> The independent city councilor [Céline Forget] has personally taken upon herself the thankless task of monitoring these regulations. Not her job, but having been personally responsible for the law's enactment, it's only right that she see to its enforcement as well. So there she is, meticulously recording every screw that goes in, then sending copious notes to City Hall noting the day and time that Reisner [a resident]'s *sukkah* went up. In the course of two weeks, Reisner will receive three notices from City Hall: the first informing him of the date and time his *sukkah* went up, the second reminding him when it must be taken down, and the third a warning that if it isn't down by then he will be fined—heavily. Woe to the *Yidden* should the first and last days of this two-week period fall on Shabbos. (Fisher, "Malice" 50)

The readership of *Ami*, who can only feel empathy for the "*Yidden*" of the article, know exactly why Forget's insistence on turning these sukkahs into her personal white whale is so harmful to the Hasidim of Outremont. The time limitation is deeply problematic, as the two-week period can prove insufficient. The Hasidim must have their sukkahs up before the eight-day holiday and take them down when it is done. There is only a four-day period between Yom Kippur and Sukkoth (when Jews traditionally build their sukkahs), and they are not allowed to build on Saturday because it is *their* day of rest or on Sunday in Quebec because it is the *provincial* day of rest (this deference to Catholic Sabbath observance is treated by the state as historic and national, just like the crucifix above the speaker's chair in the Quebec National Assembly; only minorities' religions require accommodation).

In "Squeezing in a Succah," Zipora begins her story, like many of her other ones, by explaining the Jewish- or Hasid-specific holiday or event at hand. In this case, she defines Sukkoth as "the holiday of remembrance of the Jewish exodus from Egypt and their travel through the desert" (152). But Zipora's story is neither about the Jews and their exodus nor about modern Montreal Jews celebrating. Instead, she actually begins at the close of the holiday: "The little huts perched on the balconies of the houses in the city of Outremont during the holiday of Succoth with their roofs of bamboo and ferns have all been packed away" (152). This is the story of a sukkah that has not, according to the law, been taken down—"to the chagrin," she writes, "of many of the non-Jewish Outremont dwellers who are accustomed to a city that is as well groomed as the poodles and pedigreed canines that they elegantly lead around the streets" (152). She knows that "if it stands around a few days longer, there are sure to be complaints from neighbors whose sensitive tastes cannot tolerate any impairment to the aesthetic air of this neighborhood" (153). Despite this satirical language and the repeated barbs at Outremont's elitism in the piece, "Squeezing in a Succah" offers a serious intervention in Hasidic-Quebecois relations. For one, Zipora attempts to see what resentful Quebecois (i.e., Celine Forget) see when they notice the Hasidim's rites and rituals. "It looks more like a tent for camping out," she writes, "or perhaps a tarpaulin covering a snow blower or a tank" (153). She can see that "this particular *succah* is a real klutz" (153).

But if the sukkah appears as a real klutz, that means it has been "looked at only with the eye and without the heart" (153). What if the sukkah could be looked at with the "heart" instead? What if instead of worrying about "taste" that is sensitive to "aesthetic" violations, citizens regarded the sukkah through its spirituality, through a love of community and family? This is what Zipora is arguing for in "Squeezing in a Succah," wherein Zipora's daughter, Sheindl, and Sheindl's husband, Shulem, try to erect a halachic sukkah on their balcony—a feat that seems impossible.

Much of the story follows Shulem and his male cohort's work with an air of suspense (Will they make it? Or will they fail?), taking us back in time to the days and hours leading up to the holiday:

> Two days before Succot . . . Shulem begins scrounging around for supplies. . . .
> The day before the holiday . . . Shulem . . . realizes that building a *succah* does
> not just involve randomly banging in nails. . . . By three o'clock with the help
> of neighbors the *succah* is up. . . . With three hours to the holiday . . . the *succah*
> as erected is rendered not kosher. . . . Two hours before sunset, the *dayan* him-
> self, accompanied by Talmudic students with Shulem and his friends tagging
> behind, come to study the *succah*, and figure out how it can be constructed in a
> way that would render it kosher. . . . His friends arrive from all directions with
> new supplies. . . . Sheindl lights the candles exactly ten minutes after Shulem
> throws the last tool into the tool box. (154–158)

We are reading a mystery story with no real mystery. Because the story begins with
the description of the klutz of a sukkah, we are assured of its success in the end.
And yet, a reader is made to sit on the edge of her seat, wondering how the victory
will be achieved, how the miracle, perhaps, will occur. The klutzy sukkah gathers
significance as readers, even those who had not known the term *sukkah* a few
pages back, are made to share the breathless anticipation of building and tearing
down and rebuilding the sukkah until the final creation, imagined by the reader,
leaps from the page as a model of perfection.

Yet there is more to the story than the men's labor. The rest of the story follows
the women's roles: cooking, consulting with each other, preparing backup plans,
recleaning the apartment every time a new troupe of Talmudic scholars comes
through. The women, per typical Haredi discourse, are spiritually ignorant ("I
do not have at my fingertips the fine points and complex rules for Succoth,
nor do I profess to understand the technical part of this particular 'learned succah' [*lomdishe succah*]"; "I am no Talmudic scholar. To me this *succah* is the odd-
est looking one I have ever seen") even as the women are more practical in every
way that would be understandable to a non-Hasidic reader (153, 159). It is the
women to whom the reader relates; the Hasidic women understand that the sukkah is ugly and know that it seems strange to build and destroy and rebuild a new
sukkah worse-looking than its predecessor. They are the ones who complete all
of the necessary preparations (cleaning, cooking, planning). And they are also
the ones who tell the non-Hasidic reader why the things that the men do should
also be appreciated—their abilities to parse the dense law, to solve complicated
problems, and to work *together* to serve their communal needs (perhaps the most
important lesson). Zipora's conclusion sets aside the frantic tone of the piece to
show the grandeur of the result, even as she continues to move deftly between
the opposing perspectives: "It is amazing how beautiful something so techni-
cally coarse could be. There is no way that the neighborhood of Outremont
will accept the *thing* as anything but trash. Eight days of this eyesore is too much.
But to the owners of this *succah*, it has special qualities and the holiday is just way
too short" (159). Of course, what was once merely an "eyesore" to readers is no

longer. It is now endowed with meaning and feeling. For Quebecois readers, the little huts are now symbolic of the history and work of their Jewish neighbors.

Moreover, the practicality, effectiveness, and relatability of women (without discounting the spiritual usefulness of men) in "Squeezing in a Succah" revises the images of Hasidic women for non-Jewish readers whose concerns about the roles of women in minority cultures helped lead to the Taylor-Bouchard Commission on Reasonable Accommodation of Minorities in Quebec.

## IV. Reasonable Accommodations

*A woman may, among other things: drive a car, vote freely, sign checks, dance,*
*decide for herself, express herself freely, clothe herself as she wishes while respect-*
*ing the standards of decency that have been decided democratically and accord-*
*ing to public safety, walk alone in public places, study, have a profession, possess*
*property, dispose of her property at will.*
   —from *Le Code de Vie d'Hérouxville* (January 25, 2007, my translation)

In teaching awareness beyond her own community, Zipora entered the fraught discussions in Quebec that hit their peak in 2006–2007 with the reasonable accommodation commission. The commission, according to Pierre Anctil and Howard Adelman's detailed account in *Religion, Culture, and the State: Reflections on the Bouchard-Taylor Report*, "was mandated to take stock of existing practices with respect to diversity within Québec society . . . conduct a broad process of consultation . . . [and] propose recommendations to the government to make sure that solutions already found and others to be implemented conformed to the core values of Québec as a pluralistic, democratic, and egalitarian society" (Adelman and Anctil 6). The commissioners traveled around the province and recorded responses on the ground and in the media to cultural conflicts: the YMCA window exchange, the purchase of Miramont-sur-le-Lac, and the "code of conduct" published in January 2007 by the small (white, Catholic, immigrant-free) town of Hérouxville and sent to the provincial and federal governments stating, "It is forbidden to stone women in public" and "Burning women alive or burning them with acid is not considered acceptable" (Drouin). The reaction to the YMCA, the purchase of lake property, and the code, as well as many other practices and declarations, revealed an anxiety about multiculturalism, with particular regard to the treatment of women by immigrant and other ethnic groups. While it was common to read the Hérouxville injunctions as anti-Muslim sentiment,[14] it was clear that Hasidim were also likely targets. The code, which addressed woman's attire (alluding to the modesty concerns of both Islam and Hasidism), was immediately linked in the press to the YMCA's "tempest in a teapot" and other "accommodations" for Hasidim (such as providing male examiners when Hasidic men took their driving tests and male police officers when interrogating Hasidic men).[15]

Quebecois were asking the question: Are these people a part of us? In "Hassidim and the 'Reasonable Accommodation' Debate in Quebec," Shaffir analyzes the responses of Quebec's Hasidim to the reasonable accommodation publicity, much of which intimated that Hasidim make poor neighbors. A Tosher woman tells him, "We don't want to be influenced from the outside. . . . We're trying to shelter our kids," and a Satmar woman says, "We are not a friendly group. . . . We stayed this way to stay the way we are" (41–42). Concludes Shaffir, "For hassidim, protection and preservation require erecting fences or enclosures and there must be full implementation at street level" (42). These responses and Shaffir's analysis suggest that the answer to "Are these people a part of us?" is "no"—not from the side of the Quebecois, with their codes of conduct keeping out foreign practices and implying that those who do not share their values and follow their ways ought to "choose another province," and not from the side of the Hasidim, who are busy erecting fences. But "fences" do not necessarily mean exclusion; if the proverb "good fences make good neighbors" were ever relevant, it might be here. In fact, the lack of assimilation of the Hasidim of Quebec is neither a call for special treatment nor even an indication of poor relations. Shaffir quotes one Hasidic woman as saying, "In *Ethics of our Fathers*, it says you should greet all your neighbours. I know all the neighbours on the block, even the biggest anti-Semite, because that's the kind of person I am" (40). Furthermore, how "friendly" one Hasid is might not be an indication of guidelines set in the community. A Hasidic woman complains about a Hasidic neighbor and then tells Shaffir, "Hasidim are people. Forget about what they look like. Some are friendly and some are not. And to generalize because one person doesn't say hello!" (40).

Ironically, write Anctil and Adelman, the term *accommodement* (accommodation) was widely misunderstood by the public giving their briefs to the Taylor-Bouchard Commission as well as the media reporting on it. "Reasonable accommodation," they explain, is a legal concept, "which appeared when federal courts judged that the provisions designed to protect various minorities from discrimination could miss their targets." It was *not* cases of "open-ended negotiation without legal significance, as in the case of the avenue du Parc YMCA" (Adelman and Anctil 9). The crisis, they argue, never really took place: "Brief after brief from social and public health organizations reached the Commission stressing the artificial nature of the debate supported by Bouchard and Taylor. They claimed that ways and means to accommodate the time of immigration had long been reached in Montreal. Cultural diversity and religious pluralism in certain neighbourhoods of Quebec's largest city had become commonplace, and examples of adjustment and adaptation [were] simply more widespread than instances of conflict or confrontation" (13). Despite the media's tempest—and what were perhaps real ideological differences—Anctil and Adelman, on the ground, determined that differences were being worked out. I would add that these negotiations were often done by women.

Zipora entered these discussions as both a Hasidic woman *and* a Canadian. In one of the best-known documentaries about Hasidic life, *A Life Apart*, Rabbi Arthur Hertzberg, a great scholar of American Judaism, declares, "Hasidim don't consider themselves American." Hasidism and nationality are rendered cleft. This claim is certainly questionable, as the permeability of cultural borders is evident in the cultural productions of American Hasidim. Nonetheless, Zipora makes no such statement about her national identity. Her identification as a Canadian is deeply significant for a book that is both a series of personal anecdotes and a political intervention. And her Canadianness is established through everyday actions, similar to her *Shabbos* reliance on her feet to get her places. "Winter is a unifying experience," begins one story (81). The paragraph continues with the use of the first-person plural: "We make up for the falling temperature by producing inner warmth, as we become one big family of fellow sufferers" (81). Continuing the familial metaphor, Zipora says of a neighbor who admonishes her for her lack of gloves, "She becomes my mother" (81). This neighbor is a fellow Hasidic woman, but Zipora makes clear that the "one big family of fellow sufferers" extends beyond the Hasidic community: "The below zero temperatures have made us Canadians a friendlier society . . . our main athletic pastime becomes pushing cars with revved up engines and spinning wheels out of snow banks. . . . When scientists threaten and warn us to change our lifestyles to avoid global warming, we Canadians dismiss them and advise them to address their concerns to the nomads in the Sahara desert" (82). Otherwise hostile neighbors find a point of common contention: "Instead of picking on each other, the weather becomes the punching bag" (86). In her conclusion, she returns to the kinship theme: "Why feel handicapped when we know this is part of the ritual that leads into spring? We are all part of that plan, and we should celebrate and relate to one another like one big family" (88). Using the language of "ritual" and the idea that Canadians are "all part" of a (predestined, ordained) plan, Zipora suggests that the weather that encourages her to address her readers as "fellow brothers and sisters" is God's intervention into Outremont's hostilities (88). Canadians, including Hasidim, have more uniting them than dividing them. Also, it's too cold to fight, so everyone should just get along. It might not be the sharpest political tool, but in a Montreal winter, it makes sense.

## V. Hasidic Women's Voices in Dialogue

*The situation has to change, and the best way to change things is to give yourself a voice. The most important thing is dialogue, because without dialogue, we will never find a solution.*

—Mindy Pollak, interview in *La Presse* (July 3, 2013)

QUEBECOIS GIRL 1:  How do you perceive us?

QUEBECOIS GIRL 2:  What are your prejudices?

HASIDIC GIRL 1:  We don't have prejudices. We don't judge someone before knowing her.

HASIDIC GIRL 2:  How about you? How do you see us all?

QUEBECOIS GIRL 3:  I think, at first, we had many prejudices because the truth is, at our school, Jews are badly perceived. That's unfortunate because we realize right away that it's not— [Her friends nod and smile.]

QUEBECOIS GIRL 4:  We hear lots of things and we don't know if it's true or false. The first time I saw you I said, "Wow, you're beautiful!" [Hasidic girls giggle.] For sure when we see Jews dressed in their black outfits, we say, "We don't know if they're beautiful because we can't see much." [Hasidic girls laugh and nod heads.]

QUEBECOIS GIRL 5:  You don't feel oppressed by this religion?

HASIDIC GIRL 3:  We're not so isolated. We see the world, we go out.

QUEBECOIS GIRL 5:  It's as if you were less free.

HASIDIC GIRL 1:  We live in the world, not just in our rooms, our synagogues.

QUEBECOIS GIRL 6:  Do you have internet, like Facebook? [Everyone laughs.]

HASIDIC GIRLS 2 AND 4:  Yes—even our principal!

—Scene from *Shekinah: The Intimate Life of Hasidic Women* (2013)

In recounting the story of Zipora's plan to meet the press, Mathilde Singer, writing in the French magazine *Voir*, explained the Hasidic author's terms of engagement: "Malka Zipora was willing to meet journalists at the Outremont library to celebrate the launch of her collection of short stories titled, *Lekhaim! Chroniques de la vie hassidique à Montréal*, published by Éditions du Passage, on the condition that there were only women at the press conference and no one took a photo" (my translation). For many, it was acceptable to defer to the preferences of the woman being celebrated; after all, if Van Halen can demand that all brown M&Ms be removed from their band's candy bowl backstage, it seems not out of the question that a religious woman could ask that her audience comply with a request to accommodate her religious principles. One might even consider the gathering of fellow professional women a feminist manoeuver, not so different from the hundreds of professional women's networks that have been established across the globe to help women empower fellow women. We might view it as the creation of a safe and supportive women-only space—an idea, as we shall see, that is touched on in *Kaaterskill Falls* in the fictional vision of a Catskills grocery store where women are given the chance to congregate as men do in their religious studies. Such a request is also a reality in the cinemas and concert halls in which Orthodox women filmmakers and rock bands restrict male entry to their productions and performances.

For some, Zipora's attempt at bridge building—on her own terms—was not and could not be good enough. A decade after the book's publication, Pierre Lacerte's French-language blog *Accommodents Outremont*, its sole aim to catalogue and condemn what he sees as the cultural, political, and ethical violations of the Hasidim of Outremont, harshly reminded readers of Zipora's request as a painful historical event to be remembered along with the French defeat by the English at the Plains of Abraham. "Allo le pont, toi!" (Hail the bridge, you!) snarked Lacerte in his entry on January 22, 2017. The suggestion inherent in his criticism is obvious: without Zipora fully conforming to ancestrally Catholic, French-speaking, France- and Quebec-descending, secular, "pur laine" attitudes and behaviors (and blood, ideally), her attempts at a "bridge" should be resolutely rejected. Lacerte, however, is in the minority. As he admits, the "soil of the internet has been germinated" (with a tone that implies "contaminated") with blogs preaching "inclusive love":

> Since Mindy Pollak, of the Vishnitz sect, and Project Montreal, launched *Friends of Hutchison Street* in 2011, under the tutelage of the ultra-Orthodox lobbyist Mayer Feig, there followed, in 2012, the sites *Bill 613* and *Outremont Hassid* [one created by a Hasidic rabbi, the other by ultra-Orthodox activists], then *Rue Hutchison*, a blog posted in 2013 by Christian Aubry, a French resident calling himself an atheist. In 2014, even the *Daughters and Sons of an Open Quebec* joined this select club that preaches sincere dialogue, social peace, compassion, harmony with the Hasidic community, multiculturalism galore, virtue [who can be against virtue?], peace in the world. Since November 2016, in the aftermath of the referendum campaign, a new wave of inclusive love and openness has begun to unfold online. *Citizens for an inclusive Outremont, The Bridge of Outremont,* and the *Committee for the Promotion of Pluralism within the Outremont Schools* have appeared in the neighborhood's blue flower landscape. This last closed group, that has 32 members, was unveiled to us at the last meeting of the borough council (my translation).

Ironically, Lacerte's January 22, 2017, blog post fails as a condemnation of Hasidim and Hasidic allies and acts instead as a testament to the tremendous outpouring of virtual "inclusive love." And this *virtual* love does not even account for the groups that meet in person, the political achievements, and the daily interpersonal interactions between Quebecois and Hasidic Quebeckers.[16]

Indeed, the community efforts that have ensued in the wake of Zipora's book suggest how inspirational her short stories were. The continued tensions, however, explain why such inspiration might be required. Less than a year after Zipora's book was released, in 2008, a new anti-Semitic incident occurred in the Laurentians: On August 16, a father and three sons, all wearing yarmulkes, were en route to a synagogue in Sainte Agathe, when a group of teenagers approached them, threw pennies at them, and then struck the eldest of the sons in the face, causing him to bleed (Arnold, "Assault"). Rather than use this latest incident as yet another weapon for the stockpile and further entrench both sides, a bride-to-be called Hana Sellem suggested her wedding be used to continue "bridge building." On August 30, two weeks after the assault, an article by journalist Jeff Heinrich appeared in the *Montreal Gazette* titled, "Hasidic Couple Invites Town to Wedding," with the subheading, "Ste. Agathe Residents Are Asked to Bring an Open Mind to Help Build a Bridge between Two Cultures" (Heinrich, "Hasidic Couple"). Sellem was an immigrant from France, a doctoral student, and the vice-principal at Beis Moshe Chaim Teachers' Seminary (BMC) in Sainte-Agathe-des-Monts. She created pamphlets explaining the Hasidic wedding rituals to the town, shifting the nature of the event from personal to educational and public.

If Sellem felt pamphlets were necessary to explain unfamiliar terms, much like Zipora with her "A Little More Information," defining words like *kugel* and *rebbe*, there was also, for Sellem, a Ziporan stress on familiar sentiments. Ruth Roumani, Sellem's mother, told the media that she thought the public nature of the wedding was "a good thing, because we have more in common with each other than we believe" ("Hasidic Couple Hosts"). Even the location of the event was chosen to foster the wedding's role in Hasidic-Quebecois relations. Rather than book the wedding at the synagogue run by the local Lubavitch rabbi, Sellem said, "I went to the town and asked them if they could lend me their building for the wedding.... They told me it was for cultural events, not private, but I told them I wanted to make my wedding into a cultural event, and they liked the idea" (Heinrich, "Hasidic Couple"). Sellem approached the mayor of Sainte Agathe as well. "I think it's a great opportunity to get more openness on everybody's part," she told the *Gazette*. "From every community, everyone can learn something from it, and I'm sure they're going to enjoy it" (Heinrich, "Hasidic Couple"). She publicized the "cultural event" through the media, giving interviews to both French and English newspapers, as well as CBC Radio and CBC Television.

The town officials echoed Sellem's sentiment, and the wedding took place surrounded by "curious onlookers" who "gathered by the lake," where Sellem and her groom "were married in an unusually public Hasidic Jewish ceremony" (Heinrich, "Very Public Wedding"). Although Heinrich describes the religious beliefs of the couple as "fundamentalist," he notes that the "ceremony was meant not only for them but for Ste. Agathe.... The wedding was deliberately public." Heinrich recognizes Sellem's attempt "to demystify her Chabad-Lubavitch brand of Jewish ultraorthodoxy in this otherwise nominally Roman Catholic town" (Heinrich, "Very Public Wedding"). Moreover, the reaction, according to Heinrich, was positive. He writes, "Mission accomplished," and quotes a francophone neighbor, who felt that the wedding united the neighbors, who had previously been strangers: "'I hope this event will inspire others—it should have been done

a long time ago, because it's so necessary to bring our nationalities together,'
said retired nurse Marie Fortin, who lives in a condo complex next to the park
and whose downstairs neighbours are Jews from Texas" (Heinrich, "Very Public
Wedding").[17]

And if art could inspire real-world activism in the fraught Quebecois-Hasidic
relations of twenty-first-century Quebec, the reverse is true as well. The Sellem
story caught the eye of filmmaker Abbey Jack Neidik, whose large oeuvre of
documentaries has covered humanitarian stories the world over: honor kill-
ings in Kurdistan, mental illness, Tibetan refugees, the effects of industrial wind
turbines, Romanian orphans after the fall of Ceausescu, and Hurricane Katrina
evacuees. He has currently moved beyond our world to examine the privatization
of outer space. In 2013, after several years of visiting BMC Seminary, he produced
a film about the Hasidic women of Quebec (specifically Chabad). *Shekinah: The
Intimate Life of Hasidic Women*, which captivated both non-Hasidic and Hasidic
audiences and won the best documentary award at the Crown Heights Film Festival in 2014, is a romantic vision of Hasidic women. At the center is not Sellem
(though she is a gateway into the "intimate life") but the founder and director of
her seminary, Rebbetzin Chanie Carlebach.

Carlebach is a force of nature—on screen and in person. Originally from New
York, Carlebach, wife of Rabbi Emanuel Carlebach, the rabbi of Sainte Agathe's
House of Israel synagogue (where my father-in-law *davens* every *Shabbos* during the summer months), opened her seminary in 2001, a year after the death
of her infant son, Moshe Chaim, for whom the seminary was named. Carlebach has eleven children besides Moshe Chaim; in the film, she says, "People
sometimes say, 'Awww, you're just a baby machine,' and I always say to them,
'I'm happy the machine works.'" But her work at the seminary is no side job.
In a slightly tense moment of the film, Carlebach, who otherwise only speaks
well of her family and community, admits, "Funny . . . sometimes my husband
feels that, you know, everything I'm doing takes away from the kids. I say . . . oh
wow . . . you know [laugh] 'That's nice.'"

Neidik's film, at least at the outset, conforms to every imaginable stereotype
about Hasidim. He begins with a long shot of Hasidic Jews (a woman in an ankle-
length skirt; a man in a *shtreimel*, which is not even Chabad attire; another man
in a velvet *kippah* and *peyos*) and then cuts to a close-up of himself, a noticeably
secular man with uncovered head and blue jeans. We know he is the eye of the
film because we see him polishing his camera. A voiceover tells us, "I was raised
by my grandmother, who came from a poor Jewish shtetl in Russia." With this
pronouncement, Neidik links twenty-first-century New World Hasidim with the
time of his grandmother and the Old World. Furthering this trope of anachronization, Neidik digs through black-and-white and sepia pictures and announces,
"If you ever saw *Fiddler on the Roof*, that's how it was growing up with her." He
cuts to a scene of a boy, his back to us, a black hat on his head, *peyos* hanging by

his ears, cars whizzing past (we're not in the Old World, after all!), and he says wistfully, "There is wisdom in tradition, but most of the Old World is gone now. That's why I'm fascinated with the Hasids in my neighborhood."

If Neidik's opening grates me, it likely entices viewers more accustomed to thinking that Hasidim really are walking anachronisms or deserters from the set of *Fiddler on the Roof.* So perhaps it is not a bad opening. Over the course of the film, we get to know the Hasidic girls more "intimately," and we discover that they are worldly and knowledgeable, much like those from Crown Heights that Stephanie Levine, in *Mystics, Mavericks, and Merrymakers,* comes to know and render "intimately." The girls at BMC come from countries far and wide to attend the seminary, and even during their time there, they are not confined to the small mountain town where they learn. The film follows Carlebach to Paris for the wedding of one of her alumnae and to New York when the BMC girls visit "770," as Chabad headquarters is known.

Juxtaposed against local non-Jewish Quebecois girls, the BMC girls appear and sound sophisticated and polished. No longer contemporaries of Neidik's grandmother, Carlebach and the girls, by the film's end, come across as women poised for the adventures of the twenty-first century. They are smart and diplomatic and know how to engage in meaningful dialogue—dialogue that makes the young Quebecois girls who "had many prejudices because . . . at our school, Jews are badly perceived" realize their Hasidic counterparts are not "isolated" or "oppressed" or less free. Rather, they are cosmopolitan women who plainly demonstrate their broad perspectives to their neighbors and Neidik's viewers through their response to the Quebecois girls: "We see the world, we go out. . . . We live in the world, not just in our rooms, our synagogues." Musing over Neidik's time with her and the seminary, Carlebach tells me that she likes the way his vision of Hasidic girls and women changed over his time with them. But she also worries that his vision will replace the Chabad women's vision of themselves, so she made her own short video for the seminary website, where her voice is the one to speak on behalf on Chabad women. And it begins with a list that gives viewers a sense of her idea of women's roles—in an order that should not be ignored: "Women as Leaders, Women as Teachers, Women as Wives, Women as Mothers" (BMC). The women might be pleased if the machines work, but they also know that the machines are complicated devices. As they tell us, they are made for more than babies.

To conclude this story of Quebec's Hasidic women gaining their voices and engaging in dialogue in books, on screen, and in personal interactions, I want to look at a development on the political front. On November 3, 2013, Mindy Pollak, a Vishnitzer,[18] became the first Hasidic woman to hold political office. Her journey to the seat of borough councillor of Claude-Ryan in Outremont was both fraught and historically significant. It would be three years until Pollak had an American counterpart—Rachel ("Ruchie") Freier, who once responded, damningly, in *The Forward* to Judy Brown's critique of the biological imperative to procreate that turns Hasidic women into "vessels." A lawyer, activist, volunteer for Ezras Nashim (an all-female Orthodox women's EMT ambulance service, which featured in the 2018 documentary *93Queen*), and mother of six, Freier became an elected official as a civil court judge in Brooklyn in November 2016.[19] As for Pollak, she was a mere twenty-four years old when she ran for office, and she had already made inroads into harmonious relations between Hasidic and non-Hasidic neighbors. Along with a non-Jewish neighbor, she ran the food blog *Esseat* (a title that mixes the words for *eat* in Yiddish and English), and she cofounded with Palestinian Canadian filmmaker and novelist Leila Marshy the aforementioned Friends of Hutchison St. (Les Amis de Hutchison), an organization whose mission is to support a continuing dialogue between the residents.[20]

Pollak ran because she found Outremont's situation untenable. For years, as the article on sukkahs claims, the borough councillor, Céline Forget, did everything in her power to make the Hasidic community of Outremont as uncomfortable as possible. In 1999, she lobbied to have a synagogue closed down. In 2001, she took the Hasidim to court claiming their *eruv* impeded her ability to fly a kite in the neighborhood. In 2007, she charged at a Hasid with her car after arguing with him on the street. In 2011, she started a flyer campaign to encourage residents to vote against a bathroom renovation at an old Bobover synagogue. In 2012, she had a moratorium put on all public processions for a little over a month to block the procession of the visiting high rabbi of Skver Hasidim. Pollak, who ran against Lacerte, the blogger, centered her campaign on communication and unity. And she won.

There is more work to be done to build and rebuild the proverbial bridges in Quebec, and perhaps there is no bridge long enough or strong enough to sustain the many and varied attacks on Quebec's minorities—Hasidim primarily, though not exclusively, among them. But writers and filmmakers are trying to help by putting down building blocks: Malka Zipora, Myriam Beaudoin, Abla Farhoud, Abby Neidik, and Maxime Giroux (whose *Félix et Meira* ends with the rather Zangwillian melting-pot union of the Hasidic woman and Quebecois neighbor). The combination of blocks does not necessarily form a cohesive or stable base. Pollak, for example, could hardly see herself in line with Giroux's depiction of a Hasidic woman. "Do I seem meek to you?" Pollak demanded to know when asked about Meira's portrayal in Giroux's film. According to the reporter who interviewed Pollak about becoming Montreal's first Hasidic city councillor, "It was admittedly difficult to imagine the bright and animated city councillor as anything but determined and expressive." Neither would Pollak allow Hasidic women to be imagined as shut up in their homes. "We're entrepreneurs, comedians, singers, and doctors," she said (Chandrachud).

But Meira does represent a piece of the story. Before she abandons her community for freedom (New York, Venice, a new clean-shaven man), Giroux's Meira, shut up in her home, spends her time heavy-handedly snapping mousetraps. She is not permitted to listen to the music she enjoys. The film shows her with her eyes downcast, and she tells Félix, "I'm not allowed to look men in the eye." This is not how Hasidic women necessarily want to see themselves represented. "We aren't all oppressed," Pollak insisted (Chandrachud). Still, Giroux's Meira is one kind of block—a reminder of a feeling, thinking, shivering-from-the-cold woman living in Quebec, perhaps a neighbor to a viewer of the film. And a big enough pile of blocks—of all kinds—can help support the piers and abutments of blogging communities, the girders of politicians, and most of all, the foundations created by the citizens of the province, all of whom are finding their voices and learning how to engage in dialogue.

Through the range of voices, in other words, bridges are built, and these bridges are good for both the alienated communities and the communities that alienate. Some of these bridges improve the Jewish community. Some diversify Orthodox women's images. And some enhance the lives of the people on the other end of the bridge: the non-Jewish neighbors. As a borough councillor, Mindy Pollak plays an important role in enriching the city of Montreal through her unique history and set of values, and many people benefit from her work. On a sunny day, you can see her neighbors joining her in the community-driven activities she leads, from cleaning up the city to planting trees (not quite planting a vineyard, but Montreal is urban, after all).

Because they are *not* confined to the home, Orthodox Jewish women have many opportunities to contribute to the societies they inhabit—socially, politically, and economically. And in the next chapter, I will consider the last of these—the ability of Orthodox women to enter and master the workaday world.

CHAPTER 4

# She Senses That Her Enterprise Is Good

REPRESENTATIONS OF ORTHODOX BUSINESSWOMEN

## I. Introduction

*Emma Barnett is 29 and Women's Editor of the Daily Telegraph. She regards herself as a feminist; she demands equality in the workplace and in all aspects of her secular life. But she has a secret: as an orthodox Jew, when attending synagogue, she is happy to sit separately from the men, not to take part in the service and finds it hard to embrace the concept of women rabbis.*

—BBC Radio 4, March 7, 2014

*A rising star at the agency, Neuberger, 39, has worked at the Pentagon, helped plan the U.S. military's Cyber Command and served as NSA liaison to private tech companies. But what makes her story unique is where she came from. . . . As a girl, Anne Neuberger . . . grew up in a Hasidic neighborhood in Brooklyn, N.Y., largely segregated from the secular world. She spoke Yiddish at home and attended an all-girls Jewish school, where half the day was devoted to religious instruction. A woman in her ultra-Orthodox community was expected to think of herself first as a wife and mother. It was not an environment that normally supported professional aspirations.*

—NPR Radio, July 12, 2015

Turn on the radio in England or the United States, and you might hear a startling confession. "I have a bit of an embarrassing secret," begins Emma Barnett in a quiet, almost conspiratorial voice in her March 2014 two-part "One to One" talk on BBC Radio 4. By twenty-nine, Barnett had done well in her field: the women's editor of the newspaper, the *Daily Telegraph*; creator of "Wonder Women," the *Telegraph*'s digital women's section; and a judge on *BBC Woman's House* power list in 2014. She was a paragon of young, empowered womanhood in a field dedicated to the elevation of women. It seems impossible that a woman who would spend her time writing such articles as "Women Lose Custody of Their Ambition—and Don't Even Know It" (July 2015) and "The Slow Death of Sexism: Women Must Stand Their Ground" (October 2015) would choose to be a part of a misogynistic religious group. Yet we can only imagine Orthodoxy is precisely that, listening to her hushed tone as she reveals her "embarrassing secret."

In her BBC Radio 4 interviews with a barrister, a fellow professionally successful Orthodox Jewish woman, and a female rabbi, Barnett attempts to account for the glaring discrepancies between feminist professional ambition and Jewish Orthodoxy. Listeners wait for these women to solve what can only be a paradox or defend their hypocritical choices. But the result of their endeavors seems feeble, particularly if passed through the echo chamber of American history. The barrister hesitantly explains that while she would never accept a limit put on her professional life due to gender, within Judaism, she accepts that "there are some things that I believe are different but equal," a position Barnett takes as her own.

Across the Atlantic, Anne Neuberger was appointed by the National Security Agency as chief risk manager in 2015, a high-ranking position and the first of its kind, created in the aftermath of the Edward Snowden leaks. Neuberger offers a similar admission: despite her professional achievement, she too is an Orthodox Jewish woman. To the mainstream American listeners of NPR's profile of the NSA's "rising star" (as to the mainstream British listeners of the BBC's "One to One" with Emma Barnett), this conjunction is presented as highly unlikely. Radio host Tom Gjelten says of Neuberger, "A woman in her ultra-Orthodox community was expected to think of herself first as a wife and mother. It was not an environment that normally supported professional aspirations."

Yet here is Neuberger, a Washington powerhouse, committed to her faith, which Americans are now told, "helps explain her rise to the top." Neuberger's voice intervenes to justify this claim: "The discipline and rigor, the restrictions on what one can eat, the restrictions on how one behaves, I hope I bring that in values, living true to one's values, trying to bring that integrity into the way you approach your job each day and how you interact with people, every single day" (Gjelten). Rather than a separation of spheres or nonoverlapping magisteria, in the manner of Barnett, Neuberger insists on a synergistic relationship, suggesting the principles of success in her work are drawn directly from those of her strict Orthodoxy.[1]

In their radio talks, both Barnett and Neuberger acknowledge the tension between their professional aspirations and faith and offer two distinct accounts of reconciliation. The disjuncture of their resolutions might lie, in part, in national discrepancies. Barnett and her colleagues imply that they live in a country where proclaiming religion at all, and particularly the Jewish religion, is seen as slightly vulgar. "Britons shudder at public piety," according to David Voas and Rodney Ling, sociologists of religion, who did a comparative study of British and American attitudes toward religion (65). The British barrister says, "Judaism, in this country, as opposed to perhaps in the States, it's like saying the word 'cancer.' You say [here she whispers] *I'm Jewish.*" Barnett admits that she and her generation refer to themselves as "'Wej's [Jew backward] as code when we're out."[2] In the United States, conversely, religious affiliation is rarely considered "vulgar" (the halls of academe aside) but rather a staple of mainstream culture. In every election, we see again how it is a *requirement* of the country's leadership. Thus in his June 21, 2016, attack on Democratic presidential candidate Hillary Clinton, Republican presidential candidate Donald Trump ominously declared, "We don't know anything about Hillary in terms of religion. Now, she's been in the public eye for years and years, and yet there's no—there's *nothing out there*" ("Donald Trump Questions"). Perhaps this American commitment to faith, even if "faith" is generally metonymic of "Christian faith," is what allows Gjelten to conclude of Neuberger's success: "Her professional achievements have come not in spite of her faith. They've come because of it."

Yet the straightforwardness of this claim is one we ought to regard with some suspicion. Neuberger's faith is *not* Christian; it does not even sit comfortably in the hazier and more generic rhetoric of "Judeo-Christian faith." It's unfamiliar, even to most American Jews. In some ways, the NSA uses this foreignness to its advantage. As an Israeli newspaper noted, Neuberger is being "exposed as part of the NSA's PR face" (Benhorin). By including Neuberger, the NSA, and the United States at large, appears open-minded and cosmopolitan. And this inclusion is easy in part because of the generalizability of the values Neuberger cites—discipline, rigor, and integrity. But as philosopher Kwame Anthony Appiah argues, fundamentalisms (and/or neofundamentalisms) are forms of countercosmopolitanism due to their insistence on cultural purity and "one right way," and thus they are not easily co-opted by the dominant culture (Appiah 144).[3] Ultimately, Gjelten's logic is (or, at least, *should be*) surprising, because any further knowledge of Neuberger's community would suggest the universalizability of her experiences and practice ends with the familiar terms she trots out.

Neuberger, as Gjelten's introduction informs listeners, grew up in the Satmar Hasidic sect, which is known for its insularity and strict gender roles that lead to limited professional possibilities for women. This genre of stringent Jewish Orthodoxy was rarely in the spotlight before the publication of Deborah Feldman's *Unorthodox* (an *Oprah Magazine* top pick!), when Satmar suddenly became a household word. At that point, anyone with access to a television or internet would have been exposed to Feldman's angry diatribes against the Satmars: Feldman was interviewed on ABC's *The View*, CNN's blog ("Inside the World of Satmar Jews"), *Anderson Live*, and other televised media. By late 2012, Satmars were still in the news and had developed an even *more* sinister ring with the Weberman trial. Thus although the lives of Satmars were (and still are) an enigma for most Americans, listeners of Gjelten's program would have understood that Neuberger was not raised in a liberal environment that sent girls to academically excellent, private, nondenominational high schools that encouraged them to be the best in their fields and included alumnae like the famous suffragist Pankhurst sisters— as was Emma Barnett.[4] At Satmar schools, according to Feldman, "they censor the word [college] out of our textbooks. Education, they say, leads to no good" (81). After marriage, women "spend their days shuttling back and forth between their parents' home and their new apartment, busying themselves with daughterly and wifely duties" (136). They are forbidden the reading of secular books, driving, painting their nails, showing their hair, seeing movies, wearing jeans, speaking their minds ("Women have no real place in a conversation. They should be busy serving food and cleaning up," explains Feldman [200]). If the values of "discipline and rigor" or the ability to cope with "restrictions" have an essential place in the Satmar woman's vocabulary (and clearly they do), these terms hold meanings rather distinct from those circulating in mainstream diction.

In this chapter, I want to explore the logic that Orthodox women become successful *because*, not *in spite of*, their religious belief. This logic can be found in contemporary fiction about Orthodox Jewish women who are professionally ambitious, such as Allegra Goodman's *Kaaterskill Falls* (1998), a novel that broke new ground in its representation of working womanhood within a potentially feminist Orthodox Judaism. Whereas the previous chapters of this book have explored areas of empowerment for women largely in the sphere of community (traditionally a more "feminine" sphere), this chapter turns to paid work as the site of inquiry, a crucial testing ground for a religious community that has been deemed anachronistic, complete with prefeminist limitations on women's professional roles. Like Thomas Hardy, who used his novel *Tess of the D'Urbervilles* a century earlier to revise the model of womanhood from the frail, dependent "angel in the house" to the strong, independent "New Woman" using the woman of valor from Proverbs 31, Goodman also constructs the image of the contemporary Orthodox businesswoman using the same source. Her protagonist, Elizabeth Shulman, is unusual. She is, in some ways, a descendent of the protagonist of *The Rise of David Levinsky*, Abraham Cahan's version of *The Art of the Deal*. Or perhaps she better resembles Edna Pontellier of Kate Chopin's *The Awakening*. Could she be the star of a latter-day sequel to Cahan's novella, *Yekl* ("Elizabeth Shulman: Gitl's Revenge")? In truth, Elizabeth does not have a clear literary precedent. What she does have are literary antagonists: characters in novels and films that employ the woman of valor to demonstrate that Orthodoxy and professional success are irreconcilable for a Jewish woman. As in the BBC and NPR interviews, however, Goodman's story rejects this model of either/or. Elizabeth offers a paradigm of both/and: both a wig-wearing observant Jewish woman and an ambitious entrepreneur.

Here as well, national context matters: Goodman makes her heroine a British woman, and perhaps this is partly why Elizabeth is, at first, hesitant in her path. But as Elizabeth becomes entrenched in the American landscape and its values, her confidence grows; she realizes the advantages of infusing commerce into her Judaism and Judaism into her commerce. Evoking and intervening in an American Jewish literary tradition, Goodman tells her story in the style of the immigrant tales that were prominent in the early twentieth century in the United States—but with a difference. Goodman's yearning immigrant is a product (and producer) of a feminist, postsecular landscape.

Yet America alone cannot solve women's challenges in Orthodoxy. For Judaism, it's the text that matters. Goodman recognizes the need to authenticate her fiction *halachically*—in accordance with Jewish law. There is no attempt to use her novel to claim perfect equality in Orthodoxy. Goodman does, however, hold up the idea of an empowered working woman as a Jewish ideal. She does so by producing a Jewish source, a piece of scripture, an indisputable text that carries great weight in affirming not only an individual woman's ability to synthesize competing ambitions but also Judaism's. Teaching readers to do a better close reading of the text, as the good scholar of literature that she is,[5] Goodman sidelines common feminist critiques of Orthodox Judaism, shifting the blame, as it were, onto the idiosyncratic implementation of the religion: the rabbis who get it wrong.

The source is (yet again) the passage from Proverbs 31. We are reminded that the ideal woman of valor was commended not only because of her religious and familial devotion but also because she "senses that her enterprise is good [profitable]." Sung every week to Jewish women by their family members, the "Eshes Chayil," which highlights the empowered businesswoman, is more than a nice *niggun*. It is a Jewish text that is more important and more *authentic* than the whims of rabbis and communities whose interpretations of Jewish law and custom might be arbitrary and overturned in the next generation.

## II. "She Anticipates the Needs of Her Household" (Only?): Or, Conflated Models of Womanhood

*"Who can find a virtuous woman? for her price is far above rubies. She riseth while it is yet night, and giveth meat to her household. She girdeth her loins with strength and strengtheneth her arms. She perceiveth that her merchandise is good; her candle goeth not out by night. She looketh well to the ways of her household, and eateth not the bread of idleness. Her children arise up and call her blessed; her husband also, and he praiseth her. Many daughters have done virtuously, but thou excellest them all."*

*When the prayers were over, his mother said—*

*"I could not help thinking how very aptly that chapter your dear father read applied, in some of its particulars, to the woman you have chosen. The perfect woman, you see, was a working woman."*

—Thomas Hardy, *Tess of the d'Urbervilles* (1891; emphasis mine)

*"Who Can Find a Valiant Woman?" was asked frequently from the pulpit and
the editorial pages. There was only one place to look for her—at home. Clearly
and confidently these authorities proclaimed the True Woman of the nineteenth
century to be the Valiant Woman of the Bible, in whom the heart of her husband
rejoiced and whose price was above rubies.*

—Barbara Welter, "The Cult of True Womanhood: 1820–1860,"
*American Quarterly* (1966; emphasis mine)

Played out in newspaper articles, novels, and films, the idea of the Orthodox
Jewish woman at the turn of the twenty-first century has been one of a woman
dedicated to her religious ideals, her modesty, her husband and children, and
her home. She is, in short, a figure from the past, a model familiar to most of
Western civilization as the prefeminist woman of the cult of domesticity, or true
womanhood, defined by Barbara Welter in her influential feminist article published in *American Quarterly* in 1966. "The attributes of True Womanhood, by
which a woman judged herself and was judged by her husband, her neighbors
and society could be divided into four cardinal virtues: piety, purity, submissiveness, and domesticity," writes Welter. "Put them all together and they spelled
mother, daughter, sister, wife—woman" (152). How else could we see Rachel,
the "good" Jewish wife and foil for Sonia (a "bad" Hasidic woman who had a
"fire burning inside" her), in Boaz Yakin's 1998 film *A Price above Rubies?* Rachel
appears in the film—hair covered, clothing modest—to coax Sonia, her difficult sister-in-law, into handing her infant son over for his ritual circumcision;
to host Shabbat dinner; to help Sonia decorate her home; to comfort family
members; to be, always, surrounded by and caring for children.[6] Sonia, in contrast, munches on an eggroll with pork, neglects her baby, feeds her husband TV
dinners, and is never as happy as she is out and about doing business with the
cosmopolitan inhabitants of Manhattan. Also, she sleeps around. Yet the irony
of Yakin's evocative film title—we are meant to see Sonia as the truly valuable
one and Rachel as modeled on an outdated biblical ideal—rests on the assump-
tion that the Jewish woman of valor is no different from the Victorian-era true
woman.

A year after *A Price above Rubies* was released, Tova Mirvis's novel *The Ladies
Auxiliary,* written in the collective voice of the Orthodox Jewish women of Memphis, begins with the onset of the Sabbath and the men singing "Eshes Chayil."
The women are reported to think, as they listen to the words of the hymn, "As we
took in our husbands' thankful faces, we felt appreciated like no other time. We
didn't mind doing the housework, but still, a little gratitude was nice" (Mirvis,
*Ladies* 20). That this is satire—that these women are strong and powerful and
run the entire community—only becomes apparent later in the novel (to themselves, it seems, as well as readers). Mirvis interprets the Jewish woman of valor
as Yakin does—as inseparable from the Victorian true woman.

The cult of domesticity, in fact, defined itself, according to Welter, by the passage from Proverbs 31. But it was a selective reading of the woman of valor that made the true woman a "hostage in the home"—much like the eponymous heroine of British poet Coventry Patmore's 1854 "The Angel in the House" (Welter 151). "Man must be pleased," writes Patmore, "but him to please / Is woman's pleasure" (Patmore). We see Patmore's angel in the house in her various evolutions—loving, weeping, charming, smiling, leaning, pitying, and praising—but her actions, her movements, and her words are few. "Patmore adduces many details to stress the almost pathetic ordinariness of her life," write Sandra Gilbert and Susan Gubar in their seminal study, *The Madwoman in the Attic.* "She picks violets, loses her gloves, feeds her birds, waters her rose plot" (22–23).[7] Like the heroines of the nineteenth-century American magazines that Welter analyzes—"Women were the passive, submissive responders," Welter notes, while men were "the movers, the doers, the actors" (159)—Patmore's heroine plays no roles in the economic, political, or civic arenas. The "angel," Gilbert and Gubar conclude, "has no story except a sort of anti-story" (23). Possibly symbolic and arguably a deliberately artificial construction (rather than mimetic rendering) of a woman ("You, Sweet, his Mistress, Wife, and Muse, / Were you for mortal woman meant? / Your praises give a hundred clues / To mythological intent!"), the "angel" haunted real women for generations (Ward 7; Patmore).[8] In 1931, Virginia Woolf told listeners at the National Society for Women's Service, "Killing the angel in the house was part of the occupation of a woman writer" (Woolf, "Professions" 238).

Is there a similar prerequisite of "killing off" the model of womanhood to pursue a career, in writing or otherwise, in Judaism? Although the description of the woman of valor of Proverbs 31 was misread as a declaration of domestic servitude by nineteenth-century preachers and purveyors of popular culture—an idea expressed again by some contemporary Jewish artists like Yakin and Mirvis—the woman of valor found in the Bible is no hostage in the house. Domestically skilled, the original model also functions in the economic, physical, civic, commercial, and political arenas: "She considers a field and buys it. . . . She girds her loins with might. . . . She spreads out her palm to the poor. . . . Garments she makes and sells." Thanks to her prowess as a public figure, "Well-known at the gates is her husband." In nineteenth-century visions of womanhood, it is only "in religious vineyards"—that is, church work—that a woman may "labor without the apprehension of detracting from the charms of feminine delicacy," as the 1840 *Young Ladies' Literary and Missionary Report* dictated (qtd. in Welter 153). Conversely, in Proverbs 31, the vineyard is not allegorical, except inasmuch as it extends women's work to the world beyond the home. After all, it is not even a vineyard that happens to sit on her (or her husband's) property that the biblical woman of valor comes to manage. In fact, if we attend closely to the poem, we can see that she first explores her opportunities: "She considers a field." Then she conducts a financial transaction: "[She] buys it." Next, she grows her business:

with her earnings, "she plants a vineyard." At last, she "senses that her enterprise is good." This is a savvy, worldly businesswoman being described, one well suited to the twenty-first century, where women are (theoretically) on equal footing with men in many countries (even if the pay gaps and uneven progression into senior positions seem to, infuriatingly, continue apace). In other words, through its distinction *from* (rather than conflation *with*) the angel in the house, the biblical woman of valor can be read as a site of modernity.

The late nineteenth-century rise of the New Woman marked the decline of the angel in the house. In 1891, Charlotte Perkins Gilman, emerging as a prominent feminist, published "An Extinct Angel." Forty years before Woolf, Gilman criticized Patmore's model for having no "business" but "to assuage, to soothe, to comfort, to delight," for possessing "no passion whatever," and for being a domestic creature whose role was limited to "kitchen service, cleaning, sewing, nursing," and (here we see Gilman's opinion on these activities) "other mundane tasks" (48).[9]

Yet it was Thomas Hardy, that same year, who ensured that the coming extinction of the "angel" did not mean the end of the ideal of the woman of valor, even though the two mythological women seemed indistinguishable to Victorians. Hardy reintroduced the Jewish model in his masterly novel *Tess of the D'Urbervilles* (1891) in a fashion that suggested, significantly, a break from Victorian misuse. He did not just ask, "Who can find a valiant woman?" (as did so many texts in the era) but rather cited the biblical passage at length and then gave the model flesh in the form of Tess, a character deemed "actualized poetry" (Hardy 164).[10] Tess is "well-behaved" (unlike her slovenly, alcoholic parents), and she soothes and delights, but that is not the end of Tess. She is no angel. She is not selfless and submissive, not a "drawing-room wax figure" of womanhood (155). In fact, Tess has passion (and temper), as the narrator informs readers again and again. Moreover, a haymaker, a poultry keeper, a harvester, a milkmaid, a straw puller, and a thresher, she is never limited to a domestic role. On the contrary, her mother, consigned to the hard labor of a large household, strives to hold off young Tess's domestic duties. Even when Tess is herself a mother and must suckle her child, she does so out in the field, on a break from harvesting. Tess is a part of the working world and the public sphere, a woman who has set off at a young age and found employment in farms and fields afar. She holds a name that tells of a long tradition (the Durbeyfields being the last of the ancient D'Urbervilles), and yet when Angel Clare sees her, he sees not only a new woman but an "exceedingly novel, fresh, and interesting specimen of woman*hood*" (Hardy 129, emphasis mine).[11] Her end might be tragic (no place for such a woman yet?), but Hardy holds up his woman as an ideal, linking her to the original Jewish model of the woman of valor.

This explicit connection between Tess and the woman of valor is made by Hardy when Angel comes to his parents after he marries Tess, and he finds them reading the bible. "I think, since Angel has come," says his father, "that it will be more appropriate to read the thirty-first of Proverbs than the chapter which we should have had in the usual course of our reading?" "Yes, certainly," responds Mrs. Clare. "The words of King Lemuel" (Hardy, ever the champion of women, here notes parenthetically that "she could cite chapter and verse as well as her husband," assuring us that despite her lack of ordination—reserved for men—Mrs. Clare is her husband's equal). "My dear son, your father has decided to read us the chapter in Proverbs in praise of a virtuous wife," continues Mrs. Clare, and soon "Angel's father began to read at the tenth verse of the aforesaid chapter" (Hardy 262–263). Hardy, via Angel's father, quotes the biblical passage that comes to define the modern woman—a woman who is *not* the angel in the house. When the recitation ends, Angel's mother remarks tellingly, "The perfect woman, you see, was a working woman; not an idler; not a fine lady" (Hardy 263).

For a book that traipses through the ruins of past aristocracy (found in the fields and penniless, are the Durbeyfields, once grand D'Urbervilles, and the Priddles, once Paridelles) and a weary theology ("There is no institution for whose history I have a deeper admiration," says Angel, "but I cannot honestly be ordained her minister . . . while she refuses to liberate her mind from an untenable redemptive theolatry"), novelty offers the promise of hope, progress, a chance for betterment (Hardy 115). And the new model presented here is full of this promise. When laid out and clearly explicated, in fact, the *modernity* of the traditional Jewish model of womanhood, with Tess as its manifestation, is remarkable. Reclaimed from Victorian corruption, this model paves the way for the New Woman, a possibility Hardy seems to foresee in a future that has moved past the "ache of modernism" (Hardy 124).[12]

This new model is, of course, a very old one. But it appears (a)new through the recitation in Hardy's novel. And it becomes new again and again through its full recitation every week. It is resurrected, reproduced, rearticulated, and held aloft—as a beacon, a goal, a possibility—for Jewish women every Friday night in Orthodox Jewish households around the world. "At the table Isaac and the girls stand next to their chairs and sing to Elizabeth, as all the Kirshner families serenade the mother of the house on Friday night," Goodman explains at the turning point of *Kaaterskill Falls*. "Isaac smiles as he sings the verses from Proverbs. He is thinking about the words" (157). What is important—as we see in *Kaaterskill Falls*—is that those who sing the song and those to whom it is sung actually hear and think about the words.

### III. "A Woman of Valor, Who Can Find?": Or, Orthodox Businesswomen Have No Precedent

*"Don't you worry [your daughters will] become overly domestic?" asks Beatrix.*
*"Too—too little-womanish?"*

*Elizabeth shrugs and concentrates on her game. She does* look *Victorian in her long dirndl skirt and white blouse, kerchief over her hair, but running over the lawn she's much faster and* more fluid *than Beatrix.*

—Allegra Goodman, *Kaaterskill Falls* (1998; emphasis mine)

*At the table Isaac and the girls stand next to their chairs and sing to Elizabeth, as all the Kirshner families serenade the mother of the house on Friday night.* "Ashes chayil miyimtza? V'rachok mipnimim michrah . . ." *Who can find a virtuous wife? She is more precious than rubies. . . . She seeks out wool and flax, and works with eager hands. Isaac smiles as he sings the verses from Proverbs. He is thinking about the words. Is it really such a question whether a woman can start a business? This is the work of the virtuous wife, the* "Ashes Chayil" *in the ancient song:* "She considers a field and buys it; with her earnings she plants a vineyard." *And* "Ta'ama ki tov sachrah / Lo yichbeh balaila nerah. *She finds that her trade is profitable; her lamp is not snuffed at night." That could be Elizabeth, his wife, his businesswoman.*

—Allegra Goodman, *Kaaterskill Falls* (1998)

In *The Rise of David Levinsky* (1917), the eponymous hero spends much of the book hoping and planning to become a *gaon*, a great scholar of the Torah and the Talmud. But in America, it seems, the only value religion has is economic. David learns to commercialize his Jewishness and comes to understand that "an occasional quotation or two from the Talmud was particularly helpful" in striking business deals (202). And soon he is, as he says, "on the road to atheism" (230). At the end of his narrative, looking back, he realizes that twenty years before, upon coming to America, his ambition had been to "marry into some orthodox family . . . with an atmosphere of Talmudic education" (367). But the last line in the book makes it clear that the choice David made leads him to answer the question "Am I happy?" in the negative: "My past and my present do not comport well. David, the poor lad swinging over a Talmud volume at the Preacher's Synagogue, seems to have more in common with my inner identity than David Levinsky, the well-known cloak-manufacturer" (518). David chose American capitalism *over* Jewish Orthodoxy. This is a choice and a temptation that we assume Elizabeth will face as the numbers begin to add up and the rabbi's permission begins to get stretched in *Kaaterskill Falls*.

But the resolution of *David Levinsky* is representative of an American Jewish literary tradition that seems staunchly male. Historically, writers focused on men who struggled with the dilemma between business (often the key manifestation of Americanization) and their religious traditions. In these stories, Judaism rarely emerges as the victor. In tales featuring female protagonists, the choice between *consent* and *descent*, to borrow Werner Sollors's terms, also arises;

the trajectories and outcomes, however, diverge from those of men. "The Girl Who Went Right," a story by Edna Ferber, published a year after *David Levinsky*, for example, recounts the adventures of a Jewish girl who abandons her birth name (and thus Jewish identity) of Rachel Wiletzky to become Ray Willets, employee at a refined lingerie shop and woman on her way up the economic ladder. By the conclusion of the narrative, however, Rachel/Ray is not, like David Levinsky, the owner of a factory—or alienated from her roots. She has reclaimed her Jewish identity, leaving behind the fanciful world of embroidered lace, silky charmeuse, reckless spending, and wistful dreams. Similarly, Herman Wouk's Marjorie Morgenstern, raised in a traditional home, seems willing to sacrifice the synagogue for success on the stage in *Marjorie Morningstar* (1955). Yet after hundreds of pages devoted to female ambition, we read that the heroine has failed and is instead a happily married "strictly observant" suburban Jewish housewife who keeps separate dishes for milk and meat (562).[13] Conversely, for Hasidic Danny Saunders of Potok's *The Chosen* (1967), the scales tip in favor of his professional success at the expense of his beard and *peyos*.

Perhaps by way of giving the novel a feminine tradition, Goodman's *Kaaterskill Falls*—whose unsatisfied heroine, Elizabeth, strives to be more than a mother-wife—veers from Jewish traditions, evoking Louise May Alcott's *Little Women*, Kate Chopin's *The Awakening*, and Charlotte Perkin Gilman's "The Yellow Wallpaper"—nineteenth- and twentieth-century stories of American women who want to be *more* and *other*. This intertextuality becomes explicit when secular Beatrix sees Elizabeth's daughters crocheting and embroidering and criticizes Elizabeth for making her girls too "little-womanish." Goodman has Beatrix forget that principal among Alcott's "little women" is fiery, temperamental, creative Jo, who wants to go off to war with her father, writes thrilling suspense stories, dreams of having a pen for a spouse, and leaves home to pursue a career in New York (of course, Jo does eventually wed, but it's to dull Professor Bhaer, a compromise for Alcott, who fiercely resisted marrying Jo off to handsome, romantic hero Laurie).

Jo is typical of the fictional foremothers who fail to conform to their surroundings. In part, they are imagined as coming from a place apart; in the case of Chopin's Edna Pontellier, "though she had married a Creole, [she] was not thoroughly at home in the society of Creoles" (Chopin 18). The main reason they stand out, however, is their distinctness from the "angels" who surround them, "fluttering about with extended, protecting wings when any harm, real or imaginary, threatened their precious brood . . . women who idolized their children, worshipped their husbands, and esteemed it a holy privilege to efface themselves as individuals and grow wings as ministering angels" (16). Elizabeth too is different in both background and behavior. She is "unusual in her community, an Englishwoman among the Kirshners of Washington Heights. She reads Milton on her own. She's spent her pregnancies with Austen and Tolstoy" (Goodman 10). It thus seems, in drawing on these stories of suffocated artists and intellectuals, angel hostages who are hyperaware of the bars of their cages, the novel asks us to see Elizabeth's tale as a woman's liberation narrative (though Goodman chooses *not* to make her heroine an Orthodox Jewish artist, as do some of her literary peers I discuss in chapter 5). Here is a woman of imagination, of education, of ambition, locked in a community where women's roles are restricted to caring for their children, looking after their schooling and extracurricular activities, and making sure that they provide a proper Jewish home.

That this model of "ministering angels" is not actually a Jewish one comes into play when Isaac has his revelation at Friday night dinner, and it might seem that the reader must wait for his revelation, content, early in the novel, with the classic American feminist drama unfolding. However, this is not strictly true: *throughout* the novel, Goodman destabilizes the idea that Orthodox women are Victorian throwbacks, destined to be angels of the house. After all, the critical lens fixed on Elizabeth often comes to the reader vis-à-vis Beatrix, the modern, intellectual, independent working woman and Oxford scholar, whose knowledge of Orthodoxy is slim (if her assumptions are rather weighty). Beatrix acts and asks for the naive reader the questions about a religious practice that is foreign to her, and in so doing, she reveals common prejudices—rather than key facts—about Orthodoxy. How objective are we when we read Orthodox women's desires and capabilities as necessarily problematic? Do we not view the women through a judgmental secular lens? Are we so different from Beatrix and her husband, Cecil, who adamantly anachronize Elizabeth and her world, viewing Elizabeth's attire as "Victorian," her daughters as "Little Women," her literary interpretations as "archaic," and her opening a store as an act of "twiddling her toes in the twentieth century" (Goodman, *Kaaterskill* 35, 56, 243)?

Through this lens, Elizabeth's dream—"I want to open a store"—appears as a sharp conflict, an "embarrassing secret" like Barnett's, in reverse (Goodman 83). After all, many people believe that Jewish angel women, once they are mothers, don't work. *Shirleys,* Wouk called this ethnic variety of suburban housewives in the 1950s, a term that comes to include Marjorie, who eventually forgets the name of her youthful ambition that appears on the book's cover. "I don't believe I've thought of that name in a dozen years," says gray-haired, "regular synagogue-goer" Mrs. Milton Schwartz when an old visitor reminds her of her dream to become a great actress called Marjorie Morningstar (Wouk 561, 562). In *Marjorie Morningstar,* as in *Kaaterskill Falls,* the inability to balance religious and familial life with a career is told from an outside perspective. Marjorie's "Shirleyhood" is narrated by Wally Wronken—a character who dramatically idealizes (and never really knows) Marjorie. A successful playwright in adulthood, Wally sees Marjorie—a mother of four, "president of the women's branch of the local community chest," and "active in the Jewish organizations of the town"—as a failure (562). For childless, secular, professionally successful Wally, Marjorie occupies seats in the polar regions of his imagination: once a "bright vision" and now a "run-of-the-mill wife and mother" (562). The polarity is Beatrix's as well. For childless, secular, professionally successful Beatrix, Elizabeth (an athletic, studious, multitalented entertainer, educator, *and* caregiver of five children) is *nothing more* than an obedient mother-wife with a secondary school education and a kerchief on her head.[14]

But the dream of opening a store might remind us of another fictional Orthodox Jewish immigrant woman who was, perhaps, successful in her negotiation of religious practice and entrepreneurialism. I say "perhaps" because we never know the fate of Cahan's Gitl, the headstrong character who refused to abandon her faith and whose spectral presence is to be found throughout contemporary visions of the woman of valor. Yekl-now-Jake, in his final iteration—as David Levinsky in his—is written as a man of regret, a man who sold his religious birthright for a mess of secular pottage. Not so Gitl. Perhaps the great difference between Jake and Gitl, after all, is *not* their stages of Americanization, the disparity between Jake's Saturday afternoon carriage rides and Gitl's lingering lightings of *Shabbos* candles, or Jake's new name and Gitl's retention of hers ("Gertie," Yekl wants her to be called, or "Goitie," as we read, reminding readers that although ahead of Gitl, Jake also has not completed his process of Americanization). Rather, their fundamental difference might be their distinct negotiations with American culture. Jake takes on everything America demands of him. His transition from Yekl to Jake—like his progress, in the final scene, on a Third Avenue cable car—is painful, but any pause in it is only temporary. Gitl, on the other hand, resists the belief that "it is quite another world" and makes America into a world that is hers too. In the end, she refuses to "yield to Jake's demands completely"—by which we might read "America's demands" or Jake's version thereof (or more generically, a *man's* version)—and chooses not to "[go] about 'in her own hair,' like a Gentile woman'" (Cahan, *Yekl* 39).

In the "happily ever after" of the story, it is Gitl who is a picture of triumph (in spite, we are told, of her demonstrations of grief). When she faces Yekl/Jake for the last time, she is "Americanized": "The rustic, 'greenhornlike' expression was completely gone from her face and manner, and . . . there was noticeable about her a suggestion of that peculiar air of self-confidence with which a few months' life in America is sure to stamp the looks and bearing of every immigrant" (Cahan 83). Significantly, she manages this self-confidence not in a *sheitel* and not wholly in her own hair but rather in hair that was "thatched with a broad-brimmed winter hat of a brown color" (88). This Jewish American compromise is one that, we read, "nettle[s]" Jake—perhaps because it shows that Gitl has achieved what Jake could not: a negotiation between religious faith and American secularism, a solution that fits them both.

Moreover, we learn, Gitl is about to embark on a new venture, "relishing the prospect of the new life in store for her. Already on her way from the rabbi's house . . . there had fluttered through her imagination a picture of the grocery business which she and Bernstein were to start with the money paid to her by Jake" (Cahan 88–89). It is no coincidence that it is the "the rabbinical-looking man" (also rabbinical in his form of Talmudic questioning throughout), the "scholarly shopmate" Bernstein, who spends his time in the factory reading and educating himself, that Gitl has chosen as her (new) spouse (4, 5). Bernstein is "Jake's Other," in Hana Wirth-Nesher's words. "He stands for . . . some continuity of Jewish culture in the New World" (Wirth-Nesher 60). Bernstein has remained faithful to his religious practice; at mealtime, he "donned his hat, and did not sit down to the repast before he had performed his ablutions and whispered a short prayer" (Jake and his friend wink at each other while Gitl partakes in the religious ritual with Bernstein; Cahan 45–46). Gitl and Bernstein's union is a spiritual one. But it is also practical; they will work together. And what one job can satisfy the competing drives for Americanization and adherence to Orthodoxy, the needs of consent and descent? The answer is a grocery business, of course: a place where the two can foster community selling kosher food to Jewish buyers and Americanize themselves through commerce.

If *Yekl* has not been recognized by scholars as a story of the nascent Orthodox businesswoman, it is because the dominant reading of the novella as an assimilation narrative is so pervasive (even Wirth-Nesher writes, "*Yekl* is a story about Americanization" [42]). It is also due to the small space afforded by Cahan to Gitl's "picture of the grocery business" at the conclusion of his narrative, allowing this trajectory to be easily overlooked. Gitl's success or failure in the business is never determined by Cahan or the reader; it is never more than a "picture." Similarly, other writers who have interrogated the viability of the Orthodox businesswoman mostly sideline the question. In contrast to the male-coded Jewish Horatio Alger macronarrative, Jewish women's pursuits of business success appear in literary history, for the most part, as marginalia.

## IV. "A Price above Rubies": Or, the Feminist Condemnation of the Woman of Valor

The topic of businesswomen, including Orthodox Jewish ones, rose to the fore in the 1980s. It is during this era that the "Eshes Chayil" from Proverbs was used by feminists to condemn Orthodoxy as a patriarchal religion that denied women a significant role in the workplace. This was the decade that opened with a woman in Britain's highest office and socialist feminists focusing on employment. Such films as *Nine to Five* (1980) and *Tootsie* (1982) and television shows as *Family Ties* (1982–1989), *Kate and Allie* (1984–1989), and *Growing Pains* (1985–1992) were prominently highlighting working women's issues.[15] In 1983, philosopher Rebecca Goldstein published *The Mind-Body Problem*, a serious meditation on women's roles, possibilities, and the idea of women's "liberation." In the novel, Renee, a former Orthodox Jew who has gone "off the *derech*," discovers that secular life does not offer her the unlimited life options she was expecting.

As we follow the story of Renee's life and marriage to a mathematician who overshadows and fails to understand her, we begin to wonder if Renee merely exchanged one cage for another. It is crucial, however, that we comprehend the structure of these cages. To determine that in regard to the Orthodox woman, Goldstein quotes Proverbs 31 at length. Focusing on the wide-ranging jobs the woman of valor undertakes (and omitting the passages that discuss her household duties), Goldstein astutely distinguishes the Jewish model from the Victorian one. Here, the question of "liberation" is unpicked deliberately. Renee knows that while "liberated specimens among her goyish counterparts struggle against the myth of helplessness and the tradition of dependence"—think here of Patmore's angel— "the Orthodox *ayshes chayul* (woman of worth) is traditionally the sole support of her (very large) family" and "*[h]er* liberation wouldn't require her being freed from a dollhouse or lifted off a pedestal" (Goldstein, *Mind-Body* 63).[16] At the same time, she argues that the power that secular, mainstream society would afford such a woman is, paradoxically, *not* what is most valued in Orthodox society:

> The roles are reversed, but only along one dimension. Hers is still the indisput-
> ably inferior position in those matters that matter in this society: the spiritual
> and intellectual, which are one and the same. For Jews learning is the highest
> spiritual activity, but one from which women are barred. And what, I once
> asked my mother, does Judaism offer its females in the way of spiritual expe-
> riences? At the top of her list was going to *mikvah*, the ritual bath that's a
> monthly requirement for married Orthodox women. (For the men: Talmud
> and logic, while the women try to clean up their bloody messes.) In a world
> where merit is measured in the number of pages of the Talmud one has mas-
> tered, power doesn't rest in bringing home the kosher beef fry. Ask the *ayshes
> chayul*. (64)

The point here is salient, one that is taken up by other writers and sociologists who concur that although Orthodox women can and do work, their participa-tion in the marketplace is not valued in their context.[17] For Renee, this is not and cannot be enough. Leaving Orthodoxy and remaining outside its limited gender roles are essential for her, even as she fails to find true "liberation."

And yet, Goldstein's novel is nuanced and complicated. If the Orthodox woman sacrifices her ambition to her family (and community), Renee worries that the secular woman sacrifices her family for her ambition. It is the Marjorie Morningstar and David Levinsky either/or dilemma arising. Renee, who is in a fraught marriage, looks at her Orthodox brother and sister-in-law with envy. With uncharacteristic enthusiasm, she describes the "wild Chasidic dancing on both sides [of the *mechitzah*]" at their wedding, peering, it would seem, at one side and then the other. She even describes the celebration without condemning the segregated sexes, the separate spheres:

> The men did the kaztska and cartwheels, making up with exuberance what they lacked in grace. . . . Tzippy danced in the center of the women, partners constantly changing: her mother and mother-in-law, her grandmother and four sisters, the many sweet-faced friends. I too got to dance with the bride. The friends brought out a jump rope, and Tzippy and they played. The men lifted Avram on a chair, the women held up little Tzippy, and they danced around with the two of them. At one point each took hold of a corner of a handkerchief over the *mechitzah* and laughed shyly into each other's face as they were held aloft. (Goldstein, *Mind-Body* 64–65)

Significantly, Renee adds, "I watched them and was filled with disgust at my own life, which, in the glow of their purity, seemed sordid and dirty" (65). Throughout the novel, Tzippy's character, though rendered a "little" (young, benighted), playful "child-bride," is written in the soft light of longing and scented with nostalgia. "Were it possible to feel envy for Tzippy," Renee says, "I would have envied her" (173). Basking in Renee's admiration, Tzippy is the feminized "lad swinging over the Talmud volume at the Preacher's Synagogue."

It is *not* possible, though, for Renee to feel envy for Tzippy, who cannot be more than a mother-woman even if she gets a job outside the home. But *The Mind-Body Problem* was not Goldstein's last fictional meditation on the "*ayshes chayul*." Twelve years later, Goldstein offered readers an alternative viewpoint with her novel *Mazel* (1995). Goldstein's depiction of Leiba, the mother at the head of the matriarchal family of the novel, is a near-perfect manifestation of the woman of valor, and she is written with neither nostalgia nor pity. When we encounter Leiba, she has risen while it is still nighttime to prepare food for her household, and Goldstein allows us to see the sheer physical strength required of the woman of valor: her "sleeves [are] pulled up over her muscular arms as she pummel[s] the dough" of the challah she is making for her family (Goldstein, *Mazel* 51). We learn about "her business interests [that take] her into the world" (also explicitly called her "enterprises"), and we are told that because of her good work, her husband has a place of respect: "Her husband was a scholar, the crown on Leiba's head" (52). Feminist critiques of Proverbs 31:10–31 have often focused on the woman of valor being in service to and/or ornamental for her husband (like the pearls she is worthier than), but in *Mazel*, Goldstein inverts this paradigm, turning golden-haired Nachum into the decorative piece for the all-powerful woman (in much the same way that the famous seventeenth-century diarist and formidable, *pious* businesswoman Glückel of Hameln refers to her husband as the "crown of [*her*] head" [135, emphasis mine]).

In *The Mind-Body Problem*, however, the split between the respected professional woman and the religious mother is like the *mechitzah* that separates the
sexes at the wedding; one can see over the top or reach a handkerchief across it,
but the wall remains. We find a similar split in Anne Roiphe's *Lovingkindness*
(1987). In this novel, the secular mother, whose failed romantic life stands in
stark contrast to her professional success, suspects her newly Orthodox daughter
has landed on the other side of the divide and given up her professional future
through her commitment to religion. "They will find her a husband," a friend
predicts when Annie tells her that her daughter, Andrea (now Sarai), called from
a yeshiva in Israel. "They will encourage her to have twelve children" (Roiphe
3). This is not the fate Annie has chosen for her daughter. "You must be able to
work seriously if you are going to be a doctor," she said to Andrea in her youth.
"You want to be in charge, to have power, to be the one to make the important
decisions; you want to have the respect" (145). And later, she suggests, "You could
be an artist or a singer or you could have a farm with horses" (195). But now
Annie is sure that none of this will happen. "You will be a baby machine," Annie
tells Andrea, "a diaper changer, a cook, you will not have time to know any of
your children well if you have so many" (194). Orthodox women's commitment
to religion is often rendered primarily in terms of motherhood. Hence we read
about Marjorie's four children, Toby's four children, Andrea as a baby machine,
and Tzippy's desperate desire to bear a live child after two miscarriages are followed by a long period of infertility. The conflict unfolds between motherhood
and material success. Andrea will have children, therefore she won't be a doctor
or have a farm. Roiphe has the daughter conform to her mother's (and readers'?)
expectations in her response: "I will take good care of my children because that
is all that matters to me." Annie turns to her prospective son-in-law and asks
him if her daughter will "ever hold a job, talk in public, work in politics, become
a leader?" His response is also stock: "Here . . . we believe the king's daughter
should stay within. She will find plenty to do in the house" (Roiphe 224).

In Roiphe's novel, the *mechitzah* between the angel/mother and feminist/
worker seems insurmountable. To Annie, the woman of valor offers no resolutions. Annie references the hymn to suggest that the "valor women" are archaic,
oppressed, objects to be adorned, and selfless angels. "Our past had caught up
with us, overtaken us and pulled us back into a moment when the valor women
burned with the Sabbath candle and we thought of ourselves as covered with
jewels, wandering down from eternity, dispensing favors, waving gentle hands
like the Sabbath queen bringing rest to the weary," Annie thinks, watching her
daughter light *Shabbos* candles using "the shape and the sound of words [her]
grandmother and great-grandmother must have said." She imagines her daughter as a figure out of a rather confused past where angel hostages rattled around
in their Christian Victorian houses singing Jewish blessings. Sarai sounds as

if "she had an angel trapped in her nasal passages," thinks Annie, hearing her daughter recite a prayer over the candles (Roiphe 189).

Goldstein's novels are nuanced, cautious, and ambivalent about the condemnation of women who seem, at the end of the day, *happy* in their embrace of a religious lifestyle (their choice, crucially). So too is Roiphe's novel. We know this, in part, because of the perspectives we are offered. Both authors' novels explicitly foreground an outsider's perspective, even more than Wouk with Wally or Goodman with Beatrix. *The Mind-Body Problem*'s Renee cannot appreciate her sister-in-law's world. *Mazel*'s Sasha cannot understand her *ba'alat teshuva* granddaughter's world ("the reshtetlization of America," Sasha calls Phoebe's Orthodox enclave in New Jersey [354]). *Lovingkindness*'s Annie can barely recognize her daughter's world. But these outsiders sit on the verge of insiderness; they are mothers, sisters-in-law, grandmothers, relatives of some sort. Cynthia Ozick too used this convention in *Bloodshed*. Bleilip is a cousin to Toby, and it is through his mediation that we learn that Toby "used to say she would be the first lady Jewish president" but then became religious and traded in ambition for "the zealot's private pieties, rites, idiosyncrasies" and four sons (58–59). Thus the authors pose a challenge to their readers: If the relative is unable to sympathize with the Orthodox woman or comprehend her world, how likely is it that the reader, that much further afield, can?

Time and time again, Roiphe has Annie censure and Andrea stand her ground. Eventually, Annie comes to recognize that Orthodoxy is what her daughter wants. Moreover, Annie realizes that her daughter is content with life in a way she herself is not. After declaring the lifestyle and inhabitants of Andrea/Sarai's seminary, Yeshiva Rachel, "anachronistic," "fourteenth century," "a remnant of the past," Annie asks, in the novel's concluding paragraph, "But what if *I* am simply wrong, anachronistic, a figment of the enlightenment's imagination?" (Roiphe 264, emphasis mine). Still, we are left with the feeling that she is not. Or if she is, we should not rest easy. The Enlightenment, after all, liberated us (didn't it?). We have this reluctant admission in *Mazel* too, as the narrative is complicitous with Sasha and her overpowering sense of irony but also luxuriates in Phoebe's happiness, the happiness of the woman to whom a crying, loving husband earnestly sings on the final pages of the book, "Who can find a woman of valor? Her worth is far greater than that of pearls" (Goldstein, *Mazel* 354).

In the film *A Price above Rubies* (1998), in contrast, we enter from the viewpoint of the Orthodox woman and are not off to the side, unsure of our understanding of her life and her desires; from childhood through marriage and motherhood, we are so close to Sonia as to feel that we *are* Sonia. Like Hardy and Goldstein, the film cites Proverbs 31 at length. But also like its predecessors, the film stops short of reciting the poem in full, and the almost-all is always significant. We think we are hearing the whole thing but are getting a bowdlerized version fit for a selfless Victorian heroine, a version that exemplifies the angel in the house—*not* a Jewish woman. Furthermore, the film so conflates adultery with women's employment that it is hard to know which of these sins is competing with the ideal of womanhood/wifehood/motherhood. In either case, the partial recitation of the "Eshes Chayil" is not intended, as it is for Goodman's Elizabeth, to justify Sonia's role in business (the recitation of the "Eshes Chayil" transmitted to readers through Elizabeth's husband, Isaac, is also partial, but its abbreviation favors the praise of women's *non*domestic roles). Rather, it is meant to critique a religious tradition that puts unrealistic expectations on women.

"Eshes Chayil" is recited in *A Price above Rubies* by Sender Horowitz, Sonia's brother-in-law, with whom Sonia is having an affair. The affair is, at best, transactional. Sonia has been presented thus far in the film as a woman missing two key features in her life: an exciting job outside the house and sex. Her brother-in-law provides both—one in exchange for the other. When Sender approaches Sonia, it is in the aftermath of her being bored by an interior designer and irritated by a crying baby (in contrast to her husband, who is happily in his element teaching a class full of enthusiastic yeshiva students). Sender praises Sonia for her intelligence, skill, and competence. He offers her a job that will take her around New York, with occasional trips out of state to further expand her horizon. Sonia hesitates and replies, "Well . . . I'm a mother now." Sender responds, reminding her (and us) that for Orthodox women, working is not actually problematic: "Half the mothers in Boro Park are running cash businesses out of their own basements." He then further empowers her by telling her that her choice to work is her own and not her husband's. Immediately following the business agreement, he puts his hand on her breast, pushes her against the wall, lifts her dress, and penetrates her. "You start on Monday," he says as she rearranges her clothes. So much for Sender as the feminist hero of the film (#MeToo).

Sex is featured in the film's advertising and the scene that lends the film its title. It is marked as liberating and dangerous throughout. In the opening scene of the film, a young Sonia is told that she is descended from the "sin" of Baba Yitta, who disappeared one day and returned pregnant. Late in the film, we learn the fate of the great community rebbe who, after many years of restraint, gives into carnal desire and promptly dies.[18] Yet it is hard to ignore the fact that in the scene in which Sender seals the business deal he has made with Sonia—and throughout the film, which takes Sonia into jewelry shops and men's bedrooms—sex and women's work are tightly bound together. Both are about fulfilling passions—and passions, according to the film, are not part of an Orthodox woman's life. A woman must be selfless: an angel.[19]

Sonia is portrayed as a brilliant businesswoman, capable of recognizing merchandise of great worth, buying it at a steep discount, and selling it at a high premium. But it is not in a moment in which Sonia's business acumen is on display that Sender enunciates the words, "A woman of fortitude, who can find? For her price is far above rubies."[20] The sequence of scenes—Sonia proving a business dynamo, Sonia serving her sad husband a sad microwaved dinner, Sonia lying on her brother-in-law's desk, legs spread—tells the story of a woman who has made a Faustian pact (inasmuch as a woman in her situation had the authority to sign away her own soul). By reciting the poem, Sender is using the language of praise of the "Woman of Valor" to *punish* Sonia for not being one. (The immediate impetus for this punishment is Sonia's request, "Just for a moment?" as Sender finishes his violent thrusting. It is a request, presumably, to be held intimately, a sign that she wants to imagine their union as a romantic, or redeemable, act.) "When her husband relies on her, he shall lack no fortune," he says ironically, and here she shakes her head because, as is clear by their (literal) position in this scene, such familial trust has been *exchanged* for a fortune. (Sender's own role in the affair, which in scenes like the first one looks a lot more like assault and at all times hinges on a very uneven power relationship, goes unpunished in the film—it is for the viewer to condemn, along with the whole of Orthodox Judaism.) Sonia tries to cover Sender's mouth with her hand, but she does not have the power to silence him (What power, asks the film, do women in this community really have?).

As Sonia's fingers slip off Sender's mouth, Sender continues his recitation, deliberately skipping the lines that praise the woman for her professional prowess. He omits the lines that show the woman of valor taking opportunities and succeeding, such as those that appear to Elizabeth's husband in *Kaaterskill Falls* as a revelation of a Jewish woman's capability in economic pursuit: "She seeks out wool and flax, and works with eager hands" (Goodman 157). He omits the lines that speak of the power the woman of valor has in venturing out in the world in her business endeavors, the lines that prove to Goldstein's Renee that the *"ayshus chayul,"* unlike her "goyish counterpart," needs not be freed from her dollhouse: "She is like the merchant-ships; she brings her food from afar." He omits a significant and lengthy passage of the hymn, wherein the woman of valor considers a field, buys it, plants a vineyard, perceives that her merchandise is good, makes garments, sells them, and delivers them to the merchants. Of course, the ellipses silently tell what is precisely and dramatically true of Sonia. The viewer sees it: Sonia works her way through the disparate, ethnic neighborhoods (Hasidic Boro Park, Chinatown, Indian Queens, Spanish and Black Harlem) of cosmopolitan, rainbow-hued New York City—a city that becomes, for the viewer, a veritable microcosm of the planet—vigorously buying, selling, evaluating, creating, delivering.

Instead, in his condensed version of Proverbs 31, Sender highlights Sonia's failings—her domestic duties—reinforcing the idea that the woman of valor, the ideal woman of Judaism, is a woman who is only committed to her family and her home. The film has us believe that the woman of valor is the angel (hostage) in the house—or as Sender recites to Sonia, "She rises in the morning to feed her household. Strength and majesty are her raiment." As Sonia turns her head so that she faces the camera, her eyes fill with tears, and we see how poorly she, a working woman who desires fulfillment, compares to what is presented as the Jewish model. The ostensible ideal woman attends to her household and joyfully anticipates her day of judgment, a day Sonia (if she believes in the misogynistic rendering of Orthodoxy the film promotes) must fear. (*She won't believe in that backward religion much longer, dear modern, liberal viewers—don't worry!*) In the bittersweet conclusion of the film, Sonia is a successful businesswoman, but her loss of family and community is absolute: she leaves the religious community of Borough Park and is cut off from her husband, parents, in-laws, friends, and baby.

But as Allegra Goodman reminded us the same year that *A Price above Rubies* was realeased, in the Bible, the woman of valor finds that her trade is profitable *and* rises in the morning to feed her household. What Hardy once did for Victorian literature and culture by freeing the angel hostage of the house and giving her a place in the economy and the world at large, Goodman does for Orthodox Judaism. She rectifies corrupted readings of the woman of valor and thus offers us a modern, feminist midrash to redeem Judaism through the very text used to condemn it.

This is significant because few books about Haredi communities have been as close to being canonical literature as *Kaaterskill Falls*, a finalist for the National Book Award (1998), a *New York Times* Notable Book (1998), a staple of American literature syllabi, and a popular read. Many scholars and reviewers have identified Goodman as a writer who revitalized American Jewish literature with her writing. Her works stand as a retort to the 1970s through early 1990s characterizations of American Jewish literature as a dying breed and a fulfillment of the predictions of Ozick and Wisse about the liturgical direction of literature.[21] Moreover, it presents a sensitive and humane rendering of Orthodox characters in contrast to the fictional outputs literary critic Andrew Furman called a "narrative hostility toward Orthodoxy" (84).[22] As early as 1988, Ted Solotaroff identified Goodman (only twenty-one years old at the time!) as part of a new wave of American Jewish writers "who are anchored in the present-day observant Jewish community and who are drawn to the intense and growing dialogue between Judaism and modernity under the impact of feminism" (Solotaroff 31).[23] Maya Socolovsky has argued that Goodman's writing is a response to what Miriyam Glazer has called "Jewish religious . . . issues . . . as the province of the past'" (Socolovsky 28; Glazer, "Daughters" 91). Of course, we might also see Goodman as *finishing* the (*unfinished*) stories of the twentieth century—stories like that of the hat-wearing businesswoman, Gitl.

## V. "She Finds That Her Trade Is Profitable":
## Or, It's an American Story

In a feminist twist, the main plot of *Kaaterskill Falls* is Elizabeth's in a way that *Yekl's* is never wholly Gitl's: the novel centers on her. Elizabeth's plight is not a dramatic one; she simply grows tired of being dependent on her husband to bring groceries up to the remote mountain town where she resides for the summer and so conceives of the idea to open a local kosher grocery store.[24] Elizabeth requests the permission of her rabbi—Rav Kirshner—and receives it. She opens her store, and it flourishes. Eventually, Elizabeth begins to exceed the limits of the rabbi's permission, buying products not specifically sanctioned by him, and when she seeks renewal of the store's rabbinical approval—this time from the rabbi's son Isaiah, who has replaced his father at the head of their community—she is denied it. Pregnant, Elizabeth resigns herself to the domestic life she had lived before her enterprise. At the book's conclusion, however, she is working again—not only for pay but also to learn the business, to educate herself, and to—potentially—take over the store and make of it even more than her original shop. In the background of this story are Elizabeth's husband, her family, her community, and the town of Kaaterskill.

*Kaaterskill Falls* takes place in an idyllic setting of the same name, and Goodman's choice of locale grounds the book in American Jewish women's history. Though all the Kirshner Jews, around whom the novel revolves, depart gritty New York City for a Catskills mountain resort area every summer, the men must return to the city to work during the week. Thus Elizabeth is not unique in being left to her own devices on weekdays, waiting for groceries. As a rule, the women and children stay in the country all summer, whereas the men only come to the country for the weekends. There is a matriarchal structure to the society here. This practice is as true to life as its literary representation. After all, though the "Kirshners" are an imagined sect of Jews, the Catskills have long been a summer resort area for Jewish families, and the location's proximity to New York City has allowed for the weekly commute (similar to the Laurentians for Montreal Jewish families). Around the time Goodman's novel took place, my family, without my dad (it was my mom, sister, and maternal grandparents), stayed at the Concord, which sat squarely among the other fabled Catskills resorts like Kutsher's and Grossinger's; I remember tucking myself into the giant vibrating belt in the exercise room for a whole-body jiggle and sneaking into the disco to dance my red cowboy boots off among all the moms and *bubbies* and *zaidies*.

Among the many paeans to the Catskills' glory years that have been produced, no vision of Catskills-staying Jewish families—doing the merengue and the bachata, playing tennis, and learning about life—is more famous than *Dirty Dancing* (1987).[25] Here, the women-centeredness of the community is conveyed, albeit dismissively through the sexualized male gaze. In an early scene in the film, Max, the resort owner, points out Vivian Pressman to a new male guest, Dr. Houseman, the father of the film's female protagonist, Baby. Vivian is dancing with the much younger and very sensual Johnny Castle (later good Jewish girl Baby's goy-boy summer conquest). Max refers to Vivian as a "bungalow bunny" and explains to his male interlocutor: "That's what we call the women who stay here all week. The husbands only come up on weekends." This is followed by an exchange with Vivian.

MAX:  Moe coming up on Friday?
VIVIAN:  Friday.

She does not miss a dance move, and neither does she seem disturbed by her husband's absence. Clearly, Vivian is free to take a lover precisely because of this arrangement, which Max implicitly references when he looks back at Dr. Houseman and adds sarcastically, "He's away a lot. I know. It's a hardship."

*Kaaterskill Falls* takes its place among such paeans. Like *Dirty Dancing*, Goodman changes the dominant narrative of the Borscht Belt as the birthplace of secular Jewish men's entertainment by highlighting the role of the women there. And like Pearl Abraham's *The Romance Reader*, Eileen Pollack's *Paradise, New York*, and Pamela Grey's film *A Walk on the Moon* (1999), Goodman turns her attention not only to women but also to the Orthodox communities, which in the post–Lenny Bruce days have come to define the area. As testament to this fact, the I-87 Thruway has a "prayer stop" tucked in among texting/rest stops at Sloatsburg. According to a 2011 *Vos Iz Neias* article, as many as three hundred men stop for *mincha* and *ma'ariv* there each Thursday evening in the summer ("Sloatsburg").

If, at the turn of the twentieth century, by arriving in the New World, Gitl is urged to conform to a supposed Anglo-American ethic, then at the conclusion of the twentieth century, Elizabeth has no similar need: by locating her in the Borscht Belt after its golden era, Goodman writes her character into a time and space laden with Jewish history and culture. The marginal(ized) group has long taken its place at the center. So Goodman surrounds her semigarrisoned Jews with "[homes with] American flags in front and white wagon wheels," gentlemen's agreements over real estate, and a judge who is partial to his own kind, confident that readers recognize that Elizabeth is in a space that shimmers with the legacy of Jackie Mason and Sid Caesar and bungalow bunnies (42). In the margins are the white, Christian Euro-Americans whose ancestors settled the land. The journey to Kaaterskill makes this evident: to arrive at this vast milieu of Jews (Kirshner, Chabad, Conservative, *ba'al teshuva*, orthopraxic, secular), Elizabeth must traverse Washington Irving Highway and cut around Cole Mountain. The highway was named after American writer Washington Irving and the mountain after American artist Thomas Cole.

But perhaps it's fairer to say that Kaaterskill is a hybrid space, rather than one with a center and margins. Certainly, Cole's 1826 painting "Falls of the Kaaterskill" takes its place at the forefront of the novel. It features on the book's cover art and is adapted to, or merged with, Jewish ambition for Elizabeth. It becomes the surprising impetus for Elizabeth's desire to create a kosher store:

> She loves the place; she loves the painting by association. The painting is all associations. All familiar to her; reminding her, inspiring her. It brings back her own half-buried wish to capture and even recreate a place and time that beautiful. More than ever she wants to do something of her own. She has to make something; she has so much energy, she feels so strong. . . . Elizabeth looks intently at the painting, that brilliant piece of the world, and gazing at the color and the light of it she feels the desire, as intense as prayer. I want—she thinks, and then it comes to her simply, with all the force of her pragmatic soul—I want to open a store. (Goodman, *Kaaterskill* 83)

As catalyst for the main character's action that drives the plot of the novel, this vivid "piece of the [Anglo-American] world" becomes a crucial lens for the book, one that must share its space with Jewish "prayer." Thus even as *Kaaterskill Falls* is fundamentally a Jewish story—a story of the Catskills, a kosher store, contested rabbinical authority, and biblical exegesis—it's also an American story, a story of the Hudson valley, the pursuit of happiness, the lure of capitalism, and individual choice.

Initially, America might seem irrelevant to Goodman's text, as we are introduced to the Kirshner Jews as too "absorbed in their own religion" to notice the "shop windows armored with metal grilles, cement walls spray-painted pink," or "Fort Tryon Park . . . the Cloisters, with its icons and crucifixes" that surround them (4). Here, the Fourth of July involves no mention of America's revolution. In a conversation between two characters, one observes, "I hope on the Fourth it doesn't rain like this. You're coming on the Fourth?" to which his interlocutor asks, "What's on the Fourth?" and the response is, "Opening day." "Oh, of course," we read. And the narrator adds, "The Fourth of July is opening day for the Lamkins' day camp" (49). The eclipsed national day of celebration is, notably, forgotten by the characters, not the narrative (as indicated by the capitalization of "Fourth" and the syntactical construction in the narrator's aside). The characters celebrate their camp opening with potato salad and coleslaw and Torah *drashes*; the parade passes them by, a thing apart. The new young rabbi takes up the rallying call of isolationism: "Our work is to build the Kehilla like a fortress, so strong that inside it each member can devote himself to God; not to struggling against the outside, but to striving within" (226).

Yet through Elizabeth, the mythology of nationalism quickly seeps into this isolated community. As the Kirshner women order pumpernickel and chicken parts and Elizabeth slices corned beef and considers what it means to have a land-office business, "she imagines those land offices selling claims in the West; uncharted prairie overrun with game" (189). And the rhetoric of nationalism confirms this connection between her store and country when she is told by her friend Andras, after the rabbi turns down her request to keep her store, "Elizabeth, this is the United States of America. You can do whatever you damn well please" (271). This declaration is familiar to those who remember Yezierska's early twentieth-century heroine Sara Smolinsky saying, "Nobody can stop me. I'm not from the old country. I'm American!" (Yezierska 138). The main difference is that Elizabeth's own statement must be given to her. In response—like the biblical Sarah, who, past her childbearing years, laughed when told she would bear a son—Elizabeth "bursts out laughing" (Goodman, *Kaaterskill* 271). Yet in time, like Sarah, Elizabeth recognizes that this metaphorical fruit of her loins is indeed possible, and she makes the declaration on her own: when she decides to return to the world of work, these are the words that echo through her head. To overcome her uncertainty that in this life she could be whatever she wants ("businesswoman, philosopher, traveler, artist"), she hears Andras's "words, half whispered, his voice conspiratorial and dry" urging her into Grimaldi's store to ask for a job (299). Again she laughs—but this time, her laughter is not the laughter of disbelief but of possibility. And when she has gone into the store and convinced Grimaldi to hire her so she can learn the business, readers hear these words repeated for a third time at the end of the book, not only in Elizabeth's head but out of her mouth: "Elizabeth, this is the United States of America. . . . And you can do whatever you please" (323). She repeats them back to Andras, who is surprised to have the words returned to him, invested with new and powerful meaning: "It's just strange you took it so seriously," he says to the woman who laughed at his proposition. "I didn't know whether I should bother going in," Elizabeth explains, "and then I remembered what you said. I thought that you were right" (323).

Elizabeth is not American-born, and although she has not come from the old country like David Levinsky, she shares with him the immigrant's desire to fulfill her dreams through economic pursuits of happiness. The customers are "*Elizabeth's* customers," and her heart beats to her ambition (Goodman, *Kaaterskill* 171). Later, we also learn that, like David Levinsky, Elizabeth approaches her religion differently once she has achieved her commercial goal. Goodman writes of Elizabeth's decision to sell kosher food not sanctioned by her particular rabbi: "Elizabeth looks at the question differently now that she has a business. She has taken one opportunity and she can't help taking others" (202). The store is the manifestation of Elizabeth's American individualism; when the time comes to renew her permission, she resists. She feels, "The store is hers alone. Her creation, or so she'd fancied it" (237).

But in the end, Elizabeth does *not* become David Levinsky or Sara Smolinsky. As it turns out, Sara saying, "I'm going to live my own life," and Elizabeth being told, "You can do whatever you damn well please," are different. One is the ulti-mate declaration of independence, while the other suggests inclusion in a com-munity. This is not to say there is no temptation to eschew her community; at one point, Elizabeth states, "Isaac, I can do this myself" (Goodman, *Kaaterskill* 97). But the narrator makes plain that she cannot do it herself and remain a com-munity member, a fact she knows and ultimately accepts—because she is not, like Sara, willing to excommunicate herself. If the store begins as something Eliz-abeth conceives of as "something of her own," she comes to recognize that "she found something for herself and *for her community*" (83, 242, emphasis mine). Although it seems merely a justification when Isaac tells the *Rav* that her store will allow women to be able to shop for food during the week instead of wait-ing for groceries hastily bought by their husbands before the trip from the city, this reasoning comes true as her store fills with Kirshner women day in, day out. Ranen Omer-Sherman notes that the store offers "a rare social gathering place outside the synagogue" (Omer-Sherman 271). And more specifically, it offers a feminocentric Jewish gathering place. Though there are galleries for women on balconies or tucked in the back, out of sight, the Orthodox synagogue is pri-marily a man's domain. In Elizabeth's store, Mrs. Schloss chats with Mrs. Fraen-kel and a "small crowd of women cluster around the Dutch door" (Goodman, *Kaaterskill* 188). The store comes to resolve the schism that Omer-Sherman sees in the opening pages, between "the unpleasant journey from the secular world of commerce to the transcendent community of the Kirshners in Kaaterskill Falls" (Omer-Sherman 267). While this opening, the title, the book's cover, and the epigraph by John Keats about the "glorious stream" and "the thunder and the freshness" of Kaaterskill Falls all suggest that the sublime scenery of the Catskills offers a refuge from the busy, workaday world of Manhattan, Good-man, we see, prefers unions over stark contrasts. Bringing "secular ... commerce" to "transcendent ... Kaaterskill" *enriches* the Kaaterskill community rather than harms it.

The tension between American commerce and religious community is ulti-mately a creative one. Although Elizabeth is forced to close the doors of her little shop in Kaaterskill, we get a glimpse of the potential therein: a communal space, a space for women, and a space for fulfilling the religious obligation of keeping kosher through the American Dream of business. That Elizabeth's rabbi chooses to end this practice is an error: an idiosyncratic one, but a telling one. Sometimes the rabbis get it wrong.

## VI. "She Bringeth Food from Afar": But, Sunday the Rabbi Got It Wrong

*"What will she do?" the Rav asks.*

*"Mimerchak tavi lachma," Isaac quotes.*

*Elizabeth nearly forgets herself and laughs. It's such a lucky reference for him to happen on, a cardinal virtue of the virtuous wife. In "Ayshes Chayil," the song sung on Friday nights. She bringeth food from afar.*

*"She wants to bring up food from the city to Kaaterskill," Isaac says, "so women can shop during the week, instead of waiting for us to come up on weekends with all the groceries in the car."*

*The Rav nods with a pursed-lip smile.*

—Allegra Goodman, *Kaaterskill Falls* (1998)

There are multiple Orthodox communities in Kaaterskill, coming from Borough Park and Crown Heights and Washington Heights (as in the case of the Kirshners). The Kirshners, in contrast to Hasidim, appear comparatively modern (*comparatively* being key, as we read of their rabbi: "[Rav Kirshner] does not wear a long black frock coat or a streimel on Shabbes like those rabbis who dress in the garb of eighteenth-century Polish nobles. His is the modern dress of the nineteenth-century man of business, a suit with a vest and watch pocket, a large gold watch on a chain"; Goodman, *Kaaterskill* 99). Rav Kirshner is the grandson of "Jeremiah Solomon Hecht," an unmistakable allusion to Samson Raphael Hirsch (1808–1888), "the founder in Germany of neoorthodoxy" (15). Hirsch's great innovation in Judaism was *torah im derech eretz*—"Torah with the way of the land," also understood to mean "Torah and secular knowledge." The integrative attitude of this philosophy and its legacy is outlined by Goodman:

> Hecht...wrote in his elegant and stylish German, arguing that the generations to come should study science and languages, law, and mathematics—and yet none of these could come before religious law. Rav Elijah Kirshner was born in 1898, only ten years after Hecht's time, and it is said his mother was Hecht's favorite daughter. He earned a doctorate in philosophy at the University of Frankfurt am Main, and then rose to take his grandfather's place. Rav Kirshner brought Hecht's books and his community to America—only a small part of what there once was, but a remnant that he guided and strengthened. He has founded the Kirshner school and the yeshiva, sustained his people in Washington Heights, even now in the battered parks, the narrow alleyways. The Rav is an extraordinary man. And famous. He knows the mayor of New York, has led prayers in the state legislature. *The New York Times* calls him "the Reverend Doctor." (15–16)

This passage presents in the figures of Hecht and Kirshner the duality of the religious and the secular—the rabbinate and the doctorate, the man of the Jews and the man of the people. But if the duality of *Torah im derech eretz* suggests a taut rope in a game of war between these religious and secular components, Goodman recognizes it, and for the American generation to follow Kirshner, she shows the rope break and Torah and *derech eretz* become discrete entities once more. Allegorizing this split in the classical manner of opposing brothers (Cain and Abel, Romulus and Remus, Julius and Vincent in *Twins*, Jacob and The Man in Black on ABC's *Lost*...), Goodman has Rav Kirshner's two sons each embody one aspect of Hecht's philosophy and educational trajectory. The elder brother, Jeremy, is a professor of Renaissance literature, specializing in Castiglione and courtly handbooks, and the younger, Isaiah, is the inward-looking, enclavist rabbi.

But to see the Kirshner sons as mere allegory misses the larger point that Goodman is making about the individual whims of rabbis, who are, after all, mere people. Both men take their paths as logical extensions of neo-Orthodoxy's philosophy. But both are overzealous in laying claim to one of the paths. Isaiah, for example, chooses to use Elizabeth's request to renew her license for a store to assert his authority as the new rabbi when his father dies and thus denies it. Jeremy, on the other hand, blatantly flouts the basic tenets of Judaism and does so even in his father's home, driving up to the house in Kaaterskill on the Shabbat, which is strictly forbidden. These are acts of principle, to a degree, but they also suggest a habit of putting their own values above all other people's. (This calls to mind the classic Groucho Marx joke: "Those are my principles, and if you don't like them, well . . . I have others.") Furthermore, the brothers' behavior is not always connected to principle at all, and Goodman draws out the ways that they respond with typical human vanity, jealousy, and spite. Isaiah, for example, denies Elizabeth's request partly because he senses she does not respect him. Jeremy takes the antique books that his father leaves him in his will—not because he will read them but because his brother has been bequeathed everything else, and he wants to have something too (and because taking the books angers his brother, which pleases Jeremy). Jeremy seems a foil to Isaiah, but in the end, it is his similarity to his brother that is significant.[26]

As a plot device, Isaiah's pettiness ends Elizabeth's initial foray into the business world; a member in an Orthodox community, Elizabeth is subject to the decisions of her rabbi. "We are to understand that Isaiah's slight to Elizabeth's dignity is far worse than her transgression against rabbinic jurisdiction, since he is shoring up his power rather than his community or his religion," notes Wisse in her review in *Commentary* (Wisse, "Joy" 69). Although this is true, it is not the dignity of the individual that I want to highlight. Rather, it is the dignity of *women*.

Women are often at the site of conflict, the sacrifice and symbol of a rabbi's growing power. Sztokman's book *The War on Women in Israel* brings this message home powerfully, as does the film *The Women's Balcony*.[27] Deborah Feldman also tells a story in *Unorthodox* that nicely highlights this issue. "Bubby loves to tell the story of how Zeidy asked her to shave her head," she says, relating Bubby's memory: "'Husband of mine,' [Bubby] retorted indignantly, 'you went crazy in the head or what? It's not enough for you that I cover my hair with a wig, even when my own mother didn't bother back in Europe, but now you want me to shave it all too? Never in my life did I hear of such a *frumkeit*, of such a religion, that says a woman has to shave her head' . . . 'But, Fraida, the rebbe said!' [Zaidy pleaded]. 'It's a new rule. All the men are telling their wives to do it'" (Feldman, *Unorthodox* 24). The "new rules" land on both men and women, but it seems that many more of them land directly on women, who have *no say in their making*: hence Rabbi Tau's and Rabbi Aviner's respective pamphlets with new decrees on women's dress and hair covering, new signs on sidewalks indicating where women can walk, new declarations that women can't drive, and new women's image-banning leading to such peculiarities as IKEA catalogues populated with families composed of only fathers and children.[28] To see the new (and newer) iterations of Judaism as an "inevitable return to its true incarnation," which rabbis often do, is unmistakably misguided (Heilman 11).

Elizabeth knows and accepts that she needs permission from the rabbi to open a store, and in this community, it is understood that "he wouldn't even see her if she came to him alone. The Rav doesn't really speak to women. Not to women outside his family. Not women with business propositions" (Goodman, *Kaaterskill* 97). Even when Isaac does go to the *Rav* and says, "My wife and I would like to ask your permission to open a small store in Kaaterskill," the *Rav* makes it very clear who he expects to be in charge: "*In addition* your wife," the *Rav* replies to Isaac's far more egalitarian "My wife and I" (obscuring the fact that it is really just "My wife"). The *Rav* also asks about Elizabeth's role in the enterprise; being a store-owner, after all, should not interfere with the crucial duties of a woman (159).

Thus early on, expectations of Elizabeth's exclusion from the professional world are evident. Although there are moments where we see a concession to the practical requirement of outside employment for women—"They expect to marry scholars and then support them when they learn," Elizabeth thinks in relation to her daughters, even as she expresses the fervent hope that they will be *more* and *other*—in the fictional Orthodox community that Goodman constructs, we are led to understand that women do not work outside of the home (69).

This notion in Goodman's novel that Orthodox women *don't* work—but should be able to—follows on the heels of *The Romance Reader*, published three years earlier. In Abraham's novel, which similarly takes place in the 1970s in upstate New York, a husband complains, "Think how it looks. A mother of seven children, a Chassidic mother, selling fabric. A saleslady." But the practicality takes priority. "I'm not ashamed," responds his wife. "What's wrong with a saleslady? Better than a schnorrer," she says, referring to her husband's habit of asking for money rather than working for it. The husband insists, "Your mother and grandmothers never thought of going out to work. . . . They stayed home all their lives and took care of the house, of their husbands and children. They knew they had everything a woman could want" (Abraham, *Romance* 196–197). But after years of living in near poverty, the money is welcomed by the family, and the mother leads by example: the main character, Rachel, soon thereafter applies for and gets a job teaching English at a Satmar school. Her mother says, "If Rachel likes teaching, she can continue doing it after she's married. Even after she has a baby. Nowadays young women work after their first baby. They get a baby-sitter. It's better than staying home all day, cleaning and cooking. Laundry can wait. Besides, with a husband who studies, the money has to come from somewhere" (202). Here, this concept—"the money has to come from somewhere"—seems new. But it is not.

In fact, women have long been the primary earners in ultra-Orthodox communities. In Haredi writer Ruchama King (Feuerman)'s novel *Seven Blessings* (2003), we encounter Tsippi, an Orthodox woman at the helm of a grocery store, supporting her husband. "Shlomo had been a kosher slaughterer, a shochet," we read in the opening chapter, "but as he got older he no longer had the stamina for the bloody work, and so [Tsippi]'d opened [a] Makolet grocery store. In this way she had enabled Shlomo to study—not just a few hours, but full-time, like a regular yeshiva student" (King 7). Even though Tsippi also does the (paid) work so she can pursue her (unpaid) hobby of matchmaking, King suggests, that is not the "official" reason for her grocery store.

Sociologist Orna Blumen writes, in her study of gender and labor in Israel's ultra-Orthodox communities, "From the 1950s on . . . general education for girls was extended through secondary school, which in turn opened up new jobs for women teachers under ultra-Orthodox patronage. . . . Consequently, community leaders promoted a new ideal of the ultra-Orthodox family: a *kollel* student and his wife the teacher (and breadwinner)" (Blumen, "Gendered Display" 131). Blumen notes that over time, the kinds of work permissible for women have diversified. This growing diversity in Orthodox women's income stream is not unproblematic for Orthodox men. However, because the women's work enables the men's studying, the men have generally tolerated it.

In January 2007, when Haredi rabbis in Israel prohibited women's continuing education programs and severely restricted other courses of study, the Israeli newspaper *Haaretz* reported it as "a devastating economic and professional blow to thousands of women teachers, who are the primary breadwinners in the ultra-Orthodox community." The left-wing paper added, "It is also a drastic regression in haredi women's ongoing process of moving ahead in their studies and career and in improving their economic situation" (Ettinger and Rotem). This ruling occurred in a community where, in the 1990s, the labor force participation of men dropped to one-third (Berman 907). Even the Haredi newspaper *Yated Ne'eman* declared the "repercussions on the teachers and the ultra-Orthodox education system are tantamount to an earthquake," arguing that "the issues at the heart of the ultra-Orthodox society are at stake—the limits of education, the norm requiring women to be the breadwinners while their husbands study and, above all, the authority of the rabbis and functionaries to foist restrictions on the increasingly frustrated public" (qtd. in Ettinger and Rotem). The practicality of women working so men can pursue religious aims thus allows for—and even depends on—women's education, integration, and development of a secular skillset, dramatically more so than the men's.[29]

The illogicality of the prohibition is not lost on the women themselves. A 2015 *Haaretz* article chronicled the backlash against it. "I am sure the rabbis are wise and great men," says a woman interviewed. However, she concluded, they can be wrong. This Orthodox mother of seven, who was pursuing a master's degree at the Hebrew University in Jerusalem, reported, "They're saying academia is dangerous for us. In our community, we protect our society by closing ourselves. And in academia I see it myself—it's so open, there are problems there. . . . But learning in girls' high schools without getting a degree is very expensive, and for nothing, because they don't get jobs afterward. I don't agree with this decision. They're saying a woman shouldn't study, and also not work, and also should provide an apartment upon marriage? It's not logical" (Chizhik-Goldschmidt). Not wanting to be openly defiant, the women in the article insist on pseudonyms, but their words suggest a determination to do what they think is right.

Still, the men's prohibitions come from a place of concern. The more worldly the wife, the higher the chance she will want to engage in the "outside world" and the lower the chance she will be content in the Orthodox "inside" world. "The decision seems to come out of fear: fear of secularism, of education, of women as the 'foundations' of the home interacting with the world beyond and becoming," as one woman who was interviewed explained, "less deep and less concerned with Yiddishkeit" (Chizhik-Goldschmidt). In *The Romance Reader*, the wife grows into what readers might see as a dynamic, three-dimensional person through her job, learning about American culture, improving her English, and trying to balance her roles—"Now that Ma has a job, housework has become less important. The kitchen and hallway are mopped only every third day, and the old aluminum pots no longer shine like mirrors" (Abraham, *Romance* 202). It comes across as a story of progress told incrementally. We see this arc in Tova Mirvis's *The Outside World* as well, when running a grocery store counter leads Tzippy to be interested in business, which leads her to go to the library, which leads her to enroll in college, which could lead her to . . . going off the *derech*? ("If you give a mouse a cookie. . . ." goes the classic children's book.) This never happens, but the fear is there. And a similar logic is apparent in *Kaaterskill Falls*, thanks to Elizabeth's flirtation with the outside world: "The bungalow seems smaller," thinks Elizabeth, fantasizing about a larger one. She "imagines idly that maybe if the store does well they could afford it. That's what it's like when you get a wish. It breeds others" (Goodman, *Kaaterskill* 190). Where will it end? the men and rabbis seem to be asking. Blumen argues that the men in the Orthodox communities she studies weigh the advantages of women's earnings from work against "the need to restrain employed women's independence, maintain their secondary position and enforce social control over them" (Blumen, "Gendered Display" 132).

It is not out of self-interest that Isaac supports his wife, but neither is it arbitrary that it is he who comes to the conclusion that his wife could be the *eshes chayil*, could "bringeth food from afar." Perhaps Isaac is not the strongest character in the book; he lacks Elizabeth's critical eye and seems complacent. His role at times appears to be to carry on the tradition in Jewish fiction of a good but weak Jewish man. (Note that at the conclusion of *A Price above Rubies*, it is Sonia's nice if unvirile husband, Sender's foil, who reaches out to Sonia to offer her a place in her son's life despite her exile from the community, but he does not defend her publicly or offer her custody, actions that are well beyond his power.) It would seem, however, that Isaac's support of his wife is more meaningful, particularly as it materializes not only when Elizabeth sits before the rabbi asking for permission for her store but again at the book's conclusion when he encourages her to try again, not give up, and embrace her ambition.

This masculine support of the heroine's quest does not undermine the feminism of the novel. Rather, it further destabilizes the authority of the rabbis, who are meant to think deeply and understand the present in a historically and biblically informed fashion—*but do not*. It is *Isaac* who cites the lines of the "Eshes Chayil," *Isaac*, an unexceptional scholar, who remembers what the rabbis have forgotten. As should be clear throughout this book, contemporary Jewish writers have been rewriting the Jewish woman in literature and "subverting conventionalized narratives of Jewish femininity," as Helene Meyers puts it. Yet, Meyers continues, they are also "troubl[ing] gender by re-presenting masculinity and imagining Jewish men as engaged in the cultural work of healing Jewish gender relations" (Meyers, "Jewish" 323). Gittel's husband tells his wife she is the real "Eishes Chayil" in *Hush*, the men in *The Women's Balcony* defy their rabbi in support of their wives, and Isaac Shulman, against the decree of the *Rav* and the mores of the community, defends his wife for doing what is right in his eyes and his reading of Judaism. These men prove themselves to be what Meyers calls *"men* of valor" (*Identity Papers* 22).

---

"Orthodoxy," writes Heilman in his landmark text, *Sliding to the Right*, "has not remained static" (Heilman 10). It "continues to raise the ante for those who want to consider themselves truly bound to Jewish tradition" and becomes ever and "more insular and parochial as well as religiously right wing" (11, 42). To understand why, Heilman looks to the rabbis and, specifically, "the disappearance of the generation of those trained by modeling themselves after the outward-looking Soloveitchik [a spiritual descendent of Hirsch, similarly armed with a doctoral degree along with rabbinical ordination], men who sought an impressive secular education to combine with their Jewish learning" (42). And with the ruptures caused by early twentieth-century immigration and the Holocaust, according to Benor, Orthodox Jews started putting increasing faith in strong authority figures instead of uncertain family traditions.

For the Orthodox rabbis of the postwar period, those who preceded their narrow-minded descendants, Heilman contends that they sought to "contemporize" and "traditionize"—make the old new and the new old. But that did not last. "By the end of the twentieth century, and increasingly following Soloveitchik's death in 1993, newly minted rabbis would emerge with viewpoints that were far more retrograde and parochial," writes Heilman (43). Ironically, Heilman sees this as the very moment when they should have been most actively engaging the rapidly changing world: "By the turn of the millennium, the need to find a way to harmonize Orthodoxy with such thorny issues as feminism [and] homosexuality . . . the matters that rose to prominence as time passed . . . required Orthodox reinterpretations of an unprecedented complexity. But the emerging Orthodox rabbis who might offer a modern Orthodox approach to negotiating these issues were more interested in reviewing ancient texts and embedding themselves in traditional yeshiva study or values than in providing direction through the changing currents of American life" (37). It is due to the failure of the rabbis that Jewish layfolk (writers of fiction and, consequently, heroes and heroines of such fiction) have taken action. In her novel that pits a powerful rabbi against a mere mother, Goodman suggests it is the woman who is able to embody the duality of *Torah im derech eretz*. Elizabeth is an (Anglo-) American entrepreneur with a head for business. And yet Elizabeth is also wholly a part of her religion, and she knows her place in it. She is not a contradiction of terms. She is a smart, creative businesswoman for whom "becoming a mother, keeping a Jewish home is the most important thing" (Goodman, *Kaaterskill* 69). Goodman uses her male character to, as Heilman says, "[review] ancient texts," but Isaac does so precisely to achieve the ends that Heilman finds lacking: to "harmonize Orthodoxy with such thorny issues as feminism."

At the end of Goodman's novel of dramatic oppositions, we arrive at the end of the Shabbat. We are thus drawn us away from the promise the start of the Shabbat holds, with its singing of the "Eshes Chayil" and its narrative of unification, to havdalah, which harkens division (we move from sacred to profane). Perhaps sustaining the unification is too hard—too much the stuff of fairytales. But arguably, we are to see continuity even in the division: fairy tales can be part of realism, the sacred part of the secular, and working outside the home a part of a woman's "keeping a Jewish home." Goodman therefore reframes the either/or of Orthodoxy and women's professional ambition with a both/and vision.

Although *Kaaterskill Falls* is a work of fiction, it offers a solution that is grounded in a biblical text, which ought to speak to Haredi communities. Because the women of these communities are, by and large, the primary breadwinners, the solution is pragmatic—that is, it justifies an existing practice. Unsurprisingly, we see other writers happily taking up Goodman's both/and vision in their stories of Orthodox women, like Yael Levy, an (Orthodox) author of romances featuring Orthodox Jews. In *Brooklyn Love* (2012), among the stories of *shidduch*-dating (Levy does a bit of matchmaking herself), we witness a daughter flattering her mother: "How many women are stockbrokers—let alone religious mothers? Oy." The mother tries to deflect the praise: "The stress!" The daughter, however, recognizes the good in her mother's ability to be a "religious mother" and a stockbroker: "But you love it." And the mother—and narrative—concede the same, safely embedding the story of ambition in the language of domestic care: "'Yeah, I love it.' Ma sighed. 'I love that I can help support my family and marry off you and your brothers'" (Levy 17).[30] Levy, like Goodman, treats the both/and vision as a success story—yes, women can have it all! The mother here is a role model.

Elizabeth too is clearly meant to be read as a role model for her daughters as well as a corrective figure for readers who might, like Beatrix, possess prejudices about Orthodox women, imagining them unable to be businesswomen. *Kaaterskill Falls* is a rich novel, however, because Elizabeth's achievement as a wife, mother, Orthodox Jew, and businesswoman is never foregone. She has to work at all these facets of herself and integrate them. It is not enough for her to own a store and be a part of the community: the store she owns needs to *serve* the community. The novel also draws its strength from the fact that Goodman has convinced us that Elizabeth is such a woman of valor that business enterprise is only one of the paths she might take. When Elizabeth stares at Cole's painting of the Kaaterskill Falls and has her revelation—"More than ever she wants to do something of her own. She has to make something; she has so much energy, she feels so strong"—and concludes, "I want to open a store," she could have, equally, it seems, wanted to help a child, solve a crime, build a bridge, or, like Cole, paint a picture (Goodman, *Kaaterskill* 83). After all, couldn't this Orthodox woman be an artist too?

CHAPTER 5

# She Will Be Praised at the Gates by Her Very Own Deeds

## THE ORTHODOX ARTIST AND THE FRUIT OF HER HANDS

### I. INTRODUCTION: FOR WOMEN ONLY

In the popular Israeli television show *Shtisel* (2013–), the overbearing patriarch of the Haredi family after which the series is named stands before a crowd of secular Jews at an awards ceremony in honor of his son, a painter. "If you take a walk in our neighborhood and ask an old Jew what art is, and what a museum is, you know what he will say?" Shulem Shtisel asks his interlocutors. "That art," he continues, ready with his own answer, "was invented by gentiles because they didn't have the Holy Bible. And they invented museums because they didn't have a *beis midrash*." The crowd smiles appreciatively, though, of course, the joke is on them, as they share with the gentiles these deficiencies. The point is that an award for painting is no honor at all; Orthodox Jews have and need no relationship to art apart from the poetry and calligraphy of the Torah. But the message of the series is otherwise; the father might agree with the "old Jew" of the neighborhood, but if so, that is because he himself is an old Jew, out of step with modernity, narrow-minded, unimaginative, and in this instance, simply wrong. Instead, we are encouraged to wonder: Is there no history of religious Jewish art? Why is such art considered by Reb Shtisel's real-life counterparts to be a collection of golden calves? Is this sentiment, like the restriction on women's driving, yet another sign of Haredization? Can't painting, like studying Torah or *Mishnah*, be doing God's work? How about creating films? What of making music that is not to be sung in synagogue halls but rather concert halls?[1] How might an Orthodox artist confront the issues of art's lack of respect and significance in the Orthodox world? Would Moishe Shagal have become Marc Chagall had he stayed within the confines of his Lubavitch Hasidic community? What of the implications of immodesty attributed to the artist? And if we think beyond

Figure 5.1. An Orthodox Jewish woman draws John Singer Sargent's 1883 oil on canvas portrait *Albert de Belleroche* on her iPad at the Metropolitan Museum of Art in New York City. Drawing by Alexandra Gluckman (2014). The (originally anonymous) model for this drawing is Elke Reva Sudin, whose painting of a PERL concert graces the front cover of this book. Permission to publish by Alexandra Gluckman.

the male representative of Orthodox artistry in the series, what additional considerations are there for a female Orthodox artist? Why is Batsheva, who arrives in Memphis in *The Ladies Auxiliary* with a box full of paintbrushes, immediately a source of suspicion and scorn? How would an Orthodox woman artist negotiate a religious ideology that maintains an unequal separation of the sexes in the public sphere, allowing women access to images of men but not men not to those of women? After all, the reluctance to portray women's images to men—even newspaper photographs of women's faces are routinely pixelated, removed, or blurred in Haredi communities—and *kol isha*, the prohibition of women singing before men, mean that women's audiovisual art is limited in production, consumption, and distribution.[2]

To consider this last point, imagine we are attending a production at the Globe Theatre in London during the Elizabethan era, when only men (or boys) could act out all of Shakespeare's roles—including Desdemona and Juliet, Ophelia and Cordelia. How silly they might look in drag, their voices pitched high, yet the lot of us would judge the performance as credible because we determined to suspend our disbelief when we crossed the threshold into the theater. Women have no place on the stage here unless we have accidentally landed in the pages of *Cue for Treason* (1940) or on the set of *Shakespeare in Love* (1998). But now imagine a slight alteration to this scene: the audience members are all men (perhaps you will need to take leave of the Globe yourself). With its doors closed to women, the setting might begin to look more like one of the other male-occupied spaces of the era. The Bodleian, for example, in the seventeenth century was a strictly male domain—not that Oxford fared much better going into the twentieth century, as Virginia Woolf coyly reminds with her depiction of the beadle, her perpetual nemesis, in "A Room of One's Own." We might choose to envision a slightly rowdier male establishment. In any case, we can ask: as all-male productions with all-male consumption, how might Shakespeare's plays have been different? What story lines would have been altered? What messages would they then bear?

Perhaps we cannot know how Shakespeare's oeuvre would have been different with this historical revision, but if we return to the twenty-first century, a time when gender roles and sex segregation are much more rigid for large portions of the Orthodox Jewish world, we can examine audiovisual works that Orthodox women produce exclusively for women's entertainment. Not only do women play men's roles (rare and few that these parts are), but they play them *badly*, campily, refusing to allow for any suspension of disbelief. It is too dangerous for a viewer to be unsure of the biological sex of the actor. This is a world in which uncertainty is not an excuse for sin. But it is also a world where the concerns of women come first (to Judith Shakespeare, another of Woolf's figurative devices, we might say: "Come back. Your time is now."). Forget male strivings to be admitted to Ponevezh or some other eminent yeshiva, to be recognized as great scholars, to become renowned rabbis. Forget male insecurities about their lack of knowledge of women's anatomy, anxieties about their masculinity, or concerns about their abilities to financially support their families. These are real issues in the Orthodox community—but they are parked on another lot.[3] Here, in the Orthodox women's film industry, women embrace the tension that ensues in the nexus of their artistic yearnings and strict sex segregation. These women are creative, generating a rich canon of works in—to channel Woolf once more—a room of their own.

In this chapter, I consider the challenges inherent in the very idea of Orthodox women artists as portrayed in the popular imaginary. By way of response to these perceived challenges, I will then investigate the art that Orthodox women are actively producing. I am concerned with stories throughout this book, but in this chapter I turn to ones told in film, a genre that brings together visual artistry and the narrative form. Certainly, Orthodox women are engaged in internally focused literary endeavors; among Orthodox women, a solid industry exists in the United States, thanks to Feldheim Publishers, and an even stronger one flourishes in Israel.[4] Yet film has become the main vehicle through which Orthodox women transmit stories to each other. Created by and for women, the films form the backbone of the Orthodox women's exclusive entertainment industry and are adapted to the specific lifestyles of Orthodox women. Films are primarily screened on nonholy festival days (Hanukkah and *chol hamo'ed*, or the intermediate days of Passover and Sukkoth) when women are not working and their daughters are off school and can also attend. DVDs, if released, bear some variation of the label, "For Women Only" (see figure 5.2).[5]

Women take part in every level of the creation and distribution of these works, and as a result, the twenty-first century has seen the rise of a strong feminocentric cultural canon among Orthodox women. This development has offered significant opportunities for women in Orthodox communities: the establishment of new artistic varieties and genres of work in written and audiovisual fields and also the construction of discursive as well as literal women's spaces. Though women's seminaries flourish, they are not, particularly for Haredi women, like men's yeshivas, places of lifelong study and community. Instead they are more typically short-term programs or ones aimed at vocational training.[6] Yet being denied the yeshiva has not only restricted women in their attainment of closeness to God in the traditional manner of study and prayer but also advantaged men by bestowing upon them a communal setting in which to develop intimate relationships, debate questions, navigate quandaries, negotiate meaning—and drink, laugh, sing, cry, dance, and love. Isaac Bashevis Singer's Yentl does not assume male drag to ogle manly Avigdor or sing "Papa, Can You Hear Me?" (though with Barbra Streisand as her eye/mouthpiece, she does these quite well); even the misogynistic Singer can imagine why a woman would want to learn at the yeshiva rather than be consigned to the home where she is more likely to be isolated, sheltered, bored, and darning socks. The art discussed in

Figure 5.2. Cartoon from Robin Garbose's film *The Heart That Sings* (2011). Animated by Doug Bresler. Permission to reproduce by Doug Bresler.

this chapter has offered women what the communal space of the yeshiva offers men—intellectually, spiritually, emotionally, and interpersonally.

Tobi Einhorn and Robin Garbose, American filmmakers, both add to the growing diversity of Orthodox women's films. Garbose, a pioneer in the field, stages musicals that are full of song and dance; Einhorn produces serious dramas. Through a close reading of their films, we see a significant engagement with contemporary issues for Orthodox women and girls. Among the issues they examine are women needing to work while also being charged with caring for their households, girls facing prejudice and discrimination from non-Jews and fellow Jews, women coping with being without families in a community with a cultural imperative to procreate, girls being restricted in their abilities to act on their faith, women being sent to the back of the bus to avoid contact with male passengers, girls finding God through nature and art, and girls and women needing supportive female *chavurot*. The films help girls and women work through their anxieties and reassure them they are not alone—much like the advice columns of Orthodox women's magazines. "It is not written anywhere in the Torah that a mother must bake," promises Rebbetzin Horowitz in issue 320 of *Binah: The Weekly Magazine for the Jewish Woman*. Relief comes across the pages of issue 322's "Your Say" responses: "I just read Rebbetzin Horowitz's article on baking and found myself nodding along. . . . Bakeries exist for people like me," writes D. Z. "Kudos to Rebbetzin Horowitz for voicing what is the truth for many of us," proclaims an anonymous reader. "I, too, don't bake—but I'm afraid to admit it in public. I was raised to believe that a good *balabusta* has fresh cake readily available, a stocked freezer, and a home that's spic and span. Enter the reality: I'm the mother of a large family and I work full-time (and often overtime!) to make ends meet." This working mother concludes, "Thanks for the validation" ("Your Say" 6). Faced with many pressures that they cannot easily ignore, Orthodox women need the collective support of their peers. Whether reading the posts and responses of women who feel similarly or sitting in a cinema, surrounded by such women and seeing women dramatize their personal concerns on the screen, Orthodox women are given validation and comfort.

Of course, sometimes, more than anything, women just need a bit of space— to be with each other, to bond, to share their hopes and dreams, and if there's a band playing music that livens the mood while elevating the soul, to rock out. Thus this chapter concludes with another kind of Orthodox woman artist, another story of female camaraderie, and the analysis of an alt-rock indie band's song lyrics through a Lubavitcher lens.

## II. God's Art: "Bedspreads She Makes Herself; Linen and Purple Wool Are Her Clothing"

*"You're an artist," he said. . . .*

*An artist forbidden to paint. Esther lowered her gaze to her doodle in the sand. There was a large bird in flight she surely couldn't have drawn, small shells running along the spine and into the tail.*

*"Nice work," he added when she didn't reply.*

*Her toes passed through the sand to erase the bird. I'm an artist. The words banged in her head. I'm a Jerusalem maiden. A Jewess. A wife. A mother. An artist. A sister? An artist. An artist. An artist.*

—Talia Carner, *Jerusalem Maiden* (2011)

The art of Rivka Krinsky is strikingly modern, religious, and personal. Among her paintings is that of an intricate wristwatch: it is the Felipe Massa, named after the Formula 1 driver and a part of Richard Mille's exclusive collection. The wristwatch is a sleek device on a carbon nanofiber baseplate, with thirty-one jewels and a split-second chronograph. It is silver, as is the wrist on which it's wrapped and the hand at the wrist's end. The silver hand fills the center of the canvas, making a "silent fox" gesture. The painting appears futuristic and slightly alien.

Another one of Krinsky's paintings shows Rebbe Menachem Mendel Schneerson, the last Chabad rebbe, standing side by side with Krinsky's husband's grandfather, Rabbi Yehuda Krinsky, former secretary to the rebbe. Both men are looking down. The brush strokes are heavy; the palette is dark. The only light in the painting comes by way of the glow from these holy men's beatific faces.[7]

A third painting, done in blues, greens, and vibrant earth tones, shows an older woman, her hair invisible beneath a turban, her smile broad and handsome, vigorously lifting a cord that holds a wrapped package. The caption indicates that this woman was Krinsky's midwife and she was weighing Krinsky's newborn son.

Krinsky lives in an artistic world. Her husband, whom she met "through the arts," is a graphic designer. Among the Krinsky clan are several other artists and a well-known (for-women-only) singer, also named Rivka Krinsky. In addition to being an artist, Krinsky is an actress. Under her birth name, Siegel, she starred in *A Light for Greytowers* (2007), *The Heart That Sings* (2011), and *Operation: Candlelight* (2014)—in other words, director Robin Garbose's oeuvre of films. Krinsky recounts, "When I got engaged to my husband, the Krinsky female cousins and aunts told me that they had all watched *The Heart That Sings* together the night before I went to meet them." Asked about the overall reception Rivka received for her artwork and performance, Rivka replied enthusiastically, "There is no lack of support, thank G-d!" (personal correspondence).

Chabad might be exceptional in its attitude toward artists, but nevertheless, it is hard not to compare the positive experience of this real-life Orthodox artist to her fictional counterparts, Orthodox artists who struggle or do not know how to have their art recognized and validated by their communities. Another scene from the *Shtisel* illustrates this point. In the second season, we encounter Libi Shtisel, newly arrived from Antwerp. She is temporarily occupying her cousin (A)kiva's bedroom. One night, she looks under his bed. She discovers Kiva's secret cache of sketches and watercolors. Played by Hadas Yaron, an actress who has made a career of Haredi roles (she first won international acclaim starring as the adorable Haredi girl of a marriageable age in *Fill the Void*), Libi is sweet and compelling as she tells the series' hero: "If God had given me such a gift, such a talent, I'd do my best not to waste it." (Her statement is ironic for the viewer well versed in Yaron films; as a Haredi housewife in Giroux's *Félix et Meira*, Yaron was the one we saw hiding her paintings and thus rejecting God's gift.) *Shtisel* promotes the idea that art and artistic calling should be as fundamental to the lives of Haredim as anyone else.[8] Although the opportunity of a *shidduch*, or marital match, for Libi interferes with the cousins' plan to sell Kiva's art to the trendy galleries of Tel Aviv—the Orthodox Jewish woman's nuptial status, naturally, is prioritized over all, including God's gifts—by the end of that episode, Libi has inspired Kiva to follow his dream instead of resignedly teaching at a cheder under the patriarchal rule of his father (the principal). But much is sacrificed in his pursuit.

Hebrew Studies scholar Yaron Peleg critiques *Shtisel*'s secondary art story line, as he does the show's main romantic love story line, by calling it a secular fantasy glossed onto a Haredi reality. He writes, "An artistic career is not a real option in Akiva's Orthodox world." Rather, he sees it as a fiction that allows the character to "express his individuality and escape the strictures of his confining community" (Peleg 112–113). Needing to escape confining strictures is, of course, how most Haredim are depicted. To demonstrate what he sees as the unrealistic element of the artistic plot line, Peleg describes the difference between Akiva's date with a woman who does not appreciate his art and his encounter with a woman who does:

> The contrast between the two dates and the connection to art is significant here. It is perfectly acceptable, even in the Orthodox dating context, not to like someone for any reason whatever. But what Akiva hopes for is that his future wife will appreciate his art and be sensitive to it. This is not a simple request, as anything not connected to the study of scripture in the Orthodox world is considered frivolous—unworthy of time and attention. Akiva's expectation, then, that he would have an intellectual and emotional connection with his future bride and that she would appreciate his art, is uncommon. But it is unusual only in an Orthodox context—even in the Israeli Orthodox milieu, which has internalized many values of the Israeli majority culture. For Western, secular culture such concerns—true love, professional fulfillment, and especially artistic fulfillment—are of utmost importance and are the ultimate goals in life. That these are also Akiva's concerns and that they occupy center stage in a show about the Orthodox reveals the kind of cultural exchange this and other "religious" shows exhibit. (113)

For Peleg, the cultural exchange between secular and religious, represented in the themes of love, professional fulfillment, and especially artistic fulfillment, is razor thin. Ultimately, he does not see *Shtisel* as a "religious" show at all, despite the trappings.[9] It is as if *Shtisel* were a secular writer's fantasy of the Haredi world—though in fact, writer and creator Yehonatan Indursky grew up Haredi and attended Ponevezh, the "Harvard of Yeshivas" (Peleg does not remark on this fact, not even to suggest that the writer might be choosing to use his intimate knowledge of the Haredi world to pander to the secular one).[10] What is ironic in Peleg's analysis, however, is that he undoes the very work of humanizing the Orthodox community that he recognizes *Shtisel* as doing. In fact, to see the community as one in which "anything not connected to the study of scripture . . . is considered frivolous" negates an entire field of production *by* Orthodox artists, like Krinsky.

Peleg may also be wrong to read this television program as strictly for secular consumption. This was likely the original intention of the show, with Akiva's art nicely functioning as an in-text analogue to the series: just as *Shtisel*, supported by an American foundation, offers an intimate portrayal of Orthodox people for secular viewers, so too does Akiva's art, which is awarded a prize by a secular American philanthropist on the show.[11] However, Akiva's dream of becoming an artist (like his dream of falling in love) may also resonate with Haredi audiences, particularly as *Shtisel* continues to explore in depth precisely what such a dream in such a community means. Akiva's dream holds a place in all of his relationships: with God, his exacting father, his dead mother, his collection of friends, his wider community, and his bridal candidates. It influences his views of his professional future, the secular world, art history, patronage, and his own development as an individual. What do Haredim think of the show? Unfortunately, it is difficult to determine the show's popularity in the Haredi community—a community that is supposed to shun television (a fact the show indulgently uses as a story line when the Shtisel matriarch is moved into a nursing home with a television set and becomes an avid fan of *The Bold and the Beautiful*, reading promiscuous twelve-times-married Brooke Logan through her Haredi lens as a fine example of wifely devotion and motherhood). Its presence, however, is not negligible. How else would music from the fictional Haredi community of *Shtisel* appear at real Haredi weddings?[12] There is good reason to think that the trials and tribulations of the Shtisel family, including Akiva's desire to draw, appeal very much to the surreptitious Orthodox *Shtisel*-watchers.

And if a Haredi man can justify his artistic calling, even to a Haredi audience—can a Haredi woman as well? In some ways, this seems the easier sell: Orthodox women, who work and negotiate the marketplace are (and are expected to be) more engaged in mainstream culture than men. In other ways, it seems even less realistic: a woman who positions herself as an artist is self-important and not *tznius*, modest, one of the most important attributes of an Orthodox woman. This is precisely Mirvis's starting point in *The Ladies Auxiliary* with Batsheva, whose bold paintings and loud singing mark her as immodest. More problematically, a woman who turns her attention to art might not be able to play her fundamental role of mother. For "Jewish Gothic" American-Israeli writer Ragen, an artistic sensibility on a Haredi woman is akin to a scarlet letter. The author, known for her critiques of ultra-Orthodoxy, uses the artistic heroine of her 1989 novel *Jephte's Daughter* to condemn the community in which she is imprisoned like an exotic bird in a cage (a metaphor she favors).

Alongside Ragen's critique of Orthodoxy, however, there is also the establishment of a discursive space for the Orthodox woman artist (a figure with whom Ragen likely identifies), which is extended in *The Ladies Auxiliary*. In *Jephte's Daughter*, Batsheva Ha-Levi's susceptibility to beauty marks her as exceptional at a young age, and by the time she is nine years old, "she began to perceive the world as a giant canvas and God as the greatest artist of all" (28). Because this is a gothic tale, we can imagine ominous music beginning to rumble softly in the distance at this point. After the young Batsheva writes an essay exalting the fine qualities of an altarpiece glimpsed at the Metropolitan, "a shocked Rebbitzen Finegold . . . ripped it to shreds: 'Anything used for idol worship cannot be beautiful,' the woman said severely" (29). The music rises to a crescendo. Batsheva is sent off to Israel and pushed into marrying a man that is appropriate for her eminent line of descent. The reader is introduced to this man by way of his thoughts about women's roles: "The only purpose in life for a true daughter of Israel was to bear Jewish children and to make it possible for her husband to learn." Men were created to be scholars, "while woman's intelligence was given only to lighten his heavy load of Torah learning by being the wage-earner, cooking, cleaning, raising the children and keeping them disciplined and quiet" (66). (This rather sounds like Yezierska's Reb Smolinsky come back to haunt contemporary Orthodox women, doesn't it?) Our fear that our beautiful heroine is about to be victimized by this misogynist becomes palpable.

But wait—we are not entering Janet Leigh's hotel bathroom just yet. The pitch falls as the bored housewife buys herself a Leica. Batsheva discovers, through her lens, the exquisite colors and contours of Jerusalem's stone villas and narrow alleyways, the Judean hills and dense forests. We are lulled into a false sense of security and simultaneously entranced by the fictional Orthodox woman artist's photographic rendering (made visible by the living Orthodox woman artist's narrative rendering) of this majestic city. But then the beat rises again as we realize that this Leica is to be the instrument of Batsheva's doom! Next thing we know, Batsheva is wishing for death as a "way out" and running off to the sea (in the spirit of her foremothers, fictional and historical—Edna Pontellier, Virginia Woolf!). There is a suicide note, and then her gray dress, along with her son's vest, bound in seaweed and tar, wash up on the shore.

Is there no place for the Orthodox woman artist? Ragen refuses to acknowledge this impossibility as grounded in real Judaism or all Orthodoxy. In a dramatic (yet oddly unsurprising) twist, Ragen resurrects Batsheva—not as one of the undead but rather as a successful photographer (though the tableau of her death is perhaps her ultimate masterpiece). As an artist, Batsheva dazzles the celebrated art scene of London with a "one-woman show for a famous gallery" (390). The narrator compares Batsheva's photographs to those of Diane Arbus. The opening night of the gallery sees an enormous crowd; people are "genuinely impressed, genuinely glad to meet her" (395). To add to her triumph, Ragen has Batsheva divorce the Haredi villain of the novel and marry a Daniel Deronda / Peter Decker figure. At the close of the book, Batsheva realizes that she is also wedded to halacha, to Judaism, to *Orthodox* Judaism: "She could not run away from it because it was simply a part of her . . . it was not her faith in God or His Law that she lacked. *It was her faith in man, in the men who had been delegated to carry out His Law*" (424, emphasis mine). As in the "off-the-*derech*" narratives, Orthodox Judaism is reclaimed through the *indictment* of the Orthodox men who *corrupt* it. Meanwhile, Orthodox women's roles as artists are also reclaimed—and, in fact, exalted.

If Ragen's readers assumed, initially, that there was no place for the Orthodox woman artist or art in Orthodoxy, they soon learn that they share the views of only the unsophisticated Haredi Jews (here, Rebbetzin Finegold and Batsheva's husband). Our heroine (the first of Ragen's many heroines who take on what we might call the "Modern Orthodox compromise") knows better. As Batsheva wanders through the streets of gold-lit Jerusalem, Ragen presents Batsheva's photography as holy work—much as Reva Mann describes her extramarital affairs in *The Rabbi's Daughter*. (Also mirrored in these books are the accounts of failed wedding nights, ruined by men more concerned with their prayer books than their brides.) "It was true that one wasn't allowed to make statues to worship," we learn through the novel's free indirect discourse, "but that was a long way from taking photographs of the mountains, she told herself. She felt in her heart that the images she captured were a kind of psalm, a paean of praise to God for His incredible handiwork" (Ragen, *Jephte's Daughter* 142). It is through her photography that Batsheva has her "revelation" about the importance of Judaism to her soul (144).

Feminine artistry acts as a funhouse mirror on masculine piety, revealing an obverse, and *perverse*, reflection of men's Judaism. Batsheva's husband, Isaac, communes with God through prayer and punishing interpretations and implementations of biblical verse. If Batsheva, as an artist, discovers the beauty of Judaism, Isaac distorts it: "She found that Isaac Harshen was making up a lot of what he piously quoted her or seriously misconstruing it. There were laws he half fabricated, or twisted just to keep her under his thumb . . . while the clear intent of the Talmud, she had learned, was to make men charitable, generous, loving, forgiving, hospitable, and honest" (224). Guilty too are the women who support these men in their destruction of Orthodoxy; a counselor hears Batsheva's stories of emotional and physical abuse by her husband and tells her, "The man must be the head of the family, otherwise the family crumbles. Be a Woman of Valor. Bear up your hardships as a good Jewish girl must" (237). It is through her art that Batsheva sees, and allows readers to see, that (as in *A Price above Rubies*) this oppressive version of the "Woman of Valor" is misleading, having been stripped of its strength, dignity, beauty, and complexity.

The women in Mirvis's novel are similarly critiqued. Focused on clean houses and home-cooked meals, the Orthodox women of *The Ladies Auxiliary* fail to communicate the spiritual elements of Judaism to their daughters, threatening the future of Orthodoxy. It takes the arrival of an artist—unusual, threatening, and sensual—to infuse new life into the community and initiate Jewish renewal through her work (her six-foot-high menorah, her multicolored sukkah, her art lessons for the Orthodox girls' school). So what if she buys frozen microwaveable meals (like Yakin's Sonia) and stands too close to the rabbi's son? The beauty she brings to—or rather, brings out of—Judaism marks her as the holiest woman of the novel.

This possibility, however, continues to be writ as nearly or plainly untenable, as we see with Israeli American writer Talia Carner's 2011 novel *Jerusalem Maiden*, a *Künstlerroman*, or the portrait of an artist as a young *frummer*. This budding artist, Esther, thinks of her mother as a "Woman of Valor—an industrious, great *tzadeket* who helped the poor . . . a virtuous woman who knew she could bring salvation to our people by bearing many children" (Carner, *Jerusalem* 264). "What is a woman but a creator of new life?" asks Esther's sister (296). "Motherhood was the whole point of living," Esther concludes later. "That was the essence of being a Jewish woman" (323). Thus when the talented Esther is chastened by her art teacher for refusing to paint, she asks, "How can [women] dedicate themselves to art when their bodies are their destiny?" (345). By this question, she is not referring to the joys of the body, to sexual desire or satisfaction, but to the maternal condition that she is told defines the female form.

In the novel's opening pages, Carner sets up the religious expectations for girls—"to become betrothed at twelve, as every good Jerusalem maiden should upon entering mitzvah age" because "marriage was the Haredi community's building block . . . a maiden carried the promise of perpetuity for all Jews" (5, 11). Carner then constructs the diametrically opposing forces of Esther's life: her desire to be a woman of valor, as she imagines her mother to be, and an artist, whose nature is wild and passionate—the biblical model's obverse. "Nathan," she thinks of her husband late in the novel, "was such a good man. He deserved a decent wife, not a wild one who indulged her urges." Through indirect discourse or perhaps authorial assertion, we are instructed in the corollary of this indulgence: "She wasn't a Woman of Valor" (282).

To Esther's question about whether women can dedicate themselves to art, Mlle Thibaux (a wise teacher to the secular reader but a tempting Eve for the in-text Haredi community) responds, "Couldn't God be satisfied if millions of women procreated while He made an exception for a select few?" (345). She then leads Esther to a painting that Esther had created years before, now exhibited in the Louvre (by putting the juvenile Esther's painting essentially on par with the *Mona Lisa*, Carner disposes with subtlety here, as she does with Esther's relationship with Chaim Soutine and in the incidental purchase of a painting, which turns out to be an unfinished Picasso). Is there indeed a place in the Haredi world for Mlle Thibaux's "select few"? Would there be a resonance among Haredi women with a *tichel*-wearing Esther, like a black-hatted Kiva, hesitantly holding up her paintbrushes—or setting up her tripod or tuning her guitar? Carner seems to suggest that such a figure is, beyond a reasonable doubt, the stuff of the wildest imagination. In fact, on her website, Carner justifies the *strangeness* of her story by saying that it is not grounded in realism. Rather, it is the what-if life of her grandmother, a woman "whose embroidery left me breathless" because, as Carner explains pitifully of the real-life mother of six, she "channeled her astonishing talent in art into the crafts permitted to women of her generation and religious background" (Carner, "The Story"). Even in fiction framed as speculative, the author has her heroine's art career cut dramatically short: Esther's much-beloved son is trampled by a wagon and left legless, an event Esther sees as divine punishment for her sin of pursuing her passion(s).[13] Before returning to Palestine to perform her proper duty as wife and mother, Esther stops to slash all her canvases, leaving no trace of her work as an artist but for the single, haunting painting on the wall of the Louvre.

In *Jerusalem Maiden*, as in *Jephte's Daughter*, the Orthodox woman artist struggles with a version of the woman of valor that seems antithetical to the glory of the world. But Esther is attuned to the words of the biblical hymn, to the poetry, to the artistry of the hymn's form and the symmetry of its alpha- betical arrangement. This recognition gives her strength to resist the message that her community interprets from the hymn, and gives her the strength to say, "Even in the bible there isn't one true Woman of Valor" (Carner, *Jerusalem* 107). Through their creation and understanding of art, the women of these stories appear to access and disseminate a higher, purer, finer, and more beautiful spirit of Judaism.

Thus even as women's creativity is made fraught by community expectations and authorial punishments, we are asked to consider art as the vision or work of God. We are asked to consider the artist as Emerson's transparent eyeball, "a part or particle of God," or as God's apprentice. The painting of the gecko that Esther constructs in the novel can hardly be a sinful graven image when the gecko itself is a "painting" of God's: "She studied the translucency of the skin of the valiant [gecko]. . . . How did God paint their fragility?" (Carner, *Jerusalem* 4). *Shtisel's* Libi sees art as "God's gift." Ragen's Batsheva "felt in her heart that the images she captured were a kind of psalm, a paean of praise to God for His incredible handi- work" (Ragen, *Jephte's Daughter* 142). Carner's Esther is "destined by the creator," her urge to paint divine, her fingers a conduit: "Surely, this was the work of God. He must be guiding her hand" (Carner, *Jerusalem* 46). These are not merely secu- lar stories with an Orthodox veneer or attempts to subject "religious society to the cultural codes of the majority secular culture" and thus "normalize . . . Orthodox society" (Peleg 108). On the contrary, Carner, Indursky, Alon, and Ragen recog- nize the divine prism through which Orthodox men and women read the world. We might recall the heartfelt words of Quebec writer Malka Zipora, who sat down to write tales of her life as a Hasidic mom and found herself at the center of positive attention in an otherwise often openly hostile milieu. She explained that it was necessary to "believe that the details surrounding the publication of the book, leading up to it, the characters involved in its conception and its publica- tion were orchestrated by a Higher Hand" (Zipora 9). We might remember the "gratitude" Rebecca (and her author, Astaire) had for "the One Who bestows all good" when *The Disappearing Dowry* did well (*Ruby* 3).

Similarly, we see that Orthodox women's films appear to be motivated by a belief that they are not mere works of art but products of a divine spirit. As Marlyn Vinig states, "The chief protagonist of these films is God, around whom many yearnings swirl" ("Icon"). The filmmakers take seriously their mission to infuse their artistic visions with the language and spirit of God, Torah, and *Yid- dishkeit*. But Orthodox women filmmakers clearly have another mission, one not imagined in the visions of the Orthodox artist produced by Ragen, Carner, Indursky, and Alon, which present lone hero(ine)s and rugged individuals who try to capture and reproduce the art of God for the masses.

For the Orthodox woman filmmaker, films are endowed with the power to bring women closer to God and God closer to women—*and* to bring women closer to each other.

## III. DREAMERS OR DOERS? THE ORTHODOX WOMEN'S FILM INDUSTRY

*December 11, 18 and varying dates WORLDWIDE: New Film for Women!*
*"Almost a Family" by Tobi Einhorn!*

*Mekimi in conjunction with TECK Productions presents "Almost a Family" because everyone needs family. . . . A heartwarming drama by Toby Einhorn and Chavy Klein, the producers of "A Blessing in Disguise." Enjoy an evening of meaningful entertainment, a touching story with an everlasting message. Motzei Shabbat Dec 11 & 18: Boro Park, BY of BP, 1361 46th St, 8:15pm; Lakewood: Cheder Bnei Torah, 419 5th St, 8:15pm. Monsey, Motzei Shabbat Dec 18: The Atrium Plaza, 401 West Rt 59, 8:15pm. $20 admission. Professionally filmed by all women's crew Zohar Lavi-Hassan Films. L'zecher Nishmas Chaim Morde-chai ben R'Baruch. For women and girls of all ages. For more information call Mekimi 718-841-7500. Showing worldwide this December, additional shows Chol Hamoed Pesach in select cities. Upcoming Locations, see local pages for further details, admissions may vary: Gibraltar Dec 18, Golders Green London Dec 29, Manchester UK Dec 7, Stamford Hill UK Dec 25–26, Bala Cynwyd-Philadelphia PA Jan 1, Baltimore Dec 18, Dallas Tx Jan 22, Edison NJ Jan 24, Los Angeles Dec 18, South Fallsburg Jan 29, Union City NJ Dec 18. Dates TBA: Antwerp Belgium, Strasbourg France, Vienna Austria, Boston, Bridgeport CT, Cleveland, Cherry Hill NJ, Denver, Milwaukee, Passaic NJ, Queens and South Bend, IN.*

—*Atara Arts Newsletter*, "Announcements Relating to the Arts in Accordance with Torah Values," December 6, 2010

In 1908, when the first movie house opened in Jerusalem, Orthodox rabbis forbade the medium of film.[14] A hundred years later, however, the Haredi film industry is a burgeoning field, particularly for women. Men are creating action films, though these are typically of the made-for-DVD variety. Women are developing dramas and musicals made for the big screen; their work is being shown at film festivals, on the Paramount lot, in cinemas, and in the halls of synagogues and community centers internationally. Kol Neshama, in Los Angeles, was founded in 2000 as a performing arts conservatory in a "Torah-observant setting," for girls to "experience the joy and benefit of creative expression while developing their gifts with a Torah perspective" ("Kol Neshama"). The Ma'aleh School of Television,

Film and the Arts in Jerusalem has a female Orthodox clientele and is "devoted to exploring the intersection of Judaism and modern life" ("Ma'aleh"). In 2014, Ma'aleh launched an "ultra-Orthodox Women's track," which was initially limited to documentary film but then expanded its repertoire to include fiction. Another film school in Israel is entirely devoted to an Orthodox (typically Hardal) community: Torat HaChaim film and theater school uses (rabbi-approved) scenes cut from secular films to teach students cinematography and teaches men and women on separate days. Robin Garbose, who established Kol Neshama, did so to create opportunities for Orthodox girls with a "burning desire to perform" (Trappler Spielman, "Friday Film"). Similarly, Ma'aleh's website promises that if women have the "burning need to make art a significant statement," they are welcome there, and they have the encouragement and blessings of the rabbis and female educators ("Ma'aleh," my translation).

Rivka Krinsky, a graduate of a joint Stern College–Fashion Institute of Technology program in New York as well as of the Bezalel Academy of Arts and Design in Israel, told me, "When I was growing up, there was very little outlet for artistic expression. Robin Garbose pretty much had the first camp I had ever heard of. I really didn't even know I liked or was good at painting until I got to college. These days I find there is so much more being offered and incorporated into the schools" (personal correspondence). Indeed, more opportunities keep arising. In 2016, planning committees of the Jerusalem municipality proposed the Beit Yaakov Center for Performance Arts to house an Orthodox women's cinema, theater, dance space, and art galleries (Goldman).

But how and why did the Orthodox women's film industry develop? To answer this question, I turn to the work of Yoel Finkelman, who, in *Strictly Kosher Reading*, examines Haredi popular cultural productions (cookbooks, self-help guides, board games, parenting guides) through the lens of Sylvia Barack Fishman's model of compartmentalization, adaptation, and coalescence. According to Finkelman, the filtering of (desirable and adaptable) features of mainstream culture into Haredi culture is generally strategic: "To maximize Haredi consumption of Haredi culture and minimize Haredi consumption of general culture, the Haredi enclave has an interest in making available Haredi versions of whatever resources exist in general culture" (65–66). The system is one in which artists are required to flirt with the outside world to fulfill the needs—both defensive (to filter out) and developmental (to filter in)—of the inside one. The artists can be put in precarious situations: as in *Kaaterskill Falls*, rabbinical approval is not guaranteed. An innovative artist might inspire rabbis needing to assert their authority to make examples of those whose "Haredi versions" seem threatening—too close to the non-Haredi versions, too foreign, or subversive. An artist assumes she is creating a "kosher" text, and rabbis, by rejecting it, might destroy the artist's livelihood. But generally, the industry has been endorsed rather than condemned by rabbis. In an article on the Jewish Revenge men's action series, Yael Friedman and

Yohai Hakak account for the rabbinic support of such film, explaining that the filmmakers are understood to be "providing 'kosher' alternatives to those young men on the margins of Haredi society, who otherwise would be exposed to secular films, which are considered to be much worse" (51). The result, Finkelman determines, is a distinctive community with "expansive social capital and a thick cultural atmosphere" (31).

Finkelman argues that Haredi popular culture is built on an imitation game. "Haredi novels borrow literary genres and formulas from the general bestsellers and fill them with Haredi characters and values," he writes. "Imitating the most contemporary styles helps make the tradition seem sophisticated and up to date" (Finkelman 45). The argument suggests that the "outside world" is easily and regularly consumed by the insular Orthodox communities (and, in fact, there is much to support this claim, particularly in the internet era).[15] It is also important to note, however, that successful writers and filmmakers in the Orthodox community are often *ba'alei teshuva*, educated in the secular world before claiming the Orthodox world as their own, as Vinig (herself a *ba'alat teshuva*) details in *Orthodox Cinema*.[16] A case in point is Burshtein. Interviewing Burshtein after the release of *Fill the Void*, *Washington Post* columnist Emily Wax begins, "She's the first ultra-Orthodox Jewish woman to write and direct a feature-length film for a general audience—a notable achievement, since her highly insular community typically forbids watching secular television and movies"—a fact that is set to confuse readers (How can she know how a film is made if she's never even seen one?). After detailing the plot of the film for readers, Wax clears up the confusion: "Burshtein," she explains, "might be the ideal person to bring outsiders into the Orthodox world. She is what's known as a baal teshuva, a secular Jew who has returned to the faith. (Before she became religious, she graduated in 1995 from the Sam Spiegel Film and Television School, in Jerusalem, the most prestigious institution of its kind in the country.)" Wax then goes on to argue that *ba'alei teshuva* (like singer Matisyahu and actress Mayim Bialik) are essential to infusing culture into the Orthodox arts world. Inhabiting a liminal space, these artists are best positioned to speak from and to both worlds, Orthodox and secular.

But speaking to the secular world is not an essential ingredient for films that are not intended for that world. As discussed in the context of Zipora's *Lekhaim!* or *Rather Laugh than Cry*, Burshtein called her film a "window to the Orthodox world." This phrase came to define the film in the press.[17] The Orthodox themselves, of course, need no window. Burshtein explained, "They would relate to it totally because it's their world. But *Fill the Void* is not for the [Haredi] community. It's not made for them. If it was, it would be in a totally different language." Inkoo Kang, the *Village Voice*'s television critic, adds, "By this she means a different language of cinema, as the Haredim, she says, haven't seen the movies that have established the contemporary grammar of narrative features." Rather,

or more importantly, the filmmakers who choose to make "kosher" cinema
are negotiating more and greater considerations than a Hollywood filmmaker.
Although elements of artistry and wide likeability are still important (a good
Orthodox film will be screened in Orthodox communities worldwide, and some
are also available on DVD), attendance to rabbinical and communal demands is
the primary concern.

This point is nicely illuminated in Efrat Shalom Danon's 2011 documentary,
*The Dreamers* (*Ha'Cholmot*), which tells the story of the Orthodox women's
industry in Israel by focusing on two women whose filmmaking "dreams" lead to
very different realities. The genre of documentary is familiar: we could as easily
imagine a documentary that chronicles the pursuits of two young ambitious
women who come to Los Angeles with ten dollars and the desire to be famous.
At the end of such a film, no doubt one sees her name inscribed in a brass star
on the terrazzo of the Hollywood Walk of Fame; the other becomes a Skid Row
drug addict, taking shelter in a cardboard box. The two Israeli Orthodox women,
Tikvah and Ruchama, offer a variation on this theme: modestly dressed and
ensconced in houses lined with the books of the Torah and the Talmud, they are
wives, they are mothers, and they are committed to their religious communities. But similarly, by the end of the film, one of the women sees her hard work
brought to life on a big screen, and the other is addled in debt, a failure, and
worse, possibly regarded as a rebel in her community.

The documentary acts as a cautionary tale, though what it is cautioning against
is a moving target: in the opening scene, we witness Ruchama, trying to concen-
trate on her script despite the sound of a crying baby and other noisy children
in the background who continually disrupt her train of thought, which sets up a
conflict between motherhood and creativity. "How can [women] dedicate themselves to art when their bodies are their destiny?" asked the fictional Orthodox
artist Esther Kaminsky. Yet the actual tension of the film ultimately appears to be
otherwise: as in *Kaaterskill Falls* and *The Women's Balcony*, the tension is between
the women and the rabbis. Ruchama is not brought down by her family. In fact,
it is clear that her husband strongly supports her; he is cosigning loans to finance
her work. What destroys her is her inability to toe the line. Watching the documentary, we are not privy to the details of Ruchama's film, *Closed*, but we know
it involves a girl silently disagreeing with her mother. That this can be considered
transgressive becomes evident when one of the film's actresses, Hila, summarizes
the film as "dealing with authority figures," and Ruchama admits that she has had
to revise the script to make it less threatening. Ruchama, in fact, takes her script to
Vinig, a self-proclaimed "icon in the Haredi world."[18] Vinig worries that the audience will wonder where the filmmaker stands on such conflicts.

The silence, Ruchama says, of the daughter character in response to her mother's refusal to allow her to do what she wants reflects "constraints due to our

need to give the public what it wants because it'd be really inappropriate if she'd really run away[,] and take[n] one more step, this film would be inappropriate. It can't be presented that way. Many things were done here because we can't do things to the full. You see?" she asks Hila, simultaneously appealing to the audience's sympathy for the oppressed Orthodox woman. Friedman and Hakak argue that Haredi films are used as "internal communication that challenges the dominant Haredi discourse" (69). Ruchama indeed employs analogy and silence in an attempt to challenge the restrictions she faces. Yet Friedman and Hakak distinguish this raison d'être from that of most "counter-cinemas": to "undo the legacies of misrepresentation of these groups in dominant cultures by appropriating Western cinema and media forms and developing alternative practices and aesthetics" (79). Both impetuses, however, are significant—at least as is evident in American Orthodox women's cinema.

In mainstream American popular culture and media, Orthodox women have been represented as passive, limited, interpellated subjects in an oppressive patriarchal society, as I have shown throughout this book. Orthodox women in the United States, regardless of the supposed insularity of their communities, are simultaneously absorbing and internalizing and resenting and rejecting these representations. There is thus no question that the empowered Orthodox women that the American Orthodox film industry features are a retort to and revision of these depictions. In other words, a response to Orthodox women's images in the "outside world," even if that response is in the form of internal communication, plays a significant role in the Orthodox women filmmakers' alternative cinema.

Orthodox women filmmakers offer their viewers (fellow Orthodox women) opportunities to see their issues—with the outside world and the inside one—projected onto the safe space of a screen. There, battles can be fought and won, grievances aired and contained, and communities lost and reclaimed virtually, by proxy—and, in the case of Garbose's films, through song and dance.

### IV. The Films of Robin Garbose: *Torah and Girl Power!*

*While [the culture industry] claims to lead the perplexed, it deludes them with false conflicts, which they are to exchange for their own. It solves conflicts for them only in appearance, in a way that they can hardly be solved in their real lives. In the products of the culture industry human beings get into trouble only so that they can be rescued unharmed, usually by representatives of a benevolent collective; and then in empty harmony, they are reconciled with the general, whose demands they experienced at the outset as irreconcilable with their interests.*

—Theodor W. Adorno, "Culture Industry Reconsidered" (1975)

*Most central to Garbose's sensibility is a celebration of "girl power."*
—Simi Horwitz, "These Frum Filmmakers Are
Revolutionizing Orthodox Cinema" (2016)

Unlike Ruchama's *Closed* in *The Dreamers*, Garbose's films seem anything but rebellious. Garbose is a remarkably successful filmmaker in the Orthodox women's film industry and the first to create a film widely considered to be high quality. As with Burshtein, Garbose did not grow up Orthodox, receive her film training in an Orthodox school, or start her career in this milieu. In fact, Garbose, a Brown graduate, worked in theater and was the director of the sitcom *Head of the Class* before she released her debut film, *A Light for Greytowers* (2007), screened to fifty thousand women in Canada, the United States, and Israel, according to Sara Trappler Spielman at Chabad.org.[19] The movie, like her subsequent film, *The Heart That Sings* (2011), is a musical—one of the reasons the screenings need be closely guarded. "Garbose is creating a new genre in the world of women's entertainment," writes Trappler Spielman. "[They] are movie musicals featuring religious actresses, singers and dancers trained at Kol Neshama, her performing arts conservatory in Los Angeles. Because of Jewish laws of modesty that allow women to sing and dance only for other women, opportunities are sparse for talented girls and women wishing to perform professionally" (Trappler Spielman, "Frum Girls").

A *Light for Greytowers* is a big-screen adaptation of the 1992 young adult novel by Eva Vogiel and Ruth Steinberg of the same name, published by the premier American Orthodox Jewish publishers, Feldheim. The prologue takes place in Russia, where a mother and infant are on the run. The mother is singing about Torah showing her the way. A voiceover tells us that, as the father is being forced to serve in the Cossacks' army, the family is fleeing to England (this was, in fact, a time of peak immigration of Jews from Russia to England).[20] The main story takes place in a gray tower—a Victorian orphanage—in Gateshead, home to one of the most prestigious yeshivas in the world as well as a women's seminary (where Deitsch went) and thus a known site of Orthodox culture. The infant, now a child, is an inhabitant of the orphanage, and she is suffering a cruel fate. We await her redemption.

For the viewer of Hollywood cinema, the popularity of the film might be surprising: *A Light for Greytowers* can seem derivative, melodramatic, and didactic. Yet at the same time, this nineteenth-century Judaized rendition of *Little Orphan Annie* simmers with a quiet brew of female empowerment, and its repertoire of singing, dancing, and comic relief, performed primarily by students of Garbose's Kol Neshama Performing Arts Conservatory, delighted audiences. Writing in the *LA Times*, columnist Sandy Banks describes the screening at the Sherry Lansing Theater at the Paramount Pictures lot as "so packed, benches had to be hauled in to give everyone a seat." Banks, who is an African American non-Jewish woman, compares the film to *The Color Purple*, "with its cast of strong black Southern women determined to live by their own rules," whose lives more closely reflect those of her own family. For Banks, the resonances of Garbose's film are foreign, but for the Orthodox audience, she sees they could not be more personal: "I could tell these girls felt a shared sense of belonging. . . . They laughed when I didn't get the joke and passed tissues around when I wasn't tearing up. This was their story to tell."

If the film is not quite the stuff of Hollywood, that fact is lost on many of the viewers, most of whom have never seen a Hollywood film and acquired its taste. A scene in the Israeli television show *Srugim* dramatizes this point nicely: in the episode titled "Not Kosher," Nati and Amir, two Orthodox men, are in synagogue eating cake at the morning kiddush, raving about how delicious it is. "We should buy some of these," says Amir. "Where do you think they get them?" Nati says. Amir replies, "I have no idea. We could find out." As Nati picks up a second piece, smacking his lips with pleasure, another man, who has been listening to them, demands to know, "You're joking, right?" Amir and Nati stare at him curiously. "About what?" asks Nati. "The cakes," responds the stranger. "The cakes are amazing. Did you buy them?" wonders Amir. "Did *I* bring them? No!" The man snorts. Amir is bewildered. "Then I don't get what you said about the cakes," he says. The man retorts, "They're the worst cakes I've ever had in my life." Amir and Nati look at each other. Nati proceeds to stuff his mouth with yet another piece. "You don't like them?" Amir inquires. "They're awesome," adds Nati. "You should try some cakes outside of the synagogue too," the man declares self-righteously. As he walks away, Nati and Amir shrug at each other and continue eating their cake. "These secular people are so spoiled," mumbles Nati. "Wait, he's not religious?" asks Amir. "Of course not," Nati asserts. "How do you know?" Nati replies, "Because he's complaining about the food." The men laugh and each pick up another piece of cake.

This is not to suggest either that Garbose's films are "awful" or that Orthodox women are not discerning critics. It is only to say that opportunities for comparison are limited. Most of the filmmakers in the industry do not have the education and experience Garbose has. "It was a relief to watch a fast-moving film with professional looking settings and camera work," writes popular Orthodox blogger Hannah Katsman on her blog, *A Mother in Israel*. "The last movie I saw . . . out of the religious community was slow, dull and self-important. From the first song, I was impressed with the level of production and musical arrangements in 'Greytowers.'" Still, Katsman finds fault with the film, even if it is an improvement on earlier "kosher" films. Comparing the film to Dickens's *Oliver Twist* (and thus displaying her cultural literacy), Katsman criticizes the film for its "clichéd and ungrammatical song lyrics" and "American sweetness and pat ending."

The "pat ending," a staple of Hollywood cinema, is also necessary for the Orthodox women's film, which cannot leave viewers with too big a sense of doubt as to the security promised to adherents of their community, as Ruchama's story tells. As *The Matrix* (1999) begins with the terrifying idea that we are all slaves to a massive, nebulous, unseen system but concludes its enterprise in *The Matrix Revolutions* (2003) with the defeat of the machines and the victory of humanity, so *Greytowers* must free the orphan girls. In each case, viewers sigh with relief; the dark notion that the perils of the characters are our own can pass. After all, we are not in pods or a gray Victorian tower. We are, perhaps, deluded with false conflicts, which we *exchange* for our own, as Adorno argues. The films can readily solve conflicts "in appearance, in a way that they can hardly be solved in [our] real lives" (Adorno, "Reconsidered" 17). This seems to be the case in Garbose's film. Rather than deal with the many pressing problems Orthodox girls and women face in the contemporary era (such as dangerously rigidifying gender roles), the film takes us to a time and place that are remote and thus escapist (though conveniently appropriate for the Orthodox actors, who are required to wear long skirts, as Trappler Spielman points out in "No Boys Allowed"). The mistreatment and eventual adoption of the orphans, in fact, speak to the hazards of the outside world and the safety of Orthodox homes. We are not asked to think about the Orthodox men of Beit Shemesh, who attacked Orthodox schoolgirls they felt to be insufficiently modest, or the Belz mothers of Stamford Hill, who were told one day that they were no longer allowed to drive their children to school because of modesty rules. Then again, asking for a film's premise to be documentarian limits, or even undermines, the film's artistic possibilities. Indeed, though the film's conflict appears superficial, its resolution is highly suggestive, as I explain below.

The plot of the film is lifted directly from a classical favorite in American popular culture—one so unthreatening as to be acceptable viewing material for women in many Orthodox communities.[21] Garbose puts us squarely in the domain of *Annie*—though our heroine is more appropriately named Miriam. Miss Grimshaw, like Miss Hannigan, is a harsh housemistress, and the girls are starved and miserable. In response to being beaten and forced to scrub floors, the girls break out in song. When one of the younger orphans cries in the night, our heroine, Miriam (who has been renamed Maria), comforts her. When rich patrons come to visit the orphanage, the girls are cleaned and dressed in bows and aprons and put on display. A dog shows up to delight them. In the end, Miriam has a home and, furthermore, makes sure her friends benefit from her good fortune too. There is a lot more song and dance. And so concludes *A Light for Greytowers*.

Parallels to the plot, the characters (Miss Grimshaw / Miss Hannigan, Miriam/ Annie, Emma/Molly, Nero/Sandy, Mrs. Wilberforce / Daddy Warbucks—note the sex change on that one—and so on), and the genre aside, *A Light for Greytowers* offers an important revision to *Annie*. It is, of course, a Jewish revision. Miriam, we discover, is willing to defy Miss Grimshaw's rules in order to preserve her *Yiddishkeit*. Discovering that Miss Grimshaw has taken her candlesticks, for example, Miriam stealthily rescues them so that she can welcome the Shabbat on Friday night. "The only religion you'll keep here is obeying my orders!" cries Miss Grimshaw, who finds her charge with the offending ritualistic objects. To punish Miriam for disobedience, Miss Grimshaw locks the girl in a dungeon. Miriam, in turn, sings her mother's song—"Torah Shows Us the Way." And Torah *does* show her the way: Miriam suddenly realizes that, locked away in the dungeon for the whole day, she is unable to violate the Shabbat by doing the chores Miss Grimshaw would otherwise demand of her. Returned to her orphan siblings, Miriam shares with them her important lesson through song. The girls ask her about the words she uses—"*Hashem*" and "*emunah*." "*Emunah*," she explains, is the faith the Jewish people have had over centuries of persecution. "I'm Jewish!" one of the girls suddenly pipes up. A second follows suit. All at once, *all* the girls remember that they are Jewish girls!

A new world now appears at the orphanage. The meat is inspected for kashruth. The *brachas* over the food are articulated. Miriam starts a protest when Miss Grimshaw tries to make them work on Saturday. Although Miss Grimshaw retaliates by refusing the girls food, Miriam consoles the girls by telling them of sacred Jewish fasts and the endurance of Jews through history.

All of this is unsurprising. As Finkelman argues, Orthodox cultural productions hinge on the "coalescence" of "the Jewish and the non-Jewish" (44). Plots from popular culture are converted through the rabbinical magic of the artist. Annie becomes Miriam. Songs about putting faith in "Tomorrow" become songs about having "*emunah*" in "*Hashem*." The value of individuality might be replaced with community and of wealth with Torah. But significantly, for Finkelman, one of the values that replaces the modern-day mainstream American value of gender equity in the public sphere is the contemporary Orthodox value of confining women to the home: "Women are . . . encouraged by Haredi literature to dedicate themselves first and foremost to being mothers and wives" (50).[22]

Thus perhaps of greater note than the Jewish twist on the plot is the prominence and importance of women in the film—women who are not mothers or mothering. We see how the resolution of the plot applies directly to the lives of viewers. This revision goes beyond the call for an almost all-female cast and the strong leadership the heroine of the film assumes.[23] Take, for example, the small but significant role of the orphans' patrons, Lady Penelope and Lady Tilda. Tall and short, fat and thin, and full of song, they might be playing their roles for comic relief (Garbose's unlikely inspiration was the 1988 comedy *Twins*), but they also represent powerful womanhood (Soudry). Educated, they instruct the orphans on good nutrition. Conspicuously wealthy, they are generous to the orphans and are willing and able to implement change as they deem it necessary

(such as replacing the current food provider with a kosher one). Lady Penelope
and Lady Tilda are models of efficient management. In this, they are a contrast
to Anya, Miriam's mother; weak, poor, and in ill health, she is unable to par-
ent her child. And yet, even the unmothering mother is a more potent figure
than Miriam's father, who, upon discovering his child in the orphanage, fails to
reclaim her. Anya arrives at the orphanage soon after her husband and, though
in a near faint, gathers her strength and her child in her arms. In the final scene,
the mother and child look out the window and beam at the father, who has
returned with a carriage, too late to play Prince Charming and save his women.
The women have already saved themselves.

In this domain of girls and women, even the great sages have prominence only
through their women. In consoling the girls, who fear they are deeply behind
in their knowledge of Judaism, Miriam sings to them of Rabbi Akiva, the first-
century *tanna*:

> There's a teacher from the Jewish nation
> Rabbi Akiva was his name
> He wasn't always a Torah giant
> He was a shepherd poor and plain.
> Akiva was a very honest man,
> But in forty years had not been schooled. (*Greytowers*)

According to Talmudic sources, soon after he married, Rabbi Akiva left home to
study and returned, twenty-four years later, with twenty-four thousand students.[24]
Though contradictory, the different versions of Rabbi Akiva's story generally attribute this success to his wife, Rachel, whom Deborah Feldman suggests is a dangerous emblem of Jewish women's martyrdom: "Not only was Rachel, wife of Akiva,
a truly righteous woman, but she was also an exceptionally modest person, to the
point where . . . she once stuck pins into her calves to keep her skirt from lifting in
the breeze and exposing her kneecaps." Feldman reports, "I cringe when I hear that.
I can't stop picturing the punctured calves of a woman, and in my mind the prick-
ing takes place over and over again, each time drawing more blood, tearing muscle,
gashing skin. Is that really what God wanted of Rachel? For her to mutilate herself
so that no one could catch a glimpse of her knees?" (Feldman, *Unorthodox* 36).

Gone from Feldman's account is Rachel's power in selecting the shepherd boy
to patronize (according to lore, Rachel came of a wealthy family and chose Rabbi
Akiva as her groom, proposed to him, and then directed him in his course of study).
Gone is Rachel's determination to live an independent and autonomous life (she
earns her own money rather than live on her father's riches, and when her husband first returns from studying with twelve thousand students, after being gone
twelve years, she sends him out again for another twelve years, until he returns with

another twelve thousand students). In Garbose's account, Rachel stands as a model of agency, encouraging female viewers to take control of their lives.

After introducing Rabbi Akiva's humble beginnings, Miriam sings,

> Yet a rich man's daughter, Rachel, saw this man was no fool.
> Rachel said, Become a *talmid chachum*, and I will marry you.
> What could Akiva do now, but become a learned Jew?

In this version of Rabbi Akiva's life, the revered man has his entire course for life—and thus for the historical record—set in action by Rachel. As Feldman notes and Garbose agrees, Rachel does suffer for her piety. But even the suffering in Garbose's rendition demonstrates, significantly, Rachel's growing independence, not her excessive modesty. And after recounting the pain of hunger and poverty, Miriam concludes,

> Twenty-four long years go by, in which Rachel lived all alone.
> Akiva became revealed to the world, but it was to Rachel that he owed his
> *renown.*

Here, Rabbi Akiva's story is feminized and feminist: Akiva might have been "revealed to the world," *but*—and the conjunction here is telling—the true champion of the story is his wife.

Garbose's popularity in the Orthodox women's film industry positions her in an elite circle. She is not the first Orthodox woman filmmaker in the United States; this title belongs to her predecessor, Ronit Polin, whose 2006 film *Ink* bears the tagline, "*Ink* Changes Everything!" *Ink* is about a French Jewish girl in hiding during the Holocaust and was initially a play (plays have long been a staple of Orthodox Jewish girls' education and entertainment). The play, however, was transformed into the first American Orthodox woman's "drama on screen," as it was called. "I thought, why put a living room on a stage?" asks Polin in an interview with Trappler Spielman. "Why not just film in an actual living room?" (Trappler Spielman, "Orthodox Women"). It is as though the very concept of the cinema sprung from her head like Athena from Zeus—and not from living in the twenty-first century. Using female actors dressed up as Nazi men and screening the film to women in school auditoriums and synagogues, Polin did not exactly invent Orthodox women's film but rather sparked an American industry. This industry developed as a complement and counterpart to the Israeli one, which includes such filmmakers as Rechy Elias, Tali Avrahami, and perhaps most famously, Dina Perlstein, "the grande dame of frum filmmakers in Israel . . . [and] a rare example of someone who makes money from a small niche market" (Trappler Spielman, "Frum Female"). In the United States, Perlstein's films are popular (they are released in both English and Hebrew), but the

American filmmakers—the top tier including Garbose, Polin, Einhorn, and relative newcomer Yuta Silverman—are making serious inroads.

Case in point, Garbose's three films comprised almost half of the "Seven Frum Films to Look Out For" featured in a 2016 *Forward* article (Horwitz). When Garbose's second film, *The Heart That Sings*, premiered in 2011 in Los Angeles, it was sold out; six hundred mothers and daughters attended (Trappler Spielman, "Female Only"). The next day, it screened at the headquarters of the Chabad youth organization in Crown Heights, Brooklyn, and again every one of the seven hundred available seats was filled. The main character is, as in Garbose's first movie, called Miriam. The name evokes the image of a strong woman and a leader of women. Her biblical namesake is the heroine who saved baby Moses, who went on to become the great leader of the Jewish people. The Miriam of Exodus is also remembered for her music and dancing: "Then Miriam the prophetess . . . took a tambourine in her hand, and all the women went out after her with tambourines and dancing" (Exodus 15:20). We might see, then, why Miriam is the ideal archetype for Garbose's musical productions.[25] Garbose's Miriam was played by Rivka Krinsky (then Siegel), a favorite with the filmmaker. Krinsky also had the role of Miriam's mother in Garbose's earlier film and would come to star in *Operation: Candlelight*, Garbose's 2014 action film.

More polished and nuanced, *The Heart That Sings* locates us in the domain of more recent history, one that some of the older viewers could recall sharply.[26] The opening scene shows the Nazis murdering the family of a young girl. But *The Heart That Sings* takes on another issue closer to home than pogroms, Cossacks, Victorian orphanages, and even the Holocaust: Jewish intercommunity disputes. In Garbose's feminocentric microcosm of a girls' summer camp in midcentury America ("Hail, hail, the gang's all here! / Welcome to Camp Zimra!"), Judaism, apart from in the opening scene, is not under siege in the ways it has been traditionally.[27] Nazis aside, the film includes no equivalent of *A Light for Greytowers'* Miss Grimshaw, a non-Jewish figure who easily assumes the role of villain for the insular Jewish viewers used to safeguarding their faith from gentile marauders. Rather, and less comfortably, all the characters at the camp are Orthodox women and girls, including the nemeses of Miriam. They are, for the most part, upper- and upper-middle-class American and British Jewish girls and women who know their *Yiddishkeit* but also enjoy reasonably filtered popular culture. In other words, they realistically mirror the demographic segment of Garbose's audience. To be fair, the girls in the film who make Miriam's life difficult are not truly villainous. They are, however, entitled, frivolous, and snobbish—and thus in need of reform. Miriam, the refugee from Nazi Germany in the film (like Miriam, the refugee from Czarist Russia in Garbose's first film), must show her new acquaintances the way to Jewish values. She does so mostly through song, and she is helped by the other poor immigrant of the film, the camp's handywoman.

Through Miriam's efforts, the girls lose their interest in acting in a slapstick play about Native Americans (appearing as caricatured, feathered "hollering Injuns" of Wild West fantasy)[28] and embrace a plan to put on an operetta titled "The Widow's Kaddish." Like "The Mouse-Trap" in *Hamlet*, this production-within-a-production reinforces the film's messages and values, such as staying connected to the Jewish community, being generous, and keeping the faith. Based on a true story, according to Miriam, "The Widow's Kaddish" tells of a Hungarian woman who collected the names of people who had no one to say kaddish for them and then donated money so kaddish could be said for them when they died. That it is a woman who is leading the way in performing mitzvot in the story—even when it is only an obligation for men to say kaddish—is not unusual in the world of a Garbose film. Yet even formidable women fall on hard times, which is what happens to this devout woman when her husband dies, leaving her penniless, with two daughters of marriageable age. The widow pours her heart out to *Hashem*, and soon, a miracle occurs. Walking down the street one day, she meets an old man, who promptly writes her a check for the exact sum of money she needs. Two men witness the transaction. The widow then takes the check to the bank, and on seeing the signature, the bank manager faints. It turns out that the check had been signed by his father, *who had died ten years previous*. It furthermore turns out that when this father died, there had been no one to say kaddish for him, but a righteous woman in the community—this very widow—had discovered this fact and donated the money for kaddish to be said in his name. And so we see that her good deeds have been rewarded. All's well that ends well. Of course, a Jewish viewer might wonder why the son couldn't say kaddish for his father (even a minor is obligated to do so). An alternate version of this fable, which would not be appropriate for Garbose's younger audience members, relates that the bank manager had not said kaddish for his father because he had married a non-Jewish woman and abandoned his Jewish practice (but even this version has a happy ending: on seeing the check, the bank manager returned to his faith and his wife decided to convert). In *The Heart That Sings*, what is important is that good deeds, trust in God, and willingness to help fellow Jews are all rewarded at the operetta's conclusion. So too are they rewarded at the film's close.

Miriam faces many difficulties over the course of the film: she is lonely and alone, the campers find her humorless and fail to heed her, and the head counselor thinks she is ruining the camp experience and tries to have her dismissed. Still, Miriam maintains her faith and does her best to help the campers, particularly the girls who struggle with their time away from home. Chief among these is Chani, the small girl whose homesickness is apparent in her fits of tears and refusal to participate in any camp activities. Like Miriam, she seeks solace in the woods, where she can sing songs to *Hashem* amid the glories of nature. When she is upset, she is inconsolable—to all but Miriam, who patiently sits with her and calms her down. The climax of the film occurs when Chani hears that Miriam is being replaced by "full of *ru'ach*" Dini Stein. Chani is overwhelmed; Miriam goes to Chani and sings a song that her father once sang to her . . . and Chani joins in. This duet startles Chani all the more, a fact we as viewers cannot understand. Chani then bolts into the woods—in the dark of night—and in her overwhelmed state, she falls into a stream. Miriam runs after Chani and finds and saves her—in the nick of time! And as Miriam carries Chani away from danger, they realize what they (and we) should have known all along: that they are long-lost sisters. The song they both knew was written by their father and sung in the privacy of their childhood home. No one else could have known it. Miriam's entire family has not been killed in the Holocaust after all. The whole camp is in awe. The girls at last comprehend that they have been obsessing over clothes and popularity instead of celebrating their Jewish sisterhood—a sisterhood literalized in Miriam and Chani—across national, historical, and personal differences.

## V. DANGEROUS LIAISONS: THE REFORMATIONS OF TOBI EINHORN'S CAREER WOMEN

If Garbose's second film speaks to audiences more directly than her first, it at least maintains temporal distance and, as the characters are apt to break out in song and dance (as is natural only in a musical!), a sense of unreality. This is not so in the films of Tobi Einhorn, which probe directly the lives and issues of Jewish women today. Einhorn does not deal in metaphor or analogy; the conflicts of her films are the conflicts of her viewers. Einhorn is considered a "breakthrough artist" by younger Orthodox women filmmakers for her willingness to "make plays [and films] with real issues, such as going off the religious path or anorexia" (Trappler Spielman, "Frum Female"). Indeed, both *Almost a Family* (2010) and *A Matter of Chance* (2013) feature women who go "off the *derech*" before they return to Orthodoxy. Whereas in *Almost a Family*, Adele Solomon's former observance is a distant memory, in *A Matter of Chance*, we see a disgruntled Ayala (later Ally, later still Ayala once again) leave the faith and then witness her return. Single, well-dressed, and a senior editor at the *New Woman*, a mainstream women's fashion magazine, Ally, during her time "off the *derech*" looks down on her sister, who is struggling financially, widowed, and addled with four children. "To you, religion is everything," she tells her. "To me, [it is] illogical and outdated, and it's not the real world." The idea that Ally has it right and Mirel is a benighted victim of false consciousness settles like a thick dust over the set, and even Ally's skirt, meant to be a sassy sartorial statement ("Versace," she says), suddenly appears outlandishly long and incongruous.

Even more provocative than her pronouncement dismissing the life choices of her sister—and by extension Orthodox women at large—is the particular path off of Orthodoxy Ally takes as a secular woman. The *New Woman* is looking to hire an executive director, and Ally, a determined careerist, desires the position. For much of the film, it is hard to see Ally among the *neshot chayil* that Reva Mann and Judy Brown and other real "off-the-*derech*" writers described: women who open their mouths about the goings-on in Orthodox communities in order to help them. Ally's motivation is far less benevolent. At a staff meeting (all women, of course), the employees try to win over the magazine's (female) chief executive, Melissa, with original ideas for an upcoming issue. "How about we focus on women around the world?" suggests one woman. "We are not *National Geographic*," is the response, coupled with a hand wave. "Alcoholic execs?" "Bad plastic surgeries?" These ideas are also dismissed. A vision comes to Ally. It is a bus, its destination "Borough Park/Williamsburg." On the side of the bus, we see a picture of a little *frum* boy, men praying, and the words from Tehillim 72.19,

וימלא את כבודו כל הארץ אמן ואמן

(And the land shall be filled with His whole glory. Amen and Amen.)

What does it mean to fill the land with His glory? How might a bus do that work? Inferring the significance of this line to be an injunction against the immodesty of gender-mingling (rather than more generic inspirational rhetoric), Ally decides to reveal to her peers what she knows they will see as the oppressive treatment of women in Orthodox communities—and thus exploit this predicament (if that is what it is) of Orthodox women for her own gain.

The dialogue unfolds as follows:

ALLY:  You know, I just read an article about segregation in Orthodox Jewish communities.

COLLEAGUE:  Really?

ALLY:  Yes, it seems women are forced to sit at the back of the bus.

SECOND COLLEAGUE:  It's 2013, and women are still being discriminated against? Amazing!

ALLY:  It's crazy! [She lights up.]

THIRD COLLEAGUE (A WOMAN OF COLOR):  It's like the blacks in the South. It's disgusting. How do they get away with that? [She makes a face of horror.]

ALLY:  Oh, believe me, they get away with everything.

FIRST COLLEAGUE:  So typical of Jews. They're right up there with the Muslims and sharia law.

ALLY:  You're right. You know, I'm surprised they don't make their women wear burkas.[29] Honestly, it's like they're still living in the seventeenth century.

SECOND COLLEAGUE:  You mean their women don't have rights?

ALLY:  Some aren't even allowed to drive cars. The men—they're allowed to do whatever they want to. But the women—no, just stay home and take care of the kids.

THIRD COLLEAGUE: We have to expose this.

MELISSA (THE BOSS): *I think we have a winner here* . . . [To Ally] You can expose this and blow this thing wide open.

The dialogue here reveals nothing that could not be found in the mainstream newspapers by 2013, when columnists were comparing women in Orthodox communities to pre–Rosa Parks African Americans.[30] Nor could this segregation have been a surprise to the film's viewers, a good number of whom lived or live it. Still, if Ally's idea *within* the film to expose Jewish gender segregation to non-Jews is fraught, Einhorn's explicit treatment of the segregation as comparable to sharia law or living in the seventeenth century or as an indicator that "women don't have rights" is all the more so. Einhorn has no inclination to delude viewers about the nature of their conflicts or how these conflicts are interpreted by the secular, non-Jewish public. Should we view her as a real-life neoplatonic philosopher king, bringing viewers into the light and demanding the prisoners regard the state of their cave in all its dangerous glory?

The risqué nature of Einhorn's films sits in contrast to their meticulous attention to legal detail, calling to mind Vladimir Nabokov's impeccable omission of obscenities in his book about a pedophile in the wake of the *Ulysses* trial. As in Garbose's films, religious restrictions are made manifest in the limited range of settings and story lines. Much of *A Matter of Chance* takes place in magazine offices and boardrooms; conservative dress for women is the norm. Yet even in moments where it might seem bizarre to be clothed in ankle-length skirts—when Ally is jogging in Central Park, for example—the insistence on appropriate attire is maintained. Furthermore, the two male characters in the film are played by women; unlike Garbose, Einhorn does not seek out the husbands of actresses to play these roles or put male actors in separate frames. She excludes men completely.

Unsurprisingly, the dangerous messages of Einhorn's films are reined in sharply. To return to Adorno, we might think of one of his earlier claims about the working class: "Just as the ruled have always taken the morality dispensed to them by the rulers more seriously than the rulers themselves, the defrauded masses today cling to the myth of success still more ardently than the successful. They, too, have their aspirations. They insist unwaveringly on the very ideology by which they are enslaved" (Adorno and Horkheimer 106). Success, in the Orthodox world, is not about monetary capital so much as spiritual, but in many ways the structure of rulers and ruled, and the morality and ideology that act as a conduit for rule, are similar. Einhorn's films *Almost a Family* and *A Matter of Chance* act as blatant cautionary tales about the dangers that lurk in the outside world: misguided priorities and poor ethics rank among the highest.

In the outside world, one can cheat, steal from, or betray her community. One forgets the importance of family. Immodesty is acceptable, if not enforced. Yet assuming an observant lifestyle and becoming inserted in a religious community means gaining the support of loving families, friends, neighbors, and, of course, *Hashem*. The morality and the ideology of the rabbinical ruling class, internalized and reinforced by the women "enslaved" by them, keep women from rallying against their place at the back of the bus.

In *A Matter of Chance*, the culture war that ensues between Ally and her former community—also the community of the viewers of the film—is one she cannot win (not if the film is to be accepted by those viewers and is to receive rabbinical approval). A character who serves as a mouthpiece for those who feel oppressed must be presented as unlikeable (if redeemable)—someone who prefers to air dirty laundry and even side with anti-Semites rather than be a part of a beautiful, loving community. But that requirement does not and should not underplay the significance of having a mouthpiece for an idea that "challenges the dominant Haredi discourse" (Hakak and Friedman). When confronted with her younger self, who begins appearing at strategic moments in the film (there is a bit of magic within Einhorn's realism), Ally is accused of colluding with anti-Semites "who can't wait to tell the world how backward Jews are." Ally says, "Maybe I agree with them." Young Ayala is shocked. "What?" she asks. Ally responds, "Maybe there are extremists who force everyone to be like them and maybe someone has to stop them"—and she marches out the door. Maybe—the audience might entertain this idea ever so briefly—Ally is right.

The turn comes when Ally interviews an Orthodox woman whose *Forward* op-ed defending sex segregation on city buses has caught her eye (like Garbose, Einhorn engages in intra-Jewish disputes, though hers lack resolution). Ally attempts to maintain the nationally supported secular thesis with statements like "These women are being discriminated against, and being forced to sit in the back" and "This is *America* and segregation is illegal."[31] But her Orthodox counterpart has a different viewpoint, one that begins to sound compelling:

ESTHER: From my side, I don't think these women are being discriminated against. We practice it everywhere—in shuls, at weddings, in schools—why can't we practice it on a bus?

ALLY: Oh, come on, Esther. You know, off the record . . . [She turns off her tape recorder.] You know that men are more valued than women. There's a difference, and that's a fact.

ESTHER: Yes, there is a difference. But not in value. The Jewish woman is equal in value to any man, but she doesn't need a title or to sit in the front of the bus to prove her value.[32]

ALLY: OK, so why put her at the back? Let the men sit at the back of the bus.

ESTHER: Oh, it's not about the back or the front or the side. It's not the
   issue.
ALLY: So what is?
ESTHER: It's being separate. That's the issue. Look—the Torah says that min-
   gling between men and women is dangerous. That's the nature of mankind.
   Look at your secular society.

If the separate-but-equal argument begins to have some merit here, it comes as
part of a package deal: soon Esther is inviting Ally over for *Shabbos* dinners and
to play with her sweet daughters. She is a friend and confidante: precisely what
Ally has been missing. Viewers might start to wonder if making a fuss over those
segregated buses is worth the loss of community.

   Furthermore, this idea that "mingling between men and women is dangerous" gains credence, and the people to suffer from this mingling are the
women. It is an enticingly feminist claim—one that is common to Orthodox
calls for modesty and not unfamiliar to the citizens of secular societies—that
the immodesty of secular culture often leads to the objectification and sexual-
ization of women.[33] "The general stress on tznius is an equal and opposite reaction to the crudeness of society," Rabbi Avi Shafran, director of public affairs
for Agudath Israel of America, is quoted as saying in a 2016 *New York Times*
article about the rise of Borough Park shops selling accessories and adorn-
ments to "*kasher*" clothes bought in regular stores. "Despite the ostensible
feminist arc of our society," he says, "women's bodies are still being used to sell
beer and attract people to television shows and movies" (Maslin Nir). No one
living in a secular country—the United States, Canada, England, France, even
Israel—could dispute this claim.

   In *A Matter of Chance*, Ally is told to wear something "smashing" to impress
Robert, an important businessman, leading her young alter ego to ask, "Aren't
you supposed to be impressing them with your brain?" After dinner with Robert,
Melissa (Ally's boss) praises Ally and says Robert wants to work more closely
with her. She sidles up to Ally and adds, conspiratorially, "This is the way we
move to the top." With this picture of female advancement in mind, the case
for gender segregation becomes rapidly more persuasive (predatory senior-level
lesbians are apparently not cause for concern). An all-women work environment is imagined as positive, nurturing true meritocracy; a coed one is sexist
and damaging to women. Ultimately, Ally is convinced that she was wrong. She
rips up her article, titled "Secret Disgrace" ("Sorry—but I'm not playing in your
world anymore"), and dramatically quits her job at the *New Woman*. She happily
remembers that there are a lot of good Jewish publications she could be working
for ("Think of all the good you could be doing," young Ayala reminds her older
self. "You're wasting your talent here. This place is against everything Jewish"). In

the final scene, Ally is married and *sheiteled* and presumably employed by *Binah Magazine* (or *Mishpacha*, or *Ami* . . .). The message of female empowerment within Orthodoxy (the inverse of female empowerment outside of it) resounds through this image and Ally's concluding words to Melissa: "It's like you said, Melissa, *you* do whatever you have to do to get ahead. It doesn't matter who you hurt. . . . And, uh, by the way—the Jewish women? They're not riding at the back of the bus. *They're driving the bus.*"

There is no doubt that Einhorn's films are very didactic, and at first glance, the lessons they offer grossly justify and reinforce the patriarchal norms of contemporary Orthodoxy (Hello, Aunt Lydia). Unlike Garbose's films, where girls band together to sing and dance and rejoice in their *Yiddishkeit*, their togetherness, and their shared indomitable spirit, it is sometimes difficult to see Einhorn's films as celebrations of "girl power." On the contrary, the overt messages in these films—women belong at the back of the bus, women should not be career-driven—seem to negate the very basic principles of feminism and even border on misogyny. But that is not the whole picture. Einhorn is every bit as fueled by the desire to show her female viewers their strength and courage as Garbose. But to do so, she also needs to show them the real conflicts they experience.

Adele Solomon, the main character in *Almost a Family*, is another of Einhorn's secular, ambitious women in need of reform. Adele, when we meet her, is struggling with the difficulties of balancing her career and childcare. She is looking to hire a nanny. Once this feat is accomplished, much of the plot revolves around Adele's desire to be promoted to president of Carleton House, the company she works for (the other half of the plot shows the nanny mothering the daughters—as a *real mother* should). "We all know you should be president," one of Adele's female colleagues tells her, reminding her of all her hard work. The man against whom she's competing, Jeffrey (played by a woman), maintains that Adele should not become president. This is not because Adele lacks the skill or effort; in fact, we see her winning an account with Kleinfeld's, the upscale bridal emporium of *Say Yes to the Dress* fame—a massive boon for Carleton House. Rather, it is because she belongs at home with her daughters. "I don't believe you, Jeffrey!" she retorts. "I have a right to this job just as much as you do! I . . . have earned this promotion on my own merit." (Of course, as Einhorn asserts, there is no such thing as a meritocracy in a mixed-gender work environment.) Adele also questions Jeffrey's time at home with *his* children, a notion he dismisses by saying it doesn't matter how much time he is there because his wife is at home.

At the film's conclusion, Adele realizes that Jeffrey had been right all along. Furthermore, she appreciates that she could take a leaf from her nanny's book by learning to sew and cook as a proper woman/mother must. Adele relinquishes her claim to the company presidency and returns home to her daughters, who are delighted to have their mother back where she belongs.

Much the same way that *A Light for Greytowers* is a Jewish *Annie,* so *Almost a Family* is a Jewish *Mary Poppins*—the film version, more specifically (no one would accuse P. L. Travers of creating that travesty of a tale that punishes a woman for being a suffragist). A working mother with two children needs the help of a nanny. She has tried several before, and they have all left. But as the film begins, she is at last in luck; a British nanny appears, ready to take on the children with a bright smile and a spoonful of sugar. Einhorn is not coy about her use of *Mary Poppins.* The reference to the staple of mainstream popular culture is explicit: when Evie, the film's British nanny, arrives, one of the girls says, "Oh great! Mary Poppins is going to be our nanny!"

Of course, Jewish Mary Poppins does more than help the medicine go down. Like Garbose's Miriams, Evie has a missionary spirit. She sees that Adele's daughters, Julie and Alex, are missing Judaism in their lives, and she sets out to introduce them to *Hashem,* to whom they can turn when in trouble; to notions of *tzniut* ("Remember when we talked about modesty?" Evie asks Julie when Julie comes downstairs in a skirt that is meant to be seen as short. "There are laws, Julie, and they're for our own good." Julie responds, "I'm not hurting anyone," but Evie says, "Yes, you are. You're hurting yourself. And you're hurting *Hashem.*"); and to *Shabbos.* In the film's closing tableau, mother, daughters, and nanny (who has not only dispensed warmth and wisdom but—unlike her singing solitary predecessor who leaves with the same umbrella on which she arrived—gained a family in the process) are dressed in their best *Shabbos* finery, lighting candles.

If the reclamation of Judaism is sweetened through family love, the denial of women's ambition in the workplace still seems a bitter pill to swallow. Consider the viewers of the film, many of whom work, as the writer to *Binah* proclaimed, "full-time (and often overtime!) to make ends meet." Adele might be able to afford a nanny, according to the film's logic, but she has not had an easy path: we learn she is the daughter of Holocaust survivors and a single mother because her husband died. Surely the filmmakers themselves, who work round the clock on their films, know what it is to be working women. Is it possible to see this film as supporting rather than chastising working women?

The answer lies in the ending of the film, which offers a careful negotiation of women's roles when Adele Solomon makes her grand pronouncement to the Solomon daughters:

> ADELE: I thought we should celebrate. I got the promotion.
> ALEX AND JULIE [DISAPPOINTED]: Congratulations.
> ADELE: BUT I didn't take it. I gave the position to Jeffrey instead. And—I took another position. [Girls maintain looks of disappointment.]

ADELE: President of Solomon House . . . This is the only house I want to be
in, and the only position that I want is mother of the two most wonderful
girls in the entire world.

This is an announcement that is in line with Haredi ideology, which puts mothering first for a woman. It is also one that would cause most feminists to cringe.
More than fifty years ago, Betty Friedan was lamenting such depictions of American women, citing the magazine *Look*'s image of the ideal woman—"She gracefully concedes the top jobs to men"—as making its own "fiction of fact" and
damning women in the process (Friedan 52–53). Is Orthodox Judaism really, as
Ally says, "illogical and outdated, and . . . not the real world"? Does it offer nothing more than oppressive imagery and impossible limitations?

Or is this film remarkably contemporary, an Orthodox woman's own *Lean
In*, a *frummified* "Why Women Still Can't Have it All," artfully filtered, adapted,
and coalesced? Is Einhorn weighing in on the cultural debates of her American
female peers? One cannot help, after all, but note how similar Einhorn's resolution is to her secular, non-Jewish contemporaries' resolutions. We might recall
Sheryl Sandberg's opening anecdote in *Lean In*, where she marches into a meeting with Larry Page and Sergey Brin of Google and tells them to accommodate
her pregnancy with closer parking spaces for expecting mothers, or her chapter "The Myth of Doing It All," when she says that she vacates the office at five
thirty every day and is "vigilant" about having dinner with her children. There
is also Anne-Marie Slaughter's story of leaving her powerful government position: "When people asked why I had left government, I explained that I'd come
home . . . because of my desire to be with my family and my conclusion that jug-
gling high-level government work with the needs of two teenage boys was not
possible." Slaughter further adds:

I am hardly alone in this realization. Michèle Flournoy stepped down after
three years as undersecretary of defense for policy, the third-highest job in
the department, to spend more time at home with her three children, two
of whom are teenagers. Karen Hughes left her position as the counselor to
President George W. Bush after a year and a half in Washington to go home
to Texas for the sake of her family. Mary Matalin, who spent two years as an
assistant to Bush and the counselor to Vice President Dick Cheney before stepping down to spend more time with her daughters, wrote: "Having control
over your schedule is the only way that women who want to have a career and
a family can make it work."

Of course, neither Sandberg nor Slaughter calls for women to abandon
their careers. Slaughter points out, "I have not exactly left the ranks of full-time

career women: I teach a full course load; write regular print and online columns on foreign policy; give 40 to 50 speeches a year; appear regularly on TV and radio; and am working on a new academic book." Still, she calls for compromise, negotiation, and recognition of the demands of parenthood *in conversation with* the demands of work—as Einhorn does. She also calls for increased female leadership—a role we might see the filmmakers, like Einhorn, as taking on.

It would thus, I believe, be short-sighted not to identify Einhorn's film as doing complex cultural work. When Alex asks, "Does that mean you're not going to work anymore?" Adele responds, "Well, Alex, I still have to support you." Julie states, "But not so much," to which Adele replies, "As president, Jeffrey made some new rules I think you're going to like. Number one: I can only work four days a week. Number two: I need to be home every night by five o'clock. Number three: I may never, ever bring work home. And here's the best one. Number four: vacations are mandatory." If we put aside the maleness of Jeffrey—who is played in such obvious drag that viewers will have difficulty associating him with man's rule in any case—what we see here is an attempt at the work/life balance that so many women of the twenty-first century are seeking. All that is missing is Jeffrey's own realization that he needs to spend time with his children, regardless of his wife's choice to be a stay-at-home mother. But that, perhaps, belongs in the domain of male Haredi films. It is nonetheless arguable that the conclusion of *Almost a Family* is not regressive but actually progressive. Vacations should be mandatory for all of us.

"It's a world forged through the gaze of women who were educated within it," explains Vinig, regarding Orthodox women's films. "It's their language and their life," she writes, "and the dilemmas and conflicts are part of that picture" (Vinig, "Icon"). This alternative cinema of Orthodox women is created by and in a world apart from mainstream cinema, and its distinctness becomes all the more apparent when we try to apply the questions of feminist film studies to these films. For half a century, feminist film scholarship has investigated the problematic roles of women on the screen, the power of the male gaze, and gender inequality in film production. In "Feminist Film Criticism in the 21st Century," Shelley Cobb and Yvonne Tasker argue that despite tremendous progress in the field, "film criticism notices the scandal of women's marginalization. It responds to that marginalisation [*sic*] in multiple ways—in detail, in outline, through engagement with history or writing about the contemporary moment" (1). But what meaning does this criticism have in a film industry that has women playing every role (ironically, even that of the domineering male)? How can we apply it to films that are screened for women only and allow no opportunity for scopophilia, for "women as image, man as bearer of the look," as Laura Mulvey famously pronounced? Or ones that have no gender inequality in film production, being "professionally filmed by all women's crew[s]" (*"Announcements Relating"*)? That are replete with the concerns of women—and not just those in relation to men? Regardless of the sentiments expressed in these *frum* women's films, some of which are problematically antifeminist, the productions of Garbose, Einhorn, and their peers are a testament to the possibility of an alternative cinema that fosters a community of women creators and consumers, one that sidelines, if not defies, more than a hundred years of patriarchal legacy.

### VI. Bulletproof Stockings and a Far-Out Farbrengen

*An all-female, all-Hasid rock band from Crown Heights is living the dream most women can only yearn for: they've managed to banish all the dicks from the dance-floor for their upcoming gig at Arlene's Grocery on the Lower East Side.*

—Enid Shaw, "A Female Hasidic Rock Band," *Gawker* (2014)

More than *Binah* or *Ami*, online magazines like Fabologie.com—featuring high fashion, beautiful clothes and shoes, and "parsha foodporn" (weekly recipes) along with headlines like "Why More Is More," "An Inspired Sole: Christopher Kane for Yom Kippur '16," "Zelda Hair Is Revamping the Wig Industry," "Ladies Who Latke," and "Guccification of the Sukkah"—seem to be made for the strikingly sexy yet completely modest women who comprised Bulletproof Stockings (BPS). Bulletproof Stockings was an all-female Chabad alt-rock indie band that formed in 2011 and toured mainstream venues, inspiring and uniting thousands of women. The group had an EP and was set to release their debut album, *Homeland Call Stomp*, in 2015, but that never happened, and they disbanded in 2016. At the forefront of the band was Perl Wolfe, a twice-divorced single woman who had been born into, left, and returned to Chabad Hasidism, and Dalia Shusterman, a Modern Orthodox-turned-Chabadnik, who, when the band formed, was the recent widow of a Chabad rabbi and a mother of four, including a newborn baby. The band adhered to the Talmudic prohibition against *kol isha* (literally "voice of a woman"), which argues that a woman's singing voice could distract or arouse men. It is for this reason that they insisted on playing to all-women audiences, or, as *Gawker* put it, they "managed to banish all dicks from the dance-floor" (Shaw; see figure 5.3).

Bulletproof Stockings: the name references not only the thick stockings Haredi women are required to wear but also, as the women have repeatedly averred in interviews, their own strength. Their music was never explicitly or only about women and women's concerns, as Orthodox women's films are. Instead, like a Lubavitch *farbrengen*, a gathering of souls, their concerts allowed for a room full of people to contemplate and celebrate the spirit of Hasidism, their future actions, and their ability to learn and grow from and through each other. *Farbrengen* are Lubavitch get-togethers, unique to Chabad, and traditionally for

Figure 5.3. Poster from a Bulletproof Stockings
concert tour (2015). Photo by Shervin Lainez. Poster
design by Dalia G. Shusterman. Permission to
reproduce by Dalia G. Shusterman.

men. In *The Rebbe: The Life and Afterlife of Menachem Mendel Schneerson*, Heilman and Menachem Friedman describe the *farbrengen* as "an opportunity for the *shluchim* [Chabad's version of missionaries who are sent around the world to help Jews in their religious needs] to share one another's company, compare notes, impart the wisdom of their experiences and strategy, and bond with a movement that extended in time and space" (2). Or, to quote Isaiah 41:6, as does one of the Lubavitchers interviewed for Heilman and Friedman's book, the *farbrengen* is "a vehicle for '*ish es re'eihu ya'azoru ul'eochiv yoimar chazak*,' for each and all as one to help one another and to offer strength, support and encouragement" (22). My friend Rabbi Eitan Webb, who with his wife, Gitty, runs the Chabad House in Princeton, New Jersey, offered this version: "The idea of *farbrengen*—you spend your whole day reading, speaking, intellectually connecting to various ideas. But that doesn't always affect you at an emotional level." He goes on to explain, then, the nature of the setting of a *farbrengen*, which is meant to move the heart and not just the mind and thus truly motivate change. "When you sit down with a group of friends," he says, "and you have a drink (you don't even need to drink the drink—but it's the creation of that setting), and people are warm, comfortable, you sing a song, the mood shifts. In that setting, you say to yourself, or somebody says to you, or you to say to somebody else, 'Hey, here's a change that you should consider making,' you're a lot more willing to go and make that change" (personal communication).

This space of communal empathy and exchange is inspirational, but in her book on Lubavitcher women, Bonnie J. Morris describes the *farbrengen* as an opportunity for *male* bonding only: the "Hasidic woman enjoyed certain female-only rituals, such as the *forshpil* celebration of song and dance on the evening before a young woman's marriage, but this in no way competed with the *farbrengen* experience of the male who joined his peers to eat and dance with the Rebbe himself" (24–25). Yet the Tzemach Tzedek (1789–1866) was known to include his daughters-in-law in his *farbrengen* (also known as "latkes evening"), and recently, and more widely, "women have begun to hold their own farbrengen," writes Ellen Koskoff in *New World Hasidism*, "complete with story-telling, personal reminiscences, and much spirited singing" (98). My dear friend Rebbetzin Rachel Jacobs vigorously agreed that girls and women have their *farbrengens* too—and they are many and varied. "For me," Jacobs says, "a *farbrengen* is full of togetherness, emotion, self introspection, deep chassidisch melody that connects to your soul, and pulls you from your place of comfort." Jacobs describes to me the kinds of *farbrengens* she has attended: at high school with girlfriends, on birthdays, at the big women's conferences, and in her home, with her children. And she shares with me her favorite quotation: "What a chassidic *farbrengen* can accomplish the Angel Michoel can't accomplish." She adds, "We use it as opportunity to give each other blessings for good health, children, *shidduchim*, and sustenance, and my all time favorite: *nachas* from our children" (personal correspondence).

---

After describing the range of music, English and Yiddish, at a 2014 Bulletproof Stockings concert, Darian Lusk of *CBS News* turned to Wolfe to delineate the mission of the band. "The main mission," Wolfe explained, "is to create a kosher, safe space for women to express themselves, to get in touch with their femininity and rock out in their own way." Wolfe continued, "There are so many women that appreciate this—religious, not religious, Jewish, not Jewish, women are coming out and being like 'this is awesome, this is what we want to experience!' It feels like we're really doing something" (Lusk). In fact, as Lusk, a male journalist, relates, an attendee at the concert, spying his presence there, "told [him] to get out of her way because she came 'for a women-only experience.'"

Bulletproof Stockings' concerts might not have been precisely the *farbrengens* of "770," but as Jacobs says, *farbrengens* come in many shapes and sizes. The songs and spirit allowed the female concertgoers to engage in the lively and inspiring atmosphere produced by *farbrengens*. Through the band's lyrics, the women could learn about Jewish mysticism and faith; they could share in the call for the messiah. Consider "Frigid City," a representative song in Bulletproof Stockings' oeuvre. The song begins with a figure, "Scurrying through the countryside / Like a scavenger analyzing the turf. / He surveys the premises / Rummaging

through emerald blades / And scouring the sodden lanes / Thoroughly he covers
his ground / Scouting for evidence / Hoping to align fragments back together."
Who is this (male) figure? What is he searching for? What fragments does he
hope to align? The lyrics are opaque and tinged with suspense.

As we move into the chorus, there is a shift in the beat (the drums become
more pronounced), and the lyrics take us from third person to first: "Everything
is so cluttered here I can't sleep / And when I do I awake on empty. / Could you
show your face just a little more frequently? / I didn't know it was so cold in the
city." These aural and narrative breaks separate the storyteller from the story
figure of the song, yet there is a symmetry in the figure's search for fragments
and the narrator's request for a face. There is a sense of longing in both—of
desire and despair. In fact, it is easy to hear "Frigid City" as a typical American
song about New York City—its sense of alienation, of anomie, evoking Lou
Reed or Leonard Cohen or The Ramones. When one of the audience members
at the 2013 Jewish Orthodox Feminist Alliance (JOFA) conference I attended
asked Wolfe and Shusterman how they could use "rock and roll," a genre built
on angst and anger, to transmit the positive spirit of Hasidism, the band members explained that Hasidism shares some of the angst of rock music, that in
fact the genre makes for the perfect vehicle. Shusterman explained, "As we're
in a time of *galus* [diaspora] and not *moshiach* [messiah], there is yearning in
the music."

And as the band delivers its next lyrics, the Kabbalistic underpinnings of
"Frigid City" become clear:

> Little flames of tangerine
> Burning in each window
> Emit radiance so strong.
> He stops a passerby, "How to capture those lights
> Make them pervasively bright?"
> "If you or I had the answer," the man returns,
> "We wouldn't be here; we'd be home with our lessons learned."

To those familiar with the Kabbalistic teachings of Rabbi Isaac Luria of Safed, a
sixteenth-century mystic, it is evident that this song is a retelling of the myth of
"The Shattering of the Vessels." According to Luria, God was once everywhere—the
*ein sof*, the infinity, or *ohr ein sof*, the infinite light, the light with no end—but
he contracted himself into a condensed space, a pinpoint of light, creating the
universe as a void or vacuum around him. He then poured his divine light into
ten vessels and sent these vessels into the void. But the vessels were too fragile to
hold this light, and they shattered, scattering all the holy sparks. This, according
to Luria, is why we were created—to gather up the holy sparks and restore the
broken vessels, making the world perfect. The term *tikkun olam*, repairing of

the world, which in modern liberal Jewish thought is linked to social action or social justice, originally comes from this idea of fixing the vessels.

In "Frigid City," we begin in the vacuum, feeling deserted, unable to find or see God. It is cold; there is an absence of heat or light. And as the song progresses, both lyrics and rhythm suggest there is potential for hope, because the search might be successful, the fragments aligned, the vessels restored, and humanity returned "home."

The combination of influences in the music evokes the mix of *Annie* and *emunah* and *Mary Poppins* and mitzvot in Garbose's and Einhorn's films, respectively. The border between mainstream and Orthodox (here, Hasidic) communities is again revealed to be permeable—more a blurred line than a guarded boundary. When asked at JOFA what music influenced Bulletproof Stockings, Shusterman answered, "Jane's Addiction, Nirvana, influences from when I lived in New Orleans, Hasidic influence, mostly through the piano with Perl, and Perl's also classically trained." Wolfe added, "Ella Fitzgerald, the Beatles, the Doors, *niggunim*, classical music." Like the Orthodox women filmmakers and writers and artists, they said that they saw their music and their success as divinely directed. Shusterman asserted, "Hashem [God] wanted me to be in the band." Yet the context in which this inspiration was made manifest was unmistakably human and familiar.

Perhaps the one missing piece in this music is the kind of work done by Einhorn: exploring issues that are specific to contemporary Orthodox Jewish women, negotiating them, and (if possible) resolving them. The city is cold—but not because the women have to sit at the back of the bus where the heater is broken. There is a sense of existential but not *personal* angst, though we might imagine the richness of opportunity; the front women of the band are both unwed in a community that (over)values marriage and family. The absence of women in the lyrics is surprising as well. In song after song, the gender of the speaker is unstated; the interlocutor is (likely) God; and when figures dart across the lyrical terrain, they are typically male. If we are in the domain of Jewish mythology, where is Rabbi Akiva's wife, Rachel, the heroine of Garbose's Victorian orphanage? Or the daughters-in-law of the Tzemach Tzedek? Why not the biblical archetypes of female strength that Kellerman trots out: Judith, Yael? If the band mixes Jewish music with rock music, why not include their own rendition of "Eshes Chayil" and pay tribute to the ideal Jewish woman? Or question her, or reframe her, or revise her?

Explained Wolfe at JOFA, "We're doing [what we do] because we really believe that this is our mission as women." There is no doubt that despite the failure to include specifically female figures and specifically female concerns *in* their songs, the importance of womanhood *to* Bulletproof Stockings—their image, their message—loomed large. Perhaps this is why one hears the first person "I" of "Frigid City" and "Easy Pray" ("Rock bottom is when I say stop / And I followed you all the way down to the top / And I came to the conclusion you'd present to be / Illuminate for me") in a woman's voice (and not just because there are only women singing and playing in the band). In article upon article about the band in a wide spectrum of forums, mainstream and Jewish, Wolfe repeatedly positioned the band, its music, and the context in which they played as feminocentric—and fiercely feminist. "Hasidic women are the ultimate feminists," Wolfe told the *Forward* in a 2014 publicity story. "They can keep a home *and* rock out" (Landes).[34]

"A feminist critic might read a work by an ultra-Orthodox Jewish woman and determine it to be androcentric on the basis of its silence about women's concerns or its preoccupation with ungendered issues or issues that seem to apply to men alone," observes Roller in her book, *The Literary Imagination of Ultra-Orthodox Women*. "A more contextual reading, which would attempt to approach femininity from the author's own cultural authenticity," Roller argues, "might determine that the writer's silence about women stems from the confidence of her position as a woman in the larger communal context." Roller contends that the Orthodox Jewish woman's already empowered position "gives her the freedom *not* to focus on women's issues" (9). In the two decades since Roller published her study, the field of literary and cultural productions by (ultra-) Orthodox women has exploded. Orthodox women writers are not silent about women's issues. They have tackled women's issues in a variety of ways through a variety of genres. But Roller's claim—that silence is a form of confidence—still makes for a compelling way to read the songs of Bulletproof Stockings.

In fact, when I spoke to songwriter Wolfe in February 2017, after the dissolution of Bulletproof Stockings, she explained, "My music is about women because I'm a woman—It's about *me*—it's through *my* lens, and so it's all about women—just not in a literal way." She added, "In the same way I don't write about God blatantly . . . I like that everyone can interpret the songs in their own ways. Like the Torah—it has seventy ways, seventy paths . . . we can each take our own. The music is neither specifically *about* Jews or *about* women but comes *from* the experience of both. As a Jewish woman all I write is Jewish woman's music." Wolfe told me about a song she is yet to record—"Shade of the Palm"— imagined from the moment of lighting *Shabbos* candles, when a woman covers her eyes with the shade of her palm to say the *bracha* over the candles. She can also use the time to think about what she wants for herself or her family. Wolfe paused. "I realized," she said, "I speak about a father in the song—fathers, but not explicitly women or mothers." And then she added, "But I really never felt I had to. The woman is all over it. It's from the perspective of a woman." And she repeated, emphatically, reminding me that this is always her mission in her mind, "*It's all about women.*"

And it is women—in the plural—that are at the core of the experience of the music. The band, more explicitly even than Orthodox women filmmakers, conceived its concerts as the chance for women to have a space—a room—of their own. It was a place of female camaraderie and empowerment. "We are making a conscious choice as two adult women to cut out half of our audience because we see how women are moved by an environment like that," Wolfe said in a 2014 interview. "The energy is totally different. The girls are much nicer to each other. It is like a sisterhood" (Euse).

After Bulletproof Stockings disbanded, Shusterman, along with BPS's violinist, Dana Pestun, and a number of other women, launched a project called the New Moon All Stars Party Band, a kosher cabaret/speakeasy/*farbrengen*. "It's less rock band on a pedestal, more retro song lounge party . . . For Ladies, of course," she wrote me (personal correspondence). Wolfe went on to rebrand as PERL, the band featured on the front cover of this book. PERL's members also include former BPSers violinist Pestun and cellist Elisheva Maister. Wolfe, in her new band, purports to be taking the feminocentrism of her music further. She says that although Bulletproof Stockings was influenced by male as well as female artists (such as Bob Dylan and the Red Hot Chili Peppers), her new band would follow "female artists—like Courtney Barnett and Taylor Swift—who are 'taking control of their own businesses,' in both a vocational and creative sense" (Gordon). As she told the *New York Jewish Week*, "There haven't been as many women in the music industry for quite a long time. Even though it seems like all of these women are at the top of the charts, women are still so completely outnumbered by men as far as people in the industry. I think it's just because we haven't had the same opportunities. I think it's going to change. I think women are going to take over" (Gordon). But something has not changed: like Bulletproof Stockings and the New Moon All Stars Party Band, PERL plays to women-only audiences. The legacy of a women's space to come together, to "rock out," and to enjoy the uplifting spirit of a *farbrengen* lives on.

---

In the previous chapters, I have argued for the diversity of contemporary representations of Orthodox Jewish women—in community activism, in crime fiction, in politics, and in business. In all cases, these representations suggest barriers that need to be overcome: some are real, and some perceived. The struggles of Orthodox Jewish businesswomen, such as the one in *Kaaterskill Falls*, are not necessarily greater than those in other communities, but they are, in some ways, unique. Furthermore, with limited exposure to the "outside world," the women in these communities often need to deal with these struggles internally. Orthodox women artists thus play an important role in envisioning and creating stories, paintings, photographs, films, and songs for their peers—all manner of imaginative work that inspires faith and reassurance. But they too have barriers. As film studies critic Marlyn Vinig declares in *The Dreamers* (2011), the documentary about Haredi women filmmakers, "It's a conflict. You're an artist and you're ultra-Orthodox." Yet ultra-Orthodox artists, like Hasidic city councillors, exist, and some even thrive, producing work that resonates deeply with their audiences and helping construct virtual and physical spaces of feminocentric communities.

# Coda

## MANY DAUGHTERS HAVE ATTAINED VALOR

*Power is the ability to take one's place in whatever discourse is essential to action and the right to have one's part matter.*
— Carolyn Heilbrun, *Writing a Woman's Life* (1988)

*The woman question will determine the future of Orthodoxy.*
— Helene Meyers, *Identity Papers* (2011)

In Rama Burshtein's second mainstream movie, *Through the Wall* (2016), viewers are subject to a typical rom-com marriage plot, Haredi style. The premise: Michal is a woman in her thirties, Orthodox, unmarried, and sick of the *shidduch* scene. She finally gets engaged only to discover that her fiancé does not love her. At this point, the wedding hall has already been booked, the caterer arranged, the dress purchased. So although Michal and her fiancé break up, Michal decides to hold her wedding anyway, sure that *Hashem* will find her a new groom in the nick of time. She does all the right things (pray, visit the grave of the Breslover rebbe in Uman, date anyone her matchmaker suggests). And . . . spoiler: *Hashem* makes good on Michal's faith, and she is rewarded with handsome Shimi (played by *Srugim* star, Amos Tamam). Some of us might have been rooting for a bit more of a twist ending (Lesbian wedding with one of her close female friends? Abandonment of the whole passé marriage thing for an ashram in India? Decision to establish a grass-roots organization with a Palestinian colleague devoted to peace activism?). But Burshtein came to her film with a clear agenda: to show "if a man or woman is not loved by someone from the opposite sex they are not whole" and "marriage isn't secondary to life. It is life. It's not a side dish. It's a main dish" (Schleier).

Despite the reinforcement of the heteronormative ideal that liberal audiences will find outdated and inadequate, *Through the Wall* breaks through a lot of stereotypes about Orthodox women. Michal is strong, passionate, and willful. She does not, as she is told by one of her Orthodox women peers in the film, play a "feminine" role because men supposedly prefer it. She insists that men look at her, straight in the eye. She has an unusual job: she owns a mobile petting zoo, handles snakes, and drives around in a van that looks a little like the one in the raunchy 1994 comedy *Dumb and Dumber*. She courts a diverse group of friends, including a woman with cornrows who dates a Japanese man with *peyos*. If she likes a man, she proposes marriage to him, not waiting to be asked. In a review of the film, Beth Kissileff credits her education under Carolyn Heilbrun as allowing her to view *Through the Wall* as a feminist film because in it, "a woman creates a storyline for herself" (Kissileff). Heilbrun's simple idea looms large for so many of the works discussed in *Women of Valor*, in which women are creating story lines for themselves.

"I'm . . . not a feminist," Burshtein said in an interview after the film's release (Schleier). Yet this claim, paired with the film's portrayals of empowered, eclectic Orthodox women, women who create their own story lines, suggests that Burshtein's inability to see herself within the current constructs of feminism might be a failing of contemporary feminism itself. Surely, feminism need not be a stance in competition with religious ideologies—not if it is transnational feminism or intersectional feminism. It need not insist that women have to follow a particular path. After all, Burshtein's film might endorse the heteronormative tradition of male-female weddings as an ideal, but it also advances an Orthodox womanist ideology, wherein the woman's personal development and strength are at the forefront. This is about a woman waiting to be married, not saved.

The film's conclusion exemplifies this distinction: rather than end with the wedding, the event toward which *Through the Wall* (or as its American title, *The Wedding Plan*, makes even plainer) has been building, the story ends with the *fruit* of that wedding, the seed of which was planted early on. At the beginning of the film, a matchmaker demands to know why Michal wants to be married. Every cliché answer she offers is dismissed. At last Michal says that she wants love, respect, and someone to sing "Eshet Chayil" to her. At this point, the matchmaker stops tormenting our heroine. The truth has been articulated. And thus we realize at the end that the fruit of the marriage is not a child (as we might have expected) but rather a song. Shimi sings to his new wife "Eshet Chayil," the "Woman of Valor." Michal, the interlocutor, appears before us, her hair tucked up beneath a beautiful pink headscarf, her face aglow with the pleasure of being praised for the woman of fortitude that she is. Perhaps we will think it unfortunate that a husband is a prerequisite for the recognition of Michal's strength. Yet that thinking does not take away from Burshtein's creation; what it demonstrates instead is that we do not share Burshtein's worldview. It shows that we judge Orthodox women and their empowered creations through a secular, Western, *narrow* lens. If we want to practice transnational feminism, Chandra Mohanty writes, "Diversity and difference are central values—to be acknowledged and respected, not erased in the building of alliances" (7).

If we can better appreciate the variety of women in the world, if we can listen attentively to voices that are not like our own and look with respect at women who happily drape headscarves or wigs over their heads, we might find we have a lot to learn. After all, as the Orthodox Jewish women, fictional and real, of *Women of Valor* demonstrate, there are many kinds of Orthodox women, and they have much they can teach us. The singular figure of the Orthodox woman has come a long way from her dowdy predecessors who once simmered beneath the weight of their wigs on Hester Street or in London's East End, apparently hoping to be liberated by modernity. The heterogeneity of the women, the retentions and revisions of rituals and attire deemed anachronistic, and the insistence on untranslatable worldviews like Burshtein's reframe and broaden our understanding of both Orthodox Jewish women *and* modernity. Ghostly Gitls still hover—dead in the freezers or quarry pits of mystery novels, confined as mice in traps on the silver screen, deprived of their ability to move or speak in sensationalist newspaper stories. But now these Gitls have illustrious company, often directly countering the images of old. Even Wonder Woman, that mythical superhero, princess of the Amazon and a great warrior, has been marked by Israeli popular culture as a form of the *eshet chayil*, though if we recall that *chayil* means not only "valor" but also "warrior," we should not be terribly surprised.[1]

The religious woman has been in the crossfire of many culture wars these first years of the twenty-first century. There is no denying the growing Haredization of Judaism, on par with the increasing fundamentalism in other religions. There is no denying that women often suffer most from this trend. In a video clip from 1958 circulating as an internet meme during the writing of this book, Gamal Abdel Nasser, then president of Egypt, gives a speech about his attempt to compromise with the Muslim Brotherhood "if they were willing to be reasonable." But Nasser soon makes it clear that the very first request of the Muslim Brotherhood was in fact *un*reasonable: "The first request was to make wearing a hijab mandatory." Nasser laughs at this request. The crowd laughs at this request. "Let him wear it!" someone shouts ("Gamal Abdel"). Then Nasser laughed, and Rav Soloveitchik said, "Ask her." Now, most Egyptian women wear headscarves, and Rav Aviner wants to measure the coverage of a woman's skirt when she puts one leg on a chair. What was unimaginable sixty years ago is common practice today. (Of course, so too is the *banning* of the burka common practice—and this also targets religious women.)

I note the example of the hijab because it is, clearly, not only under the banner of Orthodox Judaism that we see women subject to increasingly stringent decrees. It is also not only under the banner of Orthodox Judaism that we see women standing up to the decrees that limit them and the popular images that flatten them. This is significant because, in essence, it shows that—in contrast to Gayatri Spivak's famous pronunciation to the contrary—the subaltern today *can* speak. Perhaps we should make more of an effort to understand her. Though Latifa's *My Forbidden Face* might have been a tool of war, it was also a solid

reminder, as Latifa says time and again, that the women who resisted the Taliban
were not women who disputed Islam but the deliberate misinterpretations the
Taliban applied to the Koran. Latifa writes her story because she is told, "Women
listen to other women" (172). Also, she is an aspiring journalist; while advancing
her career, why not also use her story to potentially save lives? Jean Sasson's Princess books might similarly have been used as propaganda, but again Sasson and
"Princess Sultana" make clear that Islam is not their target. "Sultana" condemns
"men of religion who purposely twist the words of our beloved prophet, Prophet
Muhamad . . . for the sole purpose of keeping women in a subservient position"
(20). And Sasson exploits the platform of popular fiction to present to the world
"Sultana"—a smart, feisty, strong Saudi woman.[2] There is no doubt that these
narratives—and similarly I am Malala, which I am currently reading alongside
my twelve-year-old son—teach readers that Muslim girls and women are three-
dimensional and diverse, that women are more than mere victims of patriarchal
religious ideologies, and that their voices contribute to a growing body of religious feminist discourse.

In sum, we might say that the number of times religious girls and women have
been given decrees is roughly equivalent to the number of times they have reinvented themselves. If sent to the back of the bus, the Orthodox Jewish woman
might learn how to drive the bus—even if only metaphorically and in a film. If
separated in the synagogue and the school and banned from singing in front of
men and attending men's farbrengen, she might create a room of her own and
there sing her own songs among her female peers. Her woman-centered world,
ironically, becomes a little like the "matriarchal heaven" (as reviewers called it) in
Smurfs: The Lost Village (2017) that Smurfette—that figure of dangerous allure
to the minds of some Orthodox rabbis—discovers. It is in this "lost village,"
under the tutelage of valiant female characters who don't understand themselves
in terms of and under the gaze of their male counterparts, that Smurfette ascer-
tains and develops her strengths and talents. There is, perhaps, as Fader argues
emphatically, something to be gained from the sex segregation that exists in the
lives of religious people. In response to her own question of what America could
learn from Hasidic girls, Fader offers, "Some small-scale sex segregation early in
life just may help mainstream America transcend gender constraints" (209). Do
the women really "rock out" in a more comfortable, honest manner at all-women
concerts because there are no men? Does the segregation, albeit temporary,
give them a sense of self-worth that they would otherwise struggle to muster?
Is mainstream society finding this appealing? And useful? An opportunity for
women and girls? Smurfs: The Lost Village is not the only contemporary film to
answer yes to this question. In Wonder Woman, we encounter another cinematic
feminist utopia, suggesting that this genre of fantasy fiction is showing signs of a
revival a century after its peak.[3] In the big screen version of the comic superhero

story, women are strong, powerful, and free of the dangers men pose. They work together to achieve their ends. They teach and learn and build and aspire. Even when Diana leaves Themyscira (Paradise Island), she is better off than her female peers in mixed society. Her superhuman strength has its advantages, but more importantly, her refusal to know her place (i.e., as a woman during the Great War, she ought to accept that she is barred from important meetings, political negotiations, the battlefield, real conversation, or close contact with men—but she does not) marks her as a good female role model within the film and without, for humans as well as demigods.

It might be a stretch to compare animated blue beings and superheroes to Orthodox girls and women, of course, but in some ways, it is not. Smurfette, half a century after she first appeared (in fairness to the rabbis, as a creature who is dangerous for male smurfs), finally had her feminist awakening—primarily in a feminocentric space. We might say that Orthodox women, long (and often increasingly) restricted in their roles and images and spaces, are also coming into their own. "Many daughters have attained valor," declares Proverbs 31, and it is hard to say who the "you" who has surpassed them all might be. There are so many possibilities. The girl is a troll fighter; the woman is a crime writer. The girl is a sleuth; the woman is a community leader. She is a mother and a teacher and a businesswoman. She is an artist. She is a rock star. She gathers souls. She cites the Torah. She goes to the mikvah.

And she is not alone. G. Willow Wilson's Muslim Pakistani American heroine Kamala Khan, the new brown counterpart to Marvel Comics' Captain Marvel, appeared as a cameo in the pages of *Captain Marvel* in August 2013 and has since gone on to star in her own series, *Ms. Marvel*, which debuted in February 2014. The first volume of the series—in which we see Kamala struggling with being a part of an immigrant family, questioning her sheikh's choice to silo girls and women in the mosque, and using a burkini for her superhero costume—won the Hugo Award for best graphic story in 2015. I think Wonder Woman of Themyscira and Kamala of Jersey City and Mirka, the troll-fighting Orthodox girl from Hereville, could be great friends. They are sassy heroines who perform gallant feats and, in the case of the latter two, take their eggs without a side of bacon. And this is the key: women (and their fictional counterparts) do not have to abandon their commitment to their religious principles and practices to be awe-inspiring or to join the conversations and debates of contemporary culture.

Mirka, with her long braids and long skirt, is the picture of Jewish "tradition." She is a modestly dressed girl who stands in the glow of the *Shabbos* candles that her stepmother, Fruma, lights, learning to be an Orthodox Jewish woman. She is also "*Yet Another* Troll-Fighting 11-Year-Old Orthodox Jewish Girl"—which suggests there is a part of the "traditional" Orthodox Jewish girl or woman that we have forgotten. But this forgetting is an error. We need to return to the or the "Woman of Valor." We need to remember all the praises sung to jewish women on Friday nights. Then we can see Mirka the troll fighter and Molly Blume the crime writer and Perl Wolfe the rock star as embodiments of the woman of valor. It is, after all, the woman of valor who has emerged as the paradigm of the twenty-first century for writers and artists who are challenging stereotypes and refiguring the image of the religious woman as an empowered model of contemporary womanhood.

# Acknowledgments

Over the years, I have met many people far and wide who have become my rocks as I tossed about on this great tumultuous ocean of academia. Ranen Omer-Sherman, Jonathan Freedman (*refuah shleima*), Mary Doyno, and my Facebook writing support groups—you were my virtual cheerleaders from across the ocean. Locally, Gavin Schaffer: you have been my number one supporter and favorite Jew on campus, as well as a faithful if grumbly reader and listener. And I will never forget that you came to my house and intrepidly removed a dead fox from my garden (Who can write a book with a dead fox in her garden?). Fellow ex-pats Rebecca Mitchell, Steve Hewitt, and Nathan Cardon, your feedback has come with friendship and normality in this bonkers country. Courtney J. Campbell, you too—what would I have done without you? You're my second sister. Herjeet Marway and Lauren Traczykowski, you got me through the end stages with Tinder pics and laughter. Thanks also, in early days, to my colleagues in the Princeton Writing Program and later my educational development colleagues at HEFi (Clare, Sarah, Marios, Petia, Chris, and David), and all the students/participants in my courses, who kept me grounded.

My life during this writing period has been thoroughly enriched by friends and colleagues not only in academia, at Princeton University and University of Birmingham, but also outside it in all the other places where my favorite people live (special shout-out to Michelle, Alina, Chloe, Cara, Andrea, Leila, Felicia, Natalie, and all my other amazing lady friends in Birmingham, Tel Aviv, Toronto, Montreal, Budapest, Suwon, NYC, Princeton, and Edmonton, and Alex, who is not a lady friend, in Haifa). I don't think I would have survived without my friend-therapy Whatsapp group "Steeles and Bathurst," who helped with everything from finding me Wonder Woman internet sites in Hebrew to offering opinions on dresses, shoes, vacations, and other highly important issues in my life. So thank you, Dorit Geva and Shlomit Weisblum! I am also ever grateful to my brilliant collaborator, Lori Harrison-Kahan, who has allowed me to spend much-needed time working on things that are *not* related to Orthodox women in literature, and Rachel Harris, with whom I will take this work in new directions.

I bothered a good number of people with queries about this research, and so many of these poor souls have discussed them with me at length. Among them are Rebbetzin Rachel Jacobs (a true woman of valor—in six-inch heels!) and Rabbi Yossi Jacobs, Rabbi Eitan Webb, Rachel Kaminetsky, Rabbi David Wolkenfeld, Zohar Lavi-Hassan, Perl Wolfe, Leah Lax, Rivka Siegel Krinsky, Robin Garbose, Marc Bellemare, Julie Rak, Shulem Deen, Yoel Finkelman, Batsheva Neuer, Fran Hendrick, Colin Lang, Yehudis Fekete, Pierre Anctil, Chantal Ringuette, Chaya Deitsch, Mindy Pollak, Shayna Weiss, Katherine Brown, Leila Marshy, Machla Abramovitz, Rebbetzin Chanie Carlebach, and Gil Magen-Cohen.

I also requested and was granted permission to use the wonderful work of a number of artists. Thanks to Frieda Vizel, Barry Deutsch, Chris Floyd, Julie Landreville, Doug Bresler, and Dalia G. Shusterman for permission to use their work and Perl Wolfe for permission for her lyrics. Two of the artists involved in this project deserve an extra word of thanks: Elke Reva Sudin, whose spectacular image of PERL (the current band of Perl Wolfe, formerly of Bulletproof Stockings) I am so grateful to have on the cover of this book, and Alex Gluckman, whose beautiful drawing of Elke made me realize how incredible the story of art really is. To think that in the twenty-first century, a Jewish American Barnard student went to the Met one day and chose as the model for her sketch another patron—the Orthodox Jewish artist Elke Reva Sudin—while Elke herself chose as the model for *her* iPad painting a portrait of Welsh Edwardian-era painter and lithographer Albert de Belleroche—who had been chosen as a model by the well-known American ex-patriot, gay, "painter of the Jews" artist John Singer Sargent. It is a story of the influence of art and artists over time on gender, religion, sexuality, and nation. And a reminder that if this book is about the emerging genre of feminocentric liturgical arts, it is also about all the literary, cultural, artistic, and historical forces that surround it.

My deepest gratitude goes to Elisabeth Maselli at Rutgers University Press for her tremendous enthusiasm for the project from the moment she read my proposal and to my two reviewers, whose anonymity is no longer: Ranen (again!) and Wendy Zierler, your kind words were incredibly encouraging and your suggestions keen and insightful. Thanks to Lauren Conkling and Josh Wilkerson at Scribe for your hard work copyediting this book. And to my unofficial reviewers who read part or all of the manuscript—my mom, my mother-in-law, my husband, Courtney, Gavin, and Rachel, as well as Matthew Hilton, Nora Rubel, and Sara Wolkenfeld (who also gave me all the Faye Kellerman books I could dream of)—thank you too for offering outstanding advice.

Additionally, I want to thank all the people who have heard me speak and given me feedback and support in person. The first seed of this project was planted during my internship at CLAL (The National Jewish Center for Learning and Leadership), which gave me the chance to meet with rabbinical students and discuss contemporary issues pertaining to observance and representation. Over the years, I have been fortunate to present my research to brilliant colleagues, friends, and community members at a number of research series and academic conferences, as well as regional Limmuds and the Birmingham Hebrew Congregation. I am so very grateful for all the people who listened to, questioned, and critiqued my ideas.

I am also thankful to *Shofar* and *Open Library of Humanities* for publishing some of this research and to funding bodies that have financially supported me. Essential funding to travel to Israel came by way of the William H. Tuck Memorial Fund Grant for Travel and Research and to Montreal by way of the Canadian Studies Research Grant, both from Princeton University.

There are a lot of people who helped me in a lot of different ways, and I owe them all an enormous debt of gratitude, but my family has been my first and best support system. Mom, when I gave a talk about this research in Birmingham, what a star you were for coming straight to my talk from an overseas flight and sitting there in a jetlagged stupor trying to keep your eyes open! You've always had my back. Dad, I lost you during the last stages of writing this book, but I know that you were proud of me and what I have accomplished in my career and my life. You always inspired me with your adherence to tradition and your faith: every morning you put on your tefillin and prayed, like your father and his father before him. When you were in the hospital for the surgery that would extend your life for another decade (though we didn't know it yet), you reassured me saying, "It'll be OK. God is my friend." Speaking of friends, Sister, you are my best friend, and you have supplied me with sanity and clothes for many years (which reminds me: I'm due to go shopping in your closet). All the Skinazis have given me love and strength: Rochelle Skinazi; Isaac Skinazi, z"l; Frances Skinazi; Neal Mortensen; and my nephews and niece, Jake, Max, Justin, and Lilah. I am also so grateful to the family that became mine through marriage: the Ludvigs. Eva Ludvig, with your Orthodox lifestyle, two master's degrees, prominent government job, and many important community leadership roles: you're like a character out of the books I discuss! And my best customer: You were the first to pre-order *Women of Valor*! Abe Ludvig, you are a wellspring of Jewish knowledge and a great role model for your sons. And to the rest of the Ludvigs, I am also so grateful for all your support, advice, and good guacamole: Jason Ludvig, Keren Fyman Ludvig, Daniel Ludvig, Jessica Dick Ludvig, and my three nieces and one nephew (to date), Julia, Shia, Avery, and Noa.

And of course, my greatest source of encouragement, love, inspiration, and joy (and anxiety and insanity and exhaustion) has been from the Skinazi-Ludvig household: Elliot Ludvig, my husband and *bashert*, and our very own wolf pack, Lucas and Jasper Ludvig and Morien Skinazi. When this book is out in the world, "La La Land" won't blare through the house at 5 a.m. anymore. I promise. Also, Elliot, I want to take this opportunity to publicly apologize to you for *not* calling the book "Under the *Sheitel*," a title meant to be sung to the tune of "Under the Boardwalk" (or better yet, to the tune of Schlock Rock's "Under the *Chuppah*"), as you hoped. Still, it was you who inspired the title long ago at our wedding—when you got down on one knee and serenaded me with "Eshes Chayil," all your buddies joining in for the chorus. It was one of the most perfect moments of my life. Obviously, I could not have written the book without your boundless support, love, mad editing skills, and partnership in parenting. Also, apikores though you are, your Orthodox upbringing came in handy many times, so thank you for tolerating my ignorance when I asked my thousands of stupid questions.

# Notes

## INTRODUCTION

1. Christine Yoder, for instance, reads the text as personifying Wisdom, though she also contextualizes the poem in the socioeconomic activities of women in the Achaemenid Empire. For a review of contemporary biblical exegeses of the poem (which is, however, heavily critical of feminist approaches), see Fox. A little known and fascinating interpretation of the text belongs to Yisrael Ya'akov Al-Gazi, chief rabbi of Jerusalem in the eighteenth century. Al-Gazi argued for women's equality with men in the religious sphere, and he used his strongly feminist interpretation of the "Woman of Valor" to do so. He wrote that the poem reveals a woman with a very high level of proficiency in the study of Torah, whose knowledge gives her the authority to judge things for herself, including her right to wear a *tallis* (a prayer shawl) and *tefillin* (phylacteries). See Zohar for an analysis of Al-Gazi's interpretation of the text.

2. Joskowicz and Katz provide a specifically Jewish account of secularism and its discontents and offer a compelling explanation of its necessity, arguing that Jews have been left out of, and in fact have acted as the foil for, the secularization thesis (of broader Western culture).

3. *Hester Street* predates a number of other films that similarly attempt to transport viewers into an earlier time through monochrome: among them, *Schindler's List* (1993), *Ed Wood* (1994), *Pleasantville* (1998), *The Man Who Wasn't There* (2001), *The Saddest Music in the World* (2003), and *The Artist* (2011).

4. What she finds instead is a cohort of strong, playful, confident, bold, thoughtful, and centered young women. Though Levine, too, tantalizes readers with the offer of a "window into a universe few outsiders have glimpsed," the sight inside is one that inspires replication, not dread, and Levine concludes her book with a long, polemical chapter calling on mainstream America to learn from the Hasidim's ability to "add to the feminist project" (25, 26).

5. Pogrund's 2017 British *Times* article about escapees from Haredi communities suggests an enigma ("To shut out secular distractions, the particular Haredi sect . . . speaks Yiddish, bans mass media and mobile phones and sends its children to illegal religious schools. This," the article adds ominously, "in the London borough of Hackney"). It also

uses pictures from the carnivalesque holiday of Purim as if they represent the everyday lives of Haredim. A contemporaneous *New York Times* article takes the sense of the paradoxical a step further, almost insinuating the Skverers of New York into the *Twilight Zone* by claiming, "Perhaps it's easiest to think of them as living in a *different dimension*" (Brodesser-Akner, emphasis mine).

6. *Mystics, Mavericks, and Merrymakers* is refreshingly positive, but at the same time, Levine has a tendency to romanticize her subjects.

7. See, for example, the article entitled "Hearts of Darkness" published in the magazine *Mishpacha*, a pan-Orthodox publication aiming to give voice to Hasidic, Yeshivish, Modern Orthodox, and Sephardic communities (with a circulation of about fifty thousand people). On the other hand, *Ami Magazine*, which serves a similar demographic, took umbrage with *Mishpacha*'s depiction (even as they clarified that they were not endorsing the lifestyle of Lev Tahor). The Lev Tahor community was ultimately raided, and a number of children were removed from their families. Most members fled the province. Helbrans was found dead in July 2017 in Guatemala.

8. Similarly, in 2016, the *New York Times* penned a harsh editorial criticizing a Brooklyn pool for offering gender-segregated swimming hours, which it had been doing for *about twenty years* ("Everybody in the Pool"). The *New York Times* was, in turn, censured by many readers for its blatant hypocrisy; after all, only four months earlier, the same newspaper lauded Toronto swimming pools for accommodating diversity by offering gender-segregated swim times (Levin). See also the discussion of the YMCA windows in chapter 3.

9. Lest we be unsure of his politics from the nature of his art, on his website, Deutsch divides his cartoons into such categories as "feminist cartoons," "anti-racist cartoons," "environmental cartoons," "LGBT cartoons," and "imperialism and war cartoons" (leftycartoons.com). He also dedicates a good deal of his blog to his feminism (amptoons.com/blog/).

10. Most critics see Jewish renewal as part of a larger picture of, as Benor calls it, an "expanding 'spiritual marketplace'" (20). Benor also notes that the growing popularity of Limmud conferences dedicated to Jewish learning is a sign of "renewed interest in Jewish observance and education" (20). See also Joskowicz and Katz.

11. This seeking can be found everywhere from the 2013 Israeli television series *Mekimi*, about a secular woman who, with her boyfriend, becomes a Breslov Hasid, to the 2014 American television series *Transparent*, in which secular Jews are continually engaging with religious Jewish ritual, from mikvah immersion to searching for blood dots in eggs.

12. Of course, this was the very limitation of American choice demarcated by philosopher Horace Kallen, who wrote in "Democracy vs the Melting Pot," his 1915 manifesto of cultural pluralism, "Men may change their clothes, their politics, their wives . . . but they cannot change their grandfathers" (194).

13. Across America in the postwar period, Orthodox communities formed enclaves; created schools, yeshivas, and other fundamental institutions; and developed cultural and political power. See Diamond; Liebman; Heilman; and Finkelman.

14. Rubel's book captures the cultural anxiety surrounding this text and similar ones.

15. New Square, New York, established in 1954, is the all-Hasidic village of the Skverers.

16. In her comparison of "Eli, the Fanatic" and "Bloodshed," Ruth Wisse notes the key difference is location but sees the location of the latter as a place of *myth* rather than reality: "Writers like Ozick . . . who feel the historic, moral, and religious weight of

Judaism, and want to represent it in literature, have to ship their characters out of town by Greyhound or magic carpet, to an unlikely *shtetl* . . . in search of pan-Jewish fictional atmospheres" (45). That mysterious quality of the American *shtetl* is far less palpable now, though novels with such settings, such as Julia Dahl's 2015 *Run You Down*, set in the fictional upstate New York Orthodox town of Roseville, still market their books as offering insights into unknown, insular worlds.

17. Janet Burstein credits Rosenbaum with coining the "new wave" and describes it as writing that "reverses the flight from ethnic identity so common in earlier American Jewish writing" and "participates in what [Rosenbaum] calls a kind of 'neurotic millennial return' to religious and/or cultural commitments rebelled against by immigrant writers and all but abandoned by writers of the fifties, sixties, and seventies" (803).

18. On the popularity of Potok's novel, see McClymond. Strikingly, Ozick and Wisse make no mention of Potok, clearly a popular but often critically disregarded novelist.

19. The shofar is blown in the synagogue during the month leading up to Rosh Hashana, the Jewish New Year, as well as to signal the end of Yom Kippur, the Day of Atonement.

20. Contemporary writer Dara Horn cites Ozick's essay as inspiration for her "liturgical" novel, *In the Image* (2005; Horn 473–474).

21. In *The Modern Jewish Canon*, Wisse revises her claim about the new wave of Jewish writing, saying it was less of a sea change than a "trickle" (though perhaps if asked today, she might revise her revision; 26).

22. In Orthodox parlance, *return* is the term used to indicate a shift from secularity to observance (what a Christian might call *born again*).

23. Whether or not Stern was actually Jewish is debatable. In *Slippery Characters*, Laura Browder argues that Stern had no connection to Jewishness and was in fact the daughter of a German Lutheran and Welsh Baptist.

24. See Harrison-Kahan and Skinazi, "The 'Girl Reporter' in Fact and Fiction," "Feminist Collaboration," "Miriam Michelson's 'Yellow Journalism,'" "Miriam Michelson, American Jewish Feminist," and "Miriam Michelson."

25. Excellent work has been done on the British Victorian *idea(l)* of Jewish women by Nadia Valman. Contrasting the image of the Jewish woman with her male counterpart, Valman writes, "The Jewess was often . . . an idealised representation of femininity." It is interesting to note that the image was that of "the beautiful or *spiritual* Jewess" (emphasis mine, 3).

26. Sztokman's book *The War on Women in Israel: A Story of Religious Radicalism and the Women Fighting for Freedom* (2014) catalogues a series of statements, events, policies, and responses marking "the disturbing trend happening in Israel in which religion increasingly is used as a stultifying force in women's lives to control and oppress them" (xxiv). At times sensationalistic, deeply polemical, and somewhat problematically uncritical of the press's rendering of the affairs she chronicles, the book still offers important insights into the recent developments in Orthodox Judaism (within but also well beyond Israel's borders).

27. See Blundy; Saul; and Deardon. Like the swimming pool scandal, however, it should be noted that the street signs, erected for crowd control during a Simchas Torah parade, were not at all a clear-cut sign of women's oppression, though of course they appeared that way in the media.

28. My contention here is to be careful that we do not fall into the trap that Chandra Talpade Mohanty warns of with regard to "Western" feminists' writing about the "Third

World Woman": the co-opting (or discursive colonization) leading to a "suppression" of the "heterogeneity of the subject(s) in question" and the "production of a singular monolithic subject" (333). Judith Butler reiterates Mohanty's claims in *Precarious Life* and concludes: "Mohanty's critique is thorough and right—and it was written more than a decade ago" (47). I would add that this thinking is still contemporary and critical and as relevant to the women of the fringe communities of the "first world" as those of the "third."

29. Shalit's article might have missed the mark, but as Horowitz rightly asks, "Who would have imagined that such a debate about Jewish American letters would ensue as we plunge into the twenty-first century? Not so long ago, virtually all scholars read Jewish literature in North America as a secular discourse" (235).

## CHAPTER 1 — A G-D-FEARING WOMAN, SHE SHOULD BE PRAISED

1. Liora Batnitzky argues effectively in *How Judaism Became a Religion* that Moses Mendelssohn (1729–1786) "*invents* the modern idea that Judaism is a religion," albeit using a Protestant notion that did not and does not perfectly accommodate Judaism (13).

2. A modified segment of this chapter was published in *Open Library of Humanities*, vol. 3, issue 2, 2017, 1–27.

3. This is a fact that is not lost on most inhabitants. In 2012, Orthodox Jews filled the New York Mets' Citi Field stadium to its forty-thousand-person capacity rallying against the internet; an additional stadium was rented out for the overflow. Ironically, the event was for men only, so women had to watch it via live stream . . . on the internet.

4. Neither are modern, Jewish secular heroes beyond Auslander's sacrilegious satire; in *Hope: A Tragedy* (2012), Anne Frank is an old, twisted, manipulative beast that terrorizes a young family and is triumphant in her everlasting survival.

5. McClintock observes that in colonial discourse, journeys forward in space (i.e., into the interior of Africa) are presented as backward through time. "The . . . movement," she writes, "presents . . . regression backward to what I call anachronistic space . . . from white, male adulthood to a primordial, black degeneracy" (9). Add the word "hat" to "black" and change Africa to Brooklyn and this rhetoric seems eerily akin to contemporary discourse pertaining to Haredi communities.

6. Finkelman's *Strictly Kosher Reading* does a superb job of identifying how mainstream cultural artifacts are remade to fit the Orthodox world. Also see chapter 5.

7. The Marble Arch Synagogue merged with the Western Synagogue in 1991 to become the Western Marble Arch Synagogue.

8. Ironically, the particular passage invoked by Mann has far greater resonance for Christians, who see it as prophesying Christ's words on the cross.

9. Benor offers an excellent analysis of code-switching in the Orthodox world, showing the ways that FFBs (*frum* from birth) will accommodate BTs (*ba'alei teshuva*) or those whom they expect to have less knowledge about Judaism by either defining terms or using English equivalents to the more commonly used Yiddish and Hebrew loanwords prevalent in Orthodox Jewish English (Benor 87). Ironically, in Mann's book, it is the BT who appears to be accommodating the FFB—which only makes sense if we recognize that this conversation should be taken as a literary performance for the reader rather than a verbatim account.

10. Plaskow explores female embodiment in the context of Jewish theology. For a detailed study of timebound commandments, see Alexander.

11. *Awful Disclosures of Maria Monk, or, the Hidden Secrets of a Nun's Life in a Convent Exposed* (1836) was a sensationalist faux memoir about the horrors of the Hotel Dieu Nunnery in Quebec. The text, a bestseller in the United States, functioned to fuel already virulent anti-Catholic sentiment.

12. This blog acts as an interesting afterlife of Vizel's first blog, *Shpitzle Shtrimpkind*, published in 2006–2007, while Vizel was still in the Hasidic community in Kiryas Joel.

13. This list could go on. Dawkins, Dennett, Hitchens, and Harris have been called the "four horsemen" of the movement.

14. At the turn of the twenty-first century, Mormonism has become a touchstone of popular culture. Although Mormonism has appeared in cultural productions—typically less than favorably—for over a century (think Arthur Conan Doyle's *A Study in Scarlet*), more recent productions such as Tony Kushner's two-part play *Angels in America*, later an all-star cast HBO movie (2003); the HBO television series *Big Love* (2006–2011); and the religious satire *The Book of Mormon*, which opened on Broadway to wild acclaim in 2011, suggest that Mormonism has occupied a disproportionately large space in the cultural imagination of late.

15. As discussed in the introduction, there are many parallels between the depictions of the Amish and Haredi Jews. PBS's *American Experience: The Amish* proffered a romanticized view of a culture that Haredim would find familiar. It opens with the enticing claims "They're in our world, but they're not part of our world" and "The Amish represent something true and virtuous about American life that some others of us have lost." Slow old-world music plays, and images of seemingly timeless figures in homespun clothing stream by via horse and buggy (the only thing marring the image of the timeless landscape being the telephone wires above their heads).

16. With irony surpassing that of Reich, I. L. Peretz relates this tale of "righteousness" in his 1904 short story, "Three Gifts." In Feldman's version, as discussed in chapter 5, the legend is attributed to Rachel, wife of the great *tanna*, Rabbi Akiva.

17. Photoshopping, pixelating, and cropping women's faces from Haredi newspapers have become common practices. See Tessler; Berkenwald; and Sztokman. A social media backlash began in 2017, with the hashtag #FrumWomenHaveFaces.

18. After the era of assimilation literature, Jewish authors created a generation of characters who spoke English, succeeded in business, and lived in the suburbs. Jewishness did not disappear—though many read the midcentury novels as universal representations of humanity, wherein Jewishness figures as a form of contemporary alienation—but it served, more or less, as background noise.

19. Masculinity studies have been very influential in Jewish studies, and much has been written about the feminized image of Jewish men (along with, in some cases, the counterimage of the *Muscle Jew*, a term coined by Max Nordau in 1898) in both anti-Semitic lore as well as within Jewish culture. Scholarship includes, but is not limited to, works by Gilman; Boyarin; Breines; Schaffer; Rubel; Dekel; Presner; Davison; and Benor.

20. Contemporary ethnographic research on Orthodox Jews at times replicates this gendering, while obscuring the limits of its methodology. Benor writes, "Some male researchers purport to paint a portrait of an entire Orthodox community even though they had very little access to women's lives." She notes that William Helmreich's book *The World of Orthodox Jewry* "would be more accurate as *The World of the Yeshiva: An Intimate Portrait of Orthodox Men*" and that Heilman "makes several statements about how

he assumes women feel (e.g., about not participating in the rebbe's tish) without offering evidence that he observed their reactions or interviewed them extensively" (25).

21. Many scholars have examined the erotics of the veil and the Muslim/Orientalized woman. See, for example, Said on Flaubert; Ahmed's "The Discourse of the Veil"; and Mohanty.

22. Michaels's story is dark and multilayered. The boys have literally murdered no one, but many victims are made by their game of peeping tom, not the least of whom is their friend Arnold, who slides off the roof to his death.

23. Sztokman frequently compares the two, but I would urge caution against uncritical comparisons. A passage from Sztokman belies the problem here: after recounting to readers the disappointment of a girl who was not permitted to play basketball against a religious boys' team and who dissolved into tears, Sztokman explains, "The lives of youth form a major battleground in religious cultural wars across the globe. Take Tunisia, for example, where radical Islamists in Nabeul attempted to kill the headmaster of Lycée Menzel Bouzelfa for refusing entry to a student wearing a niqab" (64–65). Whereas it is unfortunate and perhaps *wrong* that a ten-year-old girl was denied her opportunity to show off her slam dunks, a cancelled game is not, and ought not be, on par with attempted murder.

24. Pratt writes that in autoethnography, "colonized subjects undertake to represent themselves in the colonizer's own terms" (7).

25. The term *unveiling* itself has a very different connotation in Judaism than in neocolonialist Western discourse, as it refers to the religious service during which a tombstone is erected over a grave.

26. Although a man's narrative, the text is very much concerned with the lives and limitations of Orthodox women as well, and the title of the book is a modified version of a biblical expression that foregrounds the dangers of immodest women: *Kol bo'eho lo yeshuvun* (All who go to her do not return). Explains Deen, linking women's immodesty and heresy: "So says the Bible regarding a woman of loose morals. So said the rabbis of the Talmud regarding heresy" (116).

27. It is tempting to read these images of women in *tallises* as evoking the pictures of the "Women of the Wall" that have come to be a staple in newspapers and social media, but this reading would be misguided. There are no references to this movement or similar in the books, and I would contend that the men's ritualistic practices within Judaism are not what these women are seeking.

28. On Orthodox women's blogs, see Lieber's "A Virtual Veibershul." Lieber notes the journalistic accounts of these blogs, in both the United States and the United Kingdom, tended to be sensationalist, promising a kind of women's revolution against Orthodox patriarchs, which reflected the readers' desires for exposure and condemnation as opposed to the writers' attempts to extend their private spheres (622). The language of these articles—she cites, for example, the article "How the Internet Is Lifting the Veil from Orthodox Jewish Women"—echoes the kind of Western feminist misreading of the texts discussed here.

29. See Rubel's chapter "The New Jewish Gothic" for an in-depth discussion of these tropes.

30. Ragen has gone on, however, to work as an activist outside of the domain of novel writing, making her name as an outspoken protester against bus segregation in Israel. See Sztokman, chapter 1.

31. Mavar and GesherEU are the British/European equivalents of Footsteps.

32. Fader offers evidence that the Hasidic communities in New York she was observing were attuned to mainstream publications (including *The Village Voice*), discussing them despite the claim that they avoid secular reading materials (84).

33. Although the term *Eshes Chayil* is gendered in a way that makes it ill-fitting for Deen, he takes on a similar role (perhaps we can simply call him a *mensch*—a term that means both "man" and "good man"). We see that he is working for a remedy not only for himself but also for his community. His memoir records his experiences as typical of Hasidic men, who are undereducated and underemployable. Despite the expectation for them to have large families, they have great difficulties supporting those families. Ironically, poor education is one of the problems Hasidic women have less to complain about (which is not to say it's not an issue), as women are given secular educations superior to men's in most of the communities. Deen avers the importance of including men's voices and distinct concerns, noting, "Although equally of interest is the amount of focus on women's literature within the orthodox world (and certainly the OTD world) given that the bulk of the material seems to me . . . mostly by and about women[,] accounts of the male lived experiences [are] very meager" (personal communication).

34. The use of the term *sodomy* to denote a crime is curious. Why is there a distinction between vaginal and anal rape? In fact, the term *sodomy* does not necessarily indicate *rape* at all and seems to be an artifact of the American justice system's homophobic past. But the distinction is even more problematic in the Israeli present. "Rape in Israel was defined as sex between a man and a woman," according to Orbach, "and Mondrowitz's case, homosexual rape, was not an extraditable offense."

## CHAPTER 2 — A WOMAN OF VALOR WHO CAN FIND

1. There is also the American writer Yael Levy, who wrote *Starstruck* (2013); popular British writer Ruthie Pearlman, who pens seminary thrillers; and no shortage of writers who offer kosher Nancy Drews (sometimes in pairs, more like the Hardy Boys) for the younger crowd: R. Leverton (*Enter with Caution: A Chavi and Chevi Mystery Thriller*), Rivkah Small ("Double Trouble" children's mystery series), and Chaya Hubner (*A Mystery from Afar and Other Leah Lamdan Holiday Mysteries*), who also writes as Carol Korb Hubner (*The Devora Doresh Mysteries*)—and more.

2. The Keren Ariel Women's Halachic Institute, an arm of Nishmat, The Jeanie Schottenstein Center for Advanced Torah Study for Women, began training women to be *yoetzot* in 1997.

3. In addition to his *Father Brown* series, for which he is best known, Chesterton was a lay theologian and wrote about his faith extensively, publishing texts like *Heretics* (1905) and *Orthodoxy* (1908) and, after his conversion to Catholicism, *St. Francis of Assisi* (1923), *The Everlasting Man* (1925), and *The Catholic Church and Conversion* (1926).

4. Mosley himself is not only black but also Jewish, though his writings are rarely included in discussions of the American Jewish literary canon. See Heft.

5. See also Zierler's "A Dignitary in the Land?," 263–266. Zierler makes the acute observation that though femininized, Small and the series at large are far from feminist.

6. Of course, the protagonist also *becomes* the very image he fears. Roth's story is a nuanced one.

7. In a less significant way, Kemelman uses this plot device in *Conversations with Rabbi Small*, including a woman who comes to the rabbi to convert only to discover her mother was Jewish. The metaphorical role of this plot device is evident when the rabbi says his job (and we might also say the author believes his job) consists of "converting Jews to Judaism" (105). Dahl, who offers us her heroine, Rebekah Roberts, born to a Haredi mother and raised by a Christian father, closely followed Kellerman's example, and one even wonders if Waldman's choice to name her mommy-track mystery series' Jewish protagonist's Christian husband Peter is a coincidence or a tribute to Kellerman.

8. Also see Deykin Baris.

9. Much can be said about Kellerman's yeshiva and the other settings in her series. In her depictions of New York (in *Day of Atonement*, *Sanctuary*, and *Stone Kiss*), we get glimpses of the all-encompassing Orthodox communities that exist there, and in *The Forgotten*, Rina enters her old neighborhood, an area of Los Angeles that is a lesser version of the Boro Park or New Square variety: "The area had become so Jewish that, except for the palm trees, it felt as regional as Brooklyn" (211). She calls the valley's *frum* community "self-contained"—complete, as it is, with kosher bakeries and butchers, Jewish bookstores, and yeshivas—though of course it is not as self-contained as the yeshiva. Kellerman chooses *not* to locate Rina and her family in this neighborhood, as she does not leave her in the yeshiva, but rather moves her to a space more "of the world." There is an evolution we follow: we begin with Rina in the relatively closed Haredi community, where her place is uncertain; we see her (unhappy) in no community (on Peter's ranch, a far walk from the synagogue); and finally, Kellerman puts Rina in what she clearly depicts as an ideal in-between space, and that is the *open* but *tight-knit* Modern Orthodox community.

10. *Niddah* is a hot topic in Kellerman's books and one that attracts considerable criticism from feminist thinkers; in chapter 4, I cite Rebecca Goldstein's use of it in *The Mind-Body Problem* to demonstrate women's lack of value in Orthodox Judaism. See also Hyman and Plaskow. For a counterargument, see Hartman. Avishai takes a balanced approach by interviewing women in the Orthodox community to gauge their attitudes toward the practice.

11. Of course, this description of popular detective fiction (as of any kind of genre fiction) is something of a straw man. See Makinen.

12. Even scholars who do examine Kellerman's writing seem, on the whole, unimpressed with its offerings, apart from R. Harris, Sokoloff, and Uffen. See Deykin Baris; Ben-Merre; and L. Roth.

13. Uffen's "The Novels of Fannie Hurst: Notes toward a Definition of Popular Fiction," which touches on historical novels, gothics, mysteries, and science fiction, is likely the first piece of literary criticism on Hurst's work, now the topic of a number of dissertations, articles, and books. Anticipating Radway, Uffen argues that such novels "illuminate the character of the *reader* and not the fictional actor" and offers an examination of this body of writing that is distinct from the study of more "literary" fiction (574). Later invested in *merging* the study of popular writing with the study of the canon, Uffen reads the works of Kellerman and Zelda Popkin alongside those of Cynthia Ozick and Anzia Yezierska in *Strands of the Cable*.

14. Numerous comparisons could be made between Kellerman's generic fiction, including its mode of engaging elements of the romance, and the Christian novels that Lynn Neal discusses in *Romancing God*. Crucially, Neal argues that evangelical romances deviate from standard secular fare (and Radway's sources) by virtue of their putting the

characters' relationships with God above all else. Thus happy endings never arrive because men *magically* transform from rake to *mensch*, as it were, but because of "divinely sparked spiritual growth" and "the power of God's love" (Neal 5).

15. Adding to the gender divide is Kellerman's regular asymmetrical use of Decker/Rina (last name / first name) for the characters, as Roth also noted (L. Roth, "Unraveling" 187).

16. Kellerman makes this New Testament reference explicit in *The Forgotten* but also, in that same installment, reminds us of another (Jewish) Lazarus: Emma. She writes, "When Emma Lazarus wrote her famous words underneath the Statue of Liberty, she must have had places like the Foothills Division of the LAPD in mind, the area being a multicultural mix of displaced and struggling whites, blacks, Hispanics, Asians, and other ethnicities thrown into the immigrant salad" (230). This description, perhaps, should suggest another educational project of Kellerman. If the series is primarily committed to Jewish teachings along with telling action-packed crime tales, it also aims to recognize the many immigrant, racial, and cultural groups in America.

17. This requirement is very much in line with the evangelical romances Neal examines.

18. See Berger, "Russian Art."

19. It is notable that the bulk of feminist scholarship dedicated to crime fiction focuses exclusively on female detectives. See, for example, Gavin; Irons; and Heilbrun ("New Female").

20. Although all are customs at this point, one might distinguish between them: the immersions following ejaculation are rooted in the Torah (are, in other words, *halachic*), though in post-Temple times, the rule no longer applies, whereas the others have always been *minhags* (Wolkenfeld, personal correspondence).

21. At the end of *Dream House*, similarly, Rochelle Krich provides the recipe for Bubbie G's challah. See Weissman Joselit on the symbolic power of American Jewish recipes (*Wonders* 217).

22. This attempt is, at times, rather simplistic. When Rina visits *Ma'arat Hamachpelah*, which is a shrine to the biblical ancestors in Hebron, for example, the narrator asserts that if the Arabs permitted digging on their holy lands, we would discover the remains of Adam and Eve and other figures from Genesis, as Peter discovers the remains of Californian crime victims: "These people weren't fairy-tale characters or mythological creatures, they were *real* people" (*Sanctuary* 295).

23. If claims of authenticity feel exaggerated, they are not unusual—particularly when it comes to the Holocaust. While much ethnic literature gets subjected to debates about claims of authenticity, Holocaust literature in particular is burdened by the demands of reality and authenticity. See Horowitz.

24. For the record, the Hasidic group Honey belongs to—the *Leibben*—is a fictional one, like Waldman and Chabon's *Verbovers*. Because so few people (particularly those reading mainstream literature) are familiar with all the Hasidic groups, it is easy to make one up, and writers have the freedom to cast the fictitious group any way they like (such as giving them a prohibition on telephone use or making central to their practice a search for an unblemished sacred red cow).

25. Later, in her attempt to translate the experience of the village children to her husband, Rina falls into the same error of using the language of anachronistic space: "Peter, imagine if you lived most of your life in eighteenth-century Poland, then you were suddenly beamed into 1990s Los Angeles. They're in a time warp" (Kellerman, *Sanctuary* 103).

26. In rare circumstances, he can also remarry (though she cannot).

27. Public shaming, in the twenty-first century, includes social media. See Janofsky.

28. In *I am Forbidden*, a Satmar couple tries to conceive a child for ten years without success. After the wife has been tested and treated in every which way, she is blamed for the couple's infertility, and the husband is encouraged to divorce her. Her husband has not been tested because it is a "grievous sin" to "spill seed" for semen analysis (Markovits 174). Ultimately, the husband finds a rabbi to authorize the testing and discovers the fault is his own, but by then it is too late; the wife has used the biblical story of Tamar and Judah to justify sleeping with another man and conceives a child the husband now knows cannot be his.

29. This glossary speaks of the existence of "Orthodox English," discussed at length in Benor and in Fader (the latter, more specifically, focusing on Hasidic English). Benor sees such glossaries and definitions in "mainstream Orthodox English books and periodicals" as speaking to and aiding *ba'alei teshuva*, though we can see in Krich's books as well as Zipora's (as discussed in the next chapter) that these translations also allow for—and facilitate—a non-Jewish readership (Benor 158).

30. According to Irons, once the domain of hard-boiled dicks and (at best) spinster sleuths, fictional detectives since the 1980s "have transcended generic codes and virtually rewritten the archetypal male detective from a female perspective" (xii).

31. To understand how defined Orthodox men are by their headwear, consider the name of the popular Israeli television show *Srugim* (2008–2012), meaning *knitted* or *crocheted*, referring to their yarmulkes and suggesting an entire lifestyle of the *Friends*-like cast of characters, who could easily fit into a Modern Orthodox community in North America. Near the end of *Dream House*, Krich explains some of the distinctions for readers but suggests there is much more to know. In a parenthetical aside, she writes, "The kind of yarmulke you wear—crocheted in any color or combination thereof, with or without the wearer's initials in Hebrew or English; black suede or black velvet; teeny, medium, large—is an indicator of where you belong in the world of Orthodox Judaism." She then confesses (perhaps remembering she's supposed to be writing a mystery novel, not a primer of Orthodoxy), "But that's a chapter in itself" (Krich, *Dream* 247–248).

32. Regarding this story of Rabbi Soloveitchik's response about his wife, Tonya (Lewit) Soloveitchik, PhD, there are other versions (e.g., "She doesn't want to"), but they all point to the same thing: her agency.

## CHAPTER 3 — SHE OPENS HER MOUTH WITH WISDOM

1. A version of this chapter was published in *Shofar*, vol. 33, no. 2, 2015, 1–26.

2. In chapter 5, I discuss a more literal rethinking of *kol isha* in relation to the all-women Hasidic alternative-rock indie band Bulletproof Stockings, which played to women-only venues.

3. See Beer; and Richler (1992) in *Oh Canada! Oh Quebec!*; and Paris. Examples often come from Anatole Vanier, who wrote a number of articles in the influential magazine *L'action Nationale* about Jews in the 1930s, demanding from the government that Canada keeps it doors closed to desolate Jews in Europe and declaring, "What is happening in the new Germany is germinating everywhere where Jews are considered as intruders. And where, one way well ask, are they considered otherwise?" (trans. Paris 52).

4. Groulx published a great deal of anti-Semitic propaganda, yet in honor of his memory, a subway station in Montreal is named after him. In 1996, the League for Human

Rights of B'nai Brith Canada petitioned the Executive Committee of the Montreal Urban Community to have the station be renamed, but their request was not granted.

5. Similarly, a Quebecois graduate student named Esther Delisle, who wrote her doctoral dissertation about the anti-Semitism of Quebec nationalists around the same time, waited two years to have her thesis approved at Université de Laval and was subject to very critical press. See both Nadeau for the Quebecois media response and Caldwell's searing review of both Delisle's *The Traitor and the Jew* and Richler's *Oh Canada! Oh Quebec.*

6. Other Orthodox communities have not gone untouched, however, especially since Quebec proposed a new "Charter of Values" in 2013, forbidding public-employee Jews (e.g., doctors, professors, government workers, and teachers) from wearing skullcaps and other overt symbols of faith (see fig. 3.1). The proposal, however, failed, and the charter, in fact, was considered one of the reasons the Parti Québécois lost the election.

7. A number of people have written about this heated exchange. See Richler (1992) in *Oh Canada! Oh Quebec!*, as well as Shaffir; Herman; Stoker; and Bauer.

8. Covertly purchasing the land in his French-Canadian girlfriend's name, Duddy wins a bidding war for a piece of Ste. Agathe lake grounds against Dingelman—a wealthy, established *big macher*—because, as his girlfriend Yvette hesitantly explains, "One of the farmers . . . well, he hates Jews. He'd prefer to sell to me." Duddy exploits the French Canadian's anti-Semitism, telling Yvette, "Listen you get a hold of that farmer and tell him Dingleman is the biggest, fattest, dirtiest goddam Jew who ever lived. If he gets hold of that land he's going to build a synagogue on it. You tell him that" (Richler, *Duddy Kravitz* 288). More recently, on the south side of the border, Allegra Goodman's *Kaaterskill Falls* (1998), discussed in the following chapter, explores a similar question of property purchase in the Catskills. An Orthodox Jew wishes to buy land in Kaaterskill; the local judge, who is defined by his love of his country and his god, wishes to preserve this land from the encroachment of "cultish" people who "do not inspire his sympathy, generosity of fellow feeling" (61). Using free indirect discourse, Goodman visits the mind of the judge to confirm for readers that the Jewish suspicions of American anti-Semitism are accurate (191).

9. In Quebec, the Hasidic problem is often referred to as *la problème juive*. In East Ramapo, New York, a long-running conflict between Hasidim and their neighbors concerning the ways the public schools are run attracted the media and was the focus of an in-depth article in *New York Magazine* in April 2013, a one-hour "This American Life" episode on NPR in September 2014, and a counterargument in *Tablet Magazine* also in September 2014. The first (*New York Magazine*) article cites one student-interviewee explaining that at church, active congregants urged their peers to vote in school-board elections: "'Parents,' they'd always say, 'Let's go vote for the district, we're voting against the Jews.'" Another young woman admits, "At a young age, you hear 'Jewish' and you automatically think, *Oh, they're trying to kill my school district*" (Wallace-Wells). The later pieces demonstrate a similar and continued rhetoric.

10. Secular Jews not infrequently side against Hasidim, determined to distinguish themselves from their Hasidic counterparts. See Barbara Kay's "Not in My Backyard, Either," for example. Rubel refers to this secular Jewish anxiety as "They are us in other clothes" (Rubel, *Doubting* 147).

11. These magazines are relatively new—which is to say, late twentieth / early twenty-first century—American international cultural productions (*Mishpacha* was begun in 1984, *Binah* in 2006, and *Ami* in 2010), but arguably in the tradition of *Jeschurun* and *Der Israelit*, late nineteenth-century weekly German neo-Orthodox magazines. See Lezzi for

an interesting discussion of the didactic fiction (aiming to preserve and promote Ortho-doxy) in these periodicals.

12. In a rare exception, in December 2012, *Ami* published an interview with George Far-kas, the attorney who defended Weberman, the convicted rapist and pedophile, explain-ing that "upon consulting with leading rabbinical figures, we determined that it is impera-tive that the defendant be given the same opportunity as his accuser to present his case, not only in the court of law but also in the court of public opinion. The prosecutor's case has been given its full airing in the general media. The defense's arguments deserve equal exposure" ("On Court Street," 49). This editorial choice led to a number of readers boy-cotting the magazine and the creation of a Facebook page publicizing the effort. *Ami* also, as discussed earlier, chose to defend Lev Tahor when *Mishpacha* criticized it.

13. For an excellent reading of the billboard lawsuit, see Hammerman.

14. See Ahadi.

15. See Heinrich, "Media Stir Up Storm"; Ferguson; and Bruemmer and Dougherty.

16. One group that meets in person as well as having an online forum is The Friends of Hutchison Street / *Les Amis de la Rue Hutchison*. In Lacerte's blog post, he intentionally omits the second, and French, half of the group's name as if to suggest it is monolingual and exclusionary, instead of bilingual and inclusionary.

17. Again, here we see the slippage from Hasidim to Jews, one that some Jews are quick to trouble, if for what seem to be self-serving reasons. Victor Goldbloom, for example, a well-known Canadian politician (a Member of the National Assembly for many years and the former Commissioner of Official Languages) and president of the Quebec region of the Canadian Jewish Congress, wrote in to the *Montreal Gazette* to allay concerns that the act of violence against the visibly observant Jews be construed as general anti-Semitism, pointing out that the violence in Ste. Agathe that led to the public Sellem ceremony was anti-Hasidic as opposed to anti-Semitic (Goldbloom).

18. Although there is often a conflation of Hasidic groups, it is significant that Pollak is part of the Vishnitz Hasidim, not a more outward-facing liberal dynasty, such as Chabad.

19. On the website of Ezras Nashim, the all-female service cites their mission as stem-ming from a verse in the "Woman of Valor": "*Chagrah v'oz mosneiha vat'ametz zro'oseiha*" or "She girds herself in strength, and makes her arms strong" (www.ezras-nashim.org/our -mission/).

20. See Skinazi, "Meet Mindy Pollak."

#### CHAPTER 4 — SHE SENSES THAT HER ENTERPRISE IS GOOD

1. In remarkably similar fashion, Sarah Hofstetter, the CEO of 360i and an observant Jewish American woman, has written and spoken about the synergy of her Orthodoxy and professional success, arguing that "vulnerabilities" like hers (she names an interconnected triptych: religion, motherhood, and lack of experience) can be major assets. She often cites the rest afforded by the Sabbath as what fuels her energy during the week and the efforts involved in finding and trekking out to kosher restaurants with clients as creat-ing strong bonds. Her accounts have been chronicled by *Fortune* in their "Most Powerful Women" column, and her speech at Cannes was publicized by the popular blog "Jew in the City," which is dedicated to revising negative perceptions about Orthodoxy and has a focus on women.

2. Polls consistently show Americans to be far more theistic than Britons. That said, the lack of separation between church and state in the United Kingdom means (Christian) religion is embedded into social institutions, including schools, where religious instruction is mandatory.

3. I use the term *fundamentalism* with some hesitation. Because Judaism does not seek converts, Appiah's definition of fundamentalism can be said to exclude Judaism. *Jewish fundamentalism* (a term Samuel Heilman, for one, freely employs) is only Manichean about its own constituents, whereas Christian and Islamic fundamentalisms demand their (respective) "one right way" for all people.

4. In *Sliding to the Right*, Heilman distinguishes the (unnamed) Modern Orthodoxy we see represented by Barnett—contrapuntalist, pluralist, and able to accommodate "dissonant and competing loyalties"—from the Haredi Orthodoxy of Neuberger—contra-acculturative, enclavist, and "retrograde" (3–4). Heilman recognizes that the division is made from a line in the sand but sees the line moving in the direction of Haredi Orthodoxy (hence the title of his book), although it should be evident in the case of Neuberger, and throughout my book, that I see the line moving in both directions.

5. Goodman's academic credentials are as solid as her literary ones: she studied English and philosophy at Harvard and has a PhD in English from Stanford.

6. If there's one "cult-of-true-womanhood" attribute the film resists giving Rachel, it's submissiveness, perhaps testament to the overwhelmingly dominant stereotype of Jewish women being in control.

7. Although Gilbert and Gubar never cite Welter, it is hard not to see their points of convergence.

8. For a reading of the angel as love, see Ward 7.

9. Considering the fact that Woolf was still on a homicidal rampage forty years later, it seems important to note that the 1890s marked the "angel's" decline and not her demise. One could argue she still hovers in some dim corners of Michaels stores and playgrounds today.

10. And fleshy she is. An 1892 reviewer, in fact, objected to the heroine's physical endowment, made a source of constant emphasis in the novel (Hardy 409n12).

11. Calling the *man* Angel (he is, appropriately, idealistic, dispassionate, and righteous) is a brilliant act of gender inversion on Hardy's part.

12. The term *New Woman*, referring to a woman who decries the "home-is-the-woman's-sphere" claim, dates to 1894, three years after *Tess*, and is attributed to Sarah Grand (Grand 271).

13. No such "return" marks the film version, which features a starry-eyed Natalie Wood as the eponymous Marjorie Morningstar and Gene Kelly as her ill-cast lover. In terms of its feminist appeal, the change suggests a more optimistic ending. In terms of its Judaism, the film sits squarely with its contemporaries as a happy tale of assimilation.

14. Goodman tells us that Elizabeth was educated at Carmel College. The selective Orthodox Jewish boarding school Carmel College (1948–1997) was located not, as in the novel, in Henley (a Jewish neighborhood of London) but rather in Oxfordshire, putting Elizabeth and her education in closer proximity to Beatrix and hers than the humble description of her premarriage studies suggests. Carmel was dubbed the "Jewish Eton" in *The Observer* in 1973, shortly after the time the fictional Elizabeth would have graduated (Bermant 41).

15. Building on earlier television characterizations of young working women such as "That Girl" (1966–1971) and "The Mary Tyler Moore Show," the shows of the 1980s focused on single working mothers, women whose work was on par with their husbands', and women who worked while their husbands stayed home.

16. Andrew Furman sees this depiction of the Orthodox Jewish woman's plight as analogous to that of the African American woman (as opposed to the upper-middle-class white woman; Furman 86).

17. See, for example, Blumen's study on women's labor in the ultra-Orthodox community. Explains Blumen, "Religious male unpaid work takes priority over the hegemonic capitalist value of paid work. Hence, in accordance with women's subordination in the gender prestige system, paid work is assigned to women" ("Ultraorthodox Jewish Women" 135).

18. The unnamed Hasidim, who cluster in a neighborhood in Brooklyn and can think of no greater honor than hearing the rebbe's *farbrengen* every week, are transparently modeled on Chabad Lubavitch Hasidim (the only Hasidim who would have a *farbrengen*—the others would have a *tisch* or a *botteh*). The film, however, moves the community from Crown Heights to Borough Park and gives the old cult-of-personality rebbe who looks like the last Lubavitch rebbe, Menachem Mendel Schneerson, the slightly different name of Moshe Meyerson.

19. In Carner's *Jerusalem Maiden*, we see a similar conflation of the Orthodox woman's passions. See chapter 5 for a more detailed account of the construction of the Orthodox artist.

20. Why a woman of *fortitude* as opposed to *valor* or *virtue*? It is an aside, but perhaps a significant one, to note that each translation tells a slightly different story about the paradigmatic woman of Proverbs 31 (the translation of *fortitude* is closest to "woman warrior," a translation I suggest in the introduction).

21. Famously, Irving Howe declared, "American Jewish fiction has probably moved past its high point," and Leslie Fiedler asserted, "The Jewish American novel is over and done with" (Howe 16; Fiedler 117).

22. Furman specifically discusses Goldstein's *The Mind-Body Problem* here, though he suggests this "narrative hostility" is/was a larger trend. Shalit echoed Furman in her *New York Times* article, exempting Allegra Goodman *alone* from condemnation: "For now," concludes Shalit, "harshly satirical views of the haredi may still be too common, and novels and stories by sympathetic outsiders like Allegra Goodman too rare" (Shalit, "Observant").

23. Most, if not all, critics see Goodman's writing as heading or part of a paradigm shift. See Bell; Avery; Pinsker; Omer-Sherman; Furman; Socolovsky; Cronin; Aarons; Wisse; Meyers; and Harrison-Kahan.

24. Meyers's provocative interpretation of the feminism in *Kaaterskill Falls* focuses on the "men of valor." She argues that Isaac's consciousness raising is "inspired rather than impeded" by his Orthodoxy (*Identity* 34). Furthermore, she argues, "Rather than sacrificing Jewish continuity, feminism, in the form of Jewish men who love Jewish women and Jewish textual traditions enough to enable them to live and breathe in the modern world, ensures the future viability of traditional Jewish life" (35).

25. See Cahan's *The Rise of David Levinsky*, Wouk's *Marjorie Morningstar*, and I. B. Singer's "The Yearning Heifer," among others. A good collection is Phil Brown's *In the Catskills: A Century of Jewish Experience in the Mountains*.

26. This is not to say Isaiah's overzealousness is not indicative of a larger trend in Orthodoxy (traced by Heilman), only to say that by focusing on this individual rabbi as *son* and *brother*, Goodman illustrates what room there is in rabbinical authority for human error.

27. *The Women's Balcony* unfortunately undoes in the last third of the film some of the good work it produced in the first hour. After we are witness to the young rabbi's recommendations to the men in his congregation that are primarily directed at controlling their wives, an entirely realistic premise, we are shown the rabbi as a stock film villain when he declares (without hesitation) that forgery is acceptable and that he is happy to sign a document (that requires countersigning) with each of his hands.

28. See Lifshitz-Kliger and Becker, "Haredi Ikea Catalogue Is a No-Ma'am's Land." It is arguable that although the 2017 IKEA catalogue and other varieties of magazines and pamphlets featuring men doing all the cooking and childcare are not reflective of reality, they serve to normalize such practices and could thus be said to foster more egalitarian behavior in Haredi homes.

29. Although many of the "off-the-*derech*" memoirs discussed in chapter 1 bemoan the state of women under Orthodoxy, Deen's argues that it is men who suffer at least as much as women (if differently) by being denied the superior secular education women receive as well as job training. A December 2015 Fox News televised interview with transgender woman Abby Stein reveals a general misunderstanding of Haredi gendered education, as the interviewer remarks that Abby was lucky to have grown up male and thus receive a good education, enabling her path to Columbia University. Abby corrects the interviewer, explaining, "Definitely in my community, I wouldn't have gotten such a good Jewish education [as a girl], however, I would have gotten a way better secular education" ("Free to Be").

30. For more on Levy, see Ingall's *Tablet* article and Katsman's blog post, "Interview with Yael Levy."

CHAPTER 5 — SHE WILL BE PRAISED AT THE
GATES BY HER VERY OWN DEEDS

1. One cannot but note that a hundred years ago, Orthodoxy had one of its greatest singers filling concert halls: Cantor Yossele Rosenblatt (1882–1933), known as "the Jewish Caruso." Nevertheless, Rosenblatt famously turned down lucrative opportunities (to star in *The Jazz Singer*, for example) that could imply irreligious motivations, and he died destitute.

2. As yet another sign of "sliding to the right," the erasure of women's faces, discussed earlier, is not a long-standing Jewish tradition. Adina Bar Shalom, who is the daughter of the late Rabbi Ovadia Yosef, the founder and spiritual leader of Shas (the Haredi Sephardi political party in Israel), and an Orthodox feminist activist, recalls how her father was outraged when he discovered that in photographs, his wife and mother had been blurred out (Pileggi, "Ex-Shas").

3. For personal, cultural, linguistic, sociological, and economic approaches to Orthodox men's issues, see, among others, Deen; Finkelman; Friedman and Hakak; Benor; Heilman; Blumen, "Gendered"; and Berman.

4. Writing in 1999, Alyse Roller saw Orthodox women's fiction as the final frontier—a thinly populated discursive space with great potential. Barbara Landress's 2012 study is

more bountiful, but even she sees a limited selection on offer (comprising primarily the uses and critiques of second-wave feminism). This field is far flusher now. Arad's 2016 *Haaretz* long read chronicles the thriving industry in Israel and includes interviews with pioneering Haredi woman writer Menucha Fuchs, who has published almost four hundred children's books; Avigail Myzlik, a Breslov publisher who gave many fellow Haredi women writers their starts; Mali Avraham, a prolific writer who has published seventeen novels, sometimes as Mali Green; and other key figures in the field. Of particular note is the discussion of "the Haredi Writer's House," all of whose members are women. The forum was established by writer Leah Fried. "We meet once a month and exchange information," Myzlik says. "If a writer is stuck on a sentence, we immediately help her. There is amazing reciprocity. . . . I will get an answer to every question immediately" (Arad). Also see Shenker's scholarly examination of the theme of identity swapping in Haredi women's popular literature in Israel. It sheds light on the active decision-making processes regarding their lifestyles that Orthodox women writers foreground in their novels.

5. A related cultural production would be Orthodox women's magazines, which, too, comprise a sizeable international women-run industry, tailored to the lives of their readers. These magazines are delivered to women's homes on Fridays for leisurely Shabbos reading. Women haunt the pages of the magazines in shadowed profiles or are represented in their believed use values: pots, knitting needles, or children (girls only below the age of three). Their actual photographs, however, are absent, as, arriving in unregulated environments, no risk can be taken that men would inappropriately consume their images.

6. In Modern Orthodoxy, there are numerous places for women to study and advance their Jewish scholarship, including the Drisha Institute, a pioneer in women's scholarship, and Yeshivat Maharat, founded in 2009.

7. Appointed secretary of the movement by Rebbe Menachem Mendel Schneerson in 1990, Krinsky later became the leader of the movement, and he was ranked among the top five rabbis during all seven years (2007–2013) that *Newsweek* ran its annual list "The 50 Most Influential Rabbis in America," reaching number one in 2010 and 2011. As it turns out, both of Rivka's husband's grandfathers were secretaries to the Rebbe, the other being Rabbi Binyomin Klein. And both the Klein and Krinsky families, according to Rivka, are very supportive of her artwork.

8. Yaron's character is linked to music in both productions as well: in *Félix and Meira*, Meira is playing a recording of Wendy Rene's "After Laughter" over and over, and she makes her overture to her Québécois lover by asking to listen to music with him, after he makes *his* overture to her through her drawing; in *Shtisel*, Libi and her father connect over a Tchaikovsky melody on the radio.

9. It would be interesting to see what Peleg would make of *Shababnikim* (2017–present), the newer Israeli television show that blurs the boundaries between Haredi and secular even further, with a cast of characters who cruise the streets in a luxury SUV, flirt with young attractive secular women, drink, swear, shop at the Nespresso store, play football, text on the latest iPhone, and masturbate—all in their black, brushed Borsalinos. See Skinazi, "Black Hats."

10. For more on Ponevezh, the most renowned yeshiva of the contemporary era, see Indursky's documentary about his alma mater, *Ponevezh Time* (2014).

11. See Dardashti.

12. Columnist Jessica Steinberg describes a *niggun*, a wordless song, composed by *Shtisel* writer Ori Alon, that the grandmother hums in one episode, showing up at a

Haredi wedding soon thereafter (documented in a YouTube clip entitled "Shtisel's Emotional *Niggun* from Minsk"). Steinberg cites Alon's glee: "We made it up! . . . How would they even know about something on TV? It's a badge of honor that they watch it." See also Leibovitz.

13. As in *A Price above Rubies*, in Carner's novel, a woman's passions—professional, artistic—are subsumed in and represented by sexual excess.

14. Klein traces the history of film in Palestine/Israel (Klein 75; cited in Shohat 15).

15. See discussion in chapter 1, along with articles by N. Deutsch; Fraenkel; and Ungar-Sargon.

16. Benor's *Becoming Frum* analyzes the two-way relationship of *ba'alei teshuva* and their "FFB" peers. She argues BTs offer "alternative cultural capital outside of the religious sphere," citing Matisyahu and others with skills gleaned in the secular world (80).

17. See Glinter, "Orthodox World"; Bitton-Jackson; Agence France-Presse; Rosenberg, "Israeli Film"; Kang.

18. The author of *Orthodox Cinema* describes herself as "a ba'alat tshuva . . . , a member of the Belz Hasidic sect, mother of seven, a lecturer at a religious college and an ultra-Orthodox seminary for women, a researcher of Haredi cinema at the Hebrew University of Jerusalem and a film critic" (Shani).

19. It is hard to validate the accuracy of such figures without a traditional box-office calculation, but there is no doubt that Garbose is one of the biggest figures in Orthodox women's film.

20. The community of London's East End Jews, most of whom were refugees from the pogroms, was colorfully chronicled in Israel Zangwill's brilliant set of "ghetto" novels and plays of the 1890s.

21. What is and is not acceptable varies widely among communities and individual families.

22. The value of gender equity in the public sphere, he notes, is not only modern American but also medieval Jewish. "Women," Finkelman writes, "although also mothers, played central roles in the medieval Jewish marketplace, at a time and place when parenthood was not considered a fulltime endeavor and where raising children was perceived as requiring less moment-to-moment vigilance than it does today" (49). *The Memoirs of Glückel of Hameln*, begun in 1690 by a German Jewish businesswoman, indicates the continued importance of Jewish women in the marketplace beyond the medieval era (Glückel).

23. Garbose's cast is not entirely female, as some minor roles are played by male actors, generally not in the same scenes as women. For these inclusions, Garbose was subject to an angry diatribe at a screening in Boro Park, followed by a threat to cancel her bookings (Horwitz). "Ultimately that did not happen,'" Garbose recounts in an interview. "Instead,'" she says, "they hung posters all over Flatbush with a disclaimer in Yiddish saying, 'It's not forbidden, but it doesn't meet our standards.' That turned out to be the best publicity we could have. We sold out and had to add a 10 p.m. screening with 800 more women waiting to get in. That was our greatest victory against people on the right" (Horwitz). In her second film, Garbose begins with a husband and wife scene. Side by side in the same frame, the couple could have been seen to be scandalous; the husband and the wife in the film, however, are played by a real-life couple (Miriam Kublin and Markus Kublin), and in the opening credits, their names, along with their pictures, are presented to the viewers to make the relationship transparent.

24. See the Babylonian Talmud (*Ketubbot* 62b; *Nedarim* 50a), the Jerusalem Talmud (*Shabbat* 6:1, 7d; *Sotah* 9:15, 24c), and Avot de Rabbi Nathan (Version A, chapter 6; Version B, chapter 12).

25. Although Mirvis names her Batsheva, this singing and painting heroine in *The Ladies Auxiliary* similarly seems to walk in the path of her biblical foremother Miriam, and when Batsheva paints the image of the biblical Miriam "in a long turquoise gown holding a tambourine and leading a line of women as she danced across the dry land," the collective voice of the novels declares that "when we took a closer look, we realized that this Miriam looked suspiciously like Batsheva" (Mirvis *Ladies*, 146–147).

26. The Holocaust is a common trope in Orthodox women's cultural productions. It offers a number of suitable stock features, including an us/them Jewish/non-Jewish Manichean world and a seemingly incontestable reason to advocate for the maintenance of faith and Jewish traditions.

27. A fan of *Marjorie Morningstar*—the 1958 film—might have a hard time not noticing that Krinsky bears a resemblance to Natalie Wood as she watches unfold before her the tale of a girl going to upstate New York in the 1950s to take the position of musical director and head of drama at a Jewish summer camp. Of course, we can assume that most of the viewers of *The Heart That Sings* are not *Marjorie Morningstar* fans, but, seeing as the filmmaker is *ba'al teshuva*, I could not help but ask Garbose if *she* were a fan. "I perhaps subconsciously was thinking about Marjorie Morningstar, which I devoured as a teenager, when creating *The Heart That Sings*," she wrote me. "Ironically, as per my recommendation, my daughter is reading (and loving) MM right now!" (personal correspondence).

28. If this representation is meant to be a subversive questioning of ethnic imagery in mainstream popular culture, it is not obvious. It is no *Blazing Saddles*.

29. Actually, some Orthodox sects *do* involve women wearing attire that remarkably resembles the Muslim burka (it is derisively referred to as a *frumka*), including Lev Tahor. The practice has been promoted by a female leader, Bruria Keren. See Wagner, "Sexual Responsibility," as well as Katsman's posts "Mother Taliban" and "Hyper-Modest Abusive Mother of 12 Released" on her *Mother in Israel* blog.

30. See "Brooklyn, NY—Boro Park Williamsburg Bus Line"; Chavkin, "City Human Rights," "Sex-Segregation on Brooklyn Bus," "Women Ride in Back"; Haughney, "At front of Brooklyn Bus"; Fermino, "'Back of Bus' Furor." For the Israeli version of this event and its fallout, see Sztokman.

31. The *Jewish Daily Forward* has, in truth, published articles about Orthodox sex segregation on Brooklyn buses: see, for example, Zeveloff. Esther's response ("You know I couldn't believe that a *Jewish* newspaper would write something like that. They did this *scathing* article about how Orthodox Jews practice their religion in America. It was unbelievable") is exaggerated, though. It echoes Roller's argument about Orthodox women's literature, which she emphatically calls a "reaction to secular Jewish feminism" (52).

32. The "title" likely refers to the fact that shortly before this film was produced, the first woman "maharat" was ordained. It caused, and to date, continues to cause, fierce debates among Orthodox groups. In 2015, female ordination prompted Agudath Israel of America to denounce as dissidents all forms of Orthodoxy that accepted it.

33. This is a central tenet of Shalit's *A Return to Modesty* (1999).

34. The band might have been niche, but it garnered much media attention. Write-ups of the band can be found in *The Huffington Post*, *The Village Voice*, *The Forward*, *Gawker*, *The New York Jewish Week*, *CBS*, *Market Wired*, *Tom Tom Mag*, *Tablet Magazine*, *Times*

*of Israel, The Guardian, The Wall Street Journal, Hadassah Magazine, Vice, The New York Times, The New Yorker,* and many local papers and magazines.

### CODA

1. Although the 2017 Patty Jenkins film starring Israeli actress Gal Gadot premiered in Israel with *Wonder Woman* transliterated as the title, many Israelis remember (with a chuckle) the backlash the Israeli Broadcasting Authority received when they decided to air a new television show called *Eshet Chayil* on Friday evenings. Assuming the show featured an Orthodox woman, viewers unable to watch television on Shabbat demanded the time of the show be moved, only to discover *Eshet Chayil* was *Wonder Woman.* In 2011, there was another television show in Israel called *Eshet Chayil*, and this one *was* about Judaism and feminism (see Sharir). For a reading of the Jenkins's Wonder Woman as a woman of valor, see Abrams.

2. The author of the *Princess* books is a white American woman called Jean Sasson, former resident of Saudi Arabia. Sasson says that the details of the books are all taken straight from a Saudi princess, whom she calls Sultana.

3. Many New Woman and suffragist activists wrote in the feminist/matriarchal utopia genre at the turn of the twentieth century. Charlotte Perkins Gilman's *Herland* (1915) is best known, but there are other great examples, including *The Superwoman* (1912) by American Jewish writer Miriam Michelson and "Sultana's Dream" (1905) by Muslim Bengali writer Rokeya Sakhawat Hussain. In addition to *Smurfs: The Lost Village* and *Wonder Woman,* another recent film in this genre is *Mad Max: Fury Road* (2015), wherein the women who have been forced into being "breeders" for the ruling men seek refuge in "the green place of many mothers." These should be distinguished from speculative fiction that imagines the dangers of women's superiority (as no better than men's), such as Naomi Alderman's 2016 novel *The Power* and the 2018 French film *Je ne suis pas un homme facile* (which is in the tradition of Alice Guy's 1906 silent film *Les résultats de féminisme*).

# Bibliography

## NOVELS, SHORT STORIES, AND MEMOIRS

Abraham, Pearl. *Giving Up America*. New York: Riverhead, 1999.

———. *The Romance Reader*. New York: Riverhead, 1996.

———. *The Seventh Beggar*. New York: Riverhead, 2005.

Alderman, Naomi. *Disobedience*. New York: Touchstone, 2007.

———. *The Power*. New York: Penguin, 2016.

Antin, Mary. *The Promised Land*. 1912. New York: Penguin, 1997.

Armstrong, Karen. *The Narrow Gate: A Nun's Story*. London: Flamingo, 1997.

Astaire, Libi. *The Disappearing Dowry*. Brooklyn, N.Y.: Zahav Press, 2009.

———. *The Doppelganger's Dance*. Aster Press, 2013.

———. *The Ruby Spy Ring*. Brooklyn, N.Y.: Zahav Press, 2011.

———. *Tempest in a Teapot*. Aster Press, 2012.

Auslander, Shalom. *The Foreskin's Lament*. New York: Riverhead, 2007.

Beaudoin, Myriam. *Hadassa*. Montreal: Leméac, 2010.

Brown, Judy. *This Is Not a Love Story*. New York: Little, Brown and Company, 2015.

Bukiet, Melvin Jules. *While the Messiah Tarries*. New York: Syracuse University Press, 1997.

Cahan, Abraham. *The Rise of David Levinsky*. 1917. New York: Modern Library, 2001.

———. *Yekl and the Imported Bridegroom and Other Stories of Yiddish New York*. 1896. New York: Dover, 1970.

Carner, Talia. *Jerusalem Maiden*. New York: HarperCollins, 2011.

Césaire, Aimé. *A Tempest*. 1969. Translated by Richard Miller. New York: Theatre Communications Group, 1992.

Chabon, Michael. *The Yiddish Policemen's Union*. New York: HarperCollins, 2007.

Chayil, Eishes [Judy Brown]. *Hush*. New York: Walker, 2010.

Cohen, Robert. *The Here and Now*. New York: Scribner, 1997.

Dahl, Julia. *Invisible City*. New York: Minotaur, 2014.

———. *Run You Down*. New York: Minotaur, 2015.

Davidman, Lynn. *Becoming Un-Orthodox: Stories of Ex-Hasidic Jews*. Oxford: Oxford University Press, 2015.

Deen, Shulem. *All Who Go Do Not Return*. New York: Graywolf Press, 2015.

Deutsch, Barry. *Hereville: How Mirka Caught a Fish*. New York: Amulet, 2015.

———. *Hereville: How Mirka Got Her Sword*. New York: Amulet, 2010.

———. *Hereville: How Mirka Met a Meteorite*. New York: Amulet, 2013.

Englander, Nathan. *For the Relief of Unbearable Urges*. New York: Vintage, 2000.

Farhoud, Abla. *Le Sourire de la Petite Juive*. Montreal: VLB Editeur, 2011.

Fekete, Yehudis. "Faith in the Face of Abuse." Talk at Limmud, Manchester, United Kingdom, 29 January 2017.

Feldman, Deborah. *Exodus: A Memoir*. New York: Penguin, 2014.

———. "Once upon a Life: Deborah Feldman." *Guardian*, 29 August 2010.

———. *Unorthodox: The Scandalous Rejection of My Hasidic Roots*. New York: Simon and Schuster, 2012.

Gilman, Charlotte Perkins. "An Extinct Angel." *The Yellow Wall-Paper and Other Stories*, edited by Robert Shulman. Oxford: Oxford University Press, 1995, 48–50.

———. *Herland and Other Stories*, edited by Barbara H. Solomon. New York: Signet Classics, 1992.

Glückel. *The Memoirs of Glückel of Hameln*. Translated by Marvin Lowenthal. New York: Schocken, 1977.

Goldberg, Myra. *Whistling and Other Stories*. Cambridge, Mass.: Zoland, 1993.

Goldfarb, Daniel. *Modern Orthodox*. New York: Dramatist's Play Service, 2005.

Goldstein, Rebecca. *Mazel*. New York: Viking, 1995.

———. *The Mind-Body Problem*. New York: Penguin, 1983.

Goodman, Allegra. *The Family Markowitz*. New York: Delta, 1996.

———. *Kaaterskill Falls*. New York: Delta, 1998.

———. "Long-Distance Client." *New Yorker*, 11 July 2005.

———. *Total Immersion*. New York: Dial Press, 1989.

Grade, Chaim. *My Mother's Sabbath Days*. 1955. Translated by Channa Kleinerman Goldstein and Inna H. Grade. New York: Knopf, 1986.

Hardy, Thomas. *Tess of the D'Urbervilles*. 1892. New York: Penguin, 2009.

Harris, Eve. *The Marrying of Chani Kaufman*. Dingwall: Sandstone Press, 2013.

Himes, Chester. *A Rage in Harlem*. 1957. London: Penguin, 2011.

Horn, Dara. *In the Image*. New York: W. W. Norton, 2002.

Jacobson, Howard. *Kalooki Nights*. London: Cape, 2006.

Kellerman, Faye. *The Beast*. New York: HarperCollins, 2013.

———. *Blindman's Bluff*. New York: HarperCollins, 2009.

———. *Bone Box*. New York: William Morrow, 2017.

———. *The Burnt House*. London: HarperCollins, 2007.

———. *The Day of Atonement*. New York: Morrow, 1991.

———. *False Prophet*. New York: Morrow, 1992.

———. *The Forgotten*. New York: HarperCollins, 2001.

———. *Grievous Sin*. New York: Morrow, 1993.

———. *Gun Games*. New York: HarperCollins, 2012.

———. *Hangman*. New York: HarperCollins, 2010.

———. *Jupiter's Bones*. London: Headline, 1999.

———. *Justice*. New York: Morrow, 1995.

———. *The Mercedes Coffin*. New York: HarperCollins, 2007.

———. *Milk and Honey*. 1990. New York: HarperCollins, 2011.

———. *Murder 101*. London: HarperCollins, 2014.

———. *Prayers for the Dead*. London: Headline, 1996.

———. *The Ritual Bath*. 1986. New York: HarperCollins, 2011.

———. *Sacred and Profane*. 1987. London: Headline, 1994.

———. *Sanctuary*. New York: Morrow, 1994.

———. *Serpent's Tooth*. London: Headline, 1997.

———. *Stalker*. New York: HarperCollins, 2000.

———. *Stone Kiss*. New York: Warner, 2002.

———. *Street Dreams*. New York: Warner, 2003.

———. *The Theory of Death*. New York: William Morrow, 2015.

———. *Walking Shadows*. New York: William Morrow, 2018.

Kemelman, Harry. *Conversations with Rabbi Small*. New York: Fawcett Crest, 1990.

———. *Friday the Rabbi Slept Late*. Boston: G. K. Hall, 1964.

King, Ruchama. *Seven Blessings*. New York: St. Martin's Press, 2003.

Klinghoffer, David. *The Lord Will Gather Me In: My Journey to Jewish Orthodoxy*. New York: Free Press, 1998.

Krauss, Nicole. *A History of Love*. New York: W. W. Norton, 2005.

Krich, Rochelle. *Blues in the Night*. New York: Ballantine, 2002.

———. *Dream House*. New York: Ballantine, 2003.

———. *Grave Endings*. New York: Ballantine, 2004.

———. *Now You See Me . . .* New York: Ballantine, 2005.

Latifa. *My Forbidden Face*. Translated by Lisa Appignanesi. London: Virago Press, 2002.

Lax, Leah. *Uncovered: How I Left Hasidic Life and Finally Came Home*. Berkeley, Calif.: She Writes Press, 2015.

Levitin, Sonia. *Strange Relations*. New York: Knopf, 2007.

Levy, Yael. *Brooklyn Love*. Avon: Crimson Romance, 2012.

———. *Starstruck*. Avon, Mass.: Crimson Romance, 2013.

Lichtenstein, Rachel, and Ian Sinclair. *Rodinsky's Room*. London: Granta, 2000.

Mann, Reva. *The Rabbi's Daughter*. New York: Dial Press, 2007.

Markovits, Anouk. *I Am Forbidden*. New York: Vintage, 2012.

Metzker, Isaac, editor. *A Bintel Brief*. Introduction by Isaac Metzker. Translation by Diana Shalet Levy. New York: Doubleday, 1971.

Michaels, Leonard. "Murderers." *The Collected Stories*, edited by Katharine Ogden Michaels. New York: Farrar, Straus, and Giroux, 2007, 95–98.

Michelson, Miriam. "The Superwoman." *The Smart Set*, vol. 37, no. 4, August 1912, 1–48.

———. *A Yellow Journalist*. New York: D. Appleton, 1905.

Mirvis, Tova. *The Ladies' Auxiliary*. Toronto: Ballantine, 1999.

———. *The Outside World*. New York: Vintage, 2004.

Morton, Leah. *I Am a Woman—and a Jew*. 1926. New York: Markus Wiener, 1986.

Ozick, Cynthia. *Bloodshed and Three Novellas*. New York: Alfred A. Knopf, 1976.

Patmore, Coventry. *The Angel in the House*. 1854. London: John W. Parker and Son, 1858.

Pearlman, Ruthie. *Lockdown*. New York: Menucha, 2014.

———. *School of Secrets*. New York: Menucha, 2013.

Pollack, Eileen. *Paradise, New York*. Philadelphia: Temple University Press, 1998.

Potok, Chaim. *The Chosen*. New York: Simon and Schuster, 1967.

———. *Davita's Harp*. 1985. New York: Ballantine, 1996.

———. *The Promise*. 1969. New York: Fawcett, 1982.

Ragen, Naomi. *Jephte's Daughter*. 1989. New Milford, Conn.: Toby Press, 2001.

———. *The Sacrifice of Tamar*. New Milford, Conn.: Toby Press, 1995.

———. *The Saturday Wife*. New York: St. Martin's Griffin, 2007.

———. *Sotah*. New York: St. Martin's Griffin, 1992.

———. *Women's Minyan*. New Milford, Conn.: Toby Press, 2006.

Rapoport, Nessa. *House on the River: A Summer Journey*. New York: Harmony, 2004.

———. *Preparing for Sabbath*. New York: Bantam, 1982.

Richler, Mordecai. *The Apprenticeship of Duddy Kravitz*. Toronto: Penguin, 1959.

Roiphe, Anne. *Lovingkindness*. 1987. New York: Grand Central, 1997.

Rosen, Jonathan. *Joy Comes in the Morning*. New York: Picador, 2005.

Rosenbaum, David. *Zaddik*. New York: Mysterious Press, 1993.

Rotchin, B. Glen. *The Rent Collector*. Montreal: Véhicule Press, 2005.

Roth, Henry. *Call It Sleep*. New York: Avon, 1934.

Roth, Philip. *The Counterlife*. New York: Vintage, 1986.

———. *Goodbye, Columbus*. 1959. New York: Vintage, 1987.

————. *Portnoy's Complaint.* 1969. New York: Vintage, 1994.

Sasson, Jean. *Princess.* 1992. New York: Bantam, 2004.

Shalit, Wendy. *A Return to Modesty: Discovering the Lost Virtue.* New York: Free Press, 1999.

Singer, Isaac Bashevis. "The Yearning Heifer." *In the Catskills: A Century of Jewish Experience in the Mountains,* edited by Phil Brown. New York: Columbia University Press, 2002, 64–74.

Small, Rivkah. *Diamonds in the Boathouse.* New York: Targum Press, 2009.

————. *A Fortunate Find.* New York: Menucha, 2012.

Stanger-Ross, Ilana. *Sima's Undergarments for Women.* New York: Penguin, 2009.

Tan, Shaun. *The Arrival.* 2006. London: Hodder Children's, 2007.

Thériault, Yves. *Aaron.* 1954. Translated by W. Donald Wilson and Paul G. Socken. Waterloo, Canada: Wilfrid Laurier University Press, 2007.

Tremblay, Lise. *Mile End* [orig. *La Danse Juive*]. 1999. Translated by Gail Scott. Vancouver: Talon, 2002.

Vincent, Leah. *Cut Me Loose: Sin and Salvation After My Ultra-Orthodox Girlhood.* New York: Nan A. Talese, 2014.

Waks, Manny. "My Personal Journey." Talk at Limmud, Birmingham, United Kingdom, 27 December 2015.

Waldman, Ayelet. *The Big Nap.* New York: Penguin Putnam, 2001.

Wilson, G. Willow. *Ms. Marvel: No Normal.* Illustrated by Adrian Alphona, Marvel, 2014.

Wouk, Herman. *Marjorie Morningstar.* 1955. London: Hodder and Stoughton, 2008.

Yezierska, Anzia. *Bread Givers.* 1925. New York: Persea, 1999.

————. "Wings." *Hungry Hearts.* 1920. New York: Signet, 1996, 1–27.

Yousafzai, Malala, with Christina Lamb. *I am Malala.* London: Weidenfeld and Nicolson, 2013.

Zangwill, Israel. *Children of the Ghetto.* 1892. Edited by Meri-Jane Rochelson. Detroit: Wayne State University Press, 1998.

Zipora, Malka. *Laugh Rather than Cry: Tales from a Hassidic Household* [orig. *Lekhaim! Chroniques de la vie hassidique à Montréal*]. Montreal: Véhicule Press, 2007.


## ORTHODOX MAGAZINES AND NEWSPAPERS

*Ami Magazine*

*Binah Magazine*

*Fabologie* (http://www.fabologie.com)

*Hadar* (http://www.hadarmagazine.com)

*Hamodia: The Daily Newspaper of Torah Jewry*

*Jewish Magazine: The Magazine of the Orthodox Union*

*Mishpacha*

*The Observer*

*Yaldah*


## FILMS

*Almost a Family.* Written and directed by Tobi Einhorn, performance by Chanie Berger, Teck Productions, 2010.

*Annie Hall.* Directed and performance by Woody Allen, MGM, 1977.

*Be Fruitful and Multiply.* Directed by Shosh Shlam, Transfax Film Productions, 2005.

*The Chosen.* Directed by Jeremy Kagan, performances by Maximilian Schell and Rod Steiger, Henstooth Video, 1981.

*Dirty Dancing.* Directed by Emile Ardolino, written by Eleanor Bergstein, performances by Jennifer Grey and Patrick Swayze, Vestron Pictures, 1987.

*Félix et Meira*. Directed by Maxime Giroux, written by Maxime Giroux and Alexandre Laf-
ferière, performances by Hadas Yaron and Luzer Twersky, Metafilms, 2014.

*Fill the Void*. Written and directed by Rama Burshtein, performance by Hadas Yaron, Norma
Productions, 2012.

*The Heart That Sings*. Directed by Robin Garbose, performance by Rivka Siegel, Kol
Neshama, 2011.

*The Jazz Singer*. Directed by Alan Crosland, performance by Al Jolson, Warner Bros., 1927.

*Je ne suis pas un homme facile*. Written and directed by Eleonore Pourriat, Autopilot Entertainment, 2018.

*A Life Apart: Hasidism in America*. Directed by Oren Rudavsky and Menachem Daum, Oren
Rudavsky Productions, 1997.

*A Light for Greytowers*. Directed by Robin Garbose, Kol Neshama, 2007.

*Mad Max: Fury Road*. Directed by George Miller, Warner Brothers, 2015.

*A Matter of Chance*. Written and directed by Tobi Einhorn and Chavy Klein, Teck Productions, 2013.

*93Queen*. Directed by Paula Eiselt, Fork Films, 2018.

*One of Us*. Directed by Heidi Ewing and Rachel Grady, Loki Films, 2017.

*Ponevezh Time*. Written and directed by Yehonatan Indursky, Reshet, 2014.

*A Price above Rubies*. Written and directed by Boaz Yakin, performance by Renée Zellweger,
Miramax, 1998.

*Les résultats de féminisme*. Directed by Alice Guy, Gaumont, 1906.

*Romeo and Juliet in Yiddish*. Directed by Eve Annenberg, Vilna City Films, 2011.

*The Secrets*. Directed by Avi Nesher, Artomas Communications, 2007.

*A Serious Man*. Directed by Joel Coen and Ethan Coen, Feature Focus, 2009.

*Shekinah: The Intimate Life of Hasidic Women*. Directed by Abbey Jack Neidik, produced by
Abbey Neidik and Irene Lilienheim, DLI Productions, 2013.

*Smurfs: The Lost Village*. Directed by Kelly Asbury, Sony Pictures Animation, 2017.

*Song of Songs*. Directed by Josh Appignanesi, performance by Amber Agha, Wild Horses
Film, 2006.

*A Stranger among Us*. Directed by Sidney Lumet, performance by Melanie Griffith, Hollywood Pictures, 1992.

*Through the Wall [The Wedding Plan]*. Written and directed by Rama Burshtein, Norma
Productions, 2016.

*Trembling Before G-d*. Directed by Sandi Simcha DuBowski, Simcha Leib Productions, 2001.

*Ushpizin*. Directed by Gidi Dar, Eddie King Films, 2004.

*A Walk on the Moon*. Directed by Tony Goldyn, written by Pamela Gray, Miramax, 1999.

*The Women's Balcony*. [orig. *Yismach Hatani*]. Directed by Emil Ben-Shimon, written by
Shlomit Nehama, performances by Orna Banai and Avraham Aviv Alush, Pie Films, 2016.

*Women Unchained*. Directed by Beverly Siegel, performance by Mayim Bialik, National Center for Jewish Film, 2011.

*Wonder Woman*. Directed by Patty Jenkins, performance by Gal Gadot, Warner Bros., 2017.


TELEVISION

"America's Hidden Culture" parts 1 and 2. *Oprah's Next Chapter*. Presented by Oprah Winfrey, OWN, 12 and 13 February 2012.

"The Amish." *American Experience*. Written and directed by David Belton, season 24, episode
5, PBS, 28 February 2012.

*Extreme Wives with Kate Humble*. Presented by Kate Humble, BBC2, episode 2, 17 November
2017.

*Mekimi*. Directed by Ram Nahari, Hot, 2013.

*Real Time with Bill Maher*. Presented by Bill Maher, HBO, season 14, episode 4, 5 February 2016.

*Shababnikim*. Written by Eliran Malka and Daniel Paran, HOT, 2017–present.

*Shtisel*. Created by Yehonatan Indursky and Uri Alon. Hot, 2013–present.

*Srugim*. Directed by Eliezer Shapira. Yes, 2008–2012.

*Transparent*. Created by Jill Soloway, Amazon Prime, 2014–present.

### WEBSITES, BLOGS, FACEBOOK GROUPS, AND RADIO PODCASTS

"Announcements Relating to the Arts in Accordance with Torah Values." *Atara Arts Newsletter*, 6 December 2010, http://groups.google.com/forum/#!topic/atara/yqOXYMsM6qQ.

Aviner, Shlomo. "Modest Dress." *Be'ahava Ube'emuna (In Love and Faith)*. 25 December 2012, http://rav-shlomo-aviner.blogspot.co.uk/2012/12/blog-post_7588.html.

Barnett, Emma, presenter. "Emma Barnett." *One to One*. BBC Radio 4, 7 March 2014.

———. "Emma Barnett Talks to Rabbi Sylvia Rothschild." *One to One*. BBC Radio 4, 11 March 2014.

BMC Teachers' Seminary. http://www.seminarybmc.org. Accessed 3 May 2018.

Brown, Judy (Eishes Chayil). "Cracks in a Holy Vessel." *Forward* (New York), 11 March 2013, http://www.forward.com/articles/172568/cracks-in-a-holy-vessel.

———. "I'm a Mother, not a Baby Machine." *Forward* (New York), 14 March 2013, http://www.forward.com/sisterhood/172918/im-a-mother-not-a-baby-machine.

Calhoun, Ben. "A Not So Simple Majority" parts 1 and 2. *This American Life*. NPR/WBEZ, 12 September 2014, http://www.thisamericanlife.org/radio-archives/episode/534/a-not-so-simple-majority.

*Citoyen.n.es pour un Outremont inclusif*. Facebook, http://www.facebook.com/Citoyen.ne.s.pour.un.Outremont.inclusif. Accessed 1 May 2018.

*Comité de promotion du pluralisme au sein des écoles d'Outremont*. http://www.pluralisme outremont.wordpress.com. Accessed 1 May 2018.

Ezras Nashim. https://www.ezras-nashim.org. Accessed 5 June 2018.

*Esseat*. Weebly, http://esseat.weebly.com/. Accessed 1 May 2018.

Feldman, Charnie. Comment on "Cracks in a Holy Vessel." *Forward* (New York), 11 March 2013, http://www.forward.com/articles/172568/cracks-in-a-holy-vessel.

*Les filles et fils d'un Québec ouvert*. Facebook, http://www.facebook.com/fillesetfildunquebec ouvert/. Accessed 1 May 2018.

"Free to Be Me." *YouTube*, uploaded by Chasing News, 9 December 2015, http://www.youtube.com/watch?v=2Fc1vnqXSbA.

Freier, Rachel. "A Mother Is Who I Am." *Forward* (New York), 13 March 2013, http://www.forward.com/opinion/172778/a-mother-is-who-i-am.

*Friends of Hutchison Street*. Facebook, http://www.facebook.com/FriendsAmisHutchison. Accessed 1 May 2018.

"Gamal Abdel Nasser on the Muslim Brotherhood." *YouTube*, uploaded by Video Clips, 13 December 2015, http://www.youtube.com/watch?v=_ZIqdrFeFBk. Accessed 6 May 2018.

Gjelten, Tom, presenter. "At the NSA, a Rising Star's Commitment to Faith—and Public Service." *Parallels: Many Stories, One World*. NPR, 12 July 2015, www.npr.org/sections/parallels/2015/07/12/421816261/at-the-nsa-a-rising-stars-commitment-to-faith-and-public-service/.

*Jew in the City*. http://www.jewinthecity.com. Accessed 1 May 2018.

*Jewish Mom: Inspiration from One Jewish Mother to Another*. http://www.jewishmom.com. Accessed 1 May 2018.

Katsman, Hannah. "A Light for Greytowers: Movie Review." *A Mother in Israel*. 15 December 2008, http://www.amotherinisrael.com/a-light-for-greytowers-movie-review.

———. "Hyper-Modest Abusive Mother of 12 Released." *A Mother in Israel*. 15 June 2012, http://www.amotherinisrael.com/hyper-modest-abusive-mother-of-12-released.

———. "Interview with Yael Levy, Author of Brooklyn Love." *A Mother in Israel*. 28 November 2012, http://www.amotherinisrael.com/interview-with-yael-levy-author-of-brooklyn-love.

———. "Interview with 'Mother Taliban.'" *A Mother in Israel*. 17 February 2011, http://www.amotherinisrael.com/interview-bruria-keren-jail.

*Kol Neshama*. Kol Neshama, http://www.kolneshama.org. Accessed 1 May 2018.

Lacerte, Pierre. *Accommodents Outremont*. Blogger, http://www.accommodementsoutremont.blogspot.com. Accessed 1 May 2018.

"A Lubavitcher's Response." *Jewish Mom*, 5 November 2011, http://www.jewishmom.com/2011/11/05/a-lubavitchers-response-to-controversial-book-hush.

*The Ma'aleh School of Television, Film and the Arts*. http://www.maale.co.il. Accessed 1 May 2018.

Oppenheimer, Mark, presenter. "Sun-Rise, Sun-Get: Stuck in the Middle." *This American Life*. NPR, 17 January 2014, http://www.thisamericanlife.org/radio-archives/episode/516/stuck-in-the-middle?act=2.

*Le pont d'Outremont*. Facebook, http://www.facebook.com/pg/PontdOutremont. Accessed 1 May 2018.

*Rue Hutchison*. http://www.ruehutchison.ca. Accessed 1 May 2018.

"Shtisel's Emotional *Niggun* from Minsk." *YouTube*, uploaded by שמחה החתיך, 28 December 2015, http://www.youtube.com/watch?v=ZyO6sBH0Qos&feature=youtu.be.

Stein, Abby Chava. *The Second Transition*. Blogger, 2012–2017, http://www.thesecondtransition.blogspot.com.

Vizel, Frieda. "On Hasidic Women." *Oy Vey Cartoons*. 25 May 2012, http://www.oyveycartoons.com/2012/05/25/on-chasidic-women/.

———. *Oy Vey Cartoons*. 2012–2014, http://www.oyveycartoons.com.

———. *Shpitzle Shtrimpkind*. Blogger, 2006–2011, http://www.shtrimpkind.blogspot.co.uk.

Weiss, Cheskie. *Outremont Hassid*. http://www.outremonthassid.com. Accessed 1 May 2018.

### PERSONAL CORRESPONDENCE AND INTERVIEWS

Carlebach, Chanie. Personal interview (in Ste. Agathe, Canada). 14 August 2015.

Deen, Shulem. Personal correspondence (Facebook Messenger). 18 May 2015.

Fisher, Effy. Personal interview (in Montreal). 4 July 2013.

Garbose, Robin. Personal correspondence (email). 14 February 2017.

Jacobs, Rachel. Personal correspondence (email). 15 February 2017.

Krinsky, Rivka Siegel. Personal correspondence (email). 13 February 2017.

Shusterman, Dalia G. Personal correspondence (email). 17 October 2017.

Webb, Eitan. Personal correspondence (Facebook Messenger). 13 February 2017.

Wolfe, Perl. Personal interview (phone). 13 February 2017.

Wolkenfeld, Sara. Personal correspondence (email). 27 and 29 June 2017.

### SECONDARY TEXTS

Aarons, Victoria. "The Covenant Unraveling: The Pathos of Cultural Loss in Allegra Goodman's Fiction." *Shofar*, vol. 22, no. 3, 2004, 12–25.

Abrams, Nathan. "The Secret Jewish Origins of Wonder Woman." *Haaretz* (Tel Aviv), 11 June 2017.

Adelman, Howard, and Pierre Anctil. *Religion, Culture, and the State: Reflections on the Bouchard-Taylor Report.* Toronto: University of Toronto Press, 2011.

Adler, Ruth. "Mothers and Daughters: The Jewish Mother as Seen by American Jewish Women Writers." *Yiddish*, vol. 6, no. 4, 1987, 87–92.

Adorno, Theodor. "Culture Industry Reconsidered." *New German Critique*, vol. 6, 1975, 12–19.

Adorno, Theodor, and Max Horkheimer. *Dialectic of Enlightenment: Philosophical Fragments.* 1944. Translated by Edmund Jephcott. Stanford, Calif.: Stanford University Press, 2002.

Agence France-Presse. "Orthodox Israeli Director Opens Window on Close Society." *Guardian* (Nigeria), 25 November 2016, http://www.guardian.ng/art/orthodox-israeli-director-opens-window-on-closed-society.

Ahadi, Daniel. "L'Affaire Hérouxville in Context: Conflicting Narratives on Islam, Muslim Women, and Identity." *Journal of Arab and Muslim Media Research*, vol. 2, no. 3, 2009, 241–260.

Ahmed, Leila. *Women and Gender in Islam.* New Haven, Conn.: Yale University Press, 1992.

Alexander, Elizabeth Shanks. *Gender and Timebound Commandments in Judaism.* Cambridge, U.K.: Cambridge University Press, 2015.

Al-Othman, Hannah. "Did They Think It Was a BLUE Movie?" MailOnline. *Daily Mail*, 28 March 2017, http://www.dailymail.co.uk/news/article-4357600/Smurfette-banned-Israeli-ads-avoid-causing-offence.html.

Anctil, Pierre, Gérard Bouchard, and Ira Robinson. *Juifs et Canadiens français dans la société québécoise.* Sillery, Canada: Septentrion, 2000.

Appadurai, Arjun. *Modernity at Large: Cultural Dimensions of Globalization.* Minneapolis: University of Minnesota Press, 1996.

Appiah, Kwame Anthony. *Cosmopolitanism: Ethics in a World of Strangers.* London: Penguin, 2006.

Arad, Roy. "In Israel's Haredi Literary World, Women Rule." *Haaretz* (Tel Aviv), 9 October 2016.

Arnold, Janice. "Assault on Jewish Visitor Raises Concerns." *Canadian Jewish News*, 4 September 2008.

———. "New UdeM Course Studies Quebec Jews." *Canadian Jewish News*, 25 January 2013.

Avery, Evelyn. "Allegra Goodman's Fiction: From the Suburbs to 'Gan Eden.'" *Studies in American Jewish Literature*, vol. 22, 2003, 36–45.

Avishai, Orit. "'Doing Religion' in a Secular World: Women in Conservative Religions and the Question of Agency." *Gender and Society*, vol. 22, no. 4, 2008, 409–433.

Aviv, Caryn, and David Shneer. *New Jews: The End of the Jewish Diaspora.* New York: NYU Press, 2005.

Aviv, Rachel. "The Outcast." *New Yorker*, 10 November 2014.

Banks, Sandy. "Movie Is a Show of Faith." *Los Angeles Times*, 19 January 2008.

Batnitzky, Liora. *How Judaism Became a Religion: An Introduction to Modern Jewish Thought.* Princeton, N.J.: Princeton University Press, 2011.

Bauer, Julien. "Racism in Canada: A Symposium." *Viewpoints*, vol. 16, no. 5, 1989, 1.

———. *Les Juifs Hassidiques.* Paris: Presses Universitaires France, 1994.

Beer, Max. "The Montreal Jewish Community and the Holocaust." *Current Psychology*, vol. 26, no. 3, 2007, 191–205.

"Beit Shemesh Ultra-Orthodox Jews Clash with Police." *BBC News*, 27 December 2011, http://www.bbc.co.uk/news/world-middle-east-16335603.

Bell, Pearl. "Talmud in the Catskills." *New York Times*, 14 August 1998.

Benhorin, Yitzhak. "The Meteor from Borough Park: Meet the Hasidic Woman Who Manages Risk for the NSA." *Ynet News*, 13 September 2015.

Ben-Merre, Diana Arbin. "Murdering Traditional Assumptions: The Jewish-American Mystery." *The Detective in American Fiction, Film, and Television*, edited by Jerome H. Delamater and Ruth Prigozy. Westport, Conn.: Greenwood Press, 1998, 57–70.

Benor, Sarah Bunin. *Becoming Frum: How Newcomers Learn the Language and Culture of Orthodox Judaism.* New Brunswick, N.J.: Rutgers University Press, 2012.

————. "Talmid Chachams and Tsedeykeses: Language, Learnedness, and Masculinity among Orthodox Jews." *Jewish Social Studies*, vol. 11, no. 1, 2004, 147–170.

Berger, Alan L. "American Jewish Fiction." *Modern Judaism*, vol. 10, no. 3, 1990, 221–241.

Berger, Maurice. "The Mouse That Never Roars: Jewish Masculinity on American Television." *Too Jewish? Challenging Traditional Identities*, edited by Norman L. Kleeblatt. New York: The Jewish Museum / New Brunswick, N.J.: Rutgers University Press, 1996, 93–107.

Berger, Paul. "Russian Art Exchanges Frozen over Chabad Lawsuit." *Jewish Daily Forward* (New York), 24 August 2011, http://www.forward.com/articles/141799/russian-art -exchanges-frozen-over-chabad-lawsuit.

Berger, Zackary Sholem. "Haredi Women's Lit Explodes: The Writers and Editors behind the Astonishing Rise of Orthodox Magazines and Fiction." *Tablet Magazine*, 8 August 2012.

Berkenwald, Leah. "On the Photoshopping of a Tsnius Hillary Clinton." *Forward* (New York), 9 May 2011.

Berman, Eli. "Sect, Subsidy, and Sacrifice: An Economist's View of Ultra-Orthodox Jews." *Quarterly Journal of Economics*, vol. 115, no. 3, August 2000, 905–953.

Bermant, Chaim. "The Jewish Eton." *Observer*, 23 September 1973, 41, 43, 44, 47.

Bitton-Jackson, Livia. "Rama Burshtein: A Window into Her World." *Jewish Press* (New York), 6 December 2012.

Blain, Dominique. "Controversy Brews after Hasidic Jews Buy Resort: News of Sale Has Quebec Town Talking." *Montreal Gazette* 2 July 2007.

————. "We're Being Targeted: Jewish Community." *Montreal Gazette*, 18 June 2007.

Bloomberg, Jon. *The Jewish World in the Modern Age*. Newark, N.J.: KTAV, 2004.

Blumen, Orna. "Criss-Crossing Boundaries: Ultra-Orthodox Woman Go to Work." *Gender, Place, and Culture*, vol. 9, no. 2, 2002, 133–151.

————. "The Gendered Display of Work: The Midday Scene in an Ultra-Orthodox Street in Israel." *Nashim*, vol. 13, 2007, 123–157.

Blundy, Rachel. "Hackney Council Removes 'Unacceptable' Posters Telling Women Which Side of the Road They Should Walk On." *Evening Standard*, 19 September 2014.

Boyarin, Daniel. *Unheroic Conduct: The Rise of Heterosexuality and the Invention of the Jewish Man*. Berkeley: University of California Press, 1997.

Boyle, Louise. "'Raped, Tormented and Locked in a Room to Starve with Her Two Babies': The Shocking Claims of a Young Jewish Mother Who Found the Courage to Flee Her Husband but Is Still 'Chained' Because He Refuses to Grant Religious Divorce." *Daily Mail*, 26 June 2014.

Brauner, David. "History on a Personal Note: Postwar American Jewish Short Stories." *The Edinburgh Companion to Modern Jewish Fiction*, edited by David Brauner and Axel Stähler. Edinburgh, U.K.: Edinburgh University Press, 2015, 105–118.

Brauner, David, and Axel Stähler, editors. *The Edinburgh Companion to Modern Jewish Fiction*. Edinburgh, U.K.: Edinburgh University Press, 2015.

Brodesser-Akner, Taffy. "The High Price of Leaving Ultra-Orthodox Life." *New York Times*, 17 March 2017. Also published as "Apostates Anonymous." *Sunday Times*, 2 April 2017, MM36.

"Brooklyn, NY—Boro Park Williamsburg Bus Line Urges Schools to Advise about Schedules Due to Overcrowding." *Voz Iz Neias?*, 19 February 2009, http://www.vosizneias.com/27672/ 2009/02/19/brooklyn-ny-boro-park-williamsburg-bus-line-urges-schools-to-advice-of -schedules-due-to-overcrowding.

Browder, Laura. *Slippery Characters: Ethnic Impersonators and American Identities*. Chapel Hill: University of North Carolina Press, 2000.

Brown, Phil. *In the Catskills: A Century of Jewish Experience in the Mountains*. New York: Columbia University Press, 2002.

Broyde, Michael. "Hair Covering and Jewish Law: Biblical and Objective (*Dat Moshe*) or Rabbinic and Subjective (*Dat Yehudit*)?" *Tradition*, vol. 42, no. 3, 2009, 97–179.

Bruemmer, Rene, and Kevin Dougherty. "Herouxville: Cause Celebre: 'Isolated Case,' Charest Says, but Other Towns Mull Similar Rules." *Montreal Gazette*, 2 February 2007.

Bryden, Joan. "Trudeau Calls Harper's Niqab Comments 'Pandering to Fears' of Muslims: 'It's Unworthy of Someone Who Is Prime Minister.'" *National Post*, 20 February 2015.

Buddick, Emily Miller, editor. *Ideology and Jewish Identity in Israeli and American Literature*. Albany: SUNY Press, 2001.

Burstein, Janet Handler. "Recalling Home: American Jewish Women Writers of the New Wave." *Contemporary Literature*, vol. 42, no. 4, 2001, 803.

Butler, Judith. *Precarious Life: The Powers of Mourning and Violence*. London: Verso, 2004.

Caldwell, Gary. "The Sins of the Abbé Groulx." *Literary Review of Canada*, July–August 1994.

Cappell, Ezra. *American Talmud: The Cultural World of Jewish American Fiction*. Albany: SUNY Press, 2007.

Carmody, Denise L. *Biblical Women: Contemporary Reflections on Spiritual Texts*. New York: Crossroads, 1988.

Carner, Talia. "The Story behind the Story: My Grandmother, Myself." TaliaCarner.com, http://www.taliacarner.com/jerusalem-maiden/the-story-behind-the-story. Accessed 1 May 2018.

Carpenter, Mary Wilson. "The Apocalypse of the Old Testament: Daniel Deronda and the Interpretation of Interpretation." *PMLA*, vol. 99, no. 1, 1984, 56–71.

Chandrachud, Neha. "We Spoke with Mindy Pollak about Being Montreal's First Female Hasidic City Councillor." *Vice*, 31 March 2015.

Chase, Steven. "Niqabs Rooted in a Culture That's 'Anti-Women.'" *Globe and Mail*, 10 March 2015.

Chavkin, Sasha. "City Human Rights Commission to Examine Sex-Segregated Bus Line." *New York World*, 19 October 2011.

———. "Sex-Segregation on Brooklyn Bus Line to End, Operator Pledges." *New York World*, 25 October 2011.

———. "Women Ride in Back on Sex-Segregated Brooklyn Bus Line." *New York World*, 18 October 2011.

Chizhik-Goldschmidt, Avital. "Despite Decrees, Jewish Ultra-Orthodox Women Still Quietly Studying for Degrees." *Haaretz*, 25 December 2015.

"Church Response to Jon Krakauer's Under the Banner of Heaven." *Newsroom*, 27 June 2003, http://www.mormonnewsroom.org/article/church-response-to-jon-krakauers-under-the-banner-of-heaven.

Cobb, Shelley, and Yvonne Tasker. "Feminist Film Criticism in the 21st Century." *Film Criticism*, vol. 40, no. 1, 2016, 1.

Cohen, Debra Nussbaum. "'Gender Began Punching Me in the Face': How a Hasidic Rabbi Came Out as Trans Woman." *Haaretz* (Tel Aviv), 16 February 2017.

Cooper, Alan. Review of *Disobedience*, by Naomi Alderman. Jewish Book Council, http://www.jewishbookcouncil.org/book/disobedience. Accessed 1 May 2018.

Côté, Roch. "Outrement se découvre un 'problème juif.'" *Presse*, 13 September 1988.

"Côte-des-Neiges under Fire for Offering Gender-Segregated Swimming." *CBC News*, 14 January 2013, http://www.cbc.ca/news/canada/montreal/c%C3%B4te-des-neiges-under-fire-for-offering-gender-segregated-swimming-1.1376097.

Crisafis, Angelique. "Nicolas Sarkozy Says Islamic Veils Are Not Welcome in France." *Guardian*, 22 June 2009.

Cronin, Gloria L. "Immersions in the Postmodern: The Fiction of Allegra Goodman." *Daughters of Valor: Contemporary Jewish American Women Writers*, edited by Jay L. Halio and Ben Siegel. Newark, N.J.: University of Delaware Press, 1997, 247–267.

Daina, Sora Rivkah. Letter to the Editor. *Binah Between*, 25 February 2013, 3.

Dardashti, Galeet. "Televised Agenda: How Global Funders Make Israeli TV More Jewish." *Jewish Film and New Media*, vol. 3, no. 1, 2015, 77–103.

Davison, Neil. *Jewishness and Masculinity from the Modern to the Postmodern*. London and New York: Routledge, 2010.

Deardon, Lizzie. "'Women, Walk Wherever You Want' Posters Taken down in Stamford Hill following 'Unacceptable' Signs Separating Men and Women." *Independent*, 24 September 2014.

Deen, Shulem. "Breaking Away: Former Hasidim Find Fulfillment in the Secular World." *E-Jewish Philanthropy*, 26 April 2017, http://www.ejewishphilanthropy.com/breaking-away -former-hasidim-find-fulfillment-in-the-secular-world/.

Dekel, Mikhal. *The Universal Jew: Masculinity, Modernity, and the Zionist Movement*. Evanston, Ill.: Northwestern University Press, 2011.

Delisle, Esther. *The Traitor and the Jew: Anti-Semitism and the Delirium of Extremist Right-Wing Nationalism in French Canada from 1929 to 1939*. Montreal: R. Davies, 1993.

Deutsch, Nathaniel. "The Forbidden Fork, the Cell Phone Holocaust, and Other Haredi Encounters with Technology." *Contemporary Jewry*, vol. 29, 2009, 3–19.

Deykin Baris, Sharon. "George Eliot as Revenant in Faye Kellerman's Mysteries: American Daniel Is Alive and Well in Southern California." *Prospects*, vol. 19, 1994, 491–511.

Diamond, Etan. *And I Will Dwell in Their Midst: Orthodox Jews in Suburbia*. Chapel Hill: University of North Carolina, 2000.

"Donald Trump Questions Hillary Clinton's Religious Faith." *Wall Street Journal*, video, 21 June 2016, http://www.wsj.com/video/donald-trump-questions-hillary-clintons-religious -faith/12917E13-A362-459C-970F-D0F5D437204C.html.

Drouin, André. *Le Code de vie de L'Hérouxville. 2017: 10e anniversaire*. Trois-Rivières: Francois Lachapelle, 2017.

Eakin, Emily. "Maids of Honor: Wendy Shalit Argues That Sex Out of Wedlock Is 'Not Such a Cool Thing.'" *New York Times*, 7 March 1999.

Ehrenreich, Barbara, and Deidre English. *For Her Own Good: 150 Years of the Expert's Advice to Women*. New York: Doubleday, 1979.

Eisenberg, Robert. *Boychiks in the Hood: Travels in the Hasidic Underground*. New York: HarperCollins, 1996.

Ettinger, Yair, and Tamar Rotem. "Rabbinical Panel Bars Ultra-Orthodox Women from Continuing Education Programs." *Haaretz* (Tel Aviv), 2 January 2007.

Euse, Erica. "Hasidic Rock Band Bulletproof Stockings Just Want an All Girl Party." *Vice*, 30 August 2014.

"Everybody in the Pool." Editorial. *New York Times*, 1 June 2016.

"Exhibition Explores World of Haredi Women." *Ynet News*, 20 July 2013, http://www .ynetnews.com/articles/0,7340,L-4406790,00.html.

Fabian, Johannes. *Time and the Other: How Anthropology Makes Its Subject*. 1983. New York: Columbia University Press, 2014.

Fader, Ayala. *Mitzvah Girls: Bringing up the Next Generation of Hasidic Jews in Brooklyn*. Princeton: Princeton University Press: 2009.

"Faith, Fitness Clash in Mile End." *Montreal Gazette*, 8 November 2006.

Falk, Pesach Eliyahu. *Modesty: An Adornment for Life*. Nanuet, New York: Feldheim, 1998.

Ferguson, Liz. "A One-Year Chronology of the Province's 'Reasonable Accommodation' Controversy." *Montreal Gazette*, 3 February 2007.

Fermino, Jennifer. "'Back of Bus' Furor." *New York Post*, 19 October 2011.

Feuer, Alan. "A Piece of Brooklyn Perhaps Lost to Time." *New York Times*, 5 July 2009, LI3.

Fiedler, Leslie. *Fiedler on the Roof: Essays on Literature and Jewish Identity*. 1991. Boston: Godine, 1992.

Finkelman, Yoel. *Strictly Kosher Reading: Popular Literature and the Condition of Contemporary Orthodoxy*. Brighton, Mass.: Academic Studies Press, 2011.

Fish, Stanley. "One University under God?" *Chronicle of Higher Education*, 7 January 2005, http://chronicle.com/article/One-University-Under-God-/45077.

Fisher, Effy. "Heart of Darkness." *Mishpacha* (New York), 19 March 2014, 36–49.

———. "Malice in Montreal." *Ami Magazine* (New York), 16 May 2012, 46–55.

Fishkoff, Sue. *The Rebbe's Army: Inside the World of Chabad-Lubavitch*. New York: Schocken, 2003.

Fishman, Sylvia Barack. "American Jewish Fiction Turns Inward." *American Jewish Year Book, 1991*, edited by David Singer and Ruth Seldin. New York and Philadelphia: Jewish Publication Society, 1991, 34–66.

———. "The Impact of Feminism on American Jewish Life." *American Jewish Year Book, 1989*, edited by David Singer and Ruth Seldin. New York and Philadelphia: American Jewish Committee and the Jewish Publication Society, 1989, 3–62.

———. *Jewish Life and American Culture*. Albany: SUNY Press, 2000.

———. "Rebecca Goldstein (1950–)." *Jewish American Women Writers: A Bio-bibliographical and Critical Sourcebook*, edited by Ann R. Shapiro. Westport, Conn.: Greenwood, 1994, 80–87.

Fishman, Sylvia Barack, editor. *Follow My Footprints: Changing Images of Women in American Jewish Fiction*. Hanover, N.H.: University Press of New England, 1992.

Fontaine, Carole. "Proverbs." *The Women's Bible Commentary*, edited by C. A. Newsom and S. H. Ringe. Louisville, Ky.: Westminster / John Knox, 1992, 153–160.

Fox, Michael V. *Proverbs 10–31: A New Translation with Introduction and Commentary*. New Haven, Conn.: Yale University Press, 2009.

Fraenkel, Carlos. "Spinoza in Shtreimels: An Underground Seminar." *Jewish Review of Books*, Fall 2012, 38–43.

Freedman, Samuel. *Jew vs. Jew: The Struggle for the Soul of American Jewry*. New York: Touchstone, 2000.

Freese, Peter. *The Ethnic Detective: Chester Himes, Harry Kemelman, Tony Hillerman*. Essen: Die Blaue Eule, 1992.

Friedan, Betty. *The Feminine Mystique*. 1963. New York: Dell, 1964.

Friedman, Thomas L. *The Lexus and the Olive Tree: Understanding Globalization*. New York: Farrar, Straus, and Giroux, 1999.

Friedman, Yael, and Yohai Hakak. "Jewish Revenge: Haredi Action in the Zionist Sphere." *Jewish Film and New Media*, vol. 3, no. 1, 2015, 48–75.

Friedmann, Thomas. "Back to Orthodoxy: The New Ethic and Ethnics in American Jewish Literature." *Contemporary Jewry*, vol. 10, no. 1, 1989, 67–77.

Furman, Andrew. *Contemporary Jewish American Writers and the Multicultural Dilemma: Return of the Exiled*. Syracuse, N.Y.: Syracuse University Press, 2000.

Gani, Aisha. "Ultra-Orthodox Jewish Sect Tells London Mothers to Stop Driving." *Guardian*, 29 May 2015.

Gani, Aisha, and Jessica Elgot. "Orthodox Jewish Sect's Female Driver Ban Condemned by Nicky Morgan." *Guardian*, 29 May 2015.

Gavin, Adrienne E. "Feminist Crime Fiction and Female Sleuths." *A Companion to Crime Fiction*, edited by Charles J. Rzepka and Lee Horsley. Chichester, U.K.: Blackwell, 2010, 258–269.

Genette, Gerard. *Paratexts: Thresholds of Interpretation*. Cambridge, U.K.: Cambridge University Press, 1997.

Gilbert, Sandra M., and Susan Gubar. *The Madwoman in the Attic: The Woman Writer and the Nineteenth-Century Literary Imagination*. New Haven, Conn.: Yale University Press, 1979.

Gladwell, Malcolm. "The Young Garmentos." *New Yorker*, 24 April 2000, 70–81.

Glazer, Miriyam. "Daughters of Refugees of Ongoing-Universal-Endless-Upheaval: Anne Roiphe and the Quest for Narrative Power in Jewish American Women's Fiction." *Daughters of Valor: Contemporary Jewish American Women Writers*, edited by Jay L. Halio and Ben Siegel. Newark, N.J.: University of Delaware Press, 1997, 80–96.

———. "Orphans of Culture and History: Gender and Spirituality in Contemporary Jewish-American Women's Novels." *Tulsa Studies in Women's Literature*, vol. 13, no. 1, 1994, 127–141.

Glinter, Ezra. "Ex-Hasidic Writers Go off the Path and onto the Page." *Jewish Daily Forward* (New York), 30 May 2014.

———. "Orthodox World Provides Backdrop for Rama Burshstein's Universal Story." *Forward* (New York), 21 May 2013.

Godbout, Jacques. "Les hassidim et les 'meechim.'" *L'Actualité* (Montreal), December 1988. 180.

Goldbloom, Victor C. "Ste. Agathe Has Come a Long Way." *Montreal Gazette*, 5 September 2008.

Goldman, Mordechai. "Women Rule Shadowy World of Ultra-Orthodox Cinema." Translated by Danny Wool. *Al-Monitor*, 3 May 2016, http://www.al-monitor.com/pulse/originals/2016/05/israel-ultra-orthodox-kosher-cinema-women-movie-industry.html #ixzz4W5pHAJSd.

Goldstein, Joseph, and Michael Schwirtz. "U.S. Accuses 2 Rabbis of Kidnapping Husbands for a Fee." *New York Times*, 11 October 2013, A18.

Goodman, Allegra. "Pemberley Previsited." *American Scholar*, vol. 73, no. 2, 2004, 142.

———. "Writing Jewish Fiction in and Out of the Multicultural Context." *Daughters of Valor: Contemporary Jewish American Women Writers*, edited by Jay L. Halio and Ben Siegel. Newark, N.J.: University of Delaware Press, 1997, 268–274.

Gordon, Amanda. "Bulletproof Stockings' Co-Founder Goes Solo." *New York Jewish Week*, 11 July 2016, http://www.jewishweek.timesofisrael.com/bulletproof-stockings-co-founder -goes-solo/.

Grand, Sarah. "The New Aspect of the Woman Question." *North American Review*, vol. 158, no. 448, 1894, 270–276.

Greenstein, Michael. *Third Solitudes: Tradition and Discontinuity in Jewish-Canadian Literature*. Montreal: McGill-Queen's University Press, 1989.

Grument, Louis, and John Caher. *The Curious Case of Kiryas Joel: The Rise of a Village Theocracy and the Battle to Defend the Separation of Church and State*. Chicago: Chicago Review Press, 2016.

Gurley, George. "Wendy Shalit's Modesty Proposal Infuriates Feminists, Says Loose Sex Conduct Takes Power from Women." *Observer*, 22 February 1999.

Gurock, Jeffrey. *American Jewish Orthodoxy in Historical Perspective*. Hoboken, N.J.: Ktav, 1996.

———. *Orthodox Jews in America*. Bloomington: Indiana University Press, 2009.

Habermas, Jürgen. *Between Naturalism and Religion*. 2005. Cambridge, U.K.: Polity Press, 2008.

———. "Notes on Post-Secular Society." *New Perspectives Quarterly*, vol. 25, no. 4, 2008, 17–29.

Halio, Jay L., and Ben Siegel, editors. *Daughters of Valor: Contemporary Jewish American Women Writers*. Newark, N.J.: University of Delaware Press, 1997.

Hamilton, Graeme. "Town Uneasy about Jews' Resort Purchase." *National Post*, 9 July 2007.

Hammerman, Shaina. *Silver Screen, Hasidic Jews: The Story of an Image*. Bloomington: Indiana University Press, 2018.

Harris, Lis. *Holy Days: The World of a Hasidic Family*. New York: Touchstone, 1985.

Harris, Rachel S. "From Feminist to Housewife and Back Again: Orthodoxy and Modernity in American Jewish Women's Writing." *The Edinburgh Companion to Modern Jewish Fiction*, edited by David Brauner and Axel Stähler. Edinburgh, U.K.: Edinburgh University Press, 2015, 76–89.

Harrison-Kahan, Lori. "Total Immersion: An Interview with Allegra Goodman." *MELUS*, vol. 37, no. 4, 2012, 187–202.

———. *The White Negress: Literature, Minstrelsy, and the Black-Jewish Imaginary*. New Brunswick, N.J.: Rutgers University Press, 2011.

Harrison-Kahan, Lori, and Karen E. H. Skinazi. "Feminist Collaboration in an Era of Academic Instability." *American Periodicals*, vol. 27, no. 1, 2017, 16–20.

———. "The 'Girl Reporter' in Fact and Fiction: Miriam Michelson's New Women and Progressive-Era Periodical Culture." *Legacy*, vol. 34, no. 2, 2017, 321–338.

———. "Miriam Michelson." *Dictionary of Literary Biography 380: Writers on Women's Rights and United States Suffrage*, edited by George Anderson. Detroit: Gale Research, 2017, 221–231.

———. "Miriam Michelson, American Jewish Feminist Literary Star of the Western Frontier." *Tablet Magazine*, 24 November 2014.

———. "Miriam Michelson's Yellow Journalism and the Multi-Ethnic West" and "In Chy Fong's Restaurant." *MELUS*, vol. 40, no. 2, 2015, 182–217.

Hartman, Tova. *Feminism Encounters Traditional Judaism: Resistance and Accommodation*. Lebanon, N.H.: University Press of New England, 2007.

"Hasidic Couple Hosts Public Wedding in Ste-Agathe." *CBC News*, 3 September 2008, http://www.cbc.ca/news/canada/montreal/hasidic-couple-hosts-public-wedding-in-ste-agathe-1.725999.

Haughney, Christine. "At Front of Brooklyn Bus, a Clash of Religious and Women's Rights." *New York Times*, 19 October 2011.

Haute, Woody. *Pulp Culture: Hardboiled Fiction and the Cold War*. London: Serpent's Tail, 1995.

Heft, Harold. "America's Blackest Jewish Writer." *Tablet Magazine*, 13 May 2013.

———. "Easy Call: A Case for Walter Mosley's Inclusion in the American Jewish Literary Canon." *Tablet Magazine*, 14 April 2010.

Heilbrun, Carolyn G. "The New Female Detective." *Yale Journal of Law and Feminism*, vol. 2, no. 14, 2002, 419–428.

———. *Writing a Woman's Life*. New York: Norton, 1988.

Heilman, Samuel. *Sliding to the Right: The Contest for the Future of American Jewish Orthodoxy*. Berkeley: University of California Press, 2006.

Heilman, Samuel, and Menachem Friedman. *The Rebbe: The Life and Afterlife of Menachem Mendel Schneerson*. Princeton, N.J.: Princeton University Press, 2010.

Heilman, Samuel C., and Steven M. Cohen. *Cosmopolitans and Parochials: Modern Orthodox Jews in America*. Chicago: University of Chicago Press, 1989.

Heinrich, Jeff. "Hasidic Couple Invites Town to Wedding." *Montreal Gazette*, 30 August 2008.

———. "In Ste. Agathe, a Very Public Wedding Story." *Montreal Gazette*, 3 September 2008.

———. "Laurentian Residents Vent Anger with Hasidim." *Montreal Gazette*, 25 September 2007.

———. "Media Stir Up Storm over 'Accommodation': Some Experts Blame Chain Ownership." *Montreal Gazette*, 3 February 2007.

Herman, Dana. "'An Affair to Remember': The Outremont Dispute of 1988." *Canadian Jewish Studies*, vols. 16 and 17, 2008–2009, 139–166.

Hernandez, Eugene, and Brian Brooks. "'Trembling' Opens Strong in NYC; Sets One-Day Record." *Indiewire*, 30 October 2001.

Hirsh, David. *Contemporary Left Antisemitism*. London: Routledge, 2018.

Hofstetter, Sarah. "Why Being an Orthodox Jewish Mom Makes Me a Better CEO." *Fortune*, 25 July 2016.

Hollinger, David. *Postethnic America*. New York: Basic, 1995.

Horn, Dara. "The Future of Yiddish—in English: Field Notes from the New Ashkenaz." *Jewish Quarterly Review*, vol. 96, no. 4, 2006, 471–480.

Horowitz, Sara R. "Mediating Judaism: Mind, Body, Spirit, and Contemporary North American Jewish Fiction." *AJS Review*, vol. 30, no. 2, 2006, 231–253.

————. *Voicing the Void: Muteness and Memory in Holocaust Fiction.* Albany: SUNY Press, 1997.

Horwitz, Simi. "These Frum Filmmakers Are Revolutionizing Orthodox Cinema." *Forward* (New York), 11 July 2016.

Howe, Irving. Introduction. *Jewish American Stories*, edited by Irving Howe. New York: NAL Penguin, 1977, 1–17.

Huggan, Graham. *The Postcolonial Exotic: Marketing the Margins.* London: Routledge, 2001.

Hyman, Paula. "The Other Half: Women in the Jewish Tradition." *The Jewish Woman: New Perspectives*, edited by Elizabeth Koltun. New York: Schocken, 1976, 139–148.

Iles, Francis. "Criminal Records." *Guardian*, 14 April 1967, 8.

Ingall, Marjorie. "Not Quite a Bodice-Ripper, But . . ." *Tablet Magazine*, 14 February 2013.

Irons, Glenwood, editor. *Feminism in Women's Detective Fiction.* Toronto: University of Toronto Press, 1995.

"Is It Appropriate for a Woman to Wear a Tallit?" Chabad.org, http://www.chabad.org/library/article_cdo/aid/587787/jewish/Is-it-appropriate-for-a-woman-to-wear-a-tallit.htm. Accessed 1 May 2018.

Israel-Cohen, Yael. *Between Feminism and Orthodox Judaism: Resistance, Identity, and Religious Change in Israel.* Leiden, Netherlands: Brill, 2012.

"Israeli Film 'Gett' Nominated for Golden Globe." *Jerusalem Post*, 12 December 2014.

Janofsky, Adam. "Facebook, Unchain Me!" *Tablet Magazine*, 22 September 2014.

Johnson, James Weldon. "Double Audience Makes Road Hard for Negro Writers." *Philadelphia Tribune*, 9 November 1928.

Johnson, Jenna. "Trump Calls for a 'Complete and Total Shutdown of Muslims Entering the United States.'" *Washington Post*, 7 December 2015.

Johnson, Jenna, and Jose A. DelReal. "Trump Tells Story about Killing Terrorists with Bullets Dipped in Pigs' Blood, Though There's No Proof of It." *Washington Post*, 20 February 2016.

Joskowicz, Ari, and Ethan B. Katz, editors. *Secularism in Question: Jews and Judaism in Modern Times.* Philadelphia: University of Pennsylvania Press, 2015.

"Les juifs de Sainte-Agathe et leurs voisins se rapprochent." *La Presse* (Montreal), 3 September 2008.

Kallen, Horace M. "Democracy versus the Melting Pot" parts 1 and 2. *Nation*, 18 and 25 February 1915, 190–194, 217–219.

Kamin, Debra. "Filmmaking by and for Women Only." *International Herald Tribune*, 24 October 2012.

————. "Israeli Drama about Ultra-Orthodox Brood Gets American Treatment." *Variety*, 17 October 2016.

————. "Ultra-Orthodox Israelis Can't Watch TV, But Show Focuses on Them Anyway." *Variety*, 17 January 2014.

Kanfer, Stefan. *A Summer World.* New York: Farrar, Straus, and Giroux, 1989.

Kang, Inkoo. "Director Rama Burshtein on *Fill the Void*: It's about the Ultra-Orthodox Jewish Community but Isn't for Them." *Village Voice*, 29 May 2013.

Kaufman, Margo. "Happiness Is a Warm Subplot." *Los Angeles Times*, 22 September 1996, 8.

Kay, Barbara. "Not in My Backyard, Either." *National Post*, 10 July 2007.

Kean, Danuta. "Eve Harris: Tension of a Life without Certainty." *Independent*, 24 August 2013, http://www.independent.co.uk/arts-entertainment/books/features/eve-harris-tension-of-a-life-without-certainty-8783625.html.

Kellerman, Faye. "Peter Decker and Rina Lazarus." *The Lineup: The World's Greatest Crime Writers Tell the Inside Story of Their Greatest Detectives*, edited by Otto Penzler. New York: Back Bay, 2009, 171–196.

Kissileff, Beth. "The Radical Subtext of 'The Wedding Plan.'" *Times of Israel* (Jerusalem), 13 June 2017.

Klein, Amram. "The First Silent Picture-Show." *Kolnoa*, vol. 5, April–May 1975. Cited in and translated from the Hebrew by Shohat.

Kolker, Robert. "On the Rabbi's Knee: Do the Orthodox Jews Have a Catholic-Priest Problem?" *New York Magazine*, 22 May 2006.

Koskoff, Ellen. "The Language of the Heart: Music in Lubavitcher Life." *New World Hasidism: Ethnographic Studies of Hasidic Jews in America*, edited by Janet S. Belcove-Shalin. Albany: SUNY Press, 1995, 87–106.

Kreilkamp, Ivan. "Allegra Goodman: A Community Apart." *Publishers Weekly*, vol. 245, no. 30, 27 July 1998, 48–49.

Landes, Rachel X. "Bulletproof Hasidic Feminist Rock Out." *Forward* (New York), 15 August 2014.

Landress, Barbara Ann. *All Her Glory Within: Rejecting and Transforming Orthodoxy in Israeli and American Jewish Women's Fiction*. Brighton, Mass.: Academic Studies Press, 2012.

Larson, Thomas. *Memoir and the Memoirist: Reading and Writing Personal Narrative*. Athens: University of Ohio Press, 2007.

Lassner, Phyllis. "Jewish Exile in Englishness: Eva Tucker and Natasha Solomons." *The Edinburgh Companion to Modern Jewish Fiction*, edited by David Brauner and Axel Stähler. Edinburgh, U.K.: Edinburgh University Press, 2015, 199–209.

Leibovitz, Liel. "Israel's Hottest TV Show Is All Black Hats and Beards." *Tablet Magazine*, 26 February 2016, http://www.tabletmag.com/jewish-arts-and-culture/197980/israels-tv-show-shtisel.

Levin, Dan. "In Toronto, a Neighborhood in Despair Transforms into a Model of Inclusion." *New York Times*, 28 February 2016.

Levinson, Chaim. "Leading Religious Zionist Rabbi: A Woman's Place Is in the Home." *Haaretz* (Tel Aviv), 31 July 2012.

Lewak, Doree. "An Orthodox Woman's 3-Year Divorce Fight." *New York Post*, 4 November 2013.

Lewin, Judith. "'Diving into the Wreck': Binding Oneself to Judaism in Contemporary Jewish Women's Fiction." *Shofar*, vol. 26, no. 4, 2008, 1–20.

Lezzi, Eva. "Secularism and Neo-Orthodoxy: Conflicting Strategies in Modern Orthodox Fiction." *Secularism in Question: Jews and Judaism in Modern Times*, edited by Ari Joskowicz and Ethan B. Katz. Philadelphia: University of Pennsylvania Press, 2015, 208–231.

Lieber, Andrea. "A Virtual 'Veibershul': Blogging and the Blurring of Public and Private among Orthodox Jewish Women." *College English*, vol. 72, no. 6, 2010, 621–637.

Liebman, Charles. "Orthodoxy in American Jewish Life." *American Jewish Yearbook*, vol. 66, 1965, 21–97.

Lifshitz-Kliger, Iris, and Gahl Becker. "Haredi IKEA Catalogue Is a No-Ma'am's Land." *Ynet News*, 15 February 2017.

Lipovenko, Dorothy. "Don't Judge Women at Back of Buses." Sisterhood, *Forward* (New York), 24 November 2011.

LoBianco, Tom. "Trump Postpones Israel Trip after Netanyahu Criticism." *CNN*, 10 December 2015.

Lusk, Darian. "Meet Bulletproof Stockings: The Band That Performs to Only Women." *CBS News*, 12 September 2014.

Magid, Shaul. "'America Is No Different,' 'America Is Different'—Is There an American Jewish Fundamentalism? Part II. American Satmar." *Fundamentalism: Perspectives on a Contested History*, edited by Simon A. Wood and David Harrington Watt. Columbia: University of South Carolina Press, 2014, 92–107.

Maillot, Alphonse. *Eve ma mère: la femme dans l'Ancien Testament et dans quelques civilisations proches*. Paris: Letouzy et Ané, 1989.

Makinen, Merja. *Feminist Popular Fiction*. Hampshire, N.Y.: Palgrave, 2001.

Maslin, Janet. "Movie Review: The Chosen." *New York Times*, 30 April 1982.

Maslin Nir, Sarah. "Outfitting Hasidic Women with Stylish, Yet Modest, Fashions." *New York Times*, 21 March 2016.

McAuley, James. "Growing Anti-Muslim Rhetoric Permeates French Presidential Election Campaign." *Washington Post*, 18 April 2017.

McClay, Wilfred. "Religion in Post-Secular America." *American Thought and Culture in the 21st Century*, edited by Martin Halliwell and Catherine Morley. Edinburgh, U.K.: Edinburgh University Press, 2008, 127–143.

McClintock, Ann. *Imperial Leather*. New York: Routledge, 1995.

McClymond, Kathryn. "*The Chosen*: Defining American Judaism." *Shofar*, vol. 25, no. 2, 2007, 4–23.

McRobbie, Angela. "Feminism and the Socialist Tradition . . . Undone?" *Cultural Studies*, vol. 18, no. 4, July 2004, 503–522.

Medina, Jennifer. "Unwilling to Allow His Wife a Divorce, He Marries Another." *New York Times*, 22 March 2014, A1.

Meyers, Helene. *Identity Papers: Contemporary Narratives of American Jewishness*. Albany: SUNY Press, 2011.

———. "Jewish Gender Trouble: Women Writing Men of Valor." *Tulsa Studies in Women's Literature*, vol. 25, no. 2, 2006, 323–333.

Mezzofiore, Gianluca. "'Jewish Taliban' Lev Tahor Sect Who Kept Girls in Basement Charged with Sexual Abuse." *International Business Times*, 17 February 2014.

Miller, Danny. "Director Rama Burshtein Opens a Rare Window into an Insular World in 'Fill the Void.'" *Hit List*, 28 May 2013.

Mirsky, Yehudah. "The Difficulty of Orthodox Fiction." *Response*, vol. 65, 1996, 30–35.

Mirvis, Tova. "Orthodox Jews in Fiction." *New York Times*, 27 February 2005, 4.

Moaveni, Azadeh. "ISIS Women and Enforcers in Syria Recount Collaboration, Anguish and Escape." *New York Times*, 21 November 2015.

Mohanty, Chandra Talpade. *Feminism without Borders: Decolonizing Theory, Practicing Solidarity*. Durham, N.C.: Duke University Press, 2003.

Moran, Michael. "Why Is Smurfette Missing from Film Posters in Israel?" *Jewish Chronicle* (London), 29 March 2017.

Morris, Bonnie J. *Lubavitcher Women in America: Identity and Activism in the Postwar Era*. Albany: SUNY Press, 1998.

Mulvey, Laura. "Visual Pleasure and Narrative Cinema." *Screen* vol. 16, no. 3, 1975, 6–18.

Myers, David N., and Nomi Stolzenberg. "What Does Kiryas Joel Tell Us about Liberalism in America?" *Chronicle*, vol. 71, 2008, 49–53.

Nadeau, Jean-François. "Esther Delisle et l'abbé Lionel Groulx: une recherche incomplète et partiale." *La Presse*, 3 June 1993.

Nathan-Kazis, Josh. "Changing Face of New York Jewry." *Forward* (New York), 14 June 2012, http://www.forward.com/news/157766/changing-face-of-new-york-jewry.

———. "Exclusive: Orthodox Union Adopts New Policy Barring Women Clergy." *Forward* (New York), 2 February 2017, http://www.forward.com/news/362043/orthodox-union-adopts-policy-barring-women-clergy.

Neal, Lynn S. *Romancing God: Evangelical Women and Inspirational Fiction*. Chapel Hill: University of North Carolina Press, 2006.

Neuer, Batsheva. "Will Real Religious Zionists Leaders Please Stand Up?" *Jerusalem Post*, 8 January 2013, http://www.jpost.com/Opinion/Op-Ed-Contributors/Will-real-religious-Zionist-leaders-please-stand-up.

Newton, Michael. "Father Brown, the Empathetic Detective." *Guardian*, 18 January 2013.

Omer-Sherman, Ranen. "Tradition and Desire in Allegra Goodman's *Kaaterskill Falls*." *MELUS*, vol. 29, no. 2, 2004, 266–289.

"On Court Street." *Ami Magazine*, 19 December 2012, 48–55.

O'Neill, Brendan. "Misery Lit . . . Read On." *BBC News*, 17 April 2007, http://www.news.bbc.co.uk/1/hi/magazine/6563529.stm.

"On the Future of Conservatism: A Symposium." *Commentary Magazine*, vol. 103, no. 2, 1997, 14–43.

Orbach, Michael. "Unmolested." *Tablet Magazine*, 11 August 2011, http://www.tabletmag .com/jewish-news-and-politics/74033/unmolested.

Ozick, Cynthia. "America: Toward Yavneh." *Judaism*, vol. 19, no. 3, 1970, 264–282.

———. *Art and Ardor*. New York: Knopf, 1983.

Paris, Erna. *Jews, an Account of Their Experience in Canada*. Toronto: MacMillan, 1988.

Parker, James. "The Joy of Vex: The Godless Charm of Larry David's *Curb Your Enthusiasm*." *Atlantic*, July–August 2011, http://www.theatlantic.com/magazine/archive/2011/07/the-joy -of-vex/308546/.

Peleg, Yaron. *Directed by God: Jewishness in Contemporary Israeli Film and Television*. Austin: University of Texas Press, 2016.

Peritz, Ingrid, and Patrick Martin. "Jewish Sect Girls Ordered Back to Israel." *Globe and Mail*, 5 October 2011.

Pileggi, Tamar. "Ex-Shas Guru's Daughter: Haredi Women Might End up Veiled." *Times of Israel* (Jerusalem), 29 May 2015.

———. "UK Haredi Rabbis Ban Women Drivers." *Times of Israel* (Jerusalem), 28 May 2015.

Pinsker, Sanford. "Jewish-American Fiction in the 21st century." *My Jewish Learning*, http:// www.myjewishlearning.com/culture/2/Literature/Jewish_American_Literature/The_21st _Century. Accessed 1 May 2018.

———. "Kosher Delights." *Washington Post*, 11 November 1998.

———. "Satire, Social Realism, and Moral Seriousness: The Case of Allegra Goodman." *Studies in American Jewish Literature*, vol. 11, no. 2, 1992, 182–194.

Plaskow, Judith. *Standing Again at Sinai: Judaism from a Feminist Perspective*. San Francisco: Harper and Row, 1990.

Poe, Edgar Allen. "The Philosophy of Composition." *Graham's Magazine*, vol. 28, no. 4, 1846, 163–167.

Pogrund, Gabriel. "Meet the British Jews Who Escaped from the Haredi Community." *Sunday Times*, 2 July 2017.

Pratt, Mary Louise. *Imperial Eyes: Travel Writing and Transculturation*. London: Routledge, 1992.

Presner, Todd Samuel. *Muscular Judaism: The Jewish Body and the Politics of Regeneration*. New York: Routledge, 2007.

Rak, Julie. *Boom! Manufacturing Memoir for the Popular Market*. Waterloo, Canada: Wilfrid Laurier University Press, 2013.

Reinharz, Shulamit. "A Survey of the First Century of Jewish Women Artists: The Impact of Four Upheavals." August 2010, http://www.brandeis.edu/hbi/publications/workingpapers/ docs/reinharz.pdf.

Richler, Mordecai. *Oh Canada! Oh Quebec! Requiem for a Divided Country*. Toronto: Penguin, 1992.

Rocker, Simon. "Stamford Hill Sect Bans Women Drivers." *Jewish Chronicle* (London), 28 May 2015.

Roller, Alyse. *The Literary Imagination of Ultra-Orthodox Jewish Women*. Jefferson, N.C.: McFarland, 1999.

Rosen, Norma. *Accidents of Influence: Writing as a Woman and a Jew in America*. New York: SUNY Press, 1992.

Rosenberg, Yair. "Israeli Film 'Fill the Void' Is Jane Austen for the Jews." *Tablet Magazine*, 11 June 2013.

Ross, Tova. "How Ex-Frum Memoirs Became New York Publishing's Hottest New Trend." *Tablet Magazine*, 7 January 2014.

Roth, Laurence. *Inspecting Jews: American Jewish Detective Stories*. Piscataway, N.J.: Rutgers University Press, 2004.

———. "Unraveling 'Intermarriage' in Faye Kellerman's Detective Fiction." *Multicultural Detective Fiction: Murder from the "Other" Side*, edited by Adrienne Johnson Gosselin. New York: Garland, 1999, 185–211.

Rubel, Nora. *Doubting the Devout: The Ultra-Orthodox in the Jewish American Imagination.* New York: Columbia University Press, 2009.

———. "Orthodox Judaism and the News." *The Oxford Handbook of Religion and the American News Media*, edited by Diane Winston. Oxford: Oxford University Press, 2012, ebook, 199–213.

Said, Edward. *Orientalism*. New York: Vintage, 1979.

Sandberg, Sheryl. *Lean In: Women, Work, and the Will to Lead.* 2013. London: Penguin, 2015.

Saul, Heather. "Stamford Hill Council Removes 'Unacceptable' Posters Telling Women Which Side of Road to Walk Down." *Independent*, 20 September 2014.

Schaffer, Gavin. "Unmasking the 'Muscle Jew': The Jewish Soldier in British War Service, 1899–1945." *Patterns of Prejudice*, vol. 46, nos. 3–4, 2012, 375–396.

Schiller, Mayer. "The Obligation of Married Women to Cover Their Hair." *Journal of Halacha and Contemporary Society*, vol. 30, 1995, 81–108.

Schleier, Curt. "Rama Burshtein Has a Fundamental Belief in Marriage." *Forward*, 11 May 2017.

Schmidt, Nancy J. *An Orthodox Jewish Community in the United States: A Minority within a Minority*. London: World Jewish Congress, 1966.

Schoett-Kristensen, Lene. "Allegra Goodman's 'Kaaterskill Falls': A Liturgical Novel." *Studies in American Jewish Literature*, vol. 24, 2005, 22–41.

Senior, Jennifer. "Review: 'Here and There,' a Renunciation of a Sect, Tinged with Love." *New York Times*, 6 December 2015.

Shaffir, William. "Boundaries and Self-Presentation among the Hasidim: A Study in Identity Maintenance." *New World Hasidim: Ethnographic Studies of Hasidim in North America*, edited by Janet S. Belcove-Shalin. Albany: SUNY Press, 1995, 31–68.

———. "Hassidim and the 'Reasonable Accommodation' Debate in Quebec." *Journal of Jewish Sociology*, vol. 50, no. 1, 2008, 33–50.

———. "Montreal's Chassidim Revisited: A Focus on Change." *Essays in the Social Scientific Study of Judaism and Jewish Society*, edited by Simcha Fishbane and Jack Lightstone. Montreal: Concordia University Press, 1990, 305–322.

Shalit, Wendy. "The Observant Reader." *New York Times*, 30 January 2005.

Shani, Ayelett. "I'm an Icon in the Haredi World: Marlyn Vinig, Lecturer and Cinema Researcher, Says Ultra-Orthodox Films Are a Genre in Their Own Right, Made by and Intended for Women." *Haaretz* (Tel Aviv), 11 July 2015, http://www.haaretz.com/israel-news/.premium-1.665217.

Sharir, Moran. "A Woman of Valor, Who Can Find?" *Haaretz* (Tel Aviv), 18 December 2011, http://www.haaretz.co.il/gallery/television/1.1593983.

Shaw, Enid. "A Female Hasidic Rock Band Is Having a Women-Only Show in New York." *Gawker*, 6 August 2014, http://www.gawker.com/a-female-hasidic-rock-band-is-having-a-women-only-show-1617385157.

Shenker, Yael. "Choosing One's Life: Identity-Swapping Plot in Popular Fiction by Israeli *Haredi* Women." *Israel Studies*, vol. 22, no. 1, 2017, 189–212.

Sherwood, Harriet. "The Battle of Bet Shemesh." *Guardian*, 31 October 2011, http://www.theguardian.com/commentisfree/2011/oct/31/bet-shemesh-haredi-jews-school.

Shohat, Ella. *Israeli Cinema: East/West and the Politics of Representation*. London: I. B. Tauris, 2010.

Singer, Mathilde. "Lekhaim! Outremont Casher." *Voir*, 11 May 2006, http://www.voir.ca/societe/2006/05/11/lekhaim-outremont-casher/.

Skinazi, Karen E. H. "Are Head Coverings the New Black? Sheitels and the Religious-Secular Culture Wars in Twenty-First-Century America and Its Literature." *Open Library of Humanities*, vol. 3, no. 2, 2017, 1–27.

————. "Black Hats Are the New Black: Israeli TV Show about Cool Haredim Is a Runaway Hit." *Tablet Magazine*, 5 January 2018, http://www.tabletmag.com/scroll/252654/black-hats -are-the-new-black-israeli-tv-show-about-cool-haredim-is-a-runaway-hit.

————. "Kol Isha: Malka Zipora's *Lekhaim!* as the Voice of the Hasidic Woman in Quebec." *Shofar*, vol. 33, no. 2, 2015, 1–26.

————. "Meet Mindy Pollak, Montreal's Hasidic Candidate." *Tablet Magazine*, 25 October 2013, http://www.tabletmag.com/scroll/149687/meet-mindy-pollak-montreals-hasidic-candidate.

Slaughter, Anne-Marie. "Why Women Still Can't Have It All." *Atlantic*, July–August 2012, http://www.theatlantic.com/magazine/archive/2012/07/why-women-still-cant-have-it-all/ 309020/.

"Sloatsburg, NY—Rest Stop Offers Jewish Men Place to Pray." *Vos Iz Neias*, 27 July 2011, http://www.vosizneias.com/88157/2011/07/27/sloatsburg-ny-rest-stop-offers-jewish-men -place-to-pray.

Socken, Paul. "From Manna to Money: The Narrative Structure of Yves Thériault's *Aaron*." *Studies in Canadian Literature*, vol. 24, no. 2, 1999, 131–140.

Socolovsky, Maya. "Land, Legacy, and Return: Negotiating a Post-Assimilationist Stance in Allegra Goodman's *Kaaterskill Falls*." *Shofar*, vol. 22, no. 3, 2004, 26–42.

Sokoloff, Naomi. "Jewish Mysteries: Detective Fiction by Faye Kellerman and Batya Gur." *Shofar*, vol. 15, no. 3, 1997, 66–85.

Sollors, Werner. *Beyond Ethnicity: Consent and Descent in American Culture*. Oxford: Oxford University Press, 1986.

Solotaroff, Ted. "American Jewish Writers: On Edge Once More." *New York Times Book Review*, 18 December 1988, 1, 31, 33.

Soudry, Celia. "Film: Unorthodox Premier Launches Orthodox 'A Light for Greytowers.'" *Jewish Journal* (Los Angeles), 10 January 2007.

Spencer, William David. *Mysterium and Mystery: The Clerical Crime Novel*. Carbondale: Southern Illinois University Press, 1992.

Spivak, Gayatri. "Can the Subaltern Speak?" *Marxism and the Interpretation of Culture*, edited by Cary Nelson and Lawrence Grossberg. Urbana: University of Illinois Press, 1988, 271–313.

Stasio, Marilyn. "Tony Hillerman, Novelist, Dies at 83." *New York Times*, 27 October 2008, B17.

Steinberg, Jessica. "TV Show 'Shtisel' Subtly Changes Ultra-Orthodox Perceptions." *Times of Israel* (Jerusalem), 13 January 2016, http://www.timesofisrael.com/tv-show-shtisel-subtly -changes-ultra-orthodox-perceptions/.

Stoker, Valerie. "Drawing the Line: Hasidic Jews, Eruvim, and the Public Space of Outrem- ont, Québec." *History of Religions*, vol. 43, no. 1, 2003, 18–49.

Stolow, Jeremy. *Orthodox by Design: Judaism, Print Politics, and the ArtScroll Revolution*. Berkeley: University of California, 2010.

Sussman, Adeena. "Profile: Faye Kellerman." *Hadassah Magazine*, 14 January 2008, http:// www.hadassahmagazine.org/2008/01/14/profile-faye-kellerman/.

Sztokman, Elana Maryles. *The War on Women in Israel: A Story of Religious Radicalism and the Women Fighting for Freedom*. Naperville, Ill.: Source, 2015.

Tessler, Yitzchak. "Passover in the Haredi Press: Women Were Censored from the Warsaw Ghetto." *Ynet News*, 27 March 2013, http://www.ynet.co.il/articles/0,7340,L-4361315,00 .html.

Trappler Spielman, Sara. "Female-Only Movie Screens in 11 Cities during Passover Holiday." Chabad.org, 14 April 2011, http://www.chabad.org/news/article_cdo/aid/1497796/jewish/ Female-Only-Movie-Sets-Passover-Schedule.htm.

————. "Friday Film: Women's Only Screening in Jerusalem." *Forward* (New York), 30 December 2011, http://www.forward.com/schmooze/148863/friday-film-women-s-only -screening-in-jerusalem.

————. "Frum Female Underground Films." *Tablet Magazine*, 30 May 2012.

————. "Frum Girls Acting Out." *New York Jewish Week*, 18 April 2011.

———. "No Boys Allowed." *Tablet Magazine*, 25 November 2008, http://www.tabletmag.com/jewish-arts-and-culture/1257/no-boys-allowed.

Uffen, Ellen Serlen. "The Novels of Fannie Hurst: Notes toward a Definition of Popular Fiction." *Journal of American Culture*, vol. 1, no. 3, 1978, 574–583.

———. "The Orthodox Detective Novels of Faye Kellerman." *Studies in Jewish American Literature*, vol. 11, no. 2, 1992, 195–203.

———. *Strands of the Cable: The Place of the Past in Jewish American Women's Writing*. New York: Peter Lang, 1992.

Ungar-Sargon, Batya. "Undercover Atheists." *Aeon Magazine*, 11 February 2015, http://www.aeon.co/magazine/culture/the-double-life-of-hasidic-atheists/.

Valman, Nadia. *The Jewess in Nineteenth-Century British Literary Culture*. New York: Cambridge University Press, 2007.

Vinig, Marlyn. *Ha-kolnoah Ha-haredi (Orthodox Cinema)*. Tel Aviv: Resling, 2011.

Voas, David, and Rodney Ling. "Religion in Britain and the United States." *British Social Attitudes: The 26th Report*, edited by Alison Park et al. London: Sage, 2010, 65–86.

Wagner, Matthew. "Sexual Responsibility." *Jerusalem Post*, 13 March 2008.

Wallace-Wells, Benjamin. "Them and Them." *New York Magazine*, 21 April 2013, http://www.nymag.com/news/features/east-ramapo-hasidim-2013-4.

Walton, Priscilla L. *Detective Agency: Women Rewriting the Hard-Boiled Tradition*. Berkeley: University of California Press, 1999.

Ward, Ian. *Sex, Crime and Literature in Victorian England*. Oxford: Hart, 2014.

Wax, Emily. "Rama Burshtein Is First Ultra-Orthodox Woman to Direct for General Audience." *Washington Post*, 7 June 2013.

Weaver, Matthew, and Jane Martinson. "Ultra-Orthodox Jewish Schools Drop Ban on Mothers Driving." *Guardian*, 5 June 2015.

Weinberg, Sydney Stahl. *The World of Our Mothers*. Chapel Hill: University of North Carolina Press, 1988.

Weinreb, Tzvi Hersh. "Hush." *Jewish Action*, 13 June 2012, http://www.ou.org/jewish_action/06/2012/hush.

Weissman Joselit, Jenna. *New York's Jewish Jews: The Orthodox Community in the Interwar Years*. Bloomington: Indiana University Press, 1990.

———. *The Wonders of America: Reinventing Jewish Culture, 1880–1950*. New York: Hill and Wang, 1996.

"Welcome to Herouxville: Don't Stone Women." *Montreal Gazette*, 28 January 2007.

Welter, Barbara. "The Cult of True Womanhood: 1820–1860." *American Quarterly*, vol. 18, no. 2, Summer 1966, 151–174.

Whitlock, Gillian. "The Skin of the *Burqa*: Recent Life Narratives from Afghanistan." *Biography*, vol. 28, no. 1, 2005, 54–76.

———. *Soft Weapons: Autobiography in Transit*. Chicago: University of Chicago Press, 2007.

Wiener, Julie. "Unapologetically Orthodox." *New York Jewish Week*, 9 February 2012.

Winston, Hella. *Unchosen: The Hidden Lives of Hasidic Rebels*. Boston: Beacon, 2005.

Wirth-Nesher, Hana. "'Shpeaking Plain' and Writing Foreign: Abraham Cahan's *Yekl*." *Poetics Today*, vol. 22, no. 1, 2001, 41–63.

Wisse, Ruth. "American Jewish Writing, Act II." *Commentary Magazine*, June 1976, 40–45.

———. "The Joy of Limits: Kaaterskill Falls by Allegra Goodman." *Commentary Magazine*, 1 December 1998, 67–70.

———. *The Modern Jewish Canon: A Journey through Language and Culture*. New York: Free Press, 2000.

———. "The Virtue of Virtue." *Wall Street Journal*, 7 January 1999, A8.

Wojcik, Pamela Robertson. "Typecasting." *Criticism*, vol. 45, no. 2, 2003, 223–249.

Woolf, Virginia. "Professions for Women." *The Death of a Moth and Other Essays*. 1942. New York: Harcourt Brace, 1970, 235–242.

Yoder, Christine Roy. *Wisdom as a Woman of Substance: A Socioeconomic Reading of Proverbs 1–9 and 31:10–31*. Berlin: Walter de Gruyter, 2001.

"Your Say." *Binah: The Weekly Magazine for the Jewish Woman*, vol. 2, no. 322, 25 February 2013, 6–10.

Zeveloff, Naomi. "Sex-Segregation Spreads among Orthodox." *Forward* (New York), 28 October 2011.

Zierler, Wendy. "A Dignitary in the Land? Literary Representations of the American Rabbi." *AJS Review*, vol. 30, no. 2, 2006, 255–275.

———. "Zierler on Rubel, 'Doubting the Devout: The Ultra-Orthodox in the Jewish American Imagination.'" *H-Judaic,* January 2011, http://www.networks.h-net.org/node/28655/reviews/30777/zierler-rubel-doubting-devout-ultra-orthodox-jewish-american.

Zohar, Zvi. "'She Opens Her Mouth with Wisdom': The Qualities of the Accomplished Jewish Woman According to Rabbi Yisrael Yaakov Algazi's Exposition of 'A Woman of Valor.'" *Journal of Jewish Culture and Identity*, vol. 7, 2016, 93–121.

# Index